Africans in
Global Migration

Africans in Global Migration

Searching for Promised Lands

Edited by
John A. Arthur
Joseph Takougang
Thomas Owusu

LEXINGTON BOOKS
Lanham • Boulder • New York • Toronto • Plymouth, UK

Published by Lexington Books
An imprint of The Rowman & Littlefield Publishing Group, Inc.
4501 Forbes Boulevard, Suite 200, Lanham, Maryland 20706
www.rowman.com

16 Carlisle Street, London W1D 3BT, United Kingdom

British Library Cataloguing in Publication Information Available

Library of Congress Cataloging-in-Publication Data
The hardback edition of this book was previously cataloged by the Library of Congress
follows:

Africans in global migration : searching for promised lands / edited by John A. Arthur,
    Joseph Takougang, and Thomas Owusu.
p. cm.
Includes index
1. African diaspora. 2. Africa—Emigration and immigration. 3. Blacks —Race identity. I.
Arthur, John A.. 1959– II. Takougang, Joseph. III. Owusu, Thomas Y. (Thomas Yaw),
1961–
    DT16.5.A36 2012
    304.8096—dc23

                                                                                    2012016592

ISBN 978-0-7391-7406-7 (cloth : alk. paper)
ISBN 978-0-7391-9800-1 (pbk. : alk. paper)
ISBN 978-0-7391-7407-4 (electronic)

Printed in the United States of America

This book is dedicated to all Africans in the diaspora.

Contents

Tables and Figures

TABLES

FIGURES

Preface

The first decade of the 21st century continues to witness the massive migration of Africans from the continent. Spurred by negative economic, political and social factors that have plagued the continent since independence in conjunction with the global economy and technological revolution of the last two decades or so, these African migrants are seeking refuge in the new global village, from Asia to the Middle East and from Europe to North America. As a result of its colonial and historical ties with the continent, Europe provided opportunities for most African migrants in the decades after the independence. Recently, however, the United States and Canada have become the favorite destination in this migration trajectory. While this change might be attributed to stricter immigration policies in many European countries especially in Britain, France and Germany, the relatively benign policies in the United States, including passage by the United States Congress of the Refugee Act of 1980, the Immigration Reform and Control Act of 1986 (IRCA) and the immigration Act of 1990 have also contributed to the surge in African immigration there. It is currently estimated that there are about 1.7 million African immigrants in the United States.

In Canada, the major policy initiative that facilitated an increase in African immigration to the country was the liberalization of immigration laws in 1971, which removed all the race-based policies and other restrictions and enabled non-whites to enter into the country. The majority of African immigrants in Canada, therefore, arrived after 1970. Currently, there are about 280, 000 African immigrants in Canada. And, unlike their predecessors who came to the United States ostensibly to obtain an education before returning to their respective countries, many of these new immigrants are obtaining permanent residency status or American citizenship. According to figures from the Department of Homeland Security (DHS), 583,594 African immigrants obtained permanent residency status in the nearly four decades between 1960 and 1999 compared to 857,988 between 2000 and 2010.

These immigrants come from all regions and every country on the continent, with the largest coming from West (492,030) and East (397,262) Africa. Nigeria (209,908), Ethiopia (148,221), Egypt (138,194), Ghana (108,647), and Kenya (87,267) remain the leading nations, other nations such as Somalia, Sudan, and many of the Francophone and Lusophone states on the continent have also witnessed significant number of immigrants in recent years. While many of these immigrants are highly educated, there are also many without basic reading and writing skills. Women are also becoming important players in African migration. It is estimated that 46.6 percent of all the African immigrants in the United States are women. Indeed, these women are not just spouses who might have migrated to meet their spouses. In many cases they are pioneers in the global migration process

Regardless of their sex, country and region of origin, or their educational status, these diaspora Africans are all united by their common African origin and the quest to seek a better life for themselves and their families in the diaspora and for those still at home. The search for global economic and cultural opportunities is the primary motivation behind the migration of Africans. The intensification of this migration in recent times speaks to the increasing opportunities (technological, cultural, social, political, and economic) that are now available for Africans to engage in international travel. Persistence migration of skilled and unskilled Africans also speaks to the deterioration of opportunities for Africans to achieve their goals and aspirations. In this regard, migration has become a powerful agency of social change in Africa. Migration culminates in the fulfillment of unmet needs, structural inequalities, and the inability of African central governments to create the conditions that are conducive for Africans to thrive. Retaining their citizens at home and providing them with adequate opportunities and incentives to stay home and contribute their quota toward growth of the region will continue to prove a daunting task for African governments. The outcomes of this migration will certainly continue to impact the region, its peoples, and institutions for a long time to come.

The chapters in this volume, all by scholars trained in the humanities and social science with experience as immigrants themselves or extensive research in diaspora studies, explore various facets of the contemporary diaspora experience. The themes reflect the dynamism, complexity, and diversity of the African immigrant experiences. It explores the migration of Africans and the formation of African immigrant communities highlighting the cultural, economic, social, and political factors involved in the creation of these communities. In recognition of the complexity of the immigrant experience, the book also addresses the institutional factors in the host society that converge to shape how these immigrants define their migratory experiences. The book also explores the nature and types of transnational connections that African immigrants maintain with their homelands, the rationale for these ties, and their implications for the settlement, adaptation, and the relationships with both the host society and their homelands.

John A. Arthur, University of Minnesota, Duluth
Joseph Takougang, University of Cincinnati
Thomas Owusu, William Patterson University of New Jersey

Acknowledgments

We are delighted for the opportunity to contribute this edited work to the growing scholarship on the African diaspora. This volume is based on collaboration approached from diverse methodological and theoretical approaches. The interdisciplinary perspectives employed in this work provided us with multiple lenses from which to view the African diaspora. Today, international migration has become a powerful source of social change across Africa. Many Africans are crossing international borders to seek better economic and cultural opportunities outside the continent. The editors of this work are part of this dynamic process. So are the majority of the scholars who have contributed to this volume. Together, the editors and contributors have been guided by one central tenet: to depict the migratory experiences of African immigrants and at the same time give context to their diasporic hopes and aspirations. Special thanks to all the contributors for their tireless work and for taking the time to share their scholarship with us. We will forever remain in your gratitude.

We also remain appreciative and grateful to our various institutions and home departments for the opportunities and resources they have provided us in our professional and creative endeavors. We will like to acknowledge the Taft Foundation at the University of Cincinnati for its financial support which allowed Dr. Takougang to attend the twenty-seventh annual meeting of the Association of Third World Conference in Accra, Ghana where the paper they contributed to this book was first presented. We would also like to thank Professors Cheli Reutter and Billie Johnson of the Department of Africana Studies at the University of Cincinnati for their helpful comments on Takougang and Tidjani's chapter. We extend our gratitude to Joed Elich for granting us copyright permission to publish Dr. Mary Osirim's piece that appeared originally in volume 7, number 4 of *African and Asian Studies.*

In addition, we would also like to thank the University of Minnesota, Dr. Vince Magnuson, former Associate Vice Chancellor for Academic Affairs, and Dr. Sue Maher, Dean of the College of Liberal Arts, for their generous financial research support over the years in support of Professor Arthur's work. We are also grateful to the Benedykt Heydekorn Foundation of Toronto, the Multicultural History Society of Ontario, Canada, and the University of Toronto, Canada, for providing financial support which enabled Dr. Owusu to undertake extensive fieldwork in Toronto to collect data for his chapter in this book.

We would like to express our heartfelt thanks to Lexington Press and Rowman and Littlefield for the efficient and diligent assistance that they have provided us in the course of preparing this manuscript. We could not have completed this work without their professional guidance and stewardship. On behalf of our contributors, the editors will like to extend a special and noteworthy appreciation to Mr. Justin Race and Sabah Ghulamali both at Lexington, the editorial board, and the external reviewers who worked with us to bring this volume to a successful end. We could not have done it without your guidance.

Our final thanks and acknowledgments are due to our families and friends who provided encouragement and shared their ideas about how to improve upon our research and scholarship. We appreciate your understanding and patience as well. Thank you all very much for your kindness and unflinching support.

Chapter One

Searching for Promised Lands: Conceptualization of the African Diaspora in Migration

The aftermath of colonization brought about many social changes to the continent of Africa. One notable change is the systematic transformation and incorporation of African societies into the new global economy brought about by the dispersion of capital investments, technological innovations, improved communication and transportation systems, the ease of cross border population movements, cultural and human capital transformations (particularly the proliferation of educational institutions of and the growth in the literate population.) The postcolonial incorporation of Africa into global systems of economic and social production created new opportunities for Africans at the local and international levels. At the local level in Africa, interregional migration in the form of rural to urban migrations intensified as Africans from all walks of life started to search for better economic opportunities. Cities and commercial as well as administrative centers boomed as the rural population started drifting to the centers and spheres of economic production. This process is still unfolding in Africa today as hundreds of thousands leave their rural communities to join the caravan of urban migrants. Africa's megacities such as Lagos, Accra, Abidjan, Freetown, Nairobi, and Kampala are busting at the seams struggling to cope with the massive influx of new settlers. Upon arrival in these cities, these settlers come into contact with the new opportunities offered by the cities. Some may pursue educational goals; others may seek cultural innovation to anchor their new identities; and still others may engage in economic and commercial activities. City living and its varied forms of culture offers myriad of lenses through which to view not only what is happening in Africa but also opportunities available in far away destinations beyond the continent.

At the international level in particular, Africans started looking beyond the continent for the fulfillment of unmet needs at home. The postcolonial period

1

and the penetration of capitalist investments, coupled with improvements in human capital resources created aspirations whose fulfillment could not be had in Africa. Political and economic morass stymied the robustness of the postcolonial economic ascension of the newly independent nations. Several of the countries continued with the postcolonial monoculture economies often with the production of agricultural raw materials which were then exported to feed Europe and America's industrial and manufacturing establishments. Little or no regard was given to the development of an industrial and manu-facturing base to bring added value to the raw materials by processing of these materials into semi-finished or finished goods for local consumption. This meant that these countries were not able to create the jobs needed by graduates and nongraduates alike. Meanwhile, several of the countries con-tinued their reliance on imported manufactured goods and products from the countries that had colonized them thereby stymieing local production sectors. Without sustainable support being given to local economic and manufactur-ing production, masses of Africans continue to be unemployed and under-employed. This stagnation affects the youth and graduates from secondary and tertiary institutions of learning. For many of them who are faced with economic deprivation, outmigration from Africa (particularly to the advanced nations in the Western hemisphere) provides the best option to improve upon one's economic status and standard of living. This commenced the postco-lonial exodus and diaspora of Africans. Compared with the pre-colonial in-voluntary resettlement of Africans in the New World through the slave trade of the Trans-Atlantic Middle Passage, the arrival of Africans to the United States and Canada is predominantly voluntary interspersed with involuntary displaced stateless refuges from Ethiopia, Somalia, Liberia, Sierra Leone, and the Sudan.

Three waves of African migration to North America can be discerned. The first period consisted of Africans who were sponsored by their respective home governments to travel to the United States to pursue advanced degrees in the arts and sciences. This period started in the mid-to-late 1950s lasting until about the 1970s. During the two decades, thousands of Africans got the opportunity to travel to the United States and Canada. The postcolonial governments recognized the imperative of well-educated cadres of civil servants and skilled workers to work in both the public and private sectors following the end of colonization and the ascension of African political leaders to power. The postcolonial task of nation-building was a daunting challenge. The infrastructures of the newly-independent countries could not handle the high demand for skilled workers. In particular, the tertiary institu-tions of learning had to rely on the universities of the metropolitan colonial countries to provide further training of Africans. Governments concentrated on the provision of primary and secondary education. The massive push for a highly-trained and skilled labor force occurred simultaneously with efforts to improve existing infrastructures such as roads, hospitals, water, electricity, and housing. The majority of those sponsored by their home governments to study abroad returned home after the completion of their courses of study. Several found jobs in an expanding civil and private sectors.

The second period of Africans to emigrate started leaving after the mid-1970 as country after country in the region were roiled in political and economic conflicts. In some of the countries (particularly in Ghana and Nigeria), incessant coup d'états marked the ascendancy of the military in African political culture. Constitutional governance structures and civil order deteriorated as democratic institutions were replaced with military regimes. The fragile coexistence of tribal, ethnic, and clan groups fractured resulting in civil wars and conflicts which led to the internal displacement of millions of Africans in their own countries. Some had to flee to less troubled spots to seek haven from the violence. The conflicts stymied the economic progress that several of the countries were making immediately following the end of foreign domination. More significantly, the civil conflicts made it difficult to incorporate diverse tribal and ethnic groups into the nation-states. Unmet economic and social needs created despair among Africans. Most started looking to the West or travel to other African countries where conflicts were minimal and people could go about their day-to-day activities without the fear of threats and intimidations. This phase of African transnational migration has yet to subside. Both regular and irregular migration has come to dominate the social and economic landscapes of the continent. Migration to other countries (preferably to the advanced Western countries) dominates the lives of both urban and rural African youths, including adult men and women from all walks of life. Migration is seen as a response to and a strategy for confronting the poverty, deprivation and the general lack of economic and cultural opportunities. The outcomes often associated with international migration is that it offers the possibilities to send money home to assist extended family members in meeting barest economic needs. Migration is also rationalized as a means to facilitate incorporation into a changing global economy characterized by the movement of skilled and unskilled labor from areas of low economic and industrial production to destinations of high economic and industrial concentrations. Chronic unemployment and underemployment among graduates from secondary and tertiary educational institutions continue to cause a brain drain leaving noticeable labor shortages in areas such as education, technology, and healthcare.

By all accounts, another wave of African migration is unfolding. Starting shortly after the beginning of this millennium, this migration is becoming an important cog in the rush of Africans to join the global caravan of skilled and unskilled labor settlements in the advanced and developed countries. This migration and the mass movement of Africa's human resources and talents is a redefining moment in Africa's development. It has set in motion a never-seen-before rallying clamor and indomitable task for Africans to seek ways and strategies to become developed and share in global economic prosperity, something that has remained elusive for generations of Africans. One result of this unyielding desire to pursue global economic integration via migration and self advancement is the currently unfolding saga of the growing number of foot migrants from Africans who are bracing the harsh and unforgiving elements of the Sahara Desert with the hope of reaching a beachhead in the Mediterranean via North Africa (Libya, Morocco, Tunisia, Algeria, and Spanish North Africa). From here, the European Union (EU) countries (Italy, Spain, and Malta) are in sight. Also in sight is the United States once some of the Africans are able to reach Europe. Again, escape from economic destitute in Africa is the driving force behind this mass migration which, at its current epoch, compares favorably with the transcontinental migration of Europeans to North America during the nineteenth and twentieth centuries.

The major urban centers of Africa have become the sites where plans to engage in desert crossing are hatched and implemented. Poorly educated and economically displaced urban youths joined by the counterparts from the rural areas sketch plans about how to implement their cross-border foot migration. Despite repeated official warnings from the central governments of Africa about the perilous nature of cross-border foot migration, the appeals often go unheeded. Would-be migrants rationalize that this is their only avenue to leave Africa and join the global market of unskilled agricultural labor in the Mediterranean and in the EU. Africa's porous borders serve as the channel of illegal interstate border crossings. Poorly paid border patrol agents may take bribes to assist these migrants. This form of irregular migration is a manifestation of the frustration and the pressures to emigrate. The reality is that only a few are able to arrive safely. Information about each successful crossing relayed home strengthens the resolve of many more prospective migrants willing to risk life and limb to make it to the Mediterranean or Europe.

Desert-crossing in Africa has created its own cultural fads and normative guidelines. For many youths unable to survive the harsh realities of life in urban and rural Africa, cross-border desert crossings have become rites of passage symbolizing the autonomy or the transition to adulthood. Family members may play a role in the formation of intent to migrate. While some may provide financial assistance, others may provide moral and spiritual support. Irrespective of how they show their support, one goal is certainly clear: a successful settlement or crossing means that the migrant would remit home and provide economic support for other family members. Hundreds, if not thousands, may perish, be interdicted, incarcerated, and if fortunate will be repatriated home. Information about failed attempts resulting in deaths is usually hard to obtain. Elaborate enabling networks linking prospective irregular migrants with traffickers has become a permanent feature of the desert communities, including long distance cross-desert lorries, and fishermen. In the short and long term, the ability of governments in Africa to effectively manage irregular labor migration streams as part of a comprehensive plan to optimize the human capital resources of the region. Some of the countries like Ghana, Liberia, Sierra Leone, and Nigeria have become labor or migrant-exporting nations for both skilled and unskilled workers. Deteriorating social, economic, and political conditions and the intense need to acquire foreign capital goods and assets continue to drive hundreds of thousands out of the continent every year. Recent recessionary and cyclical fluctuations in the global economy have disproportionately affected Africa's already poor and disadvantaged population. Rising prices in staple foods, agricultural commodity prices, including energy costs have further aggravated the economic conditions of Africa's rural and urban poor. The absence of government or private social security safety nets to cushion the effects of the global economic slump on Africa's poor means that many Africans continue to be among the biggest casualties of the worldwide economic depression. Structural adjustment programs and initiatives directed by world aid bodies have failed to trickle down to the average African. In most cases, these internationally-driven efforts aimed at restructuring and repositioning Africa for economic take-off have either failed or have had limited success. When they compare their economic situation to the rest of world, many Africans see structural imbalances in the economies of their respective countries. This imbalance (chronic unemployment, over urbanization, frequent food shortages, low production capacity) is often rationalized as the main cause of poverty in Africa. International migration is seen as panacea to this structural economic imbalance.

The Africans who are leaving the continent to seek economic fortunes are not a unitary group. They reflect the cultural, political, and economic diversity and multiple heritages of the continent. Some come from the Anglophone or former British colonies in the Western, Eastern, and Southern regions of the continent. Others are from the Francophone and Lusaphone parts where French colonial influences left its cultural and economic imprints. For others, the influences came from Arabia. Linguistic, ethnic, tribal, clan, and religious differences abound. In all of these social and cultural blending can be found indigenous African cultural forms which have been interlaced with foreign or imported influences to form a hybrid or mélange of cultures that are contextually rich and distinctively pluralistic. Irrespective of which region of the African continent they come from, the African immigrants are united by a common goal: to maximize the economic and cultural opportunities available to them in the West to raise their standards of living as well as those of their extended relatives back home. The fulfillment of economic goals (for example, working to save money to remit home, to start a small business, or to build a home) is a dominant theme in the lives of the African immigrants. The transnational foci of the immigrants are therefore to improve upon their human and social capital skills and at the same time structure their migration with an eye toward the economic development of their home countries. Ultimately, several of them intend to return to Africa.

The majority of the Africans in the diaspora enter the United States, Canada and other Western countries legally as students, visitors, refugees, or to conduct business. Many overstay their visas and do not return even if it means they have to join the ranks of the twelve million undocumented and find work in the underground economy. After all, as some of them rationalize, life and survival as an undocumented is far better economically than life in Africa. The risks and benefits associated with living in North America outweigh the economic and cultural costs of living in Africa. At the same time, several of the Africans in North America with undocumented status are cognizant of the risks of working and living in the United States or Canada without legal work authorization. For such immigrants, social circles and networks are limited to fellow immigrants or trusted friends and family members. These intra-African immigrant relationships serve important functions. They channel information about job prospects, teach migrants how to secure social security cards, work permits, and provide valuable information about employers who hire undocumented migrants. Information about these networks is known only to the migrants. There is little or no trust for outsiders. The African immigrant national societies and the clan or tribal groupings that these immigrants form provide social psychological and economic support to the immigrants by serving as quasi-families whose goals are to assist the immigrants maintain their cultures by connecting them to what goes on in Africa, and at the same offer them protection and security from living in a foreign land. This group of African immigrants lives on the margins of the host society and are more likely than those with valid authorization and legal status to focus their energies on working multiple minimum wage jobs, living frugally, and eventually repatriating their assets home. Structurally, the undocumented African immigrants have become part of the growing ranks of the undocumented immigrants. While most wait in anticipation of the passage of immigration reforms by the Obama administration and Congress, some have started heading home due to the 2007 economic recession, difficulties and legal issues involved in working with invalid work documents, the fear of deportation, and the growing public antipathy toward undocumented workers and immigration culminating in the passage of Arizona's Senate Bill 1070 and similar legislations in Georgia, Alabama, and North Carolina.

Aims and Scope of this Book

The primary aim of this book is to present detailed portraits of the African immigrant experience in North America. Using an interdisciplinary focus drawn from the social sciences and humanities, the book addresses central themes related to the migration and settlement of Africans in the United States, Canada, and Europe. Multiple dimensions of the African immigrant diaspora such as cultural community formations, immigrant adaptations, social and cultural mechanisms for forging inclusion, citizenship and naturalization, representations of African identity and cultural forms, and immigrant expressions and constructions of notions of "blackness" in its varied forms. Focus is given to African immigrant family structures, labor force, work, and occupational practices, including relationships with other minority and subordinate groups. The book utilizes these themes, recognizing that the scholarly and comprehensive documentation or modeling of the African immigrant presence in North America is dynamic, complex, and varied in content and structure. Africans are not a monolithic group. Vast differences can be found in the migratory patterns, institutions, and identities that these immigrants structure to manifest their cultures and normative systems in the host society. The variety of multiple social and cultural spaces that different groups of African émigrés create and contest to manifest their migratory experiences are represented and the internal and external forces weighing against them are examined against the backdrop of both African and American exigencies. An overarching theme in this book, therefore, is to depict the African diasporas not only as a cultural epiphenomena (or interlocking communitas), but also as a process characterized by identity transformation, lived experiences and realities, including the capturing of the historical trends that are acted and played out in multiple social domains. The heart of the diaspora domain is the cultural communities which serve at the fulcrum or the center of action exemplifying the vibrant nature and the continuities inherent in the formation of the diaspora.

This book will show the underlying contextual motivations and expectations African immigrants bring to their varied migratory experiences in North America. To accomplish this goal, the book interlaces the unfolding dynamics of African transnational migration within the overall nexus of social changes in Africa and the role(s) that these immigrants see themselves playing in addressing the complex relationship between migration and development in the emerging nation-states. We examine the full range of economic and cultural underpinnings of African migrations to North America and its accompanying trajectories at the micro and macro-structural levels of social analyses. The social constructions of African migratory societies, cultures, institutions, and normative structures in North America is significant because it speaks not only to the richness and viability of African ideas and ideals but also addresses the question of how increasingly, Africans are using international migration to seek incorporation into world affairs and at the same time redefine their role(s) and the transformative impact of migration on their lives. Our goal in this regard is to provide an exposition into the social world and spaces that these immigrants create to depict what it means to be an African immigrant in the American ethnic and cultural mosaic. African migration is a manifestation of multiple states of being; each state of being folded into the other. At times, the consciousness defining the existential aspects and the borders of the migratory experiences of Africans are such that they are somewhat difficult to define or specify. This may be attributable, again, to the variables of diasporas that are simultaneously being formed. Nonetheless, it is still possible to delineate the cartographic domain and the action social and cultural sites undergirding these migratory experiences. With the gradual maturation of African migrations to North America, we define our goal in this book to map out and identify the sources and sites for the contestations of the myriad of cultural manifestations of the new African diaspora and its depictions within the totality of the shared meanings and appropriations of the essences of African-ness or African blackness. The vulnerabilities, struggles, threats (internal or external to the immigrant community), and opportunities emanating from the diasporic relationships that these immigrants structure will be highlighted and positioned within the nexus of the African dispersion to the North America and the West generally.

In this book, we view the African diaspora in terms of spatial and geographic constructions and propagations of African cultural identity and institutional forms in global domains whose boundaries are not static but rather dynamic, complex, and multidimensional. Simply stated, this means that we approach the African diaspora from a perspective that incorporates the historical as well as contemporary postmodern constructions of the Africa's dispersed communities and their associated transnational identity forms. The constructions of the African diaspora communities and their associated identities are delineated and rationalized within the broader theoretical and structural symbiotic formulations of homelands and hostlands relationships. This approach enables us to present and discuss the cultural and economic panoplies of the reconstituted African diaspora communities and their dynamic symbolic and actualized representations. Taking a contextualized approach in this book also enables us to represent the diverse forms of African diaspora and immigrant articulation and attribution of the consciousness formed by people of African descent as they attempt to straddle, occupy, and perform different roles and statuses in transnational domains and sites. In the varied and multiple contexts of the African diaspora, this book embraces Paul Zeleza's (2009:32) configuration of the African diaspora in terms of the continuous processes involved in the making, unmaking, or remaking of African identity and forms of consciousness that is lived and experienced within a given global and ever-changing terrain. In this book, the realities undergirding these diaspora formations and their manifold intended and unintended consequences are accentuated and positioned within the overall nexus and framework of African immigrant community structures and the role(s) they continue to play in shaping the multiple cameos and vicissitudes of African migrations. The subtext of these migrations, as this book will demonstrate, can be found in the elaborate primary kinship structures and the corresponding secondary associational reference groups that have come to dominate African migration today. While the sociocultural or economic differences may separate the experiences of African immigrants from that of other recent immigrants, particularly those from the Caribbean, Central and South America, and Asia, an attempt is made, where possible, to model and show the structural and individual comparability in the patterns of African migratory experiences with those of other recent immigrants to the United States.

In a nutshell, this book is aimed at positioning the importance of African migrations within the spectrum of the new forms of migrations now occurring in North America. Coming from a continent whose peoples, cultures, and institutions have been maligned and oftentimes disparaged or looked down upon, the descriptions of the multiple contexts of African migrations presented in this book is intended to show that as a group, Africans, like prior immigrant groups to the United States, yearn for global inclusiveness and opportunities to alter their economic circumstances and transform the landscapes of their respective countries by taking an active role in the day-to-day activities of their homelands even from afar. As the same time, this book offers the opportunity to reassess the newer meanings of black representations and social consciousness; and in particular, how these forms of lived immigrant or diaspora social realities or consciousness are constructed, communicated, and contested in foreign domains or migrant host societies. To be in the worldwide African diaspora connotes an existentialist ideals and symbolisms including ways of thinking that can only be experienced, defined, expressed in epiphenomenal terms and constructs. What this book seeks to do is to situate and place these varied or multiple diasporic worlds of existence being defined by Africans in North America. At the same time, we seek to raise theoretically paradigmatic questions about how to configure the complexities of the African diaspora. This means where possible, attempts will be made to develop theoretical paradigms to schematize, reconceptualize and (re)classify the African diaspora in its many forms.

The Essays and Themes in this Book

The essays in this book are a collection of works focusing on the dreams and aspirations of African immigrants who are using international migration as agency to build a better life for themselves and their families. The reasons bringing them to United States are as varied as the cultures and peoples represented in the reconstituted neo-African diaspora. And irrespective of what brings them to the United States and Canada, these Africans are united by a common goal—to find new ways of re-creating better economic and cultural opportunities for themselves and at the same time be at the vanguard of social change in Africa through their committed involvement in the affairs of their respective homelands.

Four themes underscore the essays in this book. These are: 1) the creation of African diaspora community and institutional structures; 2) the structured relationships among African immigrants, host, and homeland societies; 3) the construction and negotiation of diaspora spaces, places consciousness, and identity politics; and finally 4) the economic integration, occupational, and labor force roles and statuses. Each of the thematic groupings have been chosen with one specific goal in mind: to depict and represent the critical structural components of the reconstitution of the African diaspora in North America as a dynamic process involving what Zeleza called the "diasporization" of African immigrant settlement communities in global transnational spaces. These themes also reflect the diversities inherent in the diaspora communities and call attention to the fluid and dynamic boundaries within which the Africans create, diffuse, and engage host and home societies. In this context, the themes embody the diaspora tapestries woven by the immigrants and their families to center African social and cultural forms in North America. Collectively, the themes represent pathways for the elucidation of African immigrant portraits and snapshots.

In chapter 2, Owusu examines the post-arrival experiences and aspirations of African immigrants in Canada. The chapter illustrates the ways in which immigrants from Africa collectively organize themselves to meet the needs related to their adaptation to and settlement in a new country. Using findings from prior research as a frame of reference (see, for example, Moya, 2005; Predelli, 2008, Mensah, 2008, and Ozcurumez, 2009), Owusu examines: 1) the different types of Ghanaian associations; the timing of, and the reasons for their formation; 2) how the associations help to fulfil the economic, so-cial, cultural, and political needs of the immigrants in the new society; 3) the ways in which immigrants use the associations to contribute to community development efforts, maintain back-home ties and commitments, and to fight for political rights in the homeland; and 4) the extent to which demographic, economic, and social factors, such as length of residence, education, income, and residential location, and desire for cultural maintenance influence mem-bership in the associations. Three main types of Ghanaian associations are examined, namely: a) township (or home town) associations—those whose members originate from the same town; b) ethnic associations—comprising individuals belonging to the same ethnic grouping in Ghana and; c) national associations—which are open to all Ghanaians regardless of ethnic origin.

The African immigrant reality in the United States is a lived and shared experience. As they create their cultural communities in their host societies to reflect their identities and sense of being, African immigrants come into contact and interact with a cross-section of other social and cultural groups whose values and beliefs are similar to or different from African belief sys-tems. The interplay of such contacts and how these intercultural interactions are given specific meanings and cultural contexts is a significant feature of the composition and structure of the reconstitution of the African diaspora in the United States. For some African immigrants, the manifestation of identity is symbolized and actualized via marriage relationships.

Unions between African immigrants and African Americans present new testing ground for theories on intermarriage, identity and biculturalism. There has been a great influx of African immigrants to the United States in the past thirty-five years, a more than fourfold increase between the decades of 1971–1980 and 1991–2000 (Clark, 2006). Increased African immigration to the United States has led to increases in both intermarriages between African immigrants and Africans Americans and bicultural blacks in America (Clark, 2006). In American universities there has been a noticeable increase in the number of black students with bicultural backgrounds. African and African-American unions are also found increasingly in both feature and documentary films. Films such as *Little Senegal, Phat Girlz, Beauty Shop, Barbershop, Okra Soup*, and the documentary *The Neo African Americans* all in some way deal with romantic relationships with African immigrants and African Americans.

Clark's analyses in chapter 3 focuses on identity expression among the growing number of bicultural black immigrants in America. Her study shows how this predominantly immigrant population is adding new dimensions to discussions around identity and biculturalism in America. The chapter examines the growth in the number of bicultural blacks, showing its correlation to the increases in romantic relationships between African and African American, as well as what that means for black identity in America. Clark's research also expands on the applicability of theories of biculturalism and identity by assessing the efficacies of bicultural identity theories in explaining black immigrant identity patterns.

Chapter 4 focuses on the identity politics of Ghanaian immigrants in the Greater Cincinnati area. While the experiences of African immigrants in very large metropolitan areas such as New York City and Washington, D.C. are well documented, there is a dearth of literature on the immigrant experiences of African émigrés in small Midwestern cities such as Columbus and Cincinnati. The principal argument of Yeboah's chapter is to show how a group of African immigrants from Ghana in the Greater Cincinnati area are collectively involved in negotiating their Ghanaian (African) heritage and their American experience through associational life and socialization of second generation immigrants by means of an identity politics. Because of today's globalization, these immigrants do not become culturally assimilated. Instead, as the chapter demonstrates, these immigrants rely on their transnational ties to live not in ethnic enclaves but ethnospaces. The chapter demonstrates that as a group, African émigrés participate in an identity politics not out of a threat but out of a combination of social convenience, intimidation and immigration status. In the process, these immigrants produce and manifest new geographies and sociologies in their making and creation of their social lives or histories in the West. Their identity politics has implications for the broader ethnic and racial components of the host societies in which they seek membership.

Scholars have long posited that identity is fluid, situational, and socially constructed and that individuals have multiple identities that emerge in different social context). Building on this theme, chapter 5 by Awokoya examines how Nigerian immigrants in the United States reconcile their identity construction processes as they contend with four major identities: African, Nigerian, African American, and black. It seeks to highlight the complex and often contradictory messages that these youth receive as they attempt to understand who they are and where they belong within various racial, ethnic, and national groups.

Awokoya's chapter draws on these previous studies by viewing identity as situational, contextual, and relational (Alba, 1985; Barth, 1969; Waters, 1990). While other scholars have examined identity among black immigrants in this manner, there are a number of factors that researchers of black identities have not taken into consideration. Like Waters' work, this chapter focuses on the possibilities for multiple black identities among African immigrant youths—Nigerian, African, African American, and black. Rather than framing these identities as existing in exclusion to each other, this chapter will show that individuals may hold multiple black identities simultaneously and demonstrates that context largely determines the salience of particular identities. In addition, this inquiry highlights two other factors rarely considered in prior research on the identities of black immigrants: the media (Awokoya, 2009; Awokoya & Harushimana, 2010; D'Alisera, 2009) and the co-ethnic community (Portes & Rumbaut, 2001; Pyke and Dang, 2003).

In chapter 6, Takougang and Tidjani examined how African immigrants utilize business formation strategies to forge economic integration and labor force participation in the United States. The chapter will discuss the types of businesses that African immigrants in Cincinnati are involved in, the reasons for their involvement in such small businesses, how they acquired the initial capital for the business, the customer base of these businesses, and some of the problems that they face as businessmen and women. These issues are not new, but they have not been fully addressed as far as African businesses are concerned. In the debate on immigrant businesses, it is believed that the latter are most successful when owners rely on their own communities for initial capital (Raijman and Tienda, 2003). The issue is more complex because communities and individuals behave differently when facing identical challenges.

Whether forced to leave their home countries because of religious, social or political persecution, or motivated by the desire to seek freedom and a better life elsewhere, immigrants to the United States have always arrived with a fierce sprit and determination to succeed at all costs (Bonacich, 1987; Olson, 1979). Not only do these immigrants come with initiative, but as Danilov (1992) puts it, they are willing to "put more hours and more hard work" in whatever they need to do to survive and succeed in the United States. Often the desire to succeed has led many immigrants to take what Staring (2000) has described as the 3Ds: dirty, dangerous and difficult jobs that most natives eschew. The same spirit and desire to succeed at all costs that was evident among European and other immigrants generations ago is also evident among the vast majority of recent African immigrants to the United States, whether they are the Senegalese, Malian, or Nigerian street vendors in New York City, Ethiopian cab drivers in Chicago, or the thousands of other African immigrants working in factories, nursing homes, restaurants, construction sites and other private and public sector employment.

Chapter 7 explores the global incorporation of African migrants in the healthcare sector in the United Kingdom. Yeboah and Mambo's chapter contributes to our understanding of the geography of international migration of African-trained nurses and their work experiences using the case of Zimbabwean immigrants in the United Kingdom. The thrust of the chapter is that global labor, and for that matter nurse migration, is based on geography between places of origin and destination of migrants. This geography of migration is bound in both the trajectory of the migration process and experience of migrants. On an economic scale, immigrants benefit from migration. In the social domain, many of these immigrants have to endure complex problems associated with forging inclusion or integration into the social structures of their host countries. Often, their work experience has to do with existing historical relationships and racial differences between source and destination, how they arrive at their destinations and the kinds of employment opportunities available to them upon arrival in the West. Within this framework, this chapter addresses three research questions. First, what is the trajectory of these Zimbabwean nurse migrants, (who are they demographically and occupationally, how do they migrate, what are their settlement patterns in the United Kingdom and what are their future plans)? Second, is there specific place or destination attributes operating in both the United Kingdom and Zimbabwe responsible for explaining the movement of nurse populations from Zimbabwe to the United Kingdom? Third, what workplace experiences do Zimbabwean nurses have in the United Kingdom and how are these experiences transferred back home to aid in the economic and cultural development of Zimbabwe?

Intra- and inter-diasporic relationships forms a significant aspect of how streams of new immigrants structure their relationships with other groups with similar cultural and normative belief systems. Blyden tackles this subject in chapter 8. For African immigrants in the diaspora, relationships with American-born blacks and Caribbean immigrants is the centerpiece of how continued expressions of blackness are constructed, lived, or negotiated. The chapter is an investigation of the cultural and social psychological parameters and dimensions of the contents of the relationships that African immigrants establish with Caribbean black immigrants and American-born blacks. It uses a historical perspective to trace the intra and inter bonds of affinity and cultural ties that are fostered and propagated by African immigrants and other blacks in the United States. It contends that the sociological and cultural narratives exploring the relationship between blacks from Africa and the Caribbean with native-born black Americans have often being constructed and characterized as unpleasant and oftentimes based on fear, lack of intercultural exchanges and communication, and above all, a misunderstanding about African cultures and societies. Anchoring this chapter is a historically textured prose that attempts to explain the continued sources of conflict and cooperation among the various black diaspora groups that are represented in the United States. Social and cultural mechanisms to bridge the differences among the various groups now constituting the black African and African American diasporas are delineated and assessed for their importance in defining what constitutes "blackness" in American racial and ethnic cultural mosaic.

In chapter 9, Arthur uses data from national opinion surveys and focus group data to contextualize the attitudinal perspectives of blacks on United States immigration policies. The thrust of the chapter is to show how blacks perceive the structural economic and cultural impact of controlled and un-controlled immigration on their economic well-being as well as on their communities. As a group, blacks bear a disproportionate amount of the economic burdens caused by immigration. Urban blacks with limited education and poor job skills continue to feel an economic squeeze during periods of economic boom and recessionary cycles. This economic squeeze is manifested in the form of high black unemployment rates which is 15 percent, higher than the current national rate of 9 percent. Mapping the attitudinal perspectives of blacks toward U.S. immigration policies is significant because as a group, and due to their lower socioeconomic status relative to whites, African Americans disproportionately are affected by the cumulative social, cultural, economic, as well as the political impacts of both regulated and unregulated immigration into the country. Aspects of the impact are seen in areas of economic competition with new immigrants for scarce urban jobs, housing, and formation of immigrant-family-owned enterprises in the urban and suburban areas of the country. The continued relegation and economic dislocation of blacks as a result of massive immigration affects the overall quality of life of blacks. Politically, if current projections of Latino immigration persist, these groups of immigrants alone will overshadow the once enviable political power and capital that blacks had as a core political constituent whose voting behavior can alter the balance of congressional and presidential elections.

Chapter 10 by Okome discusses the relationships that African immigrants in the diaspora establish with their home governments and societies. The thrust of Okome's chapter is the recognition among Africans in the diaspora and development policy makers that the resources, skills, and assets that Africa's immigrants acquire while domiciled abroad can be effectively mobilized and incorporated into the development of African societies. As Okome highlights, African immigrants abroad feel that they have a role to play in assisting their home governments raise the standard of living of Africans as a whole. This altruism is buttressed on the conviction held by many African immigrants that migration does not mean severing ties with the homeland; that ultimately, several of the immigrants plan to return home. Involvement in the economic and social development efforts of their home countries is a means to ensure that that the Africa they return home to will be one that is well developed and globally positioned to face any economic and social challenges.

In chapter 11, Osirim centers the importance of gender in the new African migration to global economic and cultural markets. African migration is no longer a male preserve. African women have joined the caravan of Africans who are now travelling to seek better economic and cultural opportunities outside of the continent. Osirim discusses how these women recreate their cultural and social identities in new domains while holding on to age-old traditional African gender and cultural values. The chapter launches into a detailed expose of the structural and individualistic components of the factors that converge to depict how African female immigrant identities are formed and the underlying social outcomes of these identities.

Chapter 12 examines border issues in African diaspora literature. Kowino's chapter highlights a number of central questions in the African disapora. First, he addresses the state of the African diaspora now that Jim Crow segregation is ostensibly behind us. Second, he argues that institutionalized borders of race, class, and gender have created an exilic condition in the African diaspora. The diasporic Africans' experiences of displacement, dispossession, and second class citizenship indicate a long way from the promised land. His chapter draws on literary analysis to further our understanding of the systemic inequalities that have reduced the American dream to a nightmare for so many diasporic Africans.

Upon entering the global migratory circuits in the West and the centers of advanced economic production, African immigrants, like their counterparts from other regions of the world, are faced with a dilemma. Should they maintain a sojourner or temporary status in their host societies? Or should they strive to straddle multiple cultural and geographic territories to reflect their newfound identities with the ultimate goal of repatriating back home to Africa? The answers to these questions are significant in understanding the economic and cultural processes African immigrants utilize to inform their decisions about whether to return to Africa or not after being domiciled in the West.

Using data collected from a nonrandom sample of 105 immigrants representing 6 African countries currently residing in Milwaukee (Wisconsin), chapter 13 examines the macro-level (structural) and the micro-level (individualistic) components that account for how African immigrants structure the decision-making process regarding repatriation and resettlement in Africa. African immigrants from Nigeria, Senegal, Ghana, Sudan, Somalia, and Ethiopia currently domiciled in Wisconsin are used as case studies to illustrate the growing significance of African immigrant repatriation and the socioeconomic, cultural, and political consequences of reverse migration on macro economic development and cultural transformations in Africa. A secondary goal of this chapter is to identify any commonalities and country-specific variations and strategies African immigrants implement as they form decisions to repatriate from the United States to Africa.

Attention is given to the importance of demographic variables (age, marital status, type employment status, educational attainment, household size, total family income, gender, length of stay in the United States) , household economic variables (amount of money saved at home and in the United States, frequency of remittance flows, amount of money remitted, immigrant sense of economic opportunities in the country of origination, home ownership, small-scale business formations at home, immigrant categorization of ease of transferability of assets, number of children or grandchildren under age twenty-one, spousal labor force participation, immigrant perception about the American economy, frequency of unemployment, sector of immigrant employment), immigrant rationalization of the political culture and environment in the country of origination (home government policies to promote smooth repatriation, immigrant sense of insecurity, lack of confidence in core institutions at home, fear of social incorporation and integration, fear of violence, crime, personal safety and security).

Chapter 14 provides an overview of international migration among Africans and discusses some of the current and future policy issues that may influence the role(s) that Africans will play in the continued saga of international migration. The chapter also summarizes what we have collectively learned about African global migration in editing this volume.

REFERENCES

Alba, R. 1985. *Ethnicity and Race in the U.S.A.: Toward the Twenty-First Century (ed.)*. Boston: Routledge and Kegan Paul.

Awokoya, J. 2009. "I'm Not Enough of Anything": The Racial and Ethnic Identity Constructions and Negotiations of 1.5 and Second Generation Nigerian Immigrants. (Unpublished doctoral dissertation). University of Maryland, College Park.

Awokoya, J., and Harushimana, I. 2010. "Family–School Mediation: Righting the Mental Self-Perceptions of 1.5 and 2.0 African Youths in U.S. Schools." In Hill, N. E.; Mann, T. L.; and H. E. Fitzgerald. *African American Children's Mental Health: Prevention, Intervention and Social Policy (ed.)*. Santa Barbara, CA: ABC/CLIO Praeger.

Barth, F. 1969. *Ethnic Groups and Boundaries: The Social Organization of Cultural Difference*. Boston: Little, Brown, and Co.

Bonacich, Edna. 1987. "'Making it' in America: A Social Evaluation of the Ethics of Immigrant Entrepreneurship." *Sociological Perspectives*, Volume 30 (4): 446–466.

Clark, M. K. 2006. *The Impact of African Immigration on Pan African Relations and Black Identity in the United States*. Unpublished doctoral dissertation, Howard University: Washington, D.C.

Danilove, Dan. 1992. "The Immigrants: How They're Helping to Revitalize the United States Economy." *Business Week (July)*, 114–22.

D'Alisera, J. 2009. "Images of a Wounded Homeland: Sierra Leonean Children and the New Heart of Darkness." In Foner, Nancy. *Across Generations: Immigrant Families in America (ed.)*. New York: New York University Press, 114–34.

Mensah, Joseph. 2008. "Religious Transnationalism Among Ghanaian Immigrants in Toronto: A Binary Logistic Regression Analysis." *The Canadian Geographer*. Volume 52 (3): 309–30.

Moya, Jose. 2005. "Immigrants and Associations: A Global and Historical Perspective." *Journal of Ethnic and Migration Studies*. Volume 31 (5): 833–64.

Olson, James S. 1979. *The Ethnic Dimension in American History*. New York: St. Martin's Press.

Ozcurumez, Saime 2009. "Immigrant Associations in Canada: Included, Accommodated, or Excluded?" *Turkish Studies*. Volume 10 (2): 195–215.

Portes, A. and Rumbaut, R. 2001. *Ethnicities: Children of Immigrants in America*. Berkeley: University of California Press.

Predelli, L. N. 2008. "Political and Cultural Ethnic Mobilization: The Role of Immigrant Associations in Norway." *Journal of Ethnic and Migration Studies*. Volume 34 (6): 935–54.

Pyke, K., and Dang, T. 2003. "'FOB' and 'Whitewashed': Identity and Internalized Racism Among Second Generation Asian Americans." *Qualitative Sociology*. Volume 26 (2): 147–72.

Raijman, Rebecca and Tienda, Marta. 2003. "Ethnic Foundations of Economic and Transactions: Mexican and Korean Immigrant Entrepreneurs in Chicago," *Ethnic and Racial Studies*. Volume 26 (5): 783–801.

Staring, Richard. 2000. "International Migration, Undocumented Immigrants and Immigrant Entrepreneurship," in Rath, Jan. *Immigrant Businesses* (ed.). New York: St. Martin's Press, 182–98.

Waters, M. 1990. *Ethnic Options: Choosing Identities in America*. Berkeley: University of California Press.

Zeleza, P. T. 2009. "Diaspora Dialogues: Engagements Between Africa and its Diasporas." In Okpewho, I. and Nzegwu, N. 2009. *The New African Diaspora*. Bloomington: Indiana University Press, 31–58.

Chapter Two

The Role of Ghanaian
Immigrant Associations in Canada

INTRODUCTION

The post-arrival experiences and aspirations of immigrants in Canada and the United States, as in other immigration countries, have been the subject of considerable research effort for several decades. Several studies have examined the residential (housing) and economic aspects of the immigrant experience (Moya, 2005; Predelli, 2008; Mensah, 2008; Ozcurumez, 2009; Skarbuskis, 1996; Ray, 1994; Hulchanski, 1993). In contrast, unlike in the United States, relatively few studies have explored the social aspects of the immigrant experience in Canada, including the ways in which immigrants organize themselves to meet some of their social, cultural, and economic needs. Specifically, little is known about the formation of ethnic associations and the role they play in the settlement and adaptation of immigrants in the host country. By definition, an ethnic association is a voluntary organization formed by individuals who consciously define themselves as members of an ethnic group within a larger context (Jenkins, 1988). It fulfills a variety of economic, social, cultural, and political needs common to persons of its defined group, and its members typically see themselves as part of an ethnic community (Jenkins, 1988).

Previous studies of ethnic associations in Canada have focused primarily on the larger and well established ethnic groups, with a longer history of immigration to Canada, such as Italians, Polish, Greeks, and Portuguese (see, for example, Giberovitch, 1994; Campani, 1992; Radecki, 1979; Jensen, 1969). Thus ethnic association formation among Canada's more recent, non-European immigrant groups, particularly from Asia, Africa, and Latin America, and the extent to which these associations assist them to adapt to and settle in a new society, are not well understood. This gap in the literature is rather surprising, given that, over the last two decades, the majority of immigrants to Canada have come from these regions. Although distinctions were made among earlier groups of immigrants from Europe on the basis of cultural and racial differences from the majority (white, Euro-Canadian) population, and advantages were conferred on some groups and not others (see Harney and Troper, 1975), the more recent groups of immigrants to Canada, commonly referred to as "visible minorities," are comparatively more distinct, both culturally and racially, from the majority population. As a result, they have experienced, and continue to experience many barriers in the host society, especially racial discrimination in housing, employment, and other spheres of life (Murdie, 1996; Henry, 1994; Hulchanski, 1993).

In addition, many recent immigrants, particularly those from Africa were admitted to Canada as refugees who, partly because of the circumstances surrounding their forced migration, often arrive with little or no financial resources, low level of education and training, often lack kinship networks on which they can rely for help and, in some cases, experience psychological problems. In light of these factors, and given the recency of their arrival, they may face greater problems of adaptation, be they economic, social, or cultural. The adaptive or coping strategies they employ, therefore, including the types of associations they establish, and their role in the lives of the immigrants, can be expected to reflect their unique economic, social, cultural circumstances and needs and, therefore, be different from those of earlier groups of immigrants.

Purpose of the Study

This study investigates the role of Ghanaian associations in Canada, to illustrate the ways in which immigrants from African collectively organize themselves to meet the needs related to their adaptation to and settlement in a new country. Specifically, the study examines: 1) the different types of Ghanaian associations; the timing of, and the reasons for their formation; 2) how the associations help to fulfil the economic, social, cultural, and political needs of the immigrants in the new society; 3) the ways in which immigrants use the associations to contribute to community development efforts, maintain back-home ties and commitments, and to fight for political rights in the homeland; and 4) the extent to which demographic, economic, and social factors, such as length of residence, education, income, and residential location, and desire for cultural maintenance influence membership in the associations. Three main types of Ghanaian associations are examined, namely: a) township (or home town) associations—those whose members originate from the same town; b) ethnic associations—comprising individuals belonging to the same ethnic grouping in Ghana; and c) national associations—which are open to all Ghanaians regardless of ethnic origin. These associations are described in detail later in the chapter.

The term "adaptation" is used as an analytical framework in this chapter, following Roberts and Clifton (1990), Herberg (1989), and Richmond (1974). The term is used here to refer to the process by which particular immigrant groups attempt to organize themselves to meet their needs, and act in ways that optimize their individual and collective interests in the host society (Roberts and Clifton, 1990). It is, however, recognized that the concept and reality of adaptation are considerably broader than obtaining the basic necessities of life such as finding housing, jobs, and establishing social relationships in a new urban environment. While lacking specificity, and requiring a more precise operational definition for purposes of empirical research, the term "adaptation" has the advantage of not involving a priori value judgement concerning desirable outcomes, or conveying the same ideological overtones that have come to be associated with the notion of assimilation (Richmond, 1974). The use of this term also avoids the pitfalls of unilinear determinism, over-generalization, and insensitivity to the richly varied paths open to individuals and groups who move into a new society (Richmond, 1974). For example, some groups may wish to assimilate, while others may either be unwilling or unable to assimilate. Another major limitation of assimilation theory is that its focus is primarily on the newcomer and his/her ability to adjust, and be accepted by the host society, while the host society remains virtually untouched and unchanged in the process (Rosenthal and Auerbach, 1992).

By the use of this term, therefore, it is possible, at least theoretically, to locate the outcome of the settlement process for each immigrant group on a continuum that may range from ethnic-group separation at one end to assimilation at the other (Herberg, 1989). In this case, the convergence of an immigrant population, in time to a state of more or less complete assimilation with the host population, may be considered a special case of a certain type of adaptation, while ethnic identity and community formation, including the formation of ethnic associations, may represent another form of adaptation.

Background

It is known that soon after migration, many immigrant groups establish associations to meet wants related to their settlement in the new country. In Canada, for example, ethnic associations were formed by various groups following mass immigration at the end of the nineteenth century and the beginning of the twentieth century (Wickberg, 1982; Campani, 1992; Jensen, 1969). Many of the recent immigrant groups have also established ethnic associations. Ethnic associations can also be found in many other immigration

countries, including the United States (Takougang and Tidjani, 2009; Predelli, 2008, Moya, 2005; Jenkins, 1988; Rex et. al., 1987). Ethnic associations often comprise people from one country, or the same region, district,
town or village in that country (Burnet and Palmer, 1988; Campani, 1992).
Besides geographical origin, there may be other bases of membership in an
ethnic association. Among the Chinese in Canada, for example, one type of
association was based on surname, which was considered to connote kinship
(Wickberg, 1982). This broader definition of an ethnic association, above, is
employed in the discussion this section. The terms "ethnic associations" and
"immigrant associations" will also be used interchangeably in this section.

Irrespective of the basis of membership, ethnic associations fill an important place in the lives of those who belong to them. Ethnic associations
may be formed for various reasons. One explanation is that newcomers to a
society who are characterized by different customs and language, and form
an ethnocultural minority, may find it difficult if not impossible to enter into
certain voluntary associations of the host population, such as those in which
membership depends somehow on a high socioeconomic attainment, as determined by, for example, education, income, professional background, or
where membership requires payment of high fees. There may also be needs
that members of the ethnic group are prevented from meeting within existing voluntary organizations by linguistic barriers, discrimination, or other
obstacles (Burnet and Palmer, 1988). Besides, depending on the purposes
of such associations, new immigrants may find them unsuitable for meeting
many of their social, economic, and cultural needs in the new society. In such
cases, attempts will be made to establish and support a distinct organizational
structure which will satisfy their special interests (Burnet and Palmer, 1988).
Ethnic associations may also be formed to serve specific needs that individuals share with their own ethnic fellows but not necessarily with the native
community. These interests may include the need for contact with others
of their own language and background, and the perpetuation of a particular
language or culture (Giberovitch, 1994). Ethnic associations also serve as
important vehicles for social networking. As Norris (1975:165) has pointed
out 'immigrant associations provide new immigrants with a basis of familiar
relationships and interactions on which they begin to build their new lives.
Ethnic association formation in particular and the persistence of ethnic affiliations in general can also be understood as immigrants' responses to specific
social and economic circumstances, opportunities, and limitations (Reitz,
1994, Yancey, et. al, 1985). For example, when the immigrant experience
includes rejection, racism, and discrimination the elaboration of ethnic ties
provides a ready system of support for groups distinguishable by "race," national origin or language (Nelson and Tienda, 1983). In their study of African

immigrants in the United States, Takougang and Tidjani (2009) point out that in order to deal with racial stereotypes, new African immigrants, like other earlier groups of immigrants have developed various self-help groups and organization to help them adapt and survive in their new environment. The process of migration, therefore, often brings about new identities for people, placing them in groupings with others with whom they may not have associated in their home country. Such affiliations, by implication, can also shift according to situation and context.

Ethnic associations seldom limit their activities to one specific goal, function, or activity. They often attempt to provide the members with a number of services and opportunities, and the scope of their activities reflects most often the combination of emotional and material interests that draw and hold the members. In general, individuals who join ethnic organizations demonstrate a sense of ethnic identity, and through membership and participation, reinforce this identity (Ozcurumez, 2009; Moghaddam and Perreault, 1992). With time, however, the appeal of ethnic associations often diminishes, especially for those whose principal occupational institutions come to lie outside the ethnic framework, including wealthy businessmen, professionals, and intellectuals (Burnet and Palmer, 1988). In addition to economic status (or social class), membership in an ethnic association may be influenced by residential location, time of arrival, and attitudes toward the host society.

The preceding review suggests that the study of ethnic associations can greatly enhance our understanding of the immigrant experience. Such studies can provide insights not only into how immigrants may organize themselves in a new society, but also how they use these associations to meet their material and emotional needs. In the context of Canada's policy of multiculturalism, ethnic associations are particularly worth studying because they may reflect the strength of ethnic affiliations, and of the desire for cultural maintenance. As Rex et al. (1987:11) have suggested "in the context of an immigrant community, associations should be studied as one of the means through which the culture and value systems of that community are represented."

Data for this study were drawn from a variety of sources. Two sets of interviews were conducted. The first set involved leaders and key officials of seven (out of a total of twenty-eight) well established Ghanaian associations in Toronto, including one national association, three ethnic associations, and three township organizations. The second set involved 100 Ghanaian respondents who were selected, through a systematic random sampling technique, from a comprehensive list of 2,000 Ghanaian immigrants in Toronto.

In both sets of interviews, face to face interviews were conducted with all the respondents in their homes. The questionnaires for these interviews were partly structured, with multiple choice responses, and partly unstructured (with open-ended, but well-defined questions). In latter case, the objective was to allow respondents to provide as much details as possible about their experiences with as little bias as possible on the part of the interviewer (Hammersley, 1992). It also allowed for in-depth interviewing, and possible probing for the meaning of certain statements made by the respondents. In addition, information was collected through content analysis of newspapers, newsletters, and brochures published by the associations included in the study. Observation of, and participation in a variety of social and cultural activities organized by each of the associations included in the study also provided valuable information for this study.

Migration of Ghanaians to Canada

By Canadian standards, Ghanaians are a recent immigrant group, although they were among the earliest group of Africans to come to Canada (Naidoo, 1985). Immigration data indicate that in 1967 there were only about 100 Ghanaian immigrants in Canada. The number of new Ghanaian arrivals remained very small throughout the 1970s, averaging less than 150 per year, but it began to increase substantially in the early 1980s. As of 2001, there were about 17,000 Ghanaian immigrants in Canada (Statistics Canada, 2001). On the one hand, the influx of Ghanaian immigrants during this period may be at-tributable to changes in Canadian immigration policy in the late 1970s, which made provisions for the admission of independent immigrants, refugees, and family members. On the other hand, emigration from Ghana to Canada and elsewhere, especially since the early 1980s, has been prompted by the dif-ficult economic and political conditions there.

The Toronto census metropolitan area (CMA) is the destination of most Ghanaian immigrants in Canada. As of 2001, 67 percent of the total Gha-naian immigrant population in Canada lived in Toronto. As a result of the political situation in Ghana, a high proportion of Ghanaians who migrated to Canada in the 1980s were admitted as political refugees. Like many recent immigrants, Ghanaian immigrants have a different demographic and socio-economic profile from the rest of the Toronto CMA's population. Overall, they have limited education and low incomes. Only 7.2 percent of Ghanaian immigrants have completed university-level education compared to 17 per-cent of the Toronto population as a whole.

Ghanaian immigrants are disproportionately represented in processing and machining occupations and under-represented in professional, managerial and administrative occupations in comparison to Toronto's CMA population as a whole. Only 4.2 percent of Ghanaian immigrants were employed in manage-rial or administrative occupations, while 41 percent were in processing and machining occupations. In contrast, 16.4 percent of the population of Toronto were employed in managerial and administrative occupations, 18 percent in professional occupations, and 11 percent in processing and machining.

Like many other visible-minority and recent immigrant groups, Ghanaians have lower employment incomes than the rest of the Toronto population. Average employment income for Ghanaians was about 30 percent less than that for the population of Toronto as a whole. The economic profile of Ghanaians may reflect a set of factors including the recency of their migration, their relatively low educational levels, as well as constraints, especially discrimination, that they face in the labour market as new immigrants and as a racial minority, which tends to restrict economic opportunities. The demographic and economic circumstances of Ghanaian immigrants have implications for their socioeconomic mobility, and for ethnic community development, including the formation of ethnic associations.

Ghanaian Associations in Toronto

Although Ghanaians have been in Toronto since the late 1960s, they began to form associations only in the late 1980s. The timing of the formation of these associations was influenced by the massive influx of Ghanaians to Toronto, which provided the critical mass of people for the viability of the different associations. Ghanaian associations in Toronto fall into three broad categories as follows: township associations, ethnic associations and national association. Table 2.1 shows selected characteristics of the associations that were surveyed. Leaders of the associations are relatively well-educated, with professional occupations, and have a relatively long period of residence in Toronto. This is consistent with findings regarding the leadership profiles of other ethnic associations in Canada and elsewhere (Louis-Jaques, 1991; Radecki, 1979; Rex et al., 1987). The "elite" character of ethnic association leadership may be explained in terms of Breton's social demand hypothesis, which suggests that, since ethnic associations have to work with mainstream bureaucratic agencies (e.g. local governments, government ministries and departments) on issues as registering the associations, writing proposals for funding, submissions on immigration and social policy issues), individuals who, by their length of residence, level of education, linguistic skills, and legal knowledge or "bureaucratic competence," can play the role of intermediaries between the immigrant group and the bureaucracy of the receiving country, are the ones who are likely to be recognized and appointed as leaders (Breton, 1991). On the other hand, it can be argued that such individuals may also seek the leadership of these associations as a means of enhancing their social status and influence within the Ghanaian community in particular and the host society in general.

Table 2.1. Selected Characteristics of Seven Ghanaian Association in Toronto

Type/Name of Association	Year Established	No. of Members	Leaders stay in Toronto	Leader's Education	Leader's Occupation
National					
National Congress Of Ghanaian Canadians	1990	N/A	18 years	University degree	Engineer
Ethnic					
Ashanti Multicultural Association	1982	600	20	University degree	Foreman
Kwahuman Cultural Association	1983	340	15	University degree	Social Worker
Okuapeman Cultural Association	1989	250	14	University degree	Dentist
Township					
Manpong Cultural Association	1989	120	10	University degree	Social Worker
Nsutaman Cultural Association	1991	80	15	College diploma	Technician
Kwabre Cultural Association	19901	100	6	University degree	Pharmacist

Source: Author's survey data

ETHNIC AND TOWNSHIP ASSOCIATIONS

Ethnic Associations

The ethnic associations comprise Ghanaian immigrants who belong to the same ethnic group (commonly called "tribe" in Ghana). The proliferation of this type of association is best understood in the context of the significance of ethnicity in Ghanaian society. Ghana's population of about 22 million is ethnically diverse; some seventeen major groups can be identified on the basis of language, cultural practices, and belief systems (Hall, 1981). This ethnic diversity has had important implications for intra- and inter-ethnic relations, and for the ways in which Ghanaians organize themselves socially, both at home and abroad.

The timing of the formation of ethnic associations can be attributed not only to the influx of Ghanaians to Toronto during this period, but, more importantly, to increase in the number of the immigrants belonging to the different ethnic groups. In the early 1970s, the Ghanaian population in Toronto was not only small, but ethnically heterogeneous. At that time, therefore, national origin rather than ethnic background was the most important point of reference for the immigrants. This sense of national identity led to the formation of the Ghana Union (an association comprising Ghanaians of all ethnic backgrounds), in 1973.

In the years following the formation of the Ghana Union, especially in the early 1980s, a large number of Ghanaians of different ethnic backgrounds came to Toronto. At the same time, the Ghana Union was experiencing "internal leadership problems and the lack of a proper focus" (Boakye-Akoto, 1993). In particular, there was a feeling among its leadership and membership that "some basic needs of Ghanaian immigrants, such as fulfilling their cultural aspirations, could be better handled by individual ethnic associations rather than the Ghana Union" (Boakye-Akoto, 1993). In 1982, therefore, the Ashantis (then the largest ethnic group) established the Ashanti Multicultural Association (AMA), the first Ghanaian ethnic association in Toronto. The formation of the AMA, and the realization by other ethnic groups that they also needed to cater for their own needs, not only intensified intra-ethnic affiliations, but weakened the appeal of the Ghana Union and, ultimately, led to its demise in 1983. The salience of ethnic identification among Ghanaians in Toronto, which underlies the proliferation of ethnic associations, is captured in the following statement by a leader of a Ghanaian ethnic association in a personal interview:

> Ghanaians put their tribe first because they feel more accepted in their own tribal groups; there is a greater sense of togetherness and belonging among members of the same tribe. Also, people feel more comfortable dealing with members of their tribe because they share the same customs and beliefs, and communicate in the same language.

Township Associations

A township association comprises persons who come from the same home town in Ghana. The majority (75 percent) of Ghanaian associations in Toronto are of this type. It should be noted that each ethnic group in Ghana typically occupies an entire region, comprising several towns and villages. This means that individuals may belong to the same ethnic groups, but have different home towns. As is common among Ghanaians in Toronto, therefore, an individual may belong to both a township and an ethnic association at the same time. Generally, township associations tend to have a much smaller membership than ethnic associations. While members of a township association share a common ethnic origin, origin from a common town, rather than a common ethnic background, provides the primary point of reference for members. The most important motivation for the formation of township associations was the belief among their members that they could use them to make direct and more contribution to the social and economic development efforts in their home towns.

The process of township, ethnic, and national association formation and institutional development is influenced by the residential distribution of the ethnic population. Generally, an ethnic group which exhibits a high degree of residential concentration will find it easier to establish associations than one whose members are residentially dispersed across the city. Residential concentration allows not only for the easy communication of information about the association by informal methods, but also proximity and accessibility to associations' meeting places. As Ghanaian immigrants have come to Toronto, they have tended to concentrate in particular neighbourhoods and even in specific buildings, partly due to the channelling effects of chain migration and the reliance on friends and relatives in the housing search process. This intense residential concentration has not only provided a critical mass even for groups that are too small, but it has eased the process of ethnic association formation.

The Role of Ethnic and Township Associations

Ethnic and township associations play a vital role in the adaptation and settlement of immigrants. They fulfill a number of social, economic, cultural, and political functions. Ghanaian associations in Toronto share quite similar objectives. The key purpose of the associations is to unite Ghanaians in Toronto who belong to particular ethnic groups or come from certain town in Ghana. This objective is pursued mainly through activities that enhance social interaction including meetings, parties, picnics, and other recreational activities.

The associations do more than promoting unity and social interaction among members. They serve many important social and economic purposes, including assisting their members to find jobs and housing. The associations are aware of the housing needs of their members, particularly new immigrants including availability and cost, space and location, and discrimination. In response to these needs, ethnic and township associations members help to locate housing, intervene with landlords, advance a month's rent, and in some cases directly provide housing. Similarly, members particularly newcomers are assisted to find employment. This assistance may include providing information about jobs they have learned about through informal networks and contacts and informing them about employment opportunities in their workplaces.

Ethnic and township associations can be vital sources of financial assistance for immigrants. The associations offer direct financial assistance in the form of "soft loans" (i.e. interest-free, with flexible repayment terms) to members, especially newcomers who may be experiencing financial difficulties. Members who lose an immediate family member or close relative can rely on the association not only for emotional support, but also financial assistance. Typically, a pre-determined amount of money is donated to a bereaved member. In addition, individual members of the association make voluntary monetary donations to the bereaved member, normally during a funeral ceremony in Toronto. These donations are meant to help the bereaved member to bear the cost of the funeral, and of transporting the corpse to Ghana, where final funeral rites and burial take place. In the event of the death of an association member, the association offers a monetary donation to his or her family, and assist them to organize a funeral and send the body home. It is worth noting that members whose family members in Ghana pass away are offered similar financial support by the associations. By the same token, members who have a new baby receive financial and material support from the association. Such donations are often made during child-naming and/or christening ('outdooring') ceremonies. These donations attest not only to the economic and social importance of the associations, but also the cultural importance attached to births and deaths in Ghanaian society.

Ethnic and township associations also fulfill a vital judicial function. They help to resolve problems and disputes involving their members, thereby helping to maintain peaceful relations within their communities. Ghanaian associations help to resolve all kinds of personal, marital, and family disputes that otherwise would have ended up and police and/or court cases.. Such disputes are typically adjudicated by a committee comprising the leaders and elder members of the associations. Ghanaian traditional customs and social practices as well as legal and social norms in the new country are used as the bases for settling such disputes.

Ethnic and township associations also help to fulfil the cultural needs of their members. They provide a means for cultural promotion, expression, and preservation. The fact that all Ghanaian ethnic associations have included the word "cultural" in their names suggests that cultural issues are central to their objectives. A variety of traditional customs and rites, including the pouring of libation (to invoke ancestral spirits), as well as traditional dresses, music, drumming, and dancing characterize activities like funerals, child-naming and christening ceremonies, and festivals. For the purpose of such ceremonies and festivals, and in accordance with their desire to portray and maintain aspects of their culture, the ethnic associations have formed traditional dance groups. As a further reflection of this cultural emphasis, leaders of the ethnic associations are considered as traditional leaders and, as such, are given titles reserved for real traditional rulers in Ghana, such as *nana, togbe,* and *mantse* (these are local names for traditional leaders among the Akan, Ewe, and Ga ethnic groups in Ghana, respectively). In fact, new association leaders are installed into office in ceremonies similar to those performed during the installation of new traditional rulers in Ghana.

Interestingly, the creation of new traditional leaders in Toronto has full approval and support of the respective real traditional leaders in Ghana. They consider it not only as a means by which their subjects abroad can help maintain their traditional values and cultural norms, but also to help expose and promote the essence and cultural richness of Ghana's traditional system of governance to non-Ghanaians. It should be noted that the installation of traditional leaders outside of Ghana is largely symbolic rather than real. As such, it has not had, and is not expected to have any short- and long-term impacts on social structure and hierarchies in Ghana, or even on the Ghanaian community in Toronto.

As part of their attempt at cultural maintenance, many of the associations have established "cultural education" programs, with the purpose of teaching the youth about Ghanaian languages, traditional customs, and social norms. Concern has been growing within the Ghanaian community about the fact that the youth are either unwilling or unable to speak the local languages, and have little or no understanding of and appreciation for Ghanaian history, customs, traditional values, and social practices. Immigrants, either individually or collectively, often establish and maintain links with their homelands, and seek to contribute to their social and economic development (see Amery and Anderson, 1995; Giberovitch, 1994). This is true of Ghanaian immigrants in Toronto. A key objective of the associations is to make a contribution to the development of their hometowns and regions in Ghana. To this end they seek to mobilize financial and material resources through membership dues and fundraising activities. During interviews, association leaders proudly listed a range of projects which they have either undertaken or plan to undertake in their regions and hometowns back home. The most frequently mentioned were the provision of medical and educational supplies, financial support for the development of community centres and clinics, and the construction of trunk roads.

Membership of Township and Ethnic Associations

Immigrants tend to differ in terms of the adaptive strategies they employ. This applies to membership in ethnic and township associations. About 60 percent of respondents belonged to at least one Ghanaian association. This rate of membership is relatively high in comparison with the rates observed for other ethnic groups, at least in Canada. Breton (1990), for example, found the following membership rates for some ethnic groups in Toronto: Chinese (12 percent), West Indian (12 percent), German (9 percent), Italian (21 percent), Portuguese (14 percent), Ukrainian (51 percent), and Jewish (63 percent). In another study (Radecki, 1979), about 35 percent of Polish immigrants in Toronto were found to belong to at least one ethnic organization. Membership in ethnic and township associations tends to be influenced by a variety of demographic, economic, social, and spatial (or residential location) factors. Although the sample sizes are small, the analysis clearly revealed that length of residence, level of education, income, and residential location were the variables most closely associated with membership in a Ghanaian association. Generally, respondents with a relatively short period of residence were more likely to belong to an association than long-term residents (Table 2.2). For instance, 82 percent of respondents who have been in Toronto for one to three years belonged to a Ghanaian association, compared to only 15 percent of respondents who have been in Toronto for over ten years respectively.

This differential in membership rates is partly attributable to the varying importance that short- and long-term immigrants attach to the associations. Many of the respondents with a short period of residence indicated that they viewed the associations as important avenues for meeting others from their ethnic group or home town, and for socialization in the initial phase of settlement. Most importantly, they viewed the associations as a resource for dealing with some of their practical social and economic needs. As one respondent who came to Toronto two years ago as a refugee, stated:

> When I arrived here (Toronto), I didn't have any relative here. I was quite lonely and I missed home a lot. Sometimes I wondered if I would be able to stay for long. Then I met a Ghanaian who told about the Okwawuman Association. I went to their next meeting and joined it immediately. Members of the associa-

Table 2.2. Membership of Ghanaian Association by Length of Residence in Toronto

Membership in Ghanaian Association	*Length of Residence in Toronto*				
	1-3 years	*4-6 years*	*7-10 years*	*Over 10 years*	*Total*
No	4 (18.2%)	9 (22.5%)	17 (68.0%)	11 (84.4%)	41
Yes	18 (81.8%)	31 (77.5%)	8(32.0%)	2 (15.4%)	59
Total	22 (100.0%)	40 (100.0%)	25 (100.0%)	13 (100.0%)	100.0%

Source: Author's survey data

tion have helped me a lot. One of them helped me to get my apartment. I consider them as my extended family.

On the other hand, most of the respondents with a relatively long period of residence indicated that they had neither the interest nor time to join them due to work and other commitments. It should be noted, however, that some of them previously belonged to an association. This finding provides support for the view that long-term immigrants tend to have less need for ethnic associations (Burnet and Palmer, 1988). This may be due to their improved economic situation. It may also be that they have relatively well-established formal and informal personal networks upon which they rely to meet their needs, thus, reducing the appeal of the ethnic associations. In fact further analysis shows that membership in influenced by income (Table 2.3). Respondents with relatively low incomes were more likely to belong to an association than those with moderate or high incomes (p<.05). Similarly, level of education was found to be a determinant of ethnic association membership. For example, 71% of respondents with less than college or university education belong to a Ghanaian association, compared to 43.1 percent of those with college or university education.

While Ghanaian associations tend to be led by relatively well-educated individuals, long-term immigrants, as previously mentioned, the majority of the members are short-term immigrants, often with low levels of education. This finding is consistent with Breton's (1991) social demand hypothesis that well-educated members of an immigrant group are more likely to be selected as leaders, since are often considered by their fellow ethnics as the ones who possess the administrative knowledge and skills required to deal with mainstream agencies. At the same time, it may also be argued that such individuals take up leadership positions in the associations as a means of enhancing their social status and influence within the ethnic community in particular and the society in general, as well as in their homeland.

Residential location within the city is an important determinant of membership in an ethnic or township association. The rate of association membership

Table 2.3.   Membership of Ghanaian Association by Income Level

Membership in Ghanaian Association	Income Level			
	Low Income *<$20,000*	*Moderate Income* *$20,000-$30,000*	*High Income* *> $30,000*	*Total*
No	12 (25.0%	20 (52.6)%)	9 (64.3%)	41
Yes	36 (75.0%)	18 (47.4%)	5 (35.7%)	59
Total	48 (100.0%)	38 (100.0%)	14 (100.0%)	100.0%

Source: Author's survey data.

Table 2.4.   Membership of Ghanaian Association by Neighbourhood of Residence

Membership in Ghanaian Association	Neighbourhood of Residence		Total
	Non-Ghanaian Neighborhood	Ghanaian Neighborhood	
No	27(62.8%)	14 (24.6%)	41
Yes	16 (37.2%)	43 (75.4%)	59
Total	43 (100.0%)	57 (100.0%)	100.0%

Source: Author's survey data

for respondents living in Ghanaian neighbourhoods was higher (76 percent) than for those in non-Ghanaian neighborhoods (36 percent) (Table 2.4). This may be attributable, at least at the superficial level, to the fact that most of the associations hold their meetings at locations in or close to the Ghanaian neighbourhoods. Those living in or close to these neighbourhoods, therefore, are more likely not only to be aware of the existence of these associations, but will also find it easier to attend their meetings and participate in their activities. At the same time, the differential in membership rate may also simply reflect the fact that a high proportion of respondents living in the Ghanaian neighbourhoods are short-term residents who, as noted earlier, tend to attach a greater importance to membership in ethnic associations.

Contrary to expectation, however, the relationship between membership in a Ghanaian association and the importance attached to the desire for the maintenance of Ghanaian cultural values and norms, was not statistically significant. A high support for cultural maintenance was found for both members and nonmembers of associations. This finding does not conform to that of a previous study of Iranian immigrants in Canada (Moghadam et. al, 1987). In a study of their integration strategies, they found that members of Iranian ethnic organizations were more committed to heritage culture maintenance than non-members. This finding may indicate a relatively strong sense of ethnic self identification among Ghanaian immigrants, perhaps reflecting their strong ties to their homeland and their intention to return to it permanently, and possibly to racial identification. It also suggests that ethnic association membership may not always be a meaningful predictor of the strength of ethnic self-identification.

The National Association: Its Formation and Role

Ethnic and township associations have played an important role in meeting the settlement needs of Ghanaian immigrants. At the same time, however, they adversely affected inter-ethnic relations. In fact, relations between the various ethnic associations have often been characterized by some degree of animosity and rivalry (Boakye-Akoto, 1993). The degree of divisiveness within the Ghanaian community was expressed as follows by the leader of a Ghanaian association: "Ghanaians in Toronto were so divided along so many ethnic lines it was impossible to imagine that we come from the same country" (personal communication). This would seem to suggest that many Ghanaians attached a greater significance to their ethnic identity, and less emphasis on their national identity. Over time, however, there was a realization that this divisiveness was detrimental to the interests of the ethnic groups and the Ghanaian community as a whole. For example, individual ethnic groups had been denied funding they had sought from government departments under the multicultural program to support cultural activities, on the grounds that they were either too small and/or did not representative of the entire Ghanaian community. Most importantly, there was a realization that the Ghanaian community risked becoming increasingly marginalised partly because it did not have a "single voice" to present their collective interests at various levels of government. These concerns, among others, provided the impetus for the formation of the National Congress of Ghanaian Canadians (NCGC) in 1990. The NCGC, therefore, was established to serve as an umbrella organization that would unite Ghanaians of all ethnic backgrounds, and provide them an effective and collective mouthpiece for addressing issues of interest to, or affecting all Ghanaian immigrants. In this regard, it may be argued that needs related to immigrants' collective survival and well-being, including funding for different programs, may force the creation of identities recognized by the host country by not necessarily the immigrants themselves.

Since its establishment, the NCGC has achieved some of these objectives. It has managed to bring together Ghanaians of different ethnic backgrounds, and to improve the level of inter-ethnic cooperation. It has provided a common forum for Ghanaians to collectively discuss and address issues that face them. For instance, it has made submissions to local and provincial governments on many issues including multiculturalism, immigrant settlement and integration, and employment equity. In addition, it actively defends the rights of Ghanaian immigrants and refugees. In 1992, for instance, it successfully intervened on behalf of some Ghanaian refugee claimants who were to be deported to Ghana. Furthermore, it has compiled a list of Ghanaian immigrants whose sponsorship of relatives has been delayed for several years, and it has used it to "bolster its demands for a better handling of Ghanaian sponsorship applications" (Boakye-Akoto, 1993). It also organizes information sessions and workshops for newcomers on a variety of social, cultural, economic, and institutional issues in Canada. Through the NCGC, Ghanaians are able to express, promote, and share their rich and diverse cultural heritage with other

Canadians in the spirit of multiculturalism, through participation in major festivals celebrating Canada's cultural diversity. On occasions like Ghana's Independence day celebration, the association presents Ghana's diverse culture through cultural displays, music, dancing, and exhibitions of arts and crafts. Unlike the township and ethnic associations, the NCGC has received government grants for various cultural activities.

Like the ethnic and township associations, the NCGC is committed to making a contribution to Ghana's social and economic development, particularly in the areas of health care, education, and agriculture. Since its formation, it has mobilized funds through fundraising activities to provide medical and educational supplies worth thousands of dollars to hospitals and educational institutions in Ghana. These contributions are a further example of how immigrants may collectively seek to maintain ties and commitments to their homeland, and contribute to its development even as they adjust to a new society.

Perhaps a more striking indication of the desire to maintain back-home ties and rights of residence, is the campaign for dual citizenship, which also demonstrates that ethnic associations may organize to address political needs related not only to the host country, but also to address their political concerns in their homeland. Given its importance to the role of ethnic associations in particular, and to the understanding of the settlement and adaptation of Ghanaians in general, the next section turns to a detailed discussion of the evolution, issues, and outcome of the dual citizenship issue.

The NCGC and the Dual Citizenship Campaign

Perhaps the most significant role of the NCGC relates to campaign for dual citizenship. This campaign was prompted by a provision in the revised (1992) Constitution of Ghana which stated that a citizen of Ghana who acquires or retains the citizenship of another country shall cease to be a citizen of Ghana. By this provision, many Ghanaian immigrants in Canada automatically lost their Ghanaian citizenship (in 1994 24 percent of Ghanaians in Toronto had acquired Canadian citizenship; 68 percent were permanent residents). Though many Ghanaians expressed in the interviews their wish to acquire Canadian citizenship, it is also true that they prefer to retain their Ghanaian citizenship.

In 1993, therefore, the NCGC initiated a campaign to seek an amendment to the 1992 constitution to allow Ghanaians to have dual citizenship. As part of the campaign, special information sessions and various social events were used to inform Ghanaian immigrants about the potential implications of the constitutional provision, and to solicit their support for its amendment. Financial support for the campaign was provided by Ghanaian businesses, associations, and individuals. In 1994, a delegation of NCGC leaders and prominent members of the Ghanaian community went to Ghana and had discussions with politicians and key government officials regarding their position on dual citizenship issue.

The most fundamental argument put forward by Ghanaian immigrants was that the constitutional provision would make them "foreigners in their own country." The various arguments for dual citizenship were summarized by a prominent member of the Ghanaian community and a leader of the campaign:

> The benefits that a foreign citizenship confers on Ghanaians abroad include opportunities for education, training, professional association membership, and employment opportunities. It is these opportunities which enable Ghanaians abroad to contribute to the development of Ghana. Even for Ghanaians who wish to re-establish residence in Ghana, a second citizenship is often needed to enhance international mobility and work opportunities abroad in order to earn foreign exchange for investment purposes in Ghana.

They argued that, although they lived abroad, they still continued to make a significant contribution to Ghana's economy, an indication of their continuing commitment to the country. They cited three broad ways or areas in which they contribute to the development of Ghana: foreign exchange remittances, direct investment, and humanitarian assistance. One basis of the campaign was the fact that Ghanaians in Canada (and by extension other countries) transfer a substantial amount of foreign money to Ghana annually through remittances. In fact a World Bank report shows that, in 1992 alone, official remittances (officially recorded private transfers) from Ghanaians abroad totalled $254.9 million, representing about 16 percent of the country's foreign exchange receipts. This amount, which excludes non-official transfers, exceeds official transfers (foreign aid) which totalled $213.8 million in the same year (World Bank, 1994).

The second major argument put forth was that many Ghanaians abroad have either made or plan to make direct private investments in Ghana in sectors like transportation, manufacturing, agriculture, and real estate. These private investments, it was argued, provided not only employment opportunities in Ghana, but also opportunities for the transfer of expertise and technology to the country. On humanitarian assistance, the argument was that Ghanaian associations regularly donate equipment, drugs, and books to various institutions in Ghana. All these contributions, they argued, indicated their commitment to their homeland. As a leader of the campaign puts it: "These remittances, investments, and donations indicated that concerns about the loyalty of Ghanaians abroad were baseless" (personal communication, 1994).

Evidence from the questionnaire survey provides strong support for these claims. Almost all of the respondents (97 percent) indicated that they maintain strong ties with their family members and relatives in Ghana, and support them financially through regular remittances. Besides, majority of respondents indicated that they have invested (31 percent) or plan to invest (58 percent) in different areas of Ghana's economy including real estate, transportation, and small business). In addition, as mentioned earlier, many also contribute to local economic development efforts in Ghana through their associations.

Perhaps the strongest indication of the commitments of Ghanaian immigrants to their homeland is their intention to return to it permanently. Over 80 percent of respondents indicated that they will return to Ghana permanently in the future. In fact the campaign for dual citizenship is better understood if viewed in the context of their return migration intentions. The apparent depth of this commitment confirms the duality of the migration process and the importance of back-home linkages in understanding the immigrant adaptation process. It is worth noting that a bill allowing for dual citizenship was passed by Ghana's legislative assembly in 1997. It is expected that it will be soon be endorsed by the President of Ghana.

It should be noted, however, that international return migration intentions are not always a useful predictor of return migration behavior (Waldorf, 1995). Though many immigrants return to their homeland, many others who initially express the intention to return eventually to their homeland remain permanently in the receiving country. This may be due to the fact that, though attachment to home may increase in the early stage of immigration in response to feelings of deprivation and cultural loss (Portes and Rumbaut, 1990), return migration intentions tend to diminish as the length of stay increases and the migrant becomes more established. Interestingly, the majority (93%) of those who intend to return home, have either Canadian citizenship or permanent residence status. It remains to be seen whether the decision to return to Ghana is a myth or a real intention.

CONCLUSION

Since the late 1980s, Ghanaians in Toronto have established a relatively large network of national, ethnic, and township associations to address some of their economic, social, cultural, and political needs. The formation of these associations has been facilitated not only by the influx of Ghanaians of different ethnic backgrounds during their period, but by their residential concentration. This concentration has provided the critical mass and accessibility for groups that would otherwise be too small to support viable associations. These processes of residential concentration, association formation, and institution-building are widely viewed as a critical element in the immigrant adaptation process.

It was also expected that Canada's policy of multiculturalism, which encourages and provides financial support for ethnic-related activities, would have provided a strong incentive for the formation of associations among Ghanaian immigrants, as it has apparently done for many other ethnic groups (Louis-Jaques, 1991; Giberovitch, 1994). Leaders of the associations, however, indicated that the policy itself was of relatively minimal consequence in terms of their decisions to form associations. Some support for this claim lies in the fact that Ghanaian associations have also been formed in countries without Canada-style multicultural policies, such as the U.S., Britain, Germany, and France. According to the leaders, the formation of associations was dictated primarily by the need to organize themselves in order to strengthen intra-group ties and address, in a collective manner, the needs related to their settlement in a different environment.

The formation of associations needs to be viewed in large part as a transplantation of an age-old adaptive strategy among Ghanaian migrants at home. Historically, rural-urban migrants within Ghana have always formed associations in cities and towns. Like those in Toronto, these associations have been based on kinship, ethnicity, and common place of origin, and their primary functions have been to provide avenues for new migrants to socialize, help them to find jobs and housing, provide mutual aid and welfare services, and contribute to development in their home towns (Peil and Sada, 1984). Lloyd (1966) has suggested that these associations are often attempts by urban migrants to recapture the benefits of their membership in traditional associations and gain support from an extensive network of kin in their places of origin, which they lose upon migration to the cities. Given that a common ethnic origin is the basis for membership in some of the associations, this interpretation is also consistent with the view that the revival of ethnicity is often related to attachment to one's culture, traditional values, customs and lifestyles (Moghaddam and Perreault, 1992).

The types and functions of the associations, as expected, reflect the needs of Ghanaians immigrants in relation to the receiving country, and the desire to maintain their back-home ties and commitments. The associations serve an important welfare function and, in many respects, they may be seen as substituting for local agencies. They seek to improve the social and economic well-being of their members, by assisting them to find employment, housing and other social and economic opportunities. They also provide an avenue for social fellowship and informal networking. This is particularly important for newcomers, since it provides them with a basis of familiar relationships and interactions on which they may begin to build their new lives. Most importantly, membership enables new immigrants to tap easily into well-established ethnic networks. The associations also serve as a collective mechanism by which ethnic groups seek to preserve and express their unique cultural identities while enhancing their progress through the local system. While the associations obviously facilitate the maintenance of ties among persons who share a common ethnicity, customs, and language, they also fragment the group as a whole.

The study also demonstrates that there is a link between international migration and community development in developing countries. The associations contribute to the development of their respective home towns and regions in Ghana through the provision of financial and material assistance to hospitals, schools, community centres and the like. The national association is particularly important in terms of its political role in relation to both the host country and the homeland. It provides a framework for Ghanaians of all ethnic backgrounds to collectively discuss and address the issues they face, and provides them with a "single voice" for articulating their concerns.

In relation to the homeland, the political role of the national association is particularly significant in terms of its campaign for dual citizenship. The vigorous campaign reflects the continuing commitments and loyalty of the immigrants to their homeland, and the seriousness of their intentions to return there permanently. This suggests that the acquisition of a foreign citizenship by immigrants does not necessarily indicate a stronger attachment to that country or, for that matter, a weak commitment to their place of origin. In fact it may be motivated by the opportunities for international mobility and economic prosperity.

Membership in Ghanaian associations supports the view, mentioned earlier, that the desire for ethnic affiliation is driven, in part, by the social and economic situation of immigrants in the host country. It also reveals intra-group differences in adaptive strategies. Analysis showed that while the associations are led by those with relatively high levels of education and income, they appealed most to those who find themselves in difficult economic circumstances, namely recent arrivals, those with relatively lower levels of education and incomes, and those living in Ghanaian neighborhoods. This again suggests that individual differences in attitudes are central to the definition of adaptation strategies and the role of institutions in those strategies. Given that this segment of the Ghanaian immigrant population may face greater problems of adaptation, this finding provides some support for the view that the development of ethnic affiliations among immigrants may be a social response to their economic circumstances, including poverty, and the lack of economic opportunities (Yancey et al., 1985; Tienda, 1983; Reitz, 1980). This confirms the collective welfare function. For groups that are also racially and culturally distinctive, such as Ghanaians, prejudice, discrimination, and social isolation may also serve to intensify ethnic affiliations, and lead to the formation of associations. The complexity of the relationships involved here, however, suggests that no single explanation of association formation, institution-building, and institutional support applies to all ethnic groups, or to all members within a group.

While this study provides useful insights into the role of Ghanaians associations, and the social aspects of their adaptation in general, it raises other issues that need to be examined in future research. These issues may be explored through comparative case studies of some of Canada's more recent immigrant groups. Further research is needed regarding the extent to which membership in ethnic associations influences membership in non-ethnic voluntary associations, and the development of formal and informal networks outside the ethnic community, both in the short- and long term, and the factors involved.

More importantly, it is also worth investigating whether ethnic associations and networks are a help or hindrance to the immigrants' adaptation to, and economic and social well-being in the new society. For example, it is worth knowing the extent to which the use of ethnic networks limits the housing, employment and other opportunities that might otherwise be available to immigrants. This can provide further insight into the processes and factors that help to create ethnic occupational and residential (housing) segregation. Similarly, it is important to know the extent to which ethnic associations substitute for local agencies in the provision of social services. This can help to determine how this substitution influences the adaptation process, as well as the well-being of new immigrants. It can also help to identify possible gaps in terms of the formal delivery of services to new immigrants and, perhaps, suggest how local governments can assist ethnic associations to expand on their role as informal resources for new immigrants.

REFERENCES

Amery, H. A. and W. P. Anderson. "International Migration and Remittances to a Lebanese Village." *The Canadian Geographer* 38, no 1. (1995): 46–58.

Bengtsson, P.S. "Empowering Members of Ethnic Organizations: Tracing the political Integration Potential of Immigrant Associations in Stockholm." *Scandinavian Political Studies* Vol. 32, no. 3 (2009): 296–311.

Boakye-Akoto, W. "The Ghanaian Community in Toronto." *Ghana Connection,* (1993): 3-4.

Breton, R. "The Political Dimension of Ethnic Community Organization." *In Ethnicity, Structured Inequality, and the State in Canada and the Federal Republic of Germany.* Edited by Robin Ostrow Frankfurt am Main: Peter Lang, 1991.

Burnet, Jean. *Migration and the Transformation of Cultures* Toronto: Multicultural History Society of Ontario, 1992.

Burnet, J. and H. Palmer. *Coming Canadians: An Introduction to the History of Canada's People.* Toronto: Mclleland and Stewart, 1988.

Campani, G. "Family, Village and Regional Networks of Italian Immigrants in France and Quebec." In *Deconstructing a Nation: Immigration, Multiculturalism and Racism in '90s Canada.* Edited by Vic Satzewich., 183–207, Halifax: Fernwood Publishing, 1994.

Giberovitch, M. "The Contributions of Holocaust Survivors to Montreal Jewish Community Life." *Canadian Ethnic Studies* Vol. XXV1, no. 1 (1994): 74–84.

Hammersley, M. *What's Wrong with Ethnography?* Routledge: London, 1992.

Harney, R. and H. Troper. *Immigrants: A Portrait of Urban Experience, 1890-1930.* Toronto: Von Nostrand Reinhold, 1975.

Henry, F. *The Caribbean Diaspora in Toronto: Learning to Live with Racism.* Toronto: University of Toronto, 1994.

Herberg, E.N. *Ethnic Groups in Canada: Adaptations and Transitions.* Toronto: Nelson Canada, 1989.

Hiebert, D.J. "Ethnicity." In *The Dictionary of Human Geography*, 3rd edition. Edited by. R. J. Johnston, D. Gregory, and D. M. Smith. Oxford: Basil Blackwell, 1991.

Hulchanski, D.J. *Barriers to Equal Access in the Housing Market: The Role of Discrimination on the Basis of Race and Gender.* Research Paper no. 187 Toronto: Centre for Urban and Community Studies, 1993.

Jenkins, C. *Ethnic Associations and the Welfare State.* New York: Columbia University Press, 1988.

Jensen, C.1969. "Leadership in the Toronto Italian Ethnic Group." *International Migration Review*, Vol. 4 no 1 (1969): 25–41.

Kanungo, R. N. 1981. "South Asian Presence in the Canadian Mosaic—Impact and Potential." In *Asian Canadians Regional Perspectives.* Edited by K.V. Ujimoto and G. Hirabayashi. Halifax: Mount Saint Vincent University, 1981.

Kogler, R. K. *The Polish Community in Canada.* Toronto: Multicultural History Society, 1976.

Louis-Jaques, D. 1991. "Refugee Adaptation and Community Structure: The Indochinese in Quebec City, Canada." *International Migration Review.* Vol. 25, no. 3 (1991): 550–72.

Lloyd, P. C. *The City of Ibadan* Cambridge: Oxford University Press, 1966.

Marger, M. N. *Race and Ethnic Relations: American and Global Perspectives* Belmont: Wadsworth Publishing, 1991.

Mensah, Joseph. "Religious Transnationalism among Ghanaian Immigrants in Toronto: A Binary Logistic Regression analysis." *The Canadian Gregrapher* 52, no. 3 (2008): 309–30.

Moghaddam, F. M., D. M.Taylor, and R. N. Lalonde "Individualistic and Collective Integration Strategies Among Iranians in Canada." *International Journal of Psychology* Vol. 22. (1987): 301–13.

Moghaddam, F. M. and S. Perreault. "Individual and Collective Mobility Strategies Among Minority Group Members." *The Journal of Psychology* Vol. 132, no. 3 (1992): 343–57.

Molinaro, J. and M. Kuitunen. *The Luminous Mosaic.* Welland, Ontario: Soleil Publishing Inc, 1993.

Moya, Jose. "Immigrants and Associations: A Global and Historical Perspective." *Journal of Ethnic and Migration Studies* Vol. 31. no. 5 (2005): 833–64.

Murdie, R. A."Economic Restructuring and Social Polarization in Toronto." In *Social Polarization in Post-Industrial Metropolis.* Edited by J. Loughlin and J. Fruedrichs Berlin and New York: de Gruyter, 1986.

Naidoo, J. C. "Africans." *Canadian Encyclopaedia* Vol 1. Edmonton: Hurtig Publishers, 1985.

Nagata, J. A. "Adaptation and Integration of Greek Working Class Immigrants in the City of Toronto." *International Migration Review* Vol. 4, no. 1. (1969): 44–69.

Nelson, C. and M. Tienda. "The Restructuring of Hispanic Ethnicity." *Ethnic and Racial Studies* Vol. 6. (1983): 49–73.

Norris, J. "Functions of Ethnic Organizations." In *Functions of Ethnic Organizations.* Edited by H. Palmer, 165–76. Vancouver: Copp Clark Publishing, 1975.

Ozcurumez, Saime. "Immigrant Associations in Canada: Included, Accommodated, or Excluded? *Turkish Studies* Vol. 10, no. 2 (2009): 195–215.

Peil, M. and P. Sada. *African Urban Society.* Chichester: John Wiley and Sons, 1981.

Portes, A. and R. Rumbaut. 1990. *Immigrant America* Berkeley: University of California Press, 1990.

Predelli, Line Nyhagen. "Political and Cultural Ethnic Mobilization: The Role of Immigrant Associations in Norway." *Journal of Ethnic and Migration Studies* Vol. 34, no. 6 (2008): 935–54.

Radecki, H. *Ethnic Organizational Dynamics: the Polish Group in Toronto* Waterloo, IA: Wilfrid Laurier University Press, 1976.

Ray, B. K. "Immigrant Settlement and Housing in Metropolitan Toronto." *Canadian Geographer* Vol. 38, No 3 (1994): 262–65

Rex, J. *Immigrant Associations in Europe.* Aldershot: Gower, 1987.

Reitz, J. G. *The Survival of Ethnic Groups.* Toronto: McGraw-Hill Ryerson, 1980.

Richmond, A. H. 1991. "Foreign-born Labour in Canada: Past Trends, Emerging Trends and Implications." *Regional Development Dialogue* Vol. 12, no. 3 (1991):145–61.

———. "A Multivariate Model of Immigrant Adaptation" *International Migration Review,* Vol 8. no. 2, (1974): 193–223.

Roberts, L. W. and R. A. Clifton. "Multiculturalism in Canada: Sociological Perspectives." In *Race and Ethnic Relations in Canada.* Ed. P.S. Li, 120-147 Toronto: Oxford University Press, 1990.

Robinson, V. "Asians in Britain: A Study in Encapsulation and Marginality." In *Geography and Ethnic Pluralism.* Edited by C. Clarke, 231–57, London: Allen and Unwin.

Skarbuskis, A."Race and Tenure in Toronto" *Urban Studies* Vol. 32, no. 2 (1996): 232-252.

Simmons, A. B. "'New Wave' Immigrants: Origins and Characteristics." In *Ethnic Demography.* Edited by S.S. Halli, 14–159, Ottawa: Carleton University Press, 1990.

Takougang, Joseph and Bassirou Tidjani. 'Settlement Patterns and Organizations Among African Immigrants in the United States." *Journal of Third World Studies.* Vol. XXV1 no.1 (2009): 31–40.

Waldorf, B. "Determinants of International Return Migration Intentions." *Professional Geographer* Vol. 47, (1995): 125–36.

Wickberg, E. Ed. *From China to Canada: A History of the Chinese Communities in Canada.* Toronto: McClelland and Stewart, 1982.

World Bank. *World Tables.* Baltimore: Johns Hopkins University Press, 1994.

Yancey, W.L. "The Structure of Pluralism." *Ethnic and Racial Studies* Vol. 8. (1985): 94–116.

Chapter Three

Identity Formation and Integration among Bicultural Immigrant Blacks

Unions between African immigrants and African Americans present new testing ground for theories on intermarriage, identity, and biculturalism. There has been a great influx of African immigrants to the United States in the past thirty-five years, a more than fourfold increase between the decades of 1971–1980 and 1991–2000 (Clark, 2006). Increased African immigration to the United States has led to increases in intermarriages between African immigrants and Africans Americans and bicultural blacks in America (Clark, 2006). In U.S. universities there has been a noticeable increase in the number of black students with bicultural backgrounds. African and African American unions are also found increasingly in both feature and documentary films. Films such as *Little Senegal*, *Phat Girlz*, *Beauty Shop*, *Barbershop*, *Okra Soup*, and the documentary *The Neo African-Americans* all in some way deal with romantic relationships with African immigrants and African Americans.

The purpose of this study is to examine that growing number of bicultural blacks in America. This study will show how this population is adding new dimensions to discussions around identity and biculturalism in America. The study will examine the growth of this population, showing its correlation to the increases in romantic relationships between African and African American, as well as what that means for black identity in America. This research will also expand on the applicability of theories of biculturalism and identity on bicultural immigrant blacks.

While theories on intermarriage can and should be used to examine relationships between African immigrants and African Americans, many of these theories tend to deal with intermarriage between individuals of different racial or religious groups. Intermarriage between Africans and African Americans is interethnic, not interracial. To understand intermarriage between Africans and African Americans an analysis of the multiple, seemingly unrelated, but important social and economic changes in black America is needed. Additionally, these unions must be understood within broader discussions of Pan African consciousness and ethnic identities within a broader racial identity.

Pan Africanism in its most fundamental and broad sense refers to the self acknowledgement of a shared origin, shared history, and cultural linkage between peoples of African descent. It is from this foundation that ideas of Pan Africanism may shift according to perspective. Some see peoples of African descent as a social and political unit and seeks to unite people of African descent, promoting "pride in African values" (Esedebe, 1994; Geiss, 1974). Others link the unification of peoples of African descent to socialist economic principles. The All-African People's Revolutionary Party, an organization founded by Kwame Nkrumah, defines Pan-Africanism as "the total liberation and unification of Africa under Scientific Socialism." Still others view peoples of African descent as a homogeneous unit and embrace identities as "Africans," minimizing regional and/or ethnic identities (Geiss, 1974). The view of Pan Africanism in this chapter takes the broadest definition of Pan Africanism. That is, a focus on a shared origin, shared history, and cultural linkages between peoples of African descent. It is this perspective or definition of Pan Africanism that lends itself to the examination of relationships between African Americans and African immigrants. It is within this context of Pan Africanism that many bicultural blacks locate their identities. It is also within this context of Pan Africanism that many African Americans and African immigrants define their relationships. The expectation is that this (broad) definition of Pan Africanism will give context to the purpose of the research, and allow for new perspectives on Pan Africanism that African immigration to the United States represent.

An examination of bicultural blacks fits within the framework of biculturalism, which examines an individual's ability to effectively navigate two cultures (Padilla, 2009). Yet, there are points of departure. The case of bicultural blacks offers opportunities to study the ways scholars use biculturalism, which is often applied to individuals born into one (heritage) culture while being raised in a different (host) culture. Bicultural blacks, however, are born into two (heritage) cultures. Bicultural blacks are often impacted by, for example, the nature of their parents' relationship to both cultures and the presence of both cultures in the home. Biculturalism is best equipped to answer questions surrounding the navigation of identities among bicultural blacks through the lens of Bicultural Identity Integration (BII). BII measures the ways in which bicultural individuals manage dual cultural identities, specifically the extent to which bicultural individuals both perceive the compatibility of their two identities and integrate their two identities (Chen, Benet-Martinez and Bond, 2008). Studies of levels of BII, as outlined by Benet-Martinez & Haritatos

(2005), will aid in explaining the ways in which bicultural blacks have integrated both their dual identities and the dual cultures. Studies of BII are important when examining the ways in which bicultural blacks perceive and manage their dual cultural identities.

In addition to being able to navigate dual cultures, the ways in which bicultural blacks self-identify are important. The theory of symbolic interactionism (SI) complements theories on biculturalism in its examination of the process by which people self-identify. While biculturalism studies how people manage dual cultures/identities, symbolic interactionism provides tools for the study of why people choose to manage dual cultures/identities in the ways that they do. SI deals with the ways in which human beings see themselves and "things" around them (Blumer, 1986). How human beings interpret themselves (their identity) is derived from social interactions with others, interactions that reinforce or contradict held assumptions. In the case of bicultural blacks, those interactions are important in understanding why individuals self-identify in certain ways.

For decades scholars have put forth that race and ethnicity would disappear with the forces of modernization, but this has not happened. Scholars such as Robert Park and Milton Gordon advanced theories of assimilation which predicted the disappearance of race and ethnicity as social categories as minority groups assimilated into the larger society (Gordon, 1964; Cornell and Hartmann, 2006; Feagin and Feagin, 2009). This has not happened, the resilience of ethnicity and race as tools for self-identification and externally imposed identification remain powerful. As Cornell and Hartmann (2006: 12) point out "ethnicity and race are among the most common categories that contemporary human beings use to organize their ideas and who they are, to evaluate their experience and behavior, and to understand the world around them."

The distinction between race and ethnicity has also been examined by scholars. The link with "race" to genetics has prompted some to replace the use of "race" with "ethnicity," which is linked to history and culture (Corbie-Smith, G., Frank, E., Nickens, H., and Elon, L., 1999; Oppenheimer, 2001). Historically the ways in which people define and identify themselves have changed over time, and societies may in the future deem the terms "race" and "ethnicity" as wholly inappropriate terms in human categorization and identification. Popular culture and policy-making organizations still distinguish between race and ethnicity and this research will apply generally accepted uses for "race" and "ethnicity."

The ideas of black identity in America have traditionally been tied to a legacy of slavery and Civil Rights in America. Bicultural blacks are another dimension to that discussion and are part of the shift in the ways in which "black" is defined in America.

The influx of African immigrants to the United States has led to numerous articles, books and films on the subject of African immigrants in America. Several scholars have examined the relationships between African immigrants and African Americans. Scholars often point to the tensions between the two groups and patterns of self-segregation on the part of each (Clark, 2006; Copeland-Carson, 2004; Gunja, 2005; Nesbitt, 2002). To a lesser extent scholars have also focused on collaborations, cooperation and relationships between Africans and African Americans (Clark, 2006; Copeland-Carson, 2004; Wamba, 1999). Less of a focus are the topics of bicultural unions and bicultural blacks. The relationships between African Americans and African immigrants and the offspring of those relationships are, however, an important part of the dynamics emerging between the two groups.

Methodology

The data for this study was obtained using descriptive case studies, which included participant observation and in-depth interviews. The use of the descriptive case studies method allows for a more accurate understanding of some of the emerging patterns surrounding bicultural black identity, as well as the perceived causal relationship between set factors and self-identity and self-perception among bicultural blacks.

Nine individuals were interviewed for this study. Most were undergraduate and graduate students. The participants, both men and women, ranged in age from nineteen to twenty-eight years old. All of the students came from bicultural backgrounds with one parent born and raised in Africa and one parent born and raised in the United States. Three of the participants were born and raised in Africa and six were born and raised in the United States. All were raised in urban areas and of those born in the United States the following cities were represented: Atlanta, Houston, Minneapolis, and Washington, D.C. All of the participants lived in the United States at the time of the interviews.

All of the participants volunteered to participate in the case study and most were identified and recruited from various classes and departments within the same university. Some were recruited by word of mouth. Data used for analysis includes at least six months of participant observation and individual in-depth interviews. Participant observation included observing the behaviors of the student participants on campus and in the classroom. Student participants were observed during in-class discussions, via interactions with other classmates, and during informal conversations. Students were also observed during on-campus events, specifically at organization meetings and panel discussions that students either organized or participated in. Nonstudent participants were observed in various social settings for at least a year prior to being interviewed. Many of the nonstudent participants were observed during numerous informal conversations, as well as during social and community events; such as parties, wedding ceremonies, and organization meetings.

During the interviews students were asked a series of questions regarding their backgrounds, identities, and social interactions. The questions asked were designed to collect specific information regarding the diversity of ways in which bicultural blacks may identify as well as to determine some of the ways in which bicultural blacks interact with both African and African American communities.

Interviews were conducted with each participant individually. The results are based on both the participant answers as well as six months of participant observation. Apart from five questions pertaining to demographic data, students were also asked the following ten questions:

1. How do you identify yourself? Why?
2. How do other people identify you?
3. In which culture do you feel the most comfortable?
4. How do you see the relationship between African Americans and Africans?
5. What is your level of knowledge of, and activity in, the African American community?
6. What is your level of knowledge of, and activity in, the African community?
7. What are your parents' level of knowledge of, and activity in, the African community?
8. What are your parents' level of knowledge of, and activity in, the African American community?
9. Do you have any dating preferences?
10. Do you have any marriage preferences?

For the purpose of this study a few terms need to be defined. While many individuals of African descent embrace a broader African racial identity, in this study the term African will refer to individuals of African descent who were born and raised in Africa. The term African American will refer to individuals of African descent whose families have been in the United States for at least three generations, well before the great influx of migrants into the United States from Africa began in the 1970s. When referring to where an individual was raised, the term raised will refer to where an individual lived until at least the age of fifteen. Bicultural relations will refer to couples with one African and one African-American partner. Bicultural blacks will refer to individuals with one African parent and one African-American parent.

Bicultural Unions

In the midst of the tensions and barriers there are many Africans and African Americans who have no problems working together, being members of the same religious and civic organizations and socializing together. One trend to have emerged is the increase in the number of African immigrants and African Americans who have transcended the divisions between the two groups and developed bicultural relationships (Wamba, 1999; Arthur, 2000; Shrager, 2001).

There is more bicultural dating and marriage between Africans and African Americans than may have been previously thought (Arthur, 2000; Qian and Lichter, 2001; Clark, 2006). This is important in light of the low levels of social and professional interactions between the groups (Arthur, 2000; Njubi, 2002). This is often due to negative perceptions of each other, and this has led to tensions between the two groups (Nesbitt, 2002; Diouf; Clark, 2006; Traore, 2006). Some scholars suggest that there is more dating and intermarriage between black groups in America than between blacks and whites in America (Qian and Lichter, 2001; Fears, 2002; Pelzer-McNill, 2004; Shrager, 2001). John Arthur's 2000 study *Invisible Sojourners: African Immigrant Diaspora in the United States* surveyed African immigrants in the United States and found 24 percent of the married respondents were married to African Americans (62 percent had African spouses, 10 percent Caribbean spouses, and 4 percent had white spouses).

In 2005 and 2006 a survey was conducted in the Washington, D.C. area. In order to get a representative sample of Africans and African Americans in the area the survey was conducted at universities, religious institutions, barbershops, community organizations, community events and other locations where African immigrants and/or African Americans naturally congregated. While participants showed more conservative views on marriage than dating, the fact that more than half would consider a bicultural marriage is significant. In fact, of the African Americans who were married, 19 percent were in bicultural relationships (13 percent with African spouses and 6 percent with spouses from the Caribbean) (Clark, 2006). Fifty-six percent of the African Americans were married to other African Americans (Clark, 2006). Of the Africans who were married, 31 percent were married to African Americans, and 62 percent were married to other Africans (Clark, 2006). The 31 percent percent of Africans married to African Americans in this study compares to the 24 percent of Arthur's survey participants who were married to Africans Americans.

One of the stereotypes often applied to immigrants of all backgrounds is that they often seek to marry American citizens for a green card or permanent residence status. While there is no data to confirm how many African immigrants marry only for that reason, surely some do. The numbers of bicultural marriages between African immigrants and African Americans, given the tensions between the groups, is significant, yet not entirely surprising.

Within these bicultural unions one finds a much higher proportion of African male and African-American female unions (Qian and Lichter, 2001; Shrager, 2001, Clark, 2006). According to a study by Zhenchao Qian and Daniel Lichter Black immigrant men in general are actually more likely to marry within their race than African-American men (2001). There are three factors that lead to this trend. One, African-American women are opening up their options when it comes to dating because the pool of eligible men has changed. With the shortage of black men on university campuses and the fact that between 25–30 percent of African-American men between the ages of 20 and 29 are in jail, on probation, or on parole, African-American women seem to have increasingly looked to the black immigrant population to find a suitable mate (Amick, 2000; Hall, 1998; Smith, 2001).

In Washington, D.C., where much of the study was conducted, Lotke (1997) found that up to 50 percent of African-American males between the ages of 18 and 35 are in jail, on probation, or on parole. Given these statistics, it is not surprising that increasingly more African-American women are turning to alternative options when finding partners.

A second factor relates to the demographics of the African immigrant community in the United States. Africans are the most educated group in America, surpassing both white and black Americans as well as Asian Americans and Latin Americans (Butcher, 1994; Deane & Logan, 2003, 5; Diouf; Gordon, 1998; Nesbitt, 2002; Okome, 2002; Reddick, 1998; Takyi, 2002). The educational attainments of African men have translated into an increase of African men with university degrees in the American workplace. This increase is important when looking at the presence of African Americans in the workplace. Higher rates of educational achievement among African-American women in comparison to African-American men have corresponded to higher rates of African-American women entering the professional arena (Ruggles, Sobek, Alexander, Fitch, Goeken, Hall, King, and Ronnander, 2004; United States Census Bureau, 2004; Malveaux, 2008; Chambers, Bush, Walpole, 2010). Data comparing African-American women with African-American men reflects a larger gap in favor of African-American women (Sussman, Steinmetz, and Peterson, 1999; Murphy, 2004). The ratio of African-American men to African-American women on college campuses means that many professional African-American women in America will have to struggle to find a professional or intellectual equal in her African-American mate. With the high emphasis placed on education among African immigrants, some professional African-American women may be selecting mates among America's highly educated African immigrant community.

A third factor is that of the African immigrants coming to the United States, there is a slightly higher percentage of men than women who immigrate (Dixon, 2006; Morrison, Schiff, and Sjöblom, 2007). This means that while African-American women are finding that there is a shortage of African-American men, it is likely that African men seek African-American mates because the ratio of men to women in the African immigrant community also makes it harder for African men to find an African mate. While some African men may opt to return home to find a mate, or seek a mate in other parts of the Diaspora, many do find themselves with African-American mates.

Historically, large migrations of people have resulted in children born of relationships formed by migrants and their hosts. This is especially the case when there is a gender imbalance in the immigrant communities, leaving either women or men with fewer options within their own national group for mates. Scholars often point to the availability of mates as a primary source of mate selection (Blau, Blum, Schwartz, 1982; Blau, Beeker, Fitzpatrick, 1984). In cities such as Washington, D.C., New York, and Atlanta, the diversity of the population and size of the African immigrant community has put Africans and African Americans in shared social spaces. Blau, Blum and Swartz's (1982) article on intermarriage suggests a relationship between a city's heterogeneity and the rates of intermarriage between different cultures. Blau et al. (1982) posit that the more heterogeneous a city, the higher the likelihood of intermarriage. Blau et al. (1982) also suggests that decisions to marry outside of one's cultural group is based on an individual's preferences, the least of which may be ethnicity, even for those that may harbor stereotypes about the very group from which they find mates. In fact Blau et al. (1982) suggest that religion plays a larger role in mate selection than ethnicity. Blau et al.'s 1982 study suggests that individuals are less likely to marry outside of their religion than they are to marry outside of their ethnic, cultural or racial group.

In addition, from a Pan African perspective, a racial (macro) identity may overshadow ethnic (micro) identities. This interpretation of Pan Africanism goes beyond the "self acknowledgement of a shared origin, shared history, and cultural linkage(s)" and toward a homogenizing of peoples of African descent, a process that focuses on racial identity while minimizing ethnic identities. Among those who only identify as being African, distinguishing only between Africans born at home and Africans born in America, one would not necessarily see romantic relationships between Africans and African Americans as "intermarriage" or what Blau et al. (1982) calls "out marriage." While simply willing cultural differences away do not erase them, this perspective should be noted when looking ways in which individuals define relationships that scholars consider bicultural.

Bicultural Blacks

Participants in this study are products of unions resulting from African Americans traveling to Africa and from African immigration to the United States Wamba (1999), a product of both the pre-1985 African immigration to the United States and post-independence African-American migration to Africa, was among the first bicultural blacks to write about his experiences. Born of an African American mother, Congolese father, and raised in Tanzania, Wamba (1999) says that bicultural blacks are vehicles for bringing the groups together. Wamba's book *Kinship: A Family's Journey in Africa and America* remains the most important memoir on African and African American relations.

It is yet to be seen how bicultural blacks will impact African and African-American relationships. Given the racial dynamics of American society and the relationships among communities of African descent, the ways in which bicultural blacks identify are contingent upon a number of factors, all of which warrant further examination. Mead's theory of symbolic interactionism (SI) addresses many of the dilemmas of bicultural blacks. SI speaks to the process of identity formation as a process that incorporates both internal and external factors. SI is predicated on the idea that one's identity is informed by one's interactions with others and one's perceptions of self (Mead and Morris, 1967; Mead, 1982; Coté and Levine, 2002; Herman-Kinney, 2004). One's identity is, therefore, significantly shaped by how others perceive the person. Identities may then shift according one's social environment. For bicultural blacks an African identity may emerge in an environment dominated by other Africans (celebrations, family interactions), though such an identity may hold stigmas in other environments, which may lead to identity shifts or conflict. More stable aspects of one's identity are no less influenced by environmental factors and the natural process of self-identification.

It is the "self," objectified, that scholars say individuals seek to define (Coté and Levine, 2002; Herman-Kinney, 2004). Identity formation is, therefore, a result of the process of searching for and gaining knowledge of self. For bicultural blacks this process is influenced by African and African-American perceptions of each other, the social environments in which they are reared, and parental influences.

Bicultural blacks identify in several ways. This study brought out three important ways bicultural blacks tend to identify: a primarily African identity, a primarily African-American identity, or a integrated bicultural identity. Many bicultural blacks gravitate toward one of these three identities, though the pull in any one direction may change under certain conditions or as their own knowledge of self evolves.

Bicultural blacks offer unique opportunities for research on biculturalism, which deals with the psychosocial changes an individual experiences when

their two cultures come into contact. For bicultural blacks we find varying levels of bicultural identity integration (BII) (LaFromboise, Coleman,
Gerton, 1993; Benet-Martinez and Haritatos, 2005; Chen, Benet-Martinez,
and Bond, 2008). Meaning, bicultural blacks differ in the extent to which
they have integrated their identities, their ability to manage both cultural
identities, and in their level of capability for cultural frame switching. The
experiences of bicultural blacks are further determined by their perceptions
of African/African-American relations. BII theorists suggest that the levels of
conflict and cooperation between a bicultural individual's two cultures have
an impact on that individual's identity formation and ability to integrate their
identities (Benet-Martinez and Haritatos, 2005; Chen, Benet-Martinez, and
Bond, 2008).

Measures of biculturalism include knowing and understanding both cultures, possessing a positive perspective of each culture, being able to effectively communicate verbally and/or nonverbally in both cultures, and having
established social networks in both cultures (LaFromboise, Coleman, Gerton,
1993). This includes a degree of cultural frame switching (CFS), or the ability
to "access multiple cultural meaning systems and switching between different
culturally appropriate behaviors depending on the context" (Jackson, 2006).

Research on the topic of biculturalism has tended to focus on either the
experiences of second generation immigrants in their host cultures or on biracial individuals, and concepts of "heritage" and "host" cultures (de Anda,
1984; Davis, 1991; Kerwin, Ponterotto, Jackson, Harris, 1993; Phinney and
Devich-Navarro, 1997; Benet-Martinez and Haritatos, 2005; Rockquemore
and Brunsma, 2007; Chen, Benet-Martinez, and Bond, 2008). So while BII
focuses on the intersection of immigrant and American cultures within first
and second generation immigrants, a look at bicultural blacks uses the same
useful tool for a slightly different type of analysis.

For bicultural blacks, high levels of BII means the ability to easily shift
between African and African-American communities, celebrations and social situations. This may include speaking multiple languages and having
friendships in both communities. Bicultural blacks with low levels of BII are
often casualties of the distance between the two groups and often choose one
culture as their primary identification. For those raised in the United States
that identity of choice is often African American, the dominant culture. In
addition, the identity most imposed on bicultural blacks raised in the United
States by the outside world is that of African American, primarily because
of their American accents. African Americans are the largest numerically of
all of the Black cultural groups in America, and therefore their culture and
values dominate among blacks in America. Bicultural blacks will then always
see themselves and their own identities in relation to the dominant African-

American culture. This is a common phenomenon with biculturals who have to decide between the pressure to assimilate into the dominate culture or to maintain a distinct, even "distant" identity (de Anda, 1984; Phinney and Devich-Navarro, 1997; Lehman, Chiu, and Schaller, 2004).

The interviewees chosen for this study have all chosen to identify in varying ways, though all have been impacted in various ways by the relations between Africans and African Americans.

The names of all of the students have been changed, as have specific identifying details. After the interviews and observations, students were categorized into three forms of self-identification: African, African American, integrated/bicultural. The responses of the interviewees reflected a significant difference in identity among some of those who were raised in Africa and others who were raised in the United States. The results are thus divided by those who were raised in Africa and those who were raised in the United States.

African Raised

Similar to other studies of bicultural or biracial individuals, some of the participants indicated feeling as though they did not fit in anywhere completely (Randolph, 1999; Tizard, 2002). The binary structure of racial politics in America often means that bicultural blacks are faced with either conforming to the dominant African-American culture or navigating a multicultural identity (Berry, Poortinga, Segall, and Dasen, 2002; Shaw-Taylor, 2007).

For the interviewees raised in Africa (Malaika, Oni, and Ndaba), their mothers are all African Americans who married African men and chose to raise their children in Africa. All are fluent in both English and the primary African language spoken by their fathers. Not surprisingly most of these individuals identified more with their African culture.

Most of these participants knew little of African-American culture and history and had not taken steps to become involved in any meaningful way in the African American community. Ndaba, a thirty-something doctoral student with a Namibian father and an African-American mother, admitted that while he was partially familiar with African-American history, he had little incentive to become familiar with African-American issues or people. Ndaba was often observed at social functions and around campus engaging with Africans, white Americans and Europeans, but never African Americans.

Most of these participants socialized primarily within the African immigrant communities. Both Ndaba and Oni indicated that most of their friends were African, while Malaika indicated having friends of African, African-American, and Caribbean backgrounds. Their dating patterns were again divided. Ndaba and Oni indicated they were not interested in dating African

Americans, while for Malaika racial background was the determining factor in whom she dated, not ethnicity. The experiences and views expressed by both Ndaba and Oni are similar to those of many second generation African immigrants, who also harbored negative stereotypes associated with African Americans (Clark, 2008).

Oni, a twenty-something college student, was one of the more interesting interviewees. She held some of the negative views of African Americans that are present in the African immigrant community. During the interview Oni admitted to joining with other Africans in mocking African Americans. Oni was a Muslim student who grew up in Guinea and was very vocal on campus around issues pertaining to Africa. She was also active in student organizations that focused on Africa. Oni almost always wore hijab (headscarf) and could frequently be seen discussing African and Islamic politics with classmates. Oni seemed to socialize primarily with Africans, and often disregarded African Americans who had little or incorrect knowledge of Africa. When asked why she did not have more African-American friends, Oni remarked that her activities in African organizations have prevented her from developing strong friendships with African Americans.

Oni, who has an American accent, said that Africans would often make comments about her "impurity" in not being 100 percent African. It was clear that she was disturbed that her African identity was at times called into question, while she did not seem concerned with expressions of her African-American identity.

Of the interviewees raised in Africa, Malaika had a much higher level of BII, identifying as both Ugandan and African American. Malaika, who wore her hair locked and usually wore African jewelry, spoke with only a hint of a Ugandan accent. Malaika saw many similarities between Africans and African Americans and moved between both communities with ease. Malaika said her parents had a Pan African outlook and made a conscious effort that she and her siblings were well informed of the history of both of their cultures. Malaika was very knowledgeable of the history of both of her cultures and was observed socializing in both communities. Malaika's dating and marriage preferences reflect her Pan African outlook. She said that she prefers black men, but that culture does not matter. In order for her to decide to marry however, she said her mate would have to identify as a person of African descent and understand her need to bridge the gap between her two cultures.

American Raised

Most of these interviewees are like most bicultural blacks in America, products of Africans who came to the United States for a variety of reasons, primarily to study, and found African-American mates. In fact all of the parents of the interviewees raised in the United States, except one, met while the father was in the United States studying. Reflecting the patterns of intermarriage among African immigrants and African Americans, most have African fathers and African-American mothers. Some have African fathers who at some point separated from the mother, impacting the individual's integration of their two cultural identities. This group offers some of the greatest diversity. Not having their father in the home full-time created fluctuation among this group with regard to how much they identified with their African identities. This group had less cultural reinforcement in the home from their African parent, leading some to disregard this part of their identity or to search for it in other ways. The majority from this group identified as African Americans but had taken steps to learn more of their African cultures, primarily by taking courses related to Africa and reaching out to African family members.

Most of these participants have never been to Africa and grew up in homes where they felt there was little effort to involve them in the events and cultures of the African immigrant community to which their parent belonged. This was often the case even if those parents were themselves involved in their community. In most cases participants indicated that their African American parent had also not been to Africa and had little knowledge of Africa.

Some of these participants experienced being teased in school about their African names and/or dark skin by their African-American classmates. Some admitted to internalizing their classmates' negative views of Africans and allowing that to affect their lack of socialization with African immigrants. Chinenye, a twenty-something college student, experienced being teased because of her Nigerian name and dark skin. Chinenye said most of the teasing was done by her African-American classmates. Though Chinenye seemed to have put it behind her, in discussing the experiences, it was clear that it was a source of stress for her. Chinenye, whose parents divorced when she was young, had begun learning more about Africa. Though quiet in class discussions, the African history courses Chinenye took seemed to be part of her attempt to learn more about her father's culture.

Chinenye identified as an African American. She said it was because she lived in the United States and did not have knowledge of the traditions of her father's people. In addition, she did not grow up with her father in the house and had never been to Nigeria. After the interview Chinenye participated in a study abroad to Africa. Upon her return she spoke about the experience and indicated she really enjoyed going. During the interview when asked about visiting Nigeria during her stay in South Africa, she indicated that she had considered it. Upon her return to the United States, Chinenye admitted that she had yet to visit Nigeria, expressing some ambivalence toward visiting the country.

While all of the students recognized their African heritages, most were active almost exclusively in the African-American community. Two were members of African-American sororities and several were members of African-American community groups, and campus organizations.

Two of the participants, Missy and Chinenye, said that in recent years their fathers tried to place cultural expectations on them, leading to tensions. The fact that Missy is also a lesbian cannot be overemphasized in terms of its importance on both her identity and her relationship with her father. With widespread negative views toward homosexuality in Africa, Missy said the perception that she had brought shame to the family increased the gap between herself and her father's family and influenced her identification with only one of her cultures. In these cases the interviewees indicated that their fathers had not previously emphasized their involvement in their African immigrant community. It was not until adolescence that the participants said their fathers began to enforce African cultural expectation on them. Not surprisingly, this caused both resistance and resentment among their daughters who had essentially assimilated into the broader African-American community.

Missy says that when she was younger her father did not stress the importance of learning her African culture. While her father participated in Nigerian events, Missy had little knowledge of Nigerian culture. Missy socialized within primarily lesbian social circles and was part of a close network of lesbian students on campus, most of whom were not African. Though while Missy indicated that she identified as an African American, she did take several Africa-related courses at her university and her partner at the time was a Nigerian woman who had been in the United States since she was twelve. Missy thought her attraction to her partner was tied to her being Nigerian.

Twenty-something college graduate Kathy has a Nigerian father and an African-American mother. Kathy's parents were still together and were both very active in Kathy's life. Kathy said that while her parents tried to create a balance in their lives, she was more exposed to African-American culture and sometimes felt uncomfortable identifying as Nigerian. Kathy took African history courses and indicated that she was active in both the African and African-American communities. Most of her activities, however, were within the African-American community, including her work with the NAACP and her membership in an African-American sorority.

The final interviewee that identified as African American was Kofi. Kofi was a twenty-something college student who was born to a Ghanaian father and African-American mother. Kofi was a quiet student who, though taking an African history class, displayed only a nominal interest in Africa. He described his parents' relationship as turbulent, involving both alcohol and drugs, and having no contact with his father, identified as an African American. Kofi indicated having some Ghanaian "acquaintances," but also admitted to harboring some prejudices and negative views of Africans. While many of these interviewees expressed a hesitance in dating Africans, Kofi was the most adamant in his lack of desire to date African women.

One interviewee, Imani, had not been to Africa at all but embraced a bicultural identity and seemed to have integrated both of her cultures well. Though Imani had not been to Tanzania, her father's country, she said that her parents raised her with an emphasis on both cultures. As a result Imani was active in organizations servicing both communities, such as the university's NAACP chapter and the campus' African Students Association. Imani's case is important. Bicultural blacks who have lived within and/or in close proximity to both communities (in Africa and the United States) have more opportunities to ground themselves in both cultures. Imani is like many bicultural blacks who have been raised in America and have not been to Africa, yet she was grounded in both cultures.

One interviewee, Folabi, offered additional considerations in the effort to understand self-identification among bicultural blacks. Folabi is the only interviewee with an African (Senegalese) mother and an African-American father. Folabi identified as an African American, which he said was based on two factors: 1). his American upbringing and the culture that he had become accustomed to; and 2). he recognized that his mother's culture is a patrilineal one and traces ethnicity through the father, making him African American.

Though Folabi identified as an African American, there were other observable factors that pointed to a higher level of bicultural integration. Folabi was very active in both communities. Though his friends were primarily African American, he was very active in the Senegalese community, participating in celebrations and assuming a level of cultural responsibility independent of his mother. For example, Folabi often donated to community functions and independently attended community events and ceremonies. Folabi has also traveled to Senegal several times and is fluent in Wolof. So while Folabi self-identified as African American, it was clear that his social patterns indicated a more integrated identity.

CONCLUSION

The interviewees all displayed varying levels of BII. The individuals possessing high to medium levels of BII, Malaika, Imani, and Folabi, were fluent in at least two languages, socialized in African and African-American communities, felt a sense of belonging to both communities, and appeared well adept at cultural frame switching. All but Malaika were raised in the Untied States, but all experienced positive reinforcements from both familial and social networks, nurturing their dual identities. The role of the parents in ensuring the presence of both cultures in the home seemed to have been a determining factor. In the United States, African-American culture is the dominant culture between the two, but all three lived and/or were raised in cities with large African populations (Washington, D.C., Minneapolis, and Atlanta). The influence of proximity and length of contact to bicultural identity can play a determining factor in BII (LaFromboise, Coleman, and Gerton, 1993).

The remaining interviewees displayed low levels of BII and fell into two categories: 1) those raised in Africa and felt more comfortable with their African identities, and 2) those raised in the United States and felt more comfortable with their African American identities. All but two had internalized minor to significant negative attitudes toward one of their cultures. This negative perception of one of their cultures or compatibility of their cultures inhibits BII and makes identifying with that culture difficult (LaFromboise, Coleman, Gerton, 1993; Chen, Benet-Martinez, and Bond, 2008).

The psychosocial impacts of low levels of BII were not within the scope of this research. Research does suggest that biculturals with low levels of BII are more susceptible to familial and social conflict and are unable to display culturally appropriate behavior, reflecting impacted levels of cognitive functioning (Benet-Martinez and Haritatos, 2005; LaFromboise, Coleman, Gerton, 1993).

There is in fact a debate on the relationship between bicultural integration and psychological health and stability. There are theorists who posit that biculturalism or being bicultural can cause instability, resulting in psychological conflict, insecurity, confusion, and feelings of alienation (LaFromboise, Coleman, Gerton, 1993; Jackson, 2006). The dominant belief, however, is that high levels of BII leads to better physical health, psychological wellbeing, and stability (LaFromboise, Coleman, Gerton, 1993; Lehman, Chiu, Schaller, 2004; Jackson, 2006; Chen, Benet-Martinez, and Bond, 2008; Padilla, 2009).

Of the four interviewees who identified most as African Americans all said they had mothers who had little knowledge of Africa, but who had tried to some extent (food, clothing) to bring African cultures into the home. Three indicated that their mothers had traveled to Africa. One, Missy, says her mother had a negative experience. Another said their mother refused to go to Africa. Of the interviewees who identified most as African Americans all had fathers who were either absent or for whatever reason said their fathers did not try to incorporate African cultures into the home. Most of the participants said their African fathers were active in African communities, but had few connections to the African-American community. Some said their fathers had been resistant to learning more about African Americans and/or harbored negative views of African Americans.

Another factor in the identity question is which parent is African. The majority of bicultural relationships that involve African immigrants and African Americans are between African men and African-American women, a fact that was reflected in the backgrounds of the participants of this study. It is a widespread custom in most patrilineal African cultures that one is identified by the ethnic origin of one's father. For some of the bicultural blacks in this study, this was a source in their own identity conflict. In addition, by not embracing the customs and culture of their father in favor of African-American customs and culture, this fueled divides between many of the interviewees and their fathers and their fathers' families.

While most of the interviewees had ties to patrilineal African societies, the increase in activity of Folabi in the African community supports the theories that suggest that much of one's cultural values and traditions are passed on by our mothers, regardless of the culture of the mother, influencing the level of one's activity in, and identification with, the mother's community (Cavalli-Sforza and Feldman, 1981; Euler, Hoier, and Rohde, 2001; Schonpflug, 2008; Padilla, 2009).

For those growing up in the United States another distinction arises between those whose childhoods are a result of an African American parent living in Africa with their African spouse or are a result of an African parent living in America and with their African-American spouse. Those African Americans who chose to live in Africa, with their mates, seemed to have had at least some level of African consciousness and interest in Africa. This often translated into a strong presence of African culture in the home, even if the family later relocated to the United States. In these cases, the African-American parent also seemed to have had a stronger Pan African consciousness, which possibly contributed to stronger bicultural integration. For bicultural blacks whose childhoods are a result of an African parent living in America and with their African-American spouse, the same is not necessarily true. There may not be any Pan African consciousness with either parent. An African immigrant may or may not have any real knowledge of, or interest in African-American culture to marry or have a child with an African American. Likewise, an African-American parent may have no knowledge of, or interest in Africa. The level to which both cultures are present in the home also seems important to the development of bicultural identity among children.

The homes of children of bicultural unions vary greatly. If the parents are very active in the African community, this may impact how well the child connects with their African identity. Though, there are cases of children whose African parent is not active in the African community but has a child that seeks out that African identity. Identity is also impacted by what extent language, customs, and food from Africa have been imported to the home in America. The interviewees who said their parents consciously made efforts to incorporate their children into both cultures tended to have higher levels of BII.

The increase in African immigration to the United States began in the mid-1980s and there is sure to be continued increases in bicultural children in future generations. The research suggests that while many of these bicultural blacks could play important roles in bridging gaps, many of them represent entire generations of bicultural children with strained ties to Africa. Some of the interviewees (Oni and Folabi) discussed the feeling of alienation, of not belonging anywhere, while others (Malaika and Imani) embraced their bicultural identities as gifts. The role of bicultural children in the identity debate in Black America further complicates that debate in ways similar to second generation African immigrants. The social expectations of both communities require some level of identity with both, even when those expectations conflict.

The increasing trend of bicultural relationships and bicultural children will ultimately aid in bridging gaps between the two groups, especially in larger metropolitan areas with large African immigrant populations. Bicultural children are born with passports to both communities and if nothing else their presence demands recognition of the breaking down of the barriers and stereotypes that exist between these two groups that are increasingly sharing the same communities, schools, and jobs.

REFERENCES

All-African People's Revolutionary Party. (n.d.). Retrieved June 19, 2009, from All-African People's Revolutionary Party Official Website: http://www.aaprp-intl.org/
Amick, M. 2000. "Does Drug War Target Blacks"? *Michigan Chronicle*. Volume 63 (40): 2.
Arthur, J. 2000. *Invisible Sojourners: African Immigrant Diaspora in the United States*. Santa Barbara: Praeger Publishers.
Benet-Martinez, V. and Haritatos, J. 2005. "Bicultural Identity Integration (BII): Components and Psychological Antecedents." *Journal of Personality*. Volume 73 (4): 1015–49.
Berry, J. Poortinga, Y., Segall, M., Dasen, P. 2002. *Cross-Cultural Psychology: Research and Applications*. Cambridge: Cambridge University Press.
Blau, P., Blum. T., Schwartz, J. 1982. "Heterogeneity and Intermarriage." *American Sociological Review*. Volume 47: 45–62.
Blau, P., Beeker, C., Fitzpatrick, K. 1984. "Intersecting Social Affiliations and intermarriage." *Social Forces*. Volume 62 (3): 585–606.

Blumer, H. 1986. *Symbolic Interactionism: Perspective and Method*. Berkeley: University of California Press.

Butcher, K. F. 1994. "Black Immigrants in the United States: A Comparison with Native Blacks and other immigrants." *Industrial and Labor Relations Review*. Volume 47: 265–84.

Cavalli-Sforza, L. and Feldman, M. 1981. *Cultural Transmission and Evolution: A Quantitative Approach*. Princeton: Princeton University Press.

Chambers, C. R., Bush, V. B., Walpole, M. "Introduction". In Bush, B. V.; Muhammad, Crystal Gafford and Mary Beth Walpole. *From Diplomas to Doctorates: The Success of Black Women in Higher Education and Its Implications for Equal Educational Opportunities for All* (ed.). Sterling: Stylus Publishing: 1–20.

Chen, S., Benet-Martinez, V. and Bond, M. 2008. "Bicultural Identity, Bilingualism, and Psychological Adjustment in Multicultural Societies: Immigration-based and globalization-based Acculturation." *Journal of Personality*. Volume 76 (4): 803–37.

Clark, M. K. 2008. "Identity among First and Second Generation African Immigrants in the United States." *African Identities*. Volume 6 (2): 169–81.

Clark, M. K. 2006. *The Impact of African Immigration on Pan African Relations and Black Identity in the United States*. Unpublished doctoral dissertation, Howard University.

Copeland-Carson, J. 2004. *Creating Africa in America: Translocal Identity in an Emerging World City*. Philadelphia: University of Pennsylvania Press.

Corbie-Smith, G., Frank, E., Nickens, H., and Elon, L. 1999. "Prevalences and Correlates of Ethnic Harassment in the U.S. Women Physicians' Health Study." *Academic Medicine*. Volume 74 (6): 695–701.

Cornell, S. & Hartmann, D. 2006. *Ethnicity and Race: Making Identities in a Changing World*. Newbury Park: Pine Forge Press.

Coté, J. & Levine, C. 2002. *Identity Formation, Agency and Culture: A Social Psychological Synthesis*. Mahwah: Lawrence Erlbaum Associates Publishers.

Davis, F. 1991. *Who is Black? One Nation's Definition*. University Park: The Pennsylvania State University Press.

Deane, G. & Logan, J. R. 2003, August 15. Black Diversity in Metropolitan America. *Lewis Mumford Center for Comparative Urban and Regional Research*. Albany: University at Albany. Retrieved on March 21, 2005 from http://mumford1.dyndns.org/cen2000/BlackWhite/BlackDiversityReport/black-diversity01.htm

De Anda, D. 1984. "Bicultural socialization: Factors Affecting the Minority Experience." *Social Work*. Volume 29 (2): 101–107.

Diouf, S. n.d. "The New African Diaspora." *In Motion: The African American Migration Experience*. New York: Schomburg Center for Research in Black Culture. Retrieved March 21, 2005 from http://www.inmotionaame.org

Dixon, David .2006. "Characteristics of the African Born in the United States." *Migration Policy Institute*. Accessed April 15, 2008 from http://www.migrationinformation.org/Feature/display.cfm?id=366#10

Esedebe, Peter Olisanwuche.1994. *Pan-Africanism: The Idea and Movement, 1776–1991*. Washington, D.C.: Howard University Press.

Euler, H., Hoier, S., and Rohde, P. 2001. "Relationship-Specific Closeness of Inter-generational Family Ties: Findings from Evolutionary Psychology and Implications for Models of Cultural Transmission." *Journal of Cross-Cultural Psychology.* Volume 32: 147–58.

Feagan, J. and Feagan, C. 2009. "Theoretical Perspectives in Race and Ethnic Relations." In Gallagher, C.A. *Rethinking the Color Line: Readings in Race and Ethnicity* (ed.). Boston: McGraw Hill, 22–32.

Fears, D. 2002, February 24. "A Diverse—and Divided—Black Community." *The Washington Post*, p. A01.

Geiss, Immanuel. 1974. *The Pan-African Movement: A History of Pan-Africanism in America, Europe, and Africa.* Oxford: Taylor and Francis.

Gordon, A. 1998. "The New Diaspora—African Immigration to the United States." *Journal of Third World Studies.* Volume 15 (1): 79–103.

Gordon, M. 1964. *Assimilation in American Life: The Role of Race, Religion and National Origins.* New York: Oxford University Press.

Gunja, A. 2005, February 22. "Equal Aid for Black Students." [Electronic version]. *Washington Square News*, p. 1.

Kerwin, C., Ponterotto, J., Jackson, B., Harris, A. 1993. "Racial Identity in Biracial Children: A Qualitative Investigation." *Journal of Counseling Psychology.* Volume 40: 221–31.

Hall, C. 1998. "Challenging Selective Enforcement of Traffic Regulations after the Disharmonic Convergence: Whren v. United States, United States v. Armstrong, and the Evolution of Police Discretion." *Texas Law Review* Volume 76: 5.

Herman-Kinney, N. 2004. *Handbook of Symbolic Interactionism.* Lanham: AltaMira Press.

Jackson, J. 2006. *Encyclopedia of Multicultural Psychology.* Thousand Oaks: Sage Publishers.

LaFromboise, T., Coleman, H., Gerton, J. 1993. "Psychological Impact of Biculturalism: Evidence and Theory." *Psychological Bulletin.* Volume 114 (3): 395–412.

Lehman, D., Chiu, C., Schaller, M. 2004. "Psychology and Culture." *Annual Review of Psychology* Volume 55: 689–702.

Lotke, E. 1997. *Hobbling a Generation: Young African American Men in D.C.'s Criminal Justice System Five Years Later.* Washington: National Center on Institutions and Alternatives.

Malveaux, J. 2008, March 7. Perspectives: The Status of African-American Women. Retrieved May 15, 2010, from Diverse Issues in Higher Education: http://diverse-education.com/article/10797/perspectives-the-status-of-african-american-women.html

Mead, G. and Morris, C. 1967. *Mind, Self, and Society: From the Standpoint of a Social Behaviorist.* Chicago: University Of Chicago Press.

Mead, G. 1982. *The Individual and the Social Self.* Chicago: University Of Chicago Press.

Morrison, A.R., Schiff, M. and Sjöblom, M. 2007. Overview. In Morrison, A. R.; Schiff, M. and Sjöblom, M. *The International Migration of Women* (eds.). Washington, D. C.: World Bank Group, 1-10.

Murphy, P. F. 2004. *Feminism and Masculinities*. Oxford: Oxford University Press.

Nesbitt, F. N. 2002. "African Intellectuals in the Belly of the Beast: Migration, Identity, and the Politics of Exile." *African Issues*. Volume 30 (1): 70–75.

Okome, M. O. 2002. "The Antinomies of Globalization: Some Consequences of Contemporary African Immigration to the United States of America." *Ìrìnkèrindò: a Journal of African Migration* (1).

Oppenheimer, G. M. 2001. "Paradigm Lost: Race, Ethnicity, and the Search for a New Population Taxonomy." *American Journal of Public Health*. Volume 91 (7): 1049–1055.

Padilla, A. M. 2009. "Development Processes Related to Intergenerational Transmission of Culture: Growing up with Two Cultures." In Schönpflug, Ute. *Cultural Transmission: Psychological, Developmental, Social, and Methodological Aspects* (ed.). Cambridge: Cambridge University Press, 185–211.

Pelzer-McNill, J. 2004. "The Challenges of Multi-cultural Relationships." *Encase Magazine*, (Spring): 18–21.

Phinney, J. and Devich-Navarro, M. 1997. "Variations in Bicultural Identification among African American and American Mexican Adolescents." *Journal of Research on Adolescence*. Volume 7 (1): 3–32.

Qian, Z. and and Lichter, D. 2001. "Measuring Marital Assimilation: Intermarriage among Natives and Immigrants." *Social Science Research*. Volume 30 (2): 289–312.

Randolph, D. M. 1999. "Check One Box. " In Gaskins, P. F. Gaskins. *What Are You?: Voices of Mixed-Race Young People*. New York: Henry Holt and Co, 45–86.

Reddick, T. 1998. "African vs. African-American: A Shared Complexion Does Not Guarantee Racial Solidarity." *The Tampa Tribune*. Accessed March 26, 2006 from http://www.library.yale.edu/~fboateng/akata.htm

Rockquemore, K. and Brunsma, D. 2007. *Beyond Black: Biracial Identity in America*. Lanham, MD: Rowman and Littlefield Publishers.

Ruggles, S., Sobek, M., Alexander, T., Fitch, C. A., Goeken, R., Hall, P. K., King, M., and Ronnander, C. 2004. *Integrated Public Use Microdata Series: Version 3.0*. Minneapolis: Minnesota Population Center.

Schönpflug, U. 2008. *Cultural Transmission: Psychological, Developmental, Social, and Methodological Aspects* (ed.). Cambridge: Cambridge University Press.

Shaw-Taylor, Y. 2007. "The Intersection of Assimilation, Race, Presentation of Self, and Transnationalism in America." In Shaw-Taylor. *The Other African Americans: Contemporary African and Caribbean Immigrants in the United States* (ed.). Lanham, MD: Rowan and Littlefield, 1-48.

Shrager, H. 2001. *Widening the pool: When Black American Women Find African mates*. Retrieved March 21, 2005, from The Graduate School of Journalism at Columbia University: http://www.jrn.columbia.edu/studentwor

Smith, A. 2001. "Can You be a Good Person and a Good Prosecutor"? *The Georgetown Journal of Legal Ethics*. Volume 14 (2): 355-368.

Sussman, M., Steinmetz, S., and Peterson, G. 1999. *Handbook of Marriage and the Family*. New York: Springer.

Takyi, B. K. 2002. "The Making of the Second Diaspora: On the Recent African Immigrant Community in the United States of America." *The Western Journal of Black Studies.* Volume 26 (1): 32–34.

Tizard, B. 2002. *Black, White or Mixed Race?: Race and Racism in the Lives of Young People of Mixed Parentage.* New York: Routledge.

Traore, R. and Robert, J. L. 2006. *This Isn't The American I Thought I'd Find: African Students in the U.S. High School.* Lanham, MD: University Press of America.

United States Census Bureau. 2004. "Percent of High School and College Graduates of the Population 15 years and Over, by Age, Sex, Race, and Hispanic Origin: Table 1a: 2004: Black Alone." *Educational Attainment in the United States.* Washington, D. C.: United States Census Bureau.

Wamba, Phillipe. 1999. *Kinship: A Family's Journey in Africa and America.* New York: Dutton.

Chapter Four

Identity Politics of Ghanaian Immigrants in the Greater Cincinnati Area: Emerging Geography and Sociology of Immigrant Experiences

INTRODUCTION

Africans slaves, as forced migrants, were significant in the initial settlement of the United States by nonnatives (Roberts, 2005; Kennedy, 1996) but, African voluntary migration to the United States is a rather recent phenomenon that has gathered speed and intensity with globalization. This contemporary migration of Africans to the United States has been made possible by technologies and emerging networks associated with today's globalization and has been constructed as part of a globalized labor market (Light, 2004; Dwyer, 1999; Sassen, 1991; Okome, 2007; Yeboah 2008). Increasingly, this migration has contributed to the emergence of African diasporas in many cities of the United States, especially in places like Washington, D.C. and New York City (see N'Diaye and N'Diaye, 2007; Abbott, 2007; Takyi and Boate, 2007; Chaco, 2003). Because of differences in regional economies around the United States, small cities such as Cincinnati and Columbus are beginning to experience African Diasporic spaces (Yeboah, 2008).

By its very nature, African migration to the United States is a geographical concept that relates place-differences and opportunity gradients between places in Africa and the United States (Yeboah, 2008; Saravia and Miranda, 2004). Immigrant experiences in the United States are therefore geographical and sociological endeavors. Traditional theory has modeled the sociology and geography of migration with two models: assimilation (Gordon, 1964) and ethnic enclaves (Portes and Jensen, 1989). The expectation is that recent immigrants will assimilate into the host American society even though they will tend to concentrate in enduring ethnic enclaves (such as China towns or Little Italy) in their initial resettlement. These sociological and geographical patterns are expected because very limited interaction occurred between immigrants and their mother country. Yet, with today's globalization and the ease of communication and networking, migrants exhibit different sociological and geographical relationships between their sources and destinations. Increasingly, African and other immigrants to the United States do not have to assimilate rather, they have become transnational (Vertovec, 2003; Itzingsohn, 2000; Owusu, 2007) and they do not have to live social, economic, and political lives in ethnic enclaves, rather they operate within ethnospaces (Appadurai, 1996) which may not even be territorially bound.

How do these changing geographical and sociological contexts manifest in immigrant experiences in the United States? What are the implications of how they manifest for immigrant communities and the host American society? Based on the experience of Ghanaians in the Greater Cincinnati area, my findings are that these immigrants engage in an identity politics in their negotiation of their African heritage and their American experience and even though this may be due to their marginalization, it is more a convenient mechanism that shields some from the vagrancies of illegality in America. This identity politics is manifest in their associational life and the socialization of second generation immigrants.

Conceptual Framework

This chapter is couched within five interrelated concepts bound together by a globalized labor market. These are identity politics, assimilation, transnationalism, ethnic enclaves, and ethnospaces. Identity politics refers to the politics of minority groups or social movements who may or may not be marginalized (Kauffman, 1988, 1990, 1993; Sullivan, 1997; Bernstein, 2002). Often these groups engage in power politics organized around their own oppression. Its origins are in the civil rights struggles of the 1960s but it has been made common by popular movements such as the gay and lesbian movement (Berstein, 2002; Bickford, 1997; Fonow and Marty, 1991), feminist movement (as espoused in the Combahee River Collective Statement, 1977 of black feminists, Norman, 2007) and the environmentalist movement (Kauffman, 1993). Identity politics is associated with issues of the subaltern after Gramsci, made popular by post-colonial theorists such as Spivak (1988) in her question "can the subaltern speak?" Identity politics is thus seen as a strategy necessary to obtain liberal political goals (Sullivan, 1997).

Identity politics has been criticized on three fronts (see Bernstein, 2002's summaries of Phelan, 1993 and Kimmel, 1993 view on this). First, it has been criticized as being essentialist since it advocates invariate truths about participants (such as sexuality, race or gender). Thus, it does not make identity politics amenable to change. Identity politics, therefore, reinforces hegemonic restrictive social categorizations such as gay versus straight, black versus white, and male versus female (Seidman, 1997). Second, because of differences in what constitutes identity for different groups, identity politics has been criticized as inhibiting coalition building. Due to fragmentation associated with "organizing around their own politics," Kauffman (1993) laments that leftist politics has increasingly become ineffective and as Gitlin (1994; 1995) argues, identity politics has contributed to the decline of leftist politics. Last and perhaps more important to this chapter, identity politics has been criticized as viewing identity movements as cultural rather than political movement since it is based on the static notion of identity (e.g., race, gender, sexual orientation or immigrant status).

Immigrant groups tend to isolate their lives and politics away from their host society giving them an identity that takes on political meaning. Often this is a manifestation of their culture. In the case of Latinos in America, recent immigration debates have taken on power politics. For most Africans though, their identity has not been wrapped in power politics but mostly in the politics of negotiating their African heritage and their American experience. Yet, Chacko (2003) provides specific instances of Ethiopians in the Washington, D.C. area engaging in power politics around the Adams Morgan area. Our interest in identity politics of Ghanaians therefore is couched within their negotiating their Ghanaian heritage and the American experience as part of their isolation from mainstream American society and not necessarily a power politics of organizing around their own oppression.

Assimilation refers to the process by which immigrants change their cultural patterns to those of their host society, enter into their institutions, intermarry, and develop a sense of "peoplehood" based on the host society (Gordon, 1964; Alba and Nee, 1997; Anh, 1999). Assimilation has been the accepted mode of immigrant acculturation in the United States through the concept of a melting pot (Rumbaut, 1997; Azar, 1999) as opposed to Canada where immigrant acculturation is based on a tapestry of cultures (Nagel, 2002; Castro, 2003).

Transnationalism refers to multiple interactions that link people and institutions across national borders (Schiller, Basch and Blanc 1995; Itzingsohn, 2000; Vertovec, 2003; Gowricharn, 2009). These are recurrent, cross-border interactions that require commitment of time by participants and cut across economic, political, cultural and religious life (Portes, 1999). A transnational community is a group whose identity is not tied to a specific territory since the group has agency. An excellent example of transnational community is an immigrant group (Owusu, 2007).

Ethnic enclaves are territories associated with cultural distinctiveness of an ethnic group (Wilson and Portes, 1980; Portes and Jensen, 1989). It often centers on ethnic businesses, but also includes residences and institutions of ethnic groups (e.g. Chinatown or Little Italy). Because of globalization, territoriality is no longer the basis of ethnicity. Rather, ethnospaces or ethnic memories are. Unlike an ethnic enclave, an ethnospace refers to globalized spatial diffusion of an ethnic community (Appadurai, 1996).

These five concepts form a framework for this chapter within which to locate the concept of a globalized labor market. Traditionally, immigrants assimilate into the United States over time because of separation from the "Old Country." Because of racism in America, they create ethnic enclaves as supports for negotiating their ethnic heritage and their American experience. Today's globalization means contacts with the "Old Country" are maintained and strengthened. Therefore Ghanaian immigrants, for example, do not become assimilated but have become transnational. This implies they create ethnospaces rather than ethnic enclaves that keep one leg in the source country and the other in the destination country. Thus, immigrants establish new sociologies and geographies by creating identities that isolate them from their host society and its culture and in the process generate a politics around their identity. This is not necessarily because they are disadvantaged through a collective racism in the United States but because as individuals, they face racism at work and in their dealings with other Americans on a daily basis. In addition, technologies of globalization make it possible for Ghanaian immigrants to negotiate their ethnic heritage and their American experience through what seems to be like identity politics. Their participation in identity politics is because of convenience, illegality and individual experiences of racism and intimidation rather than group marginalization and discrimination. After all, it is difficult to identify Ghanaian immigrants as a group, per se.

PURPOSE

The questions this conceptualization raise relate to how Ghanaian immigrants in Cincinnati area engage in an identity politics and what implications this has for both the Ghanaian community and American society. Identity politics of Ghanaian immigrants plays out at two specific scales in the Ghanaian community. The first is at the macro scale through associational life such as the Ghanaian Association of Greater Cincinnati (GAGC), Ghanaian churches, Ghanaian businesses, and the Ghanaian Men's Club (GMC). The second is at the micro scale through the socialization of second generation immigrants in their identity creation, the geography of their identity creation and the history of their identity creation.

This chapter therefore presents the cultural experience of a Ghanaian immigrant group in a Midwestern city (Cincinnati) who will normally not make headlines. Experiences of African immigrants in New York City and Washington, D.C. are well documented but for those in small Midwestern cities such as Columbus and Cincinnati, very little is known of their experience. This is partly because most Africans are subsumed to be part of the African-American community by the host American society or members of African diasporas choose to blend into American society for a variety of reasons. Despite how they are constructed, most Africans in cities like Cincinnati lead lives at home that most Americans cannot imagine, let alone comprehend. This is through an identity politics in which they decide how to negotiate their African heritage and their American experience.

Based on this conceptualization, the first research questions addressed is "how do Ghanaian immigrants in Cincinnati negotiate their Ghanaian heritage and their American experience?" The second research question is "why do they adopt specific measures used in negotiating their identity and is this identity politics played consciously?" The final question is "what implication does this identity politics have for these immigrants and broader American society?"

The argument of this chapter is that Ghanaian immigrants in the Greater Cincinnati area are collectively involved in negotiating their Ghanaian heritage and their American experience through associational life and socialization of second generation immigrants by means of an identity politics. Because of today's globalization, they are not culturally assimilated but rely on their transnational ties to live in ethnospaces rather than ethnic enclaves. Effectively, the group participates in an identity politics not out of a threat but out of a combination of convenience, intimidation and immigration status. They therefore produce new geographies and sociologies in the making of their history. Their identity politics has implications not just of these recent immigrants but, also for broader American society that they have become a part of.

DATA AND METHODOLOGY

A combination of qualitative and quantitative data and methods are used in analysis in this chapter. Three sets of data are used in the analyses in this chapter. First, in-depth interviews with leaders and officials of Ghanaian institutions in Cincinnati conducted in 2002 are supplemented by intuitive knowledge of the community over the past fifteen years. Six leaders of the GAGC, four leaders of the GMC, five of the Church of Pentecost (COP) and four of International Christian Fellowship Assemblies of God (ICFAG) were interviewed on issues of associational life of the community. This data has been supplemented by a knowledge of the community gained, not just as a member but also, as a past secretary and president of the GAGC and immersing myself in both community and individual functions.

Second, data on Ghanaian businesses collected over time and my family's previous ownership of one of the leading business institutions for over nine years offers insights into the community. Because of potential conflicts of interest, a survey of Ghanaian businesses in Columbus (conducted in 2002) was used as a surrogate for the specifics of those in Cincinnati but knowledge of Ghanaian businesses in Cincinnati was acquired for this chapter. Third, a 2005 survey of fifteen Ghanaian families made up of fifteen couples and twenty-seven children provides insights into socialization of second generation migrants. These three sets of data are buttressed by a survey of thirty-seven Ghanaians in 2007. Data for this chapter has therefore evolved over a number of years and captures a longitudinal change in Ghanaian community.

Survey data were summarized, categorized (using tables and charts), and compared by simple descriptive methods (such as measures of central tendency) to identify trends and patterns within them and intuitive data was used as a context within which to interpret identified patterns and trends derived from survey data.

Associational Life and Identity Politics at the Macro Scale

At the macro scale a number of social, religious, and business institutions have emerged as the framework for identity politics of Ghanaians in the Cincinnati area (Yeboah and Ocran, 2008). These institutions include social organizations (Attah-Poku, 1996; N'Diaye and N'Diaye, 2007), churches (Kwakye-Nuako, 2007), businesses (Yeboah and Amankwah, 2007), and more recently, hometown associations (Abbott, 2007). There seems to be both inter-category and between-category competition (Odmalm, 2004; Amoako, 2007) among these institutions, although with time, cooperation seems to be the modus operandi. Competition and cooperation between immigrant institutions reflect a changing structure of immigrant communities and changing opportunity structure within their milieu (Schrover, 2006 and Vermeulen, 2005).

As Figure 4.1 shows, most of these institutions are located outside Cincinnati city limits but rather in the inner suburbs of Fairfield, and to a lesser extent, Forest Park and Hamilton. These institutions, in their efforts to provide Ghanaians a framework within which to negotiate their Ghanaian heritage and their American experience tend to accentuate the Ghanaian-ness of these immigrants. Apart from businesses, membership to these institutions is voluntary but predominantly Ghanaian. Because of the voluntary nature of these institutions, it is difficult to gauge their universal appeal to individual Ghanaians but they are available to all who wish to engage in them.

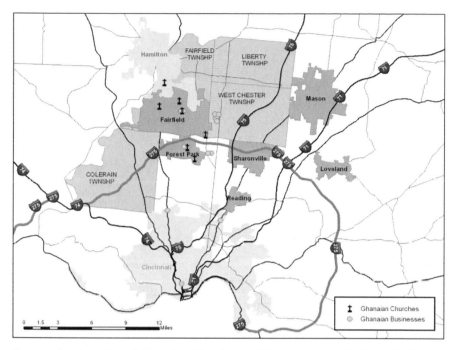

Figure 4.1.   Location of Ghanaian Churches and Businesses in Relation to their Residences

Associational Life: GAGC

GAGC is the oldest institution that Ghanaian immigrants use to engage in identity politics and has been in existence since 1992. It is a social institution (N'Diaye and N'Diaye, 2007). It has been the platform for the establishment of almost all individuals and institutions within the community (DeBiaggi, 2002) and until quite recently, it has been the most vibrant institution but its status has waned over the last six years. Its origins lie in the elite professional class (Abbott, 2007; Braken et al., 1991) of Ghanaians who first settled the region and their desire to socialize among themselves. Historically, it was the institution that was responsible for the socialization of members of the community and served the "birth to death functions" of the community (naming ceremonies, outdoorings, marriages, weddings and funerals). It is well organized with a constitution, Web site, organizes social functions such as an annual picnic and Christmas party. It served as the magnet that attracted most Ghanaians to migrate to the region (Yeboah and Ocran, 2008). Other groups that came after it have tended to copy its operations. Since its inception, it has averaged about thirty members (often, the same professional elite over the years). Membership is open to Ghanaians and their spouses so it is predominantly Ghanaian.

GAGC's hegemony had been challenged by recent developments in the community. Because of its elitist construction many recent in-migrants to Cincinnati have gravitated away from it to other institutions. Two beneficiaries of GAGC's changing status have been Ghanaian churches and the GMC. Ghanaian churches have now taken on the socialization role of the community by engaging in "birth to death" activities. GMC has also usurped the patron of GAGC and enstooled him Ghanafohene (Ghanaian Chief) in Cincinnati. This has resulted in a rift between prominent members of GAGC, on the one hand, and the former patron and Ghanaian men, on the other hand.

Despite the challenge to its hegemony, GAGC is still the organizer of overarching activities of the community (such as "Ghana @ 50" celebrations) because it has members with skills to do so. In addition, the elite and professional status of its individual members makes them attractive to chair individual and community functions such as outdooring parties and fundraisers for churches. Its role in identity politics of the community used to be the leader of the community and in settlement of recent arrivals. Even though its hegemony has declined in recent times, GAGC still leads and its individual members serve, albeit indirectly, in helping Ghanaians negotiate their Ghanaian heritage and their American experiences.

Associational Life: Christian Churches

Africans are notoriously religious (M'biti, 1991) and this is the case with the Ghanaian community in Cincinnati. For Ghanaians in Cincinnati, their religious experience is mostly Christian and Pentecostal in orientation (Kwakye-Nuako, 2007) and Christian churches have increasingly become the basis of socialization and negotiation of the Ghanaian heritage and their American experience in identity creation and politics. Eleven Ghanaian Churches currently exist in the Cincinnati area (for an estimated community population of about 2,500 people) and only four of them are Orthodox in orientation. These are mostly small churches with between twenty to fifty members. Membership in all churches is predominantly Ghanaian and even though they started out as institutions concerned with spiritual life of members, they have developed into institutions of socialization engaging in "life-to-death" functions, immigration issues and social indoctrination (Yeboah and Ocran, 2008).

Ghanaian churches in Cincinnati include Church of Pentecost (COP) which is affiliated with Church of Pentecost Ghana, International Christian Fellowship Assemblies of God (ICFAG) which was started by an individual and later loosely affiliated with the Assemblies of God Church in the United States, King's House (KH), the start-up Rhema Bible Church (RBC) and Hour of Grace (HG). The last two are splinters from ICFAG. Organizational structure and arrangements of Ghanaian churches vary. Apart from COP, most of these churches are independent but in recent times orthodox churches from Ghana have established "overseas missions" and in Cincinnati (as in other major cities) they have resulted in the emergence of a Presbyterian, Apostolic, Methodist (although the Methodists are not affiliated with a Ghanaian church but rather the Methodist Church in the United States), and a Catholic congregation which is under the tutelage of a Ghanaian Catholic priest who heads a parish in Dayton. The Ghanaian Catholic church uses the resource and facilities of an American Catholic church in Forest Park.

There exists intergroup competition between Ghanaian churches and competition with GAGC but all these churches depend on individual status of members of GAGC in chairing their functions and raising funds. By their socialization, these churches have elevated individual Ghanaians in their hierarchies to positions such as elders and deacons to the extent that some of their members refer to themselves by their church titles in public. Apart from being competitive with each other, these churches are fiercely independent. For example, a group of Ghanaians who attended a "white" Presbyterian church in Fairfield broke off from the white church and decided to incorporate their own Ghanaian church. These seven families cut all ties with their former church and even though the White church offered to cooperate with them and share facilities with them, they opted to endure the inconvenience of meeting in an individual's apartment (without a minister, sacrament, music, and other rituals of worship) until they could raise funds to rent a small warehouse to use as their sanctuary.

The majority of Ghanaian churches in Cincinnati are located within a five-mile radius in the Fairfield-Hamilton area and despite this intergroup competition and independence, there are emerging public signs of cooperation amongst them. In the last few months, church functions organized by one church make it a point to acknowledge other churches and their pastors or elders and even invite them to join the host church at the high table. My speculation is they recognize they can strategically align themselves with each other in an effort to compete.

Ghanaian churches in Cincinnati are beginning to institutionalize into mainstream America in terms of leadership and assets. Often these churches start off as renters in warehouses (which are relatively cheap and isolated from residential areas and population concentrations on Sundays and in the evenings) to buying their own premises as the COP and ICFAG, two of the oldest churches in the community have done. For instance, after meeting at the YMCA for a while, the COP bought a bank building and converted it to its church building. ICFAG rented a warehouse and later a church building from an Assemblies of God Church for a number of years. Quite recently, it has bought a Veterans Post building and converted it into a church building

In addition, they often buy vehicles for their functions and the Pentecostal ones now have permanent pastors. Whereas ICFAG has had a minister since its inception, COP has now been granted a pastor by the U.S. branch of the church, KH inherited a floating pastor after its founding pastor was deported to Ghana, RC and HG were established by pastors who were originally members of ICFAG and, the Catholic, Presbyterian, and Methodist churches do not have resident pastors.

A striking feature of these churches in their identity creation is their outward anonymity yet, their separation from the host American society. Their names do not give an indication that they are Ghanaian churches and some of them do not even have their names embossed on their premises. However, once you enter these churches, they worship in Ghanaian style, with their services stretching for as long as three to four hours on Sundays with loud music backed by instruments, and dancing. They have prayer meetings almost all days of the week and often turn to the greater Ghanaian community to raise funds for their operations. They organize youth and children activities such as summer retreats and Sunday schools. Even though they are nonprofits, they often target well-to-do and the so-called elite members of GAGC to indirectly extort large sums of money, in public settings from them. There is emerging a gender division in how they dress. Men have reverted to wearing western attire (such as suits) for Sunday service but women tend to wear Ghanaian wear (such as *kaba* and *slit* made of various fabrics such as lace, *kente*, and Dutch-wax prints). Increasingly younger women are reverting to western wear (suits).

These churches have become the basis of socialization for most Ghanaians. They influence identity formation in terms of negotiating their Ghanaian heritage and their American identity on issues of immigration, marriage, birth, death, family harmony, and even status in the community.

Associational Life: Businesses

Eight kinds of formal businesses serve Ghanaians in the Cincinnati area. These include grocery stores (e.g. Akwaaba, Asafo, Florida Skys, and recently, Kumasi), numerous mechanics (e.g. Sam's; Blackie's), used car dealers, hair products retail (e.g. Vici's and Katlyd's), tax preparers, insurance sales and travel agencies, real estate agents and loan officers, a restaurant (e.g. Adom), shipping agents (e.g. Nab), and hair dressers and a barber. To a large extent, most of these businesses are of the low-order service sector rather than manufacturing or high-order service sectors (Yeboah and Amankwah, 2008). Other individuals engage in informal businesses such as catering for functions but these are not included in this chapter.

Ghanaian businesses are not just businesses but arenas of social contact, information, communing, maintenance of Ghanaian culture and negotiating American experience. They are therefore embedded in social capital of the ethnic community (Portes and Sensenbrenner, 1993; Zhou, 1998; Poros, 2001; Raijman, 2001). Unlike Asian (e.g., Chinese) businesses in the United States, Ghanaian businesses tend to be embedded in the ethnicity of their owners rather than that of the host American community (McGlinn, 1995; Lee, 1995). Ghanaians tend to gather around these businesses, ostensibly not just for economic reasons but also social ones. It is at these businesses that they find out what is happening in the community on both an individual and institutional scale (Yeboah and Amankwah, 2008). Flyers for individual and community functions are posted on windows of businesses and sometimes tickets are sold at these businesses. In most cases word of mouth about community happenings is spread at businesses. So many Ghanaians gravitate toward grocery stores in the evenings and on the weekends, obviously to buy groceries but also to find out what is happening and many young men gravitate toward mechanics' shops and the barber shop on a regular basis (often when they are off work).

Businesses have therefore established in close proximity to residences of their customers (Figure 4.1). For example, Akwaaba African Market is located in Forest Park because this used to be the residential hub of the middle class of Ghanaians and other Africans. Also, Asafo, Florida Skys (now bought by Asafo), Kumasi, Vicki's, Adom Restaurant, and Katlyad are located close to apartment complexes in Fairfield where many working class Ghanaians reside. They have also taken advantage of the first point of International grocery shopping in Cincinnati know as Jungle Jim's. Jungle Jim's tended to be the main source of African groceries till the emergence of Ghanaian businesses (Yeboah and Amankwah, 2008). Because of zoning regulations, Ghanaian mechanics and shippers are compelled to locate in existing light industrial parks but here also, they have followed the concentration of residents in Fairfield and Forest Park and they tend to cluster in the same industrial parks. Most working class Ghanaians still reside in apartments in Fairfield and Forest Park but as they enter America's middle class, the majority of Ghanaians in the area have tended to gravitate toward West Chester, Liberty Township, and Mason in terms of their residence. Ghanaian economic activities are, however, located in the Fairfield area, especially along State Route 4 so Ghanaians trek to shop and attend church along State Route 4.

Despite their anonymity of names, the clustering of businesses close to homes and apartments of clients and customers gives the impression of an emerging ethnospace to the trained eye. In fact, a visit to Camelot and Woodridge apartment complexes will reveal many cars with Ghanaian flags as decals hanging off their rearview mirrors. This convergence of working-class residences, businesses, churches in the Fairfield area, in subtle rather than overt ways suggests the emergence of an ethnospace (Yeboah, 2008). The subtleness of this convergence is due to two factors. First, some Ghanaians have not regularized their stay in the United States and therefore would rather remain anonymous. Second, businesses and churches would like to attract more than just Ghanaian customers so it is easier to go with names such as King's House, Rhema, Vicki's, or Katlyad's.

Associational Life: Men's Club and Traditional Politics

The GMC formed as a response (of working-class men) to the perceived elite status of GAGC and currently has about thirty members. It emerged in 2000 due to a fatality and the lack of life insurance of some Ghanaians in the region but it has changed from its original intentions and membership to an opposition group to GAGC. It has corrupted and coopted the patron of GAGC to establish an abominable Chief of Ghanaians (Ghanafohene) creating division of the community as a whole. Chieftaincy in Ghana is not based on being a Ghanaian but on ethnicity (e.g., Ga, Ewe, Ashanti). Yet, the GMC has enstooled a chief for Ghanaians (Amoako, 2007; Attah-Poku, 1996).

GMC has simply replicated activities of GAGC in their effort to outcompete it (Yeboah and Ocran, 2008). It therefore organizes social functions such as a summer picnic and Christmas party. Yet it does not have the clout to bring together other institutions as the GACC does so it has not been able to organize the community-building events such as "Ghana @ 50" and celebration of Ghana's independence as GAGC does. In recent years it has embarked upon a cultural celebration through its Ghanafest.

Identity Politics of Socializing
Second Generation at the Macro Scale

At the micro scale, identity politics of Ghanaians is played out in the socialization of second generation of migrants by their parents at home, in school, and in churches (Yeboah and Yeboah, 2008), reinforcing the geography of identity politics that Ghanaian institutions facilitate. This micro-scale geography is revealed by the tension that exists between socialization and identity creation of Ghanaian children and their parents in their homes and public spaces.

Suarez-Orozco and Suarez-Orozco (2001) provide a three-category classification of second-generation immigrants (hybrid or child of one immigrant and one non-immigrant, both parents as immigrants but child born in the United States, and child born outside but brought to the United States) that is utilized in this chapter. Place of birth, age development of second generation immigrants and class status of their family influence this micro-scale geography of identity politics (Massey and Sanchez, 2007; Waldinger and Feliciano, 2004; Portes, Fernandez-Kelly and Haller, 2006; Stepick et al., 2001).

Most second-generation Ghanaian migrants are adolescents but a trend of recent arrival of college-aged Ghanaians to the region, may potentially change the socialization and identity creation of second generation immigrants and consequently the geography and sociology of identity politics of Ghanaians. This is because these college-aged Ghanaians are active in Ghanaian institutions and are beginning to provide a bridge between second generation immigrants and their parents.

Socializing Second Generation: Sociology of Identity Creation

How do parents identify their children and how do children identify themselves? A mismatch exists in self- and community-identity. Table 4.1 shows that Ghanaian second-generation children tend to self-identify as African-American in school whereas their parents community-identify them as Ghanaians at home (see Massey and Sanchez, 2007). There is therefore a difference in self-identity and community-identity of these children, within their homes. For parents, their ethnicity automatically transfers onto their children as part of their children's social capital (Shah, 2007). So, once born by Ghanaians these children will always be Ghanaian as the *Twi* saying goes "*okoto now anoma*," translated literally to "a crab does not give birth to a bird."

However, Ghanaian children's experience in the United States tends to make them think they are not Ghanaian. This is in an effort to identify with the dominant group of blacks in america. Whereas children born in the United

Table 4.1. Self Identity vs. Community Identity

Identity	Children at School	Parents at Home
Ghanaian	0	12
African-American	17	2
American	9	0
Ghanaian American	0	1
Total	25	15

Table 4.2.   Age Development and Identity Creation

Identity	Ghanaian	African-American	American
Parents	12	2	2
All Children	0	17	8
Middle Childhood	0	9	8
Adolescents	0	8	0

States tend to self-identify more as American, those born in other countries and later migrated to the United States tend to self-identify as African American. Indeed, when these children self-identity as African American, they do so in an effort to fit in and be accepted into American society (Haller and Landolt, 2005) rather than be constructed as the "other" (Hall, 1990). So, place of birth influences the self-identity of these children.

Table 4.2 shows that age also affects self-identity. All adolescents self-identify as African-American but a mixed self-identity is presented for middle childhood children with almost 50 percent of them self-identifying as African American and the other 50 percent as American. In this particular case age and place of birth are correlated. Generally speaking, most middle childhood children who self-identify as American were born in the United States, hence the correlation between place of birth and age in self-identity.

A key manifestation of identity creation lies in the name a person goes by in particular spaces, such as home and in public. Table 4.3 shows that class status influences names by which Ghanaian second-generation immigrants go by at home and in public (Kurien, 2005; Nanlai, 2005). Generally, children from families of relatively higher class status are more comfortable using both Ghanaian names whereas children form relatively lower class families are more comfortable with Western names. Children of families with relatively middle class status tend to be comfortable with the use of both Ghanaian and Western names. For some of these second generation migrants, they create segmented identities for themselves by adopting Western names that conform to their middle names and this is the name their friends call them by. For example, a child known as Kwasi will be called Quincy by their friends,

Table 4.3.   Class and Identity Creation

Class Status	High	Medium	Low
Ghanaian	4	1	3
Ghanaian & Western	4	3	1
Western	1	1	7
Nickname	0	0	0
Total	9	5	11

Table 4.4.   Place of Birth and Identity Creation

	Comfort with Ghanaian Names	Discomfort with Ghanaian Names	Comfort with Both	Total
Born in Ghana	3	2	1	6
Born in USA	4	10	0	14
Born Elsewhere	3	2	0	5
Total	10	14	1	25

or Cassidy instead of Kwakyewaa. Others adopt African-American names such as Devonte.

Place of birth also affects self-identify in identity politics of Ghanaian children in the Cincinnati area. Table 4.4 shows that place of birth influences names Ghanaian second-generation immigrants are comfortable with at home and in public. Children born in Ghana and elsewhere are more comfortable with Ghanaian names whereas those born in the United States are less comfortable with Ghanaian names both at home and in public places. This may be already because children born on Ghana may be used to Ghanaian names by the time they arrive in the United States.

Socializing Second Generation: Geography of Identity Creation

Socialization of Ghanaian second-generation migrants reveals a geography of identity creation between public and private spaces (Gagen, 2004). The geographical dimension of identity of second-generation migrants points to what Portes, Fernandez-Kelly and Haller (2005) call segmented assimilation on the ground. Place of birth influences the Ghanaian-ness of this group of second generation immigrants in public. Fifty percent of children born in the United States generally don't speak or understand any Ghanaian language. Of the other 50 percent there is a split between those who are embarrassed and those who are not embarrassed of speaking Ghanaian languages in public. Interestingly, Table 4.5 shows that children born in Ghana are embarrassed to speak Ghanaian languages in public whereas children born in countries apart from Ghana and the United States are least embarrassed of speaking Ghanaian languages in public.

Similar to place of birth, age development of second generation migrants also influences socialization and identity creation of Ghanaian second generation migrants in public, especially with respect to Ghanaian languages. Second generation immigrants tend to create hyphenated identities depending upon the place in which they are (Gibau, 2005). Table 4.6 shows that middle childhood children are generally embarrassed by Ghanaian languages in public while adolescents are least embarrassed by Ghanaian languages in public.

Table 4.5. Place of Birth and Attitude toward Ghanaian Languages in Public

Place of Birth	Don't Understand	Understand but Embarrassed	Not Embarrassed
Ghana	0	5	1
USA	7	4	3
Other	1	0	4
Total	8	9	8

Class also influences socialization and identity creation of Ghanaian second-generation immigrants in public places. Table 4.7 shows that the higher the class status of a child's family, the less embarrassed they are speaking Ghanaian languages in public. This is an indication that children from higher class families may desire to use their ethnicity as an asset in public. We also see tendencies children from lower class families being embarrassed of speaking and listening to Ghanaian languages in public. A story exists of how children in a fast food drive-through pleaded with their father to turn off African music in their car: "Daddy turn off the music, they will know we are African." Part of this is the desire for acceptance of lower class children in mainstream American society. Despite the influences of place of birth, age development and class status, a casual observation of Ghanaian children is that as they get older they become less embarrassed of Ghanaian languages and names in public.

Ghanaian second generation immigrants, just as their parents, live in two cultures and geographies simultaneously. This is especially in terms of food, clothes and music. Since they are being socialized transnationally these two cultures have a bearing on their identity creation and politics (Lutz, 2006, Gibau, 2005). This is because of what they are exposed to at home in terms of food, clothes and music. Table 4.8 shows that Ghanaian second-generation immigrants like Ghanaian music. This may be due to exposure but may also be due to quality of Ghanaian music (especially *hiplife*). However, because of their transnational socialization, they tend to like both American food and clothes as much as Ghanaian ones.

Table 4.6. Age Development and Attitude toward Ghanaian Languages in Public

Age	Don't Understand	Understand but Embarrassed	Not Embarrassed
Middle Childhood	8	7	2
Adolescents	1	1	6
Total	9	8	8

Table 4.7.   Class Status and Attitude toward Ghanaian Language in Public

Class Status	Don't Understand	Understand but Embarrassed	Not Embarrassed
High	2	2	4
Medium	4	1	0
Low	2	6	4
Total	8	9	8

Transnational socialization and identity creation of Ghanaian second-generation immigrants is also mitigated by a restricted socialization outside home and school. Table 4.9 shows that tensions exist between parents and their children in terms of socializing outside their comfort zones of home, church, Ghanaian functions and school. Ghanaian parents, just like other immigrant parents, tend to construct America as hostile (see Lutz, 2006; Zhou and Xiong, 2005; Arriaza, 2004; Stepick et al., 20001). In a sense, this is expressed in parent's desire to keep to other Ghanaians and their values (see Shah, 2007). Despite this tendency, Ghanaian children have made friends from school and, more than 50 percent have American friends. However, these children have only limited interactions with friends in their home settings. What is remarkable is that nine of the twenty-five respondent children indicate they are not allowed by their parents to visit friends, irrespective of who these friends are and even though fourteen visit American friends, these are often fellow apartment dwellers where the interaction is limited to playing video games. It is surprising that only five visit Ghanaian friends. In fact none of the twenty-five children in the survey had ever been to a sleep-over at a friend's house!

Irrespective of the limited American socialization of these children, all of them are socialized mostly through Ghanaian institutions and their spaces, especially churches (see Kwakye-Nuako, 2007). As Table 4.10 shows all but four children (belonging to one family) attend Ghanaian churches. Since the survey, this family has now left their non-Ghanaian church and joined a Ghanaian church. Interestingly, only one of the twenty-five children has ever invited a non-Ghanaian friend to a Ghanaian church. These children tend to

Table 4.8.   Transnational Living and Identity Creation

Attribute	Food	Music	Clothes
Ghanaian	0	14	0
American	1	6	7
Both	24	6	18
Total	25	25	25

Table 4.9.   Friendships and Space

School Friends	Friends All over	American Friends	Visit Ghana Friends	Visit Other Friends	Do not visit Friends
9	11	14	5	10	9

interact with other Ghanaian children they meet at church but they experience limited visits from Ghanaian friends at home. This may be because they meet Ghanaian friends at church functions such as Sunday service, youth group meetings, church picnics and parties so there is no real need to visit these friends. In addition, church members may not live close to each other or in the same apartment complex so visiting Ghanaian friends requires parents driving them. This takes away from parent's busy work schedules (Yeboah and Yeboah, 2008).

Socializing Second Generation: History of Identity Creation

Not only is space important in identity creation of Ghanaian second-generation immigrants, through time, their parents have seen change in their identity creation (Portes, Fernandez-Kelly and Haller; 2005, Gibau, 2005). As Table 4.11 shows, parents report a history or transition of identity creation amongst their children. This should be understood in the context of the emergence of first generation college-aged Ghanaian immigrants to the region who are very active in Ghanaians institutions, especially churches and may be mistaken for second-generation migrants by the untrained eye. These college-aged Ghanaians, however, seem to have provided a bridge between adolescent second-generation immigrants and their parents.

Table 4.11 summarizes longitudinal changes in both attitude and speech patterns from parent's perspective. For the twenty-five children, parents report that the majority (76 percent and 80 percent, respectively) have changed their attitude and speech patterns, acculturating away from expectations of their parents. In the three cases where the parents cannot detect changes, these children are recent arrivals to the United States. Most parents report that their children have tended to Americanizing their speech, a trend reported by South, Crowder and Chavez (2005) for other ethnic second-generation immigrants.

Table 4.10.   Socialization in Ghanaian Spaces

	Yes	No
Attend Church	25	0
Attend Ghanaian Church	21	4
Invite Non-Ghanaians	1	21

Table 4.11. **Parent's Perception of Change**

Perception	Attitude	Speech
Change	20	19
No Change	2	2
Cannot Tell	3	4
Total	25	25

The specific types of changes parents perceive in their children are summarized in Table 4.12. Parents report their children have picked up U.S. culture and mix *Twi* and English in their speech. This is reflected in their children picking up American accents and being rude and asking a lot of questions (children are supposed to be seen, not heard in Ghanaian culture). Some of these children even make fun of *Twi* and their parents when they speak it. Although some of these children either do not speak or understand *Twi*, they also make fun of their parents' accent when they speak English. This discord between parents and their children is dramatized on Facebook by African children in a "Like Page" titled "How do you know your parents are African?" Two of the postings are summarized here are responses to the question "How do you know your parents are African?"

> Answer 1: When you want to major in any other field in college, you parents say you must become a DOCTA!
> Answer 2: They constantly remind you of the sacrifices they have made for you to be in America!

Despite parents reporting these transformations in their children through time, the children live in two worlds out of necessity (Lutz, 2006; Gibau, 2005) as part of their segmented socialization. Since they live in United States, they are socialized at school and by the mass media, on one hand, and by their parents and Ghanaian institutions, on the other hand, they live as Americans

Table 4.12. **Types of Changes in Children**

Type of Change	No. of Parents
Rude and question a lot	4
Mix Twi and English in speech	7
Picked up American culture	8
Picked up American accent	4
Make Fun of Twi	2
Direct children to both cultures	2
Don't speak or understand Twi	2
Encourage children to speak Twi	3

in specific spaces their experiences reflect their changing socialization in two cultures and in different spaces (Stepick et al., 2001; Shah, 2007).

DISCUSSION

At the macro scale, Ghanaians in the Cincinnati area engage in an identity politics of associational life. This is by creating institutions that they use to negotiate their Ghanaian heritage and their American experience. Most of these institutions are geographically concentrated in Fairfield, and to a lesser extent Hamilton and Forest Park. Because of this spatial concentration, a geography of identity politics at the macro scale is emerging in the Cincinnati area. Within this geography of identity politics, Ghanaians tend commune among themselves and in isolation of the rest of the United States. They only engage American culture in their work. Their experience therefore raises the question as to the kind of sociology that these migrants are experiencing in the United States. Are Ghanaians being assimilated and acculturated into U.S. society or are they living as Ghanaians in the United States? In the context of globalization and its technologies, Ghanaians are able to engage in this identity politics at the macro scale because the reality of their transnational activities makes it possible to socialize in these two geographies with one of them being physical and the other virtual (Abbott, 2007).

In this identity politics, Ghanaian institutions tend to skew the assimilation process of Ghanaians toward their Ghanaian heritage and engage their American experience only to the extent that it facilitates Ghanaians to function economically in the United States. Thus, even though associational life is designed to negotiate their Ghanaian-and American-ness, the stress at the macro scale is more on their Ghanaian-ness (Kwakye-Nuako, 2007; N'Diaye and N'Diaye, 2007). For most Ghanaians in the region, their lives outside employment are therefore influenced by spending Saturdays shopping at Ghanaian businesses (alongside American ones out of necessity), and attending Ghanaian functions such as association meetings, outdoorings, privately organized Ghanaian parties, and funerals. Sundays are mostly spent at church.

Ghanaians work and live as any other resident in the United States yet, the locus of friends of most Ghanaians in the region is predominantly Ghanaian. A visit to any of the Ghanaian-owned mechanics or the barber shop any afternoon during the week will reveal many young men "hanging-out" at these establishments. For most of them, this is their main means of communing and socializing in the United States. Because of these institutions, Ghanaians in the region tend to have limited interaction with both black and white America, although issues of immigration (through green card marriages) have provided more avenues for interaction with black and white America.

At the micro scale, socialization of second-generation Ghanaians reveals a tension between parents and their children in identity politics in their negotiation of their Ghanaian heritage and American experience (Lutz, 2006; Gibau, 2005; Portes, Fernandez-Kelly and Haller, 2005). A geography of differential socialization and identity creations is emerging for these children (Yeboah and Yeboah, 2008). This micro-scale geography and socialization of children raises questions about an emerging sociology and geography of Ghanaian second generation migrants in the Cincinnati area.

Within homes, parents construct their children as Ghanaian, translate their ethnic values onto them (Shah, 2007), and expect them to behave Ghanaian. Yet, children self-identify more with their American-ness in the broader American society (Haller and Landolt, 2005) and therefore behave in ways that parents deem as rude and inappropriate. Place of birth, age, and class status of families affects the kind of socialization and identity creation of children of Ghanaians at the micro scale. So do geography and history. These influencers need further study as Ghanaian children grow beyond adolescence and middle childhood. For example, what will happen to Ghanaian identities as these children grow into adulthood and wish to marry? Who do they marry? Every Ghanaian they know is called either "uncle" or "auntie" so their children are "cousins." Will they be able to distinguish between their Ghanaian "cousins" and their consanguine ones?

Unlike parents who intend to retire to Ghana (at least that is their wish), second-generation Ghanaians will most probably live, work and retire in the United States. How does the tension in their socialization and identity creation between them and their parents position them in mainstream American society of the future? Speculation is that if these children are socialized by their parents' values alone they will not necessary be like other American adults in their adulthood. Yet, their socialization is being influenced by both American culture and a recent emergence of Ghanaian college-aged students who are settling in the region and have become active participants in various churches. What will be the influence of American culture and these recent arrivals on Ghanaian college immigrants in identity creation of these second-generation immigrants?

Identity politics has often been associated with groups under threat such as discrimination against an ethnic, gender, sexual-orientation or racial group (Kauffman, 1988; 1990; 1993). For the most part, such groups engage in power politics by organizing around their oppression. Ghanaian immigrants' participation in identity politics is, however not based on a threat *per se* or their marginal status. Rather it is used as a strategy to survive as Ghanaians in America.

Despite the criticism of identity politics being cultural rather than political, Bernstein (2002) questions whether there is a dichotomy between culture and politics. This chapter reinforces Bernstein's view and argues that for Ghanaian immigrants, their politics is cultural and their ability to negotiate their Ghanaian heritage and their American experience is a politically conscious process that may not necessarily involve power politics but involves their ability to make a living and live in America. Their collective and individual identities and the conflicting interests surrounding them are mitigated by their transnational circumstances that enhance their desire for convenience, intimidation of engaging American culture and for some, their illegal status. More importantly, their transnational status in today's globalized world means that first generation Ghanaian immigrants will be less assimilated to American culture and this translates into the slower and more nuanced socialization of the second generation. Ghanaian first generation immigrants can worship separately from the rest of the United States, their diets will be supplied largely by Ghanaian grocery shops, they commune in Ghanaian institutions such as ethnic associations and churches, aspire to retire to Ghana therefore invest in housing and businesses and only engage America to the extent that they have to earn a living. They do not have to interact with both black and white America (although in efforts to regularize their stay, green card marriages may necessitate such interaction). Yet, the second generation is caught in two worlds or cultures and for them, the political dilemma of how they self-identify and how community identifies them have to be negotiated.

It should be pointed out that Ghanaian immigrants have not engaged in power politics, so far, but have worked in distinctive ways to negotiate their Ghanaian heritage and their American experience in resolving these two conflicting interests. Thus, it is fair to characterize identity politics of Ghanaians as a cultural engagement based on three things. These are convenience, intimidation, and immigration status.

For most Ghanaians in the region, it is convenient and comforting to associate and commune with other Ghanaians through institutions such as GAGC and various churches. Businesses serve as points of meeting and exchange of information on community events and churches serve as a refreshing opportunity to network with each other and deal with the reality of being an alien in the United States. For others their identity politics is based on the reality of their individual experiences (rather than group experiences) of racism, discrimination and being intimidated by their American experience especially, through language barriers and problems with their legal stay. Many Ghanaians in the Cincinnati area, irrespective of socioeconomic class, can recount their individual experiences of racism in their work places and general U.S. society. These individual experiences have culminated in this group's willingness to band together in search of some form of comfort in their Ghanaian community. One argument made by members of the breakaway Presbyterian congregation is that even though they were well treated by the host church, they sometimes experienced communication problems at church. This problem is not just with language but, more importantly, with the nuances of sense of humor that go with communicating in English. It may come as a surprise to most Americans but, the nuances of communication (sense humor, gestures, etc.) are sometimes difficult for even the most urbane immigrant to grasp, let alone the working class. Despite these individual experiences of racism and discrimination, the group has not engaged in power politics because their Ghanaian-ness or culture offers them comfort and stability to live and work in America. For another group, engaging in identity politics is due to their illegal immigration status. The movie "Green Card" details the difficulty immigrants in the United States face with regularizing their stay. Some Ghanaians, like other immigrant groups in the country, are plagued by issues of illegality. For some, their engaging in identity politics is a way of shielding themselves from the vagrancies of working illegally in America. Sticking with their lot is a way of not exposing themselves to the law but also a way of finding out how to regularize their stay as well as survival strategies to ensure they earn a living.

Do Ghanaians engage in this identity politics consciously or not? At the macro scale, most Ghanaians engage in this form of communing by default. Once they arrive in the region, they are introduced to Ghanaian institutions that embrace them and make them comfortable. With the difficulty of breaking into mainstream America, these immigrants simply fall into a pattern of communing in this way. Also, businesses that specialize in Ghanaian foods and good become an attractive point of communing of recent arrivals. Class has an effect in communing. In some cases where certain middle-income families have previously communed through white or African-American churches before the emergence of Ghanaian ones in the area, there has been a tendency of these families to refocus their communing towards Ghanaian institutions. At the micro scale, parent socialization of second generation migrants toward their Ghanaian-ness has partly to do with ethnocentricity as well as a lack of trust of American values and patterns of child socialization.

CONCLUSION

Migration theory suggests that recent migrants to the United States will become acculturated and assimilate toward American culture (Gordon, 1964). Often this occurs through time and over generations. First generation migrants, however, tend to establish ethnic enclaves that encompass their institutions (businesses, churches, associations) and residence in specific spaces

(Portes and Jensen, 1989). This has been the experience of Chinese, Italians, and Latinos in the United States. Similarly, despite efforts of immigrant parents to socialize second generation immigrants in values of their source culture, second-generation migrants tend to live in two cultures and through time will become more American. Thus, there is a sociology and geography to immigration to the United States that is defined by assimilation and ethnic enclaves.

Ghanaian immigrants in the Cincinnati area subconsciously engage in a cultural identity politics at both the macro and micro scales out of a combination of convenience, intimidation and illegality of status. Their experience is transnational and, to a large extent, they have one leg in the United States and the other in Ghana (Yeboah, 2008). Thus, there is less of a likelihood of being acculturated and assimilated compared to previous immigrants. More importantly, their numbers are rather small and they tend to separate their institutions, (businesses, churches, associations) and residences. Also, socialization of Ghanaian second-generation immigrants is associated with more Ghanaian influences because of transnationalism associated with today's globalization. Ghanaian immigrant experiences therefore suggest both a new sociology and geography of transnational immigration and the emergence of ethnospaces which require a trained eye to see, rather than assimilation and ethnic enclaves.

What does this new geography and sociology mean for these immigrants and their children? Because of their engagement in identity politics, Ghanaian immigrants will tend to be less assimilated in American society. Their transnational ties and their voluntary and selective separation from mainstream American culture imply their attachment will be both to Ghana and the United States. Many of them see themselves as economic migrants who plan to retire to Ghana, although as they grow older and the children get more entrenched in America, they tend to retire transnationally between Ghana and the United States.

For their children, their micro scale socialization through the identity politics of their parents means they may miss out on what it is to be an American child and this may have impacts on them in adulthood. It should however be borne in mind that these children are also being socialized in school and by electronic media so there are more influences on them than that of their parents. This segmented acculturation of these children suggests that as adults, they will be more connected with their Ghanaian culture. Yet, they will be strongly impacted as Americans since they have to live and work in the United States. They may not be as attached to Ghana as their parents but their attachment to the United States will be tampered by their Ghanaian culture. As an indication of speculating on their bicultural lives, the 2010 World Cup soccer match between Ghana and the United States at the sixteenth round must have brought up interesting allegiances between parents and their children in American homes! By the way, Ghana won by two goals to one. One of Ghana's goals was scored by Kevin Prince Boateng (a second generation Ghanaian raised in Germany) who once represented Germany at the youth stage of competition.

What does this new geography and sociology mean for the host American society? America still assumes that immigrants will necessarily become acculturated and assimilated into mainstream society. This is what the concept of the 'melting pot' advocates. The experience of Ghanaians in the Cincinnati area suggests they will behave in more complicated ways by living transnationally. What is emerging is Ghanaian immigrants do not acculturate or assimilate totally but prefer to maintain large aspects of their source culture through their identity politics. I speculate that the policy implication of this new geography and sociology of immigrants is that the proverbial 'melting pot' of the United States will gradually be replaced with a mosaic of cultures living symbiotically with each other. This is more in line with the Canadian model. Policy makers and practitioners in this field should therefore be sensitive to changing demands such immigrant groups will make on them.

This chapter was first presented at Oberlin College as part of celebrations marking Black History Month in February, 2010.

REFERENCES

Abbott, C.W. 2007. "Nigerians in North America: New Frontiers, Old Associations?" In *The New African Diaspora in North America: Trends, Community Building and Adaptation*, edited by Kwadwo Konadu-Agyemang, Baffour K. Takyi and John A. Arthur, 141–65. Lanham, MD: Lexington Books.

Amoako, J. 2007. "Ethnic Identity, Conflict, and Diasporic Constructions in the New World: The Case of Asante in North America." In *The New African Diaspora in North America: Trends, Community Building and Adaptation,* edited by Kwadwo Konadu-Agyemang, Baffour K. Takyi and John A. Arthur, 107–20. Lanham, MD: Lexington Books.

Anh, T. L. 1999. "Self-employment and Earnings among Immigrants in Australia." *International Migration*, Volume 31: 383–412.

Appadurai, A. 1996. *Modernity at Large. Cultural Dimensions of Globalization*. Minneapolis: University of Minnesota Press.

Arriaza, G. 2004. "Welcome to the Front Seat: Racial Identity and Mesoamerican Immigrants." *Journal of Latinos and Education*, Volume 3(4): 251–65.

Attah-Poku, A. 1996. *The Socio-cultural Adjustment Question: The Role of Ghanaian Immigrant Associations in America*. Brookfield, VT.: Ashgate.

Azar, B. 1996. "Wider Path to Cultural Understanding: Researchers Move Towards a Multicultural Rather than Linear, Model of Acculturation. *APA Monitor*, Volume 30(3): 35–62.

Barkan, J. D., McNulty, M. L., Ayeni, M.A.O. 1991. "'Hometown' Voluntary Associations, Local Development, and the Emergence of Civil Society in Western Nigeria." *The Journal of Modern African Studies*, Volume 29(3): 457–80.

Bernstein, M. 2005. "Identity Politics." *Annual Review of Sociology*, Volume 31: 47–74.

———. 2002. "Identities and Politics. Toward a Historical Understanding of the Lesbian and Gay Movement." *Social Science History*, Volume 26(3): 1–51.

Castro, V. S. 2003. *Acculturation and Psychological Adaptation*: Westport, CT: Greenwood Press.

Chacko, E. 2003. "Ethiopian Ethos and the Making of Ethnic Places in Washington Metropolitan Area." *Journal of Cultural Geography*, Volume 20(2): 21 –42.

DeBiaggi, S. D. D. 2002. *Changing Gender Roles: Brazilian Immigrant Families in the US*. New York: LFC Scholarly Publishing, LLC.

Dwyer, C. "Migrations and Diasporas." In *Introducing Human Geographies* edited by Paul Cloke, Philip Crang and Mark Goodwin. London: Arnold, 1999.

Fonow, M. M. and Marty, D. 1991. "The Shift from Identity Politics to the Politics of Identity: Lesbian Panels in the Women's Studies Classroom." *NWSA Journal*, Volume 3(3): 402–13.

Gagen A.E. 2004. "Landscape of Childhood and Youth." In *A Companion to Cultural Geography* edited by Richard H. Schein, James Stuart Duncan and Nuala Christina Johnson. Boston: Blackwell Publishing.

Gibau, S.G. 2005. "Contested Identities: Narratives of Race and Ethnicity in the Cape Verdean Diaspora." *Identities*, Volume 12: 405–38.

Gitlin, T. 1994. ''From Universality to Difference: Notes on the Fragmentation of the Idea of the Left.'' In *Social Theory and the Politics of Identity* edited by Craig Calhoun, 150–174. Cambridge, MA: Blackwell.

Gordon, M. 1964. *Assimilation in American Life, the Role of Race, Religion, and National Origins*. New York: Oxford University Press.

Gowricharn, R. 2009. "Changing Forms of Transnationalism." *Ethnic & Racial Studies*, Volume 32(9): 1619–38.

Hall, S. 1990. "Cultural Identity and Diaspora." In *Identity, Community, Culture, Difference*, edited by Jonathan Rutherford. London: Lawrence and Wishart.

Haller, W. and Landolt P. 2005. "The Transnational Dimensions of Identity Formation: Adult Children of Immigrants in Miami." *Ethnic and Racial Studies*, Volume 28(6): 1182–1214.

Itzingsohn, J. 2000. "Immigration and the Boundaries of Citizenship: The Institutes of Immigrants Political Transnationalism." *International Migration Review*, Volume 34: 1116–54.

Kauffman, L.A. 1998. "How Political is the Personal?" *The Nation*, (March): 419–20.

———. 1993. "Socialism No." *Progressive*, Volume 57(4): 27–29.

———. 1990. "The Anti-Politics of Identity." *Socialist Review*, Volume 20(1): 67–80.

Kennedy, D.O. 1996. "Can We still Afford to be a Nation of Immigrants?" *The Atlantic Monthly*, Volume 56 (November).

Kimmel, M. S. 1993. "Sexual Balkanization: Gender and Sexuality and the New Ethnicities." *Social Research*, Volume 60(3): 571–87.

Kurien, P.A. 2005. "Being Young, Brown and Hindu." *Journal of Contemporary Ethnography, Volume* 34(4): 434–69.

Kwakye-Nuako, K. 2007. "Still Praisin' God in a New Land: African Immigrant Christianity in North America." In *The New African Diaspora in North America: Trends, Community Building and Adaptation,* edited by Kwadwo Konadu-Agyemang, Baffour K. Takyi and John A. Arthur, 121–40. Lanham, MD: Lexington Books

Lee, D.O. 1995. "Responses to Spatial Rigidity in Urban Transformation: Korean Business Experience in Los Angeles." *International Journal of Urban and Regional Research*, Volume 19: 40–54.

Lobo, P.A. 2007. "Unintended Consequences: Liberalized U.S. Immigration Law and the African Brain Drain." In *The New African Diaspora in North America: Trends, Community Building and Adaptation*, edited by Kwadwo Konadu-Agyemang, Baffour K. Takyi and John A. Arthur, 189 209. Lanham, MD: Lexington Books.

Light, I. 2004. "Immigration and Ethnic Economies in Giant Cities." *UNESCO*: 385–98.

Lutz, A. 2006. "Spanish Maintenance among English-speaking Latino Youth; The Role of Individual and Social Characteristics." *Social Forces*, Volume 84(3): 1417–33.

N'Diaye, D.B. and N'Diaye, G. 2007. "Creating the Vertical Village: Senegalese Traditions of Immigration and Transnational Cultural Life." In *The New African Diaspora in North America: Trends, Community Building and Adaptation,* edited Kwadwo Konadu-Agyemang, Baffour K. Takyi and John A. Arthur, 96–106. Lanham, MD: Lexington Books.

M'biti, J. 1991. *Introduction to African Religion*. London: Heinemann.

Massey, D. and Sanchez, R.M. 2007. "Latino and American Identities as Perceived by Immigrants." *Qualitative Sociology*, Volume 30(1): 81–107.

McGlinn, L. 1995. "Power Networks and Early Chinese Immigrants in Pennsylvania." *Journal of Historical Geography*, Volume 24: 430–45.

Nagel, C. 2002. "Constructing Differences and Sameness: the Politics of Assimilation in London's Arab Communities." *Ethnic and Racial Studies*, Volume 25(2): 258–87.

Nanlai, C. 2005. "The Church as Surrogate Family for Working Class Immigrant Chinese Youth: An Ethnography of Segmented Assimilation." *Sociology of Religion*, Volume 66(2): 183–200.

Norman, B. 2007. "We' in Redux: The Combahee River Collective's Black Feminist Statement." *A Journal of Feminist Cultural Studies*, Volume 18(2): 103–32.

Odmalm, P. 2004. "Civil Society, Migrant Organizations and Political Parties: Theoretical Linkages and Applications to the Swedish Context." *Journal of Ethnic & Migration Studies*, Volume 30(3): 471–89.

Okome, M.O. 2007. "The Contradictions of Globalization: Causes of Contemporary African Immigration to the United States of America." In *The New African*

Diaspora in North America: Trends, Community Building and Adaptation, edited by Kwadwo Konadu-Agyemang, Baffour K. Takyi and John A. Arthur, 29–48. Lanham, MD: Lexington Books.

Owusu, T. 2007. "Transnationalism among African Immigrants in North America: The Case of Ghanaians in Canada." In *The New African Diaspora in North America: Trends, Community Building and Adaptation*, edited by Kwadwo Konadu-Agyemang, Baffour K. Takyi and John A. Arthur, 273–86. Lanham, MD: Lexington Books.

Phelan, S. 1993. "(Be)Coming out: Lesbian Identity and Politics." *Signs*, Volume 18(4): 765–90.

Poros, V.M. 2001. "The Role of Immigrant Networks in Linking Local Labor Markets: the Case of Asian Indian Migration to New York and London." *Global Networks*, Volume 13: 243–59.

Portes, A. 1997. "Immigration Theory for a New Century: Some Problems and Opportunities." *International Migration Review* ,Volume 31(4): 799–825.

———. Fernendez-Kelly, P., and Haller, W. 2005. "Segmented Assimilation on the Ground: The New Second Generation in Early Adulthood." *Ethnic and Racial Studies*, Volume 28(6): 1000–40.

——— and Sensenbrenner J. 1993. "Embeddedness and Immigration: Notes on the Social Determinants of Economic Action." *American Journal of Sociology*, Volume 98: 1320–50.

———and Jensen, L. 1989. "The Enclave and the Entrants: Patterns of Ethnic Enterprise in Miami before and after Mariel." *American Sociological Review*, Volume 54: 929–49.

Raijman, R. 2001. "Determinants of Entrepreneurial Intention: Mexican Immigrants in Chicago." *Journal of Socioeconomics*, Volume 30:393–411.

Reger, J. Myers, D.J. and Einwohner, L. 2008. *Identity Work in Social Movements*. Minneapolis: University of Minnesota Press.

Roberts S. 2005. "More Africans Enter the U.S. than in Days of Slavery." *New York Times* (February 23). www.nytimes.com.

Rumbaut, R.G. 1997. "Assimilation and its Discontents: Between Rhetoric and Reality." *International Migration Review*, Volume 31(4): 923–60.

Sampson, E. E. "Identity Politics. Challenges to Psychology's Understanding." *American Psychologist* 48, no. 12 (1993): 1219–30.

Saravia, N.G.; 2004. Miranda, J. F. "Plumbing the Brain Drain." *Bulletin of the World Health Organization*, Volume 82(8): 608–15.

Sassen, S. 1991. *The Global City: New York, London, Tokyo*. Princeton, NJ.: Princeton University Press.

Schiller, N., Basch, L., & Blanc, C. 1995. "From Immigrant to Transmigrant: Theorizing Transnational Migration." *Anthropological Quarterly*, Volume 68(1): 48–63.

Schrover, M. 2006. "Whenever a Dozen Germans Meet . . ." German Organizations in the Netherlands in the Nineteenth Century." *Journal of Ethnic and Migration Studies*, Volume 32 (5): 847-64.

Seidman, S. 1993. "Identity and Politics in a 'Postmodern' Gay Culture: Some Historical and Conceptual Notes.'' In *Fear of a Queer Planet: Queer Politics and*

Social Theory, edited by Michael Warner, 105-42. Minneapolis: University of Minnesota Press.

Shah, B. 2007. "Being Young, Female, Laotian: Ethnicity as Social Capital at the Intersection of Gender, Generation, 'Race' and Age." *Ethnic and Racial Studies*, Volume 30(1): 28–50.

South, S. C., Crowder, K. and Chavez, E. 2005. "Migration and Spatial Assimilation Among U.S. Latinos: Classical versus Segmented Trajectories." *Demography*, Volume 42(3): 497–521.

Spivak, G. C. 1988. "Can The Subaltern Speak?" In *Marxism and the Interpretation of Culture*, edited by Cary Nelson and Lawrence Grossberg, 271–313. Urbana: University of Illinois Press.

Suarez-Orozco, C. and Suarez-Orozco, 2001. M. *Children of Immigration*. Cambridge, MA: Harvard University Press.

Sullivan, A. 1997. *Same-Sex Marriage: Pro and Con*. New York: Vintage.

Stepick, A. Stepick, C.D., Emmanuel, E., Teed, D. and Labissiere, Y. 2001. "Shifting Identities and Intergenerational Conflict: Growing Up Haitian in Miami." In *Ethnicity: Children of Immigrants in America,* edited by Alejandra Portes, and Ruben Rumbaut. New York: Russell Sage Foundation.

Takyi, B.K. and Boate, K.S. 2007. "Location and Settlement Patterns of African Immigrants in the U.S.: Demographic and Spatial Patterns." In The *New African Diaspora in North America: Trends, Community Building and Adaptation*, edited by Kwadwo Konadu-Agyemang, Baffour K. Takyi and John A. Arthur, 50–68. Lanham, MD: Lexington Books.

Vermeulen, F. 2005. "Organizational Patterns: Surinamese and Turkish Associations in Amsterdam, 1960-1990." *Journal of Ethnic & Migration Studies*, Volume 31(5): 951–73.

Vertovec, S. 2003. "Migration and other Modes of Transnationalism: Towards Conceptual Cross-Fertilization.".*International Migration Review*, Volume 37(3): 641–65.

Waldinger, R. and Feliciano, C. 2004. "Will the New Second Generation Experience 'Downward Assimilation?" Segmented Assimilation Re-assessed." *Ethnic and Racial Studies*, Volume 27(3): 375–402.

Wilson, K.L. and Portes, A. 1980. "Immigrant Enclaves: An Analysis of the Labor Market Experience of Cubans in Miami." *American journal of Sociology*, Volume 86: 295–319.

Yeboah, I.E.A. 2008. "Immigrant Trajectories and Settlement Patterns. *Black African Neo-Diaspora: Ghanaian Immigrant Experiences in the Greater Cincinnati, Ohio, Area*, 13–50. Lanham, MD: Lexington Books.

—— and Ocran K.S. 2008. "Associational Life, Acculturation, and identity Creation," In *Black African Neo-Diaspora: Ghanaian Immigrant Experiences in Greater Cincinnati, Ohio, Area*, 51–83. Lanham, MD: Lexington Books.

—— and Amankwah, B. 2008. "Ghanaian Immigrant Enterprises." In *Black African Neo-Diaspora: Ghanaian Immigrant Experiences in Greater Cincinnati, Ohio, Area*", 85–120. Lanham, MD: Lexington Books.

——— and Yeboah, S. 2008. "Second-Generation Immigrants' Identity Creation and Socialization". In *Black African Neo-Diaspora: Ghanaian Immigrant Experiences in Greater Cincinnati, Ohio, Area*", 155–199. Lanham, MD: Lexington Books.

Zhou, Y. 1998. "Beyond Ethnic Enclaves: Location Strategies of Chinese Producer Firms in Los Angeles." *Economic Geography*, Volume 74: 228–51.

Zhou, M. and Xiong, Y.S. 2005. "The Multifaceted American Experiences of the Children of Asian Immigrants: Lessons for Segmented Assimilation." *Ethnic and Racial Studies*, Volume 28(6): 1119–52.

Chapter Five

Reconciling Multiple Black Identities: The Case of 1.5 and 2.0 Nigerian Immigrants

I struggled with myself. I did not feel accepted with the white world, nor in the black world in America. . . . and I did not feel accepted with fellow Nigerians. This made me very lonely and frightened. I did not belong anywhere.

—Dayo

I would say I'm Nigerian, but . . . it depends on who I'm talking to. If I'm among a lot of Nigerians. . . . I get a little bit intimidated and . . . I won't say that I'm Nigerian. But if I'm around more people that aren't Nigerian, I will say that I'm Nigerian.

—Ama

Black, African American, Nigerian, African—I've felt that all of them describe me accurately in some capacity . . . it really depends on the context . . . If I'm around African Americans and I'm speaking specifically about African issues, I will make the distinction. If I'm around White people and I'm talking about issues that I think pertain to all Black people or what Blackness is, I will talk about myself as a Black person. So, the way identity works, I guess, some matter more depending on the context.

—Ngozi

The quotes above exemplify responses by 1.5[1] and 2.0 generation African immigrants to the common question: how do you self-identify? Influenced by their parents' cultural values, as well as various facets of U.S. society, 1.5 and 2.0 African immigrants must balance myriad social and cultural influences as they form and negotiate their identities. Furthermore, the racial milieu in the

United States gives them, as black immigrants, the added pressure of conforming to or contending with American perceptions of race. As such, they must simultaneously negotiate multiple identities and often find themselves struggling with the influences of these multiple racial and ethnic identities at different periods in their lives.

This chapter examines how eleven 1.5 and 2.0 Nigerian immigrants reconcile their identity construction processes as they contend with four major identities: African, Nigerian, African-American, and black.[2] It seeks to highlight the complex and often contradictory messages that these youth receive as they attempt to understand who they are and where they belong within various racial, ethnic, and national groups. The chapter will begin with an exploration of existing literature on black immigrants to understand their adaptation process in the United States. It will then detail the research methods employed to capture the experiences of 1.5 and 2.0 generation Nigerian youth in the present study. Next, the discussion of the findings focuses on the diverse messages that participants heard from various constituents (parents, peer networks, teachers, media, etc.) as they negotiated the four major identities examined in this inquiry. The chapter concludes with a discussion of the theoretical implications of identity reconciliations for black immigrant youth.

RESEARCH FRAMEWORK

Scholars have long posited that identity is fluid, situational, and socially constructed, and that individuals have multiple identities that emerge in different social contexts (Alba, 1985; Barth, 1969; Waters, 1990). Thus, the situation one is in and with whom one is interacting will determine the manner in which one defines oneself. Literature on black immigrant youth often reflects this perspective. Several researchers theorized that black immigrants would reject their parents' ethnicity and adopt an African American identity in response to racial similarities and the close proximity of these two groups in schools and neighborhoods (Laguerre, 1984; Vickerman, 1999; Woldemikael, 1989). Further, research suggests that in understanding U.S. racial inequalities, some black immigrants racially identify and show solidarity with African Americans (Kasinitz, 1992; Vickerman, 1999). U.S.-based black Nationalist, Pan-Africanist, and Afrocentric movements have expressed the same hope for racial solidarity (Alex-Assensoh and Hanks, 2000; Austin, 2006; Price, 2009); however, this hopefulness has yet to be fully realized, and relationships between black immigrants and African Americans often remain distant or strained (Arthur, 2000; Traore, 2003; Waters, 1999).

Mary Waters (1990, 1994, 1999), a pioneer in research on the experiences of second generation West Indians, further explores identity among Black immigrants. She posits that second generation black immigrants may adopt one of three primary identities—African American, ethnic American, or immigrant identity. Further, she found that immigrant youth that adopt an African-American identity generally identify with the racial challenges experienced by African Americans and adopt the cultural behaviors of their African-American peers. Black immigrant youth who identify as ethnic American receive encouragement to adopt this identity, from their immigrant parents, whites, and others, as a means to distinguish themselves from native blacks, whom society often perceives as lazy and unwilling to work hard to achieve educational and economic advancement. As a result, these individuals seek to differentiate themselves from African Americans, and the stereotypes held about them, by aligning with co-ethnics. Immigrant-identified individuals, Waters contends, are ambivalent about American racial and ethnic labels, and ground their identities in their native countries.

The present chapter draws on these previous studies by viewing identity as situational, contextual, and relational (Alba, 1985; Barth 1969; Waters, 1990). While other scholars have examined identity among black immigrants in this manner, there are a number of factors that researchers of black identities have not taken into consideration. Like Waters' work, this chapter focuses on the possibilities for multiple black identities among 1.5 and 2.0 immigrant youth—Nigerian, African, African-American, and black. However, rather than framing these identities as existing in exclusion to each other, this paper shows that individuals may hold multiple black identities simultaneously and demonstrates that context largely determines the salience of particular identities. In addition, this inquiry highlights two other factors rarely considered in prior research on the identities of black immigrants: the media (Awokoya, 2009; Awokoya and Harushimana, 2010; D'Alisera, 2009) and the co-ethnic community (Portes and Rumbaut, 2001; Pyke and Dang, 2003). The present study found that media-generated portrayals of immigrants, particularly Africans, and their interactions with co-ethnic community members had a significant impact on identity construction and negotiations among the participants.

As discussed further in this chapter, the relative ease that first generation Africans have in negotiating their identities,[3] proves much more complex and multilayered for their children. While first generation African immigrants discourage their children from interactions with African Americans in favor of emphasizing a distinctly Nigerian identity, African immigrant youth experience the simultaneous pressure as blacks to "fit in" and ally themselves with their African-American peers (Gans, 1992; Waters, 1999). Further, they must combat media-generated images that portray Africans as ignorant, poverty-stricken, and uncivilized and African Americans as lazy, prone to criminality, and lacking familial ties. As such, the multiple identities of 1.5 and 2.0 Nigerians largely depend on the messages they receive from various constituents (for example, family, co-ethnic community, peer networks, American authority figures), about their status, relative to other groups.

METHODOLOGY

This chapter draws data from a qualitative study conducted in 2008–2009. The study focused on the ways in which 1.5 and 2.0 Nigerians experienced the construction and negotiation of their racial and ethnic identities, at home, at school, and in their communities, from childhood to adulthood. The participants consisted of a purposeful sampling of eleven undergraduate and graduate students (eight females and three males), ages eighteen to thirty-two, of Nigerian descent in the Greater Washington D. C. metropolitan region. Nine of the participants were 2.0 generation immigrants and two were 1.5 generation. The study utilized qualitative data from individual and focus group interviews to capture and understand the participants' accounts of their racial and ethnic identity constructions and negotiations.

This chapter focuses specifically on participants' discussions about their processes of reconciling multiple, and often conflicting, identities. I carefully documented and analyzed data from interviews focusing on the messages participants received from various sources (for example parents, peers, teachers, co-ethnic community members) about their identities and the implications of these messages for participants' processes of identity development. This chapter draws upon these analyses and highlights participants' processes of reconciling four major, black identities: Nigerian, African, African-American, and black.

Findings

As stated above, data analysis revealed that participants negotiated among four major black identities—Nigerian, African, African, American, and black-around which the findings will be organized. These were identities that the participants felt they wanted or needed to embrace, they were expected by others to embrace, or that were simply ascribed to them. In each case, participants had to confront these identities and reconcile them with the way they understood themselves. The data in this study revealed that various constituents assigned to 1.5 and 2.0 generation Nigerian immigrants the terms

"Nigerian" and "African" as ethnic markers, though the term "Nigerian" is, in fact, a national, not an ethnic, identity. Similarly, the African identity is a continental identity and not an ethnic marker. In addition, constituents understood and used the terms "African American" and "black" interchangeably, though nuances existed in the ways that participants experienced these terms.

Being Nigerian

Participants reported that their parents played a fundamental role in influencing the construction of their Nigerian identity. In doing so, these parents instilled and emphasized the practice of traditional norms, values, and expectations that were in line with Nigerian culture. This focus on tradition often originates, in part, from aspirations many African immigrant parents retain of returning to their home country (Arthur, 2000). This sentiment is present in many immigrant communities, regardless of national origin. As a result, many Nigerian parents in the United States want their children to grow up to associate with either their ethnic identity (for example, Igbo or Yoruba), their national identity (Nigerian), or, at the very least, their continental African identity. Remilekun shares her parents' efforts to ensure that she maintained her Nigerian identity:

> They just always made sure to instill those Nigerian values in us because that was something that was tradition, and that was something that they wanted us to know so we could teach our kids later on. So, all that stuff in terms of . . . the food we ate . . . dance, African attire, . . . [and] the language we spoke . . . all of that was definitely still maintained even though we were here [in the United States].

This quote captures Remilekun's parents' desires to help their children observe and absorb Nigerian culture as children and put it into practice as adults. However, immigrant parents do not always have sufficient control to ensure this outcome. Maintaining Nigerian culture and practices often proved difficult as the participants became Americanized.

Scholars have attributed the cultural disconnect that many immigrant youth encounter with their ethnic communities to the Americanization process that occurs in the U.S. context (Murray, 2001; Suárez-Orozco and Suárez-Orozco, 2001). Oftentimes, tensions arise in the home and within the ethnic community when immigrant children resist their parents' attempts to socialize them into their heritage culture. For example, culturally-based norms of child-adult interactions sometimes caused conflict for many participants, particularly regarding the proper greeting of adults within the Nigerian context. Cultural norms dictate that females genuflect or kneel on the ground when encountering an adult. Similarly, males must bow in an informal meeting and, on more formal occasions, lay prostrate on the ground.

As they spent more time in the United States, several participants often found it difficult to demonstrate respect in the traditional Nigerian way among extended family and co-ethnic community members. Abimbola, for instance, recounted an incident where she did not greet a woman in her church according to tradition. The woman later reported Abimbola's transgression to her mother, saying, "Abimbola never greets me properly. Do you know how old I am? . . . I have children that are older than her." Abimbola's mother later reinforced the importance of following tradition, particularly with other Nigerian adults. Abimbola recalls, "After that, my mom emphasized that when I see people, I should kneel down or salute them in some type of way."

This incident speaks to the importance of children demonstrating respect to adults, particularly the elderly. African societies traditionally admire and revere the elderly and view them as a source of wisdom and experience. Such cultures view children who fail to properly greet adults as disrespectful and untrained, a perception that reflects poorly on the parents. Femi also expressed discomfort with greeting adults according to Nigerian tradition:

> I didn't like it when other Nigerians came over to the house and I had to bow down to them. I just felt like I had to, like they were a higher power or something . . . that's how my parents made it seem, like we just had to do this to them. You know? It just made it seem like they were God and you had to serve them. . . .

Femi's statement speaks to the internal conflict he often encountered when faced with expectations dictated by his Nigerian culture. Femi realized, as a result of his parents' training, that they expected him to bow when greeting Nigerian adults. However, influenced by the less formal adult-child interactions within the U.S. context, he began to feel uncomfortable with the overt demonstration of respect. Further, in the U.S. context, individuals often must earn the respect of others, instead of simply receiving the honor solely because of one's position in society.

Although many of the participants' parents and co-ethnic community members instilled and reinforced traditional Nigerian behaviors, participants explained that they often struggled to maintain their Nigerian identity and adhere to the expectations that came along with it, particularly as they became older. Several participants shared that they often were criticized and questioned about the authenticity of their Nigerian identity, and for the overwhelming majority, the most salient criticisms came from other Africans and co-ethnic community members.

Participants shared that they often received messages from co-ethnics that their Nigerian identity was inauthentic or invalid. Such messages frequently pertained to being born in the United States, having African-American friends, having an Afrocentric appearance (wearing traditional hairstyles, dressing in hip hop fashions), not wearing traditional African attire, and possessing an American accent. Participants often felt judged about their ethnic and cultural identities when other Africans questioned the authenticity of their Nigerian-ness.

Most participants also discussed having a "test" imposed upon them, by Nigerians or other Africans, where they had to prove their Nigerian identity. Their ability to "pass or fail" the test determined whether their peers accepted them as a "true" Nigerian or African. Adesina explained, "It's like they have these qualifications set for you and . . . if you don't meet these qualifications, they look down on you." Abimbola agreed, saying, "You know . . . they'll just say something to make me basically in some way prove that I really am from Nigeria." Bunmi shared an example of how she was tested by a Nigerian peer:

> It was the craziest experience. I just remember this one girl . . . she could not understand that I was Nigerian, and I was telling her my name. She was like, 'Well, where's your family from?' And, I was like, 'the East.' And then she asked me what state and then she asked me what town, and then she asked me what village. And when I was able to name all of those things, she kind of relented, but she never apologized nor did she explain to me why it was so difficult to believe that I was Nigerian.

According to participants, tests of ethnic authenticity included questions about their family residence in Nigeria, the number of times they had visited Nigeria, their familiarity with Nigerian culture, their traditions and experiences (for example boarding schools), their birthplace, and their ethnic language ability. Participants described a variety of emotions when their Nigerian identity was contested, including frustration, hurt, anger, loneliness, annoyance, shame, and guilt. Adesina said, "It's . . . hurtful because it's like they're trying to take away something that you believe is yours." For many participants, this doubt of their ethnic authenticity resulted in an internalized sense of not being truly Nigerian.

In sum, parents and co-ethnic community members had a significant influence on participants' Nigerian identity. Participants dealt with expectations from both constituents to maintain their ethnic and national identities as they exist in Nigeria. However, many participants came to learn that being Nigerian, as demonstrated through traditional, normative behaviors like genuflecting, proved incompatible with American culture and struggled to meet the expectations placed upon them. Further, as they became older, many encountered co-ethnics that sought to invalidate their Nigerian identity because they did not always adopt or adhere to traditional Nigerian and African cultural norms. It is important to note that participants often did not have control over many of the ways in which they were different (place of birth, American accent, ethnic language proficiency). They, therefore, found themselves in a no-win situation with their parents and the co-ethnic community members because their Nigerian identity was being held to a standard that they could not achieve.

Being African

Participants received two consistent but contradictory messages about their African identity. As Africans, they were viewed as different from African Americans and whites, and their differences were often based on the stereotypical media images that described Africans and African life as ugly, primitive, poor, and conflict-ridden. At the same time, participants also experienced positive perceptions of Africans as well-behaved, studious, and hardworking individuals, thus rendering them better than their African-American peers.

Mass media wields powerful and persuasive force in U.S. society (D'Alisera, 2009; Jacobs, 2000). In this study, participants discussed how non-African peers and others learned from, internalized, and often drew upon media depictions of Africans during personal interactions. Each of the participants discussed the Western media's depictions of Africa as an untamed jungle and of Africans as savages. In their experiences, these images influenced the way non-Africans related to and interacted with them. For instance, Adesina explained that her American peers often asked questions like, "Do you live in a jungle?" and "Do you live in huts?" Likewise, Kunle recalled being asked questions about African food and living habits such as, "Do you have to go catch your food? Do you drink the same water the animals bathe in?" Participants felt that many non-Africans internalized and drew upon non-mainstream and negative stereotypes and images to characterize and relate to them, which often led many to feel ashamed of their African heritage.

Participants also identified feelings of discomfort about their African heritage during interactions with adults, particularly their American-born, White teachers. They explained that white teachers often held simplistic, patronizing, and sympathetic views of Africa and Africans that they gleaned, for the most part, from the media. Participants cited receiving moralizing and paternalistic responses to their African backgrounds from their teachers. Ngozi, for instance, recounted a conversation with a geography teacher that left her stunned and speechless. The teacher said, "You know, the problem with Africa is that they keep sending food instead of birth control," inferring that because Africans do not control their birth rate, they should accept the blame for their own predicament.

Participants also described instances where interest in their African heritage or background sometimes came across negatively. For instance, teachers would sometimes ask questions like, ". . . your parents were refugees? How did you come here? or How is your family surviving in Africa?" Participants felt such questions were laden with negative assumptions and misinformation about Africans in Africa and the United States. In addition to combating the negative stereotypes surrounding their African identity, participants also identified discomfort when compared to other groups.

All study participants recounted situations where teachers told them, either directly or indirectly, that they were different and, in many cases, better than their African-American peers. These perceived difference pertained primarily to academics and behavior. The majority of participants reported placement in advanced or honors courses, where they often found themselves one of few black students in the class. Further, Ama noted that, "honestly, most of those students of color tend to be African, that were in those programs with me."

This preferential academic placement tended to separate participants from the larger black population in the school and resulted in their being treated differently from the other black students. Participants discussed how faculty and staff regarded them as the "good black students" in the school. Bunmi described the "good black student" as, ". . . the black student who's in these advanced classes, and doing well, and not getting into trouble, and all that stuff, and having very engaged parents who would come in." Other participants discussed how teachers noticed and often commented on the behavioral differences between the African and African-American students and described them as "respectful," "quiet," "disciplined," and "hardworking." Emeka described one such teacher, saying, "[She said] she could tell that my parents were Africans because I was disciplined and well-behaved . . . and I felt, at times, that I've been used as kind of that example, that black example." Through their praising comments, the teachers facilitated the creation of tensions between participants and their African-American peers.

Many participants expressed negative views of their teachers' focus on their African identity, particularly when those teachers used it in a divisive way to compare them to their African-American peers and when, as discussed previously, teacher perceptions perpetuated media-centered portrayals of Africans peoples. Several participants discussed that they often felt they had to explain, defend or positively characterize both African and African-American people, particularly in the presence of whites. Ngozi, for instance, illustrates her experiences:

> I'd see how white people would react watching them [African Americans], and it embarrassed me. And then I had to be in class and hear a comment that they might not even realize it was an insult, and I'd have to defend them. . . . I also had to deal with the African image in the classroom, but that was more of a covert issue, it was in the air, in the rhetoric. The questions that would arise were, "How come they [Africans] can't get it together? Why are they so poor?"

Through their own lived experiences, many participants came to understand that they shared a common relationship to oppressed minorities in the United States As 1.5 and 2.0 African immigrants, many participants had experienced discrimination based on pervasively negative images of Africans, and they had witnessed or, because they lacked the cultural identifiers of their parents, personally encountered discrimination of the African American identity. This awareness of and sensitivity to the discrimination experienced by both groups made it difficult for participants to blindly accept the favoritism that Whites often showed them because of their African identity.

Data indicate that the most salient messages that participants received about their African identities came from the media, non-African peers and their teachers. Negative perceptions held by non-African peers often reflected media depictions of Africans and African lifestyles and, according to participants, shaped their peers' interactions with them. Similarly, the participants described feeling a sense of otherness during their interactions with their white teachers. They believed that their teachers held misconceptions about Africa and Africans. Further, many participants were challenged by their teachers' tendency to compare them to their African-American peers. Although participants experienced social and cultural connections individually with their African-American counterparts, they often found engaging in racial solidarity with them to be difficult.

Being African American

All of the 1.5 and 2.0 African immigrants interviewed openly discussed their process of reconciling with the African American identity. Similar to other black immigrants, 1.5 and 2.0 Nigerian immigrants experience pressure to ally with African Americans (Kasinitz, 1992; Waters, 1999), more so than the first generation, because they are both Nigerian and American. Further, the U.S. racial hierarchy assigns to them the African-American identity. Interviews clearly show, however, that two primary agents—parents and peers—greatly informed participants' experiences with the African-American identity.

Many participants noted that their parents identified and emphasized cultural differences between Africans and African Americans. They recalled parents making comments like, "Don't be like those African American children. They don't have culture," and "You're not like those black kids." Several participants also mentioned that their parents often warned them against behaving in particular ways and associating with African-American peers they considered undesirable. Ngozi explained, "[it's] not so much that they were gonna try to bring me down, but you'll become lazy by association, was the idea. Not necessarily that they're gonna want to pull you down, but if you choose to let that lifestyle or that cultural tie affect you, then it'll happen." These statements and warnings largely appeared to be parents' attempts to steer their children away from behaviors that they perceived as disrespectful and antithetical to achievement among African-American youth. In doing so, several participants spoke of their parents' attempts to socialize them strictly with other Nigerians.

Although all of the participants commented that their parents' limited the social interactions they had with American peers, Abimbola mentioned that her parents were much more lenient when a Nigerian family moved next door. She said:

> . . . luckily, a few years after we moved here, our next door neighbors were also Nigerian, so they just automatically became our best friends . . . I spent most of my time at their house because they're a Nigerian family, they had daughters also, and they went to our church. It was easier. I could go there without having to call first and ask. They came here. We slept over each others' house. It was just easier. . . . There were definitely the same cultural expectations.

As shown in Abimbola's quote, her parents showed less concern about her peer interactions during her interactions with other Nigerians, which allowed her to freely visit her Nigerian friend's home. This example illustrates that parents' involvement in participants' social lives commonly pertained to participants' interactions with non-Nigerian peers, and that parents' concerns centered around the influences that American families and peers could have on their children. Literature on immigrant families clearly documents the fears held by immigrant parents that they will "lose" their children to American ways (Murray, 2001; Suárez-Orozco and Suárez-Orozco, 2001; Waters, 1999). Participants' parents attempted to ensure that their children developed friendships with peers who shared their values and cultural backgrounds. Many participants, however, did not have significant numbers of African students in their schools. As such, they relied heavily on their American peers, particularly their African-American peers, for friendships.

The 1.5 and 2.0 generation Nigerian Americans in this study generally were not concerned with the ethnic divisions of their parents' generation; in fact, they often sought connections with other black immigrants and/or African Americans. They understood and acknowledged their parents' preferences for other Nigerians (ideally from the same ethnic group), but this did not deter them from attempting to establish relationships outside of Nigerian communities.

Participant interviews clearly show that in order to truly be African American, participants had to adhere to the racialized expectations of their particular African-American peer culture, which comprised the majority of the black population in their respective communities, schools, and peer networks. During the focus group session, participants identified the pressure of fitting in with their African American peers as "the force." Emeka commented, "I mean, you were black, you looked black, so you should hang out with black people. Yes, it was like a force." According to the participants, "the force" was a racialized obligation or responsibility to relate to and interact with the African-American peer group. The participants' description of "the force" proved complicated, multilayered, and imbued with meanings and expectations that their peers attached to the black experience in the African American context.

Research on relationships among adolescents of color argues that they create a list of racialized markers to control, exclude, and maintain racial solidarity within their peer groups (Butterfield, 2006; Carter, 2005). Participants highlighted several racialized expectations, such as socializing strictly with black peers, listening to hip hop and rap music, not having an accent, speaking black English, etc. The underlying imperative that bound all of these expectations together was the ability to relate to and enact the behaviors expected by African-American peers. In relating to these peers, participants described having to, first, learn their peers' preferences and expectations, which many found to be difficult. Ngozi explained, "I've had moments where there have been very, very kind of highly black American contextual situations where when I was growing up, I didn't understand it. So, I would either pretend or I didn't say anything until I understand it."

The "black American contextual situations" to which Ngozi refers include the shared domestic and social experiences (for example eating traditional southern soul food, pressing hair in the kitchen, knowing particular songs, etc.) often discussed by her African-American peers. As an African immigrant child, raised by immigrant parents, Ngozi often did not understand the cultural references of African Americans. Emeka echoed Ngozi's sentiment when she said, ". . . like my group of friends that I hung out with, as African Americans they identify with each other. But when it came to me, I was fundamentally different. . . ." Participants' unfamiliarity with African-American cultural references and experiences often made them feel like cultural outsiders. African American peers often contributed to this feeling of difference when they noticed and commented on the participants' lack of understanding. Ngozi noted that her peers would say, "Give me your black card!" "Y'all, you're not black!" or 'Y'all some Africans!"

For many study participants, blackness initially was understood simply as a function of skin color. However, as Ngozi infers in the following quote, many interpret and understand blackness in a variety of ways that extend far beyond skin color. She explains, "I feel like the blackness that I have now has definitely been predominantly a social construct, something that I've had to learn. It's been a learned process for me. . . ." Here, Ngozi specifically discusses American blackness. In their attempts to avoid criticism and to fit in with their African-American peer groups, participants described having to learn how to successfully carry out their African-American peers' expectations. Several mentioned how they worked ardently to present themselves in ways that aligned with the African-American culture represented by their peer group. Abimbola, for instance, describes the particular behaviors she adopted to fit in more with her African-American peers:

> I would try to keep up with the music and things like that. . . . I would try to keep up with BET so that when they were singing songs at recess, I knew the songs also. I learned how to braid at that point so I would cornrow girls' hair, just try to do things. Joined the step team and tried to do things to make myself fit in more.

As illustrated in Abimbola's statement, "learning to be black" in the U.S. context, involved learning to be African American. For many of the participants this effort became an ongoing process of keenly observing their African-American counterparts and imitating their behaviors in acceptable ways. Reflecting on his identity, Kunle explained, "I identify myself as an African who can do African American things." Here, Kunle conveys that although he viewed himself as African, he could present himself in ways that allowed him to "pass" as African-American. For all of the participants, acceptance by African-American peers emerged as important.

According to the participants, their parents and peers had different perspectives of the African-American identity. Parents perceived a distinct difference between the African-American identity and the black identity. The African American identity held a negative connotation for parents that caused them to encourage their children to differentiate themselves from African-American peers. As immigrants from predominately black nations, blackness held little to no significance for them. Parents recognized, however, that in the Western context, black skin created certain barriers for black people. Yet, they did not apply that understanding to the underachievement and lack of respect they perceived among black youth in the U.S. context. As such, they encouraged their children to excel despite the challenges they would face as black people and to disassociate themselves from other black people, who, they felt, did not value success.

In contrast, African American peers, based their understanding of blackness on their experiences in the United States and conflated being African American with being black. African American peers communicated the message that in order to be considered truly "black," within the peer network, the participants had to embrace an African-American identity. According to the participants, their African-American peers proved well equipped in defining and policing the meanings and expectations of what it meant to be identified as black in the African American context. Participants' failure to adhere to the expectations would result in criticism, ridicule, or exclusion. This imbalanced input from parents and peers caused conflicting understandings of the participants' reconciliation of their African-American identity. It is important to note that the messages participants received about being African American also encompassed messages about being black. The next section explores the messages participants received about blackness specifically from the larger society/ media, parents and teachers.

BEING BLACK

The participants' perceptions of blackness impacted how they viewed and experienced their racial identities. What it meant to be black was explicitly and implicitly taught by others and, to varying degrees, learned by the participants. They found blackness a ubiquitous constant throughout their daily social interactions. Although participants identified various sources from which they learned about the meaning of blackness, the primary sources of those conflicting and imbalanced messages included the media, their African-born parents, and their teachers.

Participants unanimously commented that the media and larger society contributed significantly to their understanding of blackness. For example, they all referred to disparaging and gendered depictions of black people and black cultures on television and in movies and music. Participants found themselves working against negative portrayals of Blackness constructed by various forms of media and placed on them by the larger American society. The media portrayals depicted American blacks, as a whole, as lazy, apathetic, and dangerous. Abisola expressed her view of how blacks are portrayed:

The media doesn't portray – even up until now – a very good representation of African Americans. You turn the TV on now to BET, UPN, whatever, and the shows that have mostly African Americans, besides like *The Cosby Show* and *Fresh Prince of Bel-Air,* show dysfunctional families, show families living in so-called ghettos, show a girl half-naked dancing in a music video, show kids cursing, smoking, drinking, having sex.

This statement reflects the media culture that participants experienced and used to understand what it meant to be black in the United States. Further, other participants pointed out that although depictions of blackness, internationally, often pertain to African Americans, they impacted other black groups. Kunle explains:

And black Americans . . . they don't think that some of the stuff they do is broadcasted around the world, and then that's how other races will view us . . . because other races don't see us as being African, and African American, they see us as being black. And that's why other races interact with us like that.

Here, Kunle's comments draw attention to the media's ability to influence public opinions about blacks, both nationally and internationally. They also reflect his understanding that, as members of the same racial group, Africans, African Americans, and other black racial groups will inevitably encounter similar discrimination as a function of negative public portrayals of blackness. Indeed, in the global society, controlling entities behind media outlets (for example television, radio, film, and the Internet) have long exercised the power to influence and, in some instances, formulate public opinion on race, through the calculated selection and dissemination of information on racial issues (Jacobs, 2000). If not carefully wielded by responsible parties, this power can serve to reinforce existing prejudices.

In the context of this study, several of the male participants discussed how excessive media coverage connecting black men to crime contributed to the instances of racial profiling that they encountered. Three male respondents identified their blackness as the cause of the racial profiling and subsequent harassment they received from the police. Femi, for instance, shared an experienced when police officers unexpectedly stopped him and his friend and misidentified them as criminals, as they dropped off a white friend in a wealthy, predominately white area. The police officers explained that several robberies had occurred in the neighborhood, a statement Femi later learned was untrue. He explained, "Come to find out there wasn't any robberies. I guess he just saw two black dudes in a white neighborhood, so they thought we were up to no good." The racial profiling that Femi experienced is one example of the manner in which the larger society, in this case the police, conveyed the clear message that blackness is associated with criminal behavior.

Participants' parents also taught them about blackness in ways that were nuanced and multilayered. For Africans who are the racial majority in their home countries, blackness is a physical trait and, often, a non-issue. That is, being black is a nonracialized characteristic that has little to no negative connotations (Bryce-Laporte, 1972). As such, participants' parents appeared to vary in their awareness of the meaning of blackness in the U.S. context and in their ability to communicate issues of race to their children. For the majority of participants, however, their parents were acutely aware of racial barriers in the United States and the ways these barriers might impact their black children. For these parents, their experiences as racial minorities in white dominated countries (England, Canada, and the United States) raised their awareness of issues related to race and blackness in each context. For instance, Uzoma and Ngozi explained that their parents' experiences with racial discrimination taught them that their skin color placed them in the lower echelons of society. Uzoma's mother let her know that the United States "was a racist society and that whites have always thought that they were superior here."

Further, some participants shared that their parents conveyed messages that, as a black person, one has to work twice as hard as a white person to achieve success. Ngozi reflected on how she was raised to view her blackness in relation to whites, saying, "We were raised to know that we're black, and white people might think that you're inferior, and you have to be the one to, you know, prove that to them." As reflected by Ngozi's statement, several parents appeared to understand and express to their children that U.S. society views blacks as inferior and, thus, they instilled in their children the need to work harder than both their black and white peers. As Bunmi explains:

> My parents would tell me, 'You're not white so you have to be better than everyone else.' Literally everyone else, Blacks, White, Asians. . . . Like for instance I would get a 95 on a paper and they would congratulate me, but would ask, 'Where are the other five points?' They believed that I had the capability to be the best in the class and that's how you succeed in life because I was black, and because I was a foreigner. They recognized prejudices in society, particularly this society, so they wanted me to face as little prejudice as possible.

Bunmi's experiences emphasize simultaneous influences of parents and teachers on the formation of her black racial identity. Earlier in the chapter, Bunmi discussed how she often was viewed by her white teachers as the "good black student." Her parents confirmed that expectation in many ways. Her parents shaped her sense of blackness with their understanding of racial discrimination, particularly toward blacks and immigrants, and their imperative that she overcomes these challenges by excelling beyond all of her peers in school. Remilekun had a similar experience and vividly recalled being the only black person in her honors classes and that many considered her one of the few academically astute black students in her school. As such, she often felt a responsibility to demonstrate that black people could be academically successful.

> I look around and I'm the only black person here and the only African. . . . I knew I was the only black girl so I always wanted to excel and be different. . . . I always tried to be in honors reading, honors spelling, things like that because I wanted to also be different. I wanted to be distinctive.

The distinctiveness that Remilekun strived for came from her realization that she was among the few academically successful black students in her school, and she described working excessively to prove that black students can achieve success.

Each of the primary contributors to the participants' construction of Blackness—parents, teachers, and the larger society/media—gave contradictory and imbalanced messages on the meanings of blackness. According to the participants, parents' messages about blackness seemed one-dimensional and often conflicted with messages from whites. That is, as black people, they would have to work harder to achieve the same level of success that their white peers enjoyed. Among the white teachers, and in the larger society/media, participants experienced a prevalent, negative perception about Blackness. Whereas teachers would use academics and behavior to differentiate the participants from their African-American counterparts, within the larger society/media, participants experienced very little differentiation among blacks, and general society viewed blackness as threatening.

DISCUSSION: RECONCILIATION
OF MULTIPLE BLACK IDENTITIES

As participants in this study have demonstrated, 1.5 and 2.0 Nigerian immigrants must negotiate and reconcile what being African, Nigerian, African American, and black means to their own identity. Reconciling these multiple identities often proved difficult for the participants, as they sought to makes sense of disparate, contradictory messages from various sources in myriad contexts and social situations. As children, participants described feeling beholden to the expectations of others. However, as they got older, participants acquired a repertoire of responses to these various constituents and described learning processes that helped them feel more empowered when negotiating their multiple identities.

In the context of the study, participants' past experiences, and the positive and negative reactions to their identities that they have encountered from Africans and non-Africans alike, resulted in the practice of agency in the presentation of their various identities. As adults, they were not solely defined by outward messages, but rather, became active in the negotiation of their continental, national, racial and ethnic identities. For many participants, negotiation involved learning to evaluate social contexts and enacting an identity (for example African, Nigerian, African-American, or black) appropriate to the situation. This identity negotiation varied according to their desire to be accepted by the individual or group with which they interacted.

One-point-five and second generation black immigrants may also learn to respond to the multitude of messages about and expectations for identity through the development of a black, pan-ethnic identity. This identity incorporates a variety of the ethnic and cultural experiences of black peoples. This bringing together of multiple black experiences and perspectives appears in various permutations of intellectual and ideological black solidarities. Such movements seek to acknowledge cultural and political connections to the African continent. However, none of these efforts have found universal success in unifying members of the African diaspora across ethnic or cultural lines (Austin, 2006).

The identity reconciliation processes of 1.5 and 2.0 black immigrants provide the opportunity to unite African diasporic communities unlike any previous generation. Their experiences of receiving conflicting and contradictory messages from various constituents is illustrative of disconnects among black people as a whole, both within the U.S. context and globally. The lived, individual experiences of these young people highlight a great deal of intra-racial and intra-ethnic tensions that must be reconciled within black communities. Their experiences instruct, on a macro level, the challenges of bringing black groups together and the primary dilemma that arises in developing a unified African diasporic identity—the construction of black identities often develop in opposition to each other. If 1.5 and 2.0 black immigrant youth can invoke, with complete confidence, the black identity as a marker of Pan-African solidarity in the twenty-first century, they will be the ideological and intellectual hope of previous generations of black nationalists. However, in order to fulfill this hope, they must reconcile their Africanness, Nigerianness, African Americanness, and their blackness; a daunting task for one generation to undertake, but one that future generations can realize.

NOTES

1. The 1.5 generation immigrant children who are born outside of the United States (usually in their parents' country of origin) and immigrated to the United States at a

young age (age parameters vary among scholars). The 2.0 generation is defined as children of immigrants who are born and raised in the United States.

2. Although I realize that immigrant youth hold multiple identities beyond those discussed in this chapter, the participants' highlighted these four identities as the most salient in their daily lives.

3. Nigeria is a remarkably diverse nation comprised of over 250 ethno-linguistic groups, the most common of which are Yoruba, Igbo, and Hausa. Thus, when a Nigerian speaks of his or her ethnic group to other Nigerians, they often speak of their affiliation according to the classifications of the home country. In conversations with non-Nigerians, they may simply claim a national affiliation, as Nigerian, or continental, as African. Among the many complex issues the first generation faced prior to coming to the United States, race was considered very minor if not non-existent. As such, their ethnic, national, or continental affiliation equips the first generation with a more stable means of navigating the complex American racial hierarchy.

REFERENCES

Alba, R. 1985. *Ethnicity and race in the U.S.A.: Toward the twenty-first century (ed.)*. Boston: Routledge and Kegan Paul.

Alex-Assensoh, Y. M. and Hanks, L. J. 2000. *Blacks and multiracial politics in America*. New York: New York University Press.

Arthur, J. 2000. *Invisible sojourners: African immigrant diaspora in the United States*. Westport and London: Praeger.

Austin, A. 2006. *Achieving blackness: Race, black nationalism, and Afrocentricism in the twentieth century*. New York: New York University Press.

Awokoya, J. and Harushimana, I. 2010. "Family–school mediation: Righting the mental self-perceptions of 1.5 and 2.0 African youth in U.S. schools." In Hill, N. E.; Mann, T. L. and H. E. Fitzgerald. *African American children's mental health: Prevention, intervention and social policy (ed.)*. Santa Barbara, CA: ABC/ CLIO Praeger.

Awokoya, J. 2009. "'I'm not enough of anything": The racial and ethnic identity constructions and negotiations of 1.5 and second generation Nigerian immigrants. (Unpublished doctoral dissertation). University of Maryland, College Park.

Barth, F. 1969. *Ethnic groups and boundaries: The social organization of cultural difference*. Boston: Little, Brown, and Company.

Bryce-Laporte, R. 1972. "Black immigrants: The experience of invisibility and inequality." *Journal of Black Studies*. Volume 3: 29–56.

Butterfield, S.A. 2006. "To be young, gifted, Black, and somewhat foreign: The role of ethnicity in Black student achievement." In Horvat, E.M. and O'Connor, C. *Beyond acting white: Reframing the debate on black student achievement* (ed.). Lanham, MD: Rowman and Littlefield, 133–53.

Carter, P. 2003. "Black" cultural capital, status positioning, and schooling conflicts for low-income African American youth." *Social Problems*. Volume 50: 136"55.

D'Alisera, J. 2009. "Images of a wounded homeland: Sierra Leonean children and the new heart of darkness." In Foner, Nancy. *Across generations: Immigrant families in America* (ed.). New York: New York University Press, 114–34.

Gans, H. 1992. "Second generation decline: Scenarios for the economic and ethnic futures of the post-1965 American immigrants." *Ethnic and Racial Studies.* Volume 15 (2): 173–93.

Jacobs, R. 2000. *Race, media, and the crisis of civil society: From Watts to Rodney King.* New York: Cambridge University Press.

Kasinitz, P. 1992. *Caribbean New York: Black immigrants and the politics of race.* Ithaca, NY: Cornell University Press.

Laguerre, M. 1984. *American odyssey: Haitians in New York.* Ithaca, NY: Cornell University Press.

Murray, F. 2001. "Straight outta Mogadishu": Prescribed identities and performative practices among Somali youth in North American high schools. *Topia.* Volume 5: 33-60.

Portes, A. and Rumbaut, R. 2001. *Ethnicities: Children of immigrants in America.* Berkeley: University of California Press.

Price, M. T. 2009. *Dreaming Blackness: Black nationalism and African American public opinion.* New York: New York University Press.

Pyke, K. and Dang, T. 2003. "FOB" and "Whitewashed": Identity and internalized racism among second-generation Asian Americans. *Qualitative Sociology.* Volume 26 (2): 147–72.

Suárez-Orozco, C. and Suárez-Orozco, M. 2001. *Children of immigration.* Cambridge, MA: Harvard University Press.

Traore, R. L. 2003. "African students in America: reconstructing new meanings of "African American" in urban education." *Intercultural Education.* Volume 14 (3): 243–54.

Vickerman, V. 1999. *Crosscurrents: West Indian immigrants and race.* New York: Oxford University Press.

Waters, M. 1999. *Black Identities: West Indian immigrant dreams and American realities.* New York: Russell Sage Foundation; Cambridge, MA: Harvard University Press.

Waters, M. 1994. "Ethnic and racial identities of second-generation black immigrants in New York City." *International Migration Review.* Volume 28 (4): 795–820.

Waters, M.1990. *Ethnic options: Choosing identities in America.* Berkeley, CA: University of California Press.

Woldemikael, T. 1989. *Becoming Black American: Haitians and American institutions in Evanston, Illinois.* New York: AMS Press.

Chapter Six

Making-In-Roads: African Immigrants and Business Opportunities in the United States

Whether forced to leave their home countries because of religious, social, or political persecution, or motivated by the desire to seek freedom and a better life elsewhere, immigrants to the United States have always arrived with a fierce spirit and determination to succeed at all costs (Bonacich, 1987; Olson, 1979). Not only do these immigrants come with initiative, but as Danilov (1992) puts it, they are willing to "put more hours and more hard work"[1] in whatever they need to do to survive and succeed in the United States. Often the desire to succeed has led many immigrants to take what Staring (2000) has described as the 3Ds: dirty, dangerous, and difficult jobs that most natives eschew. The same spirit and desire to succeed at all costs that was evident among European and other immigrants generations ago is also evident among the vast majority of recent African immigrants to the United States, whether they are the Senegalese, Malian, or Nigerian street vendors in New York City, Ethiopian cab drivers in Chicago, or the thousands of other African immigrants working in factories, nursing homes, restaurants, construction sites and other private and public sector employment. Indeed, it is not unusual to find that same spirit and determination even among African students who are often prohibited by their immigration status as foreign students to seek employment without authorization from the Department of Homeland Security (DHS). These students often take a full load of courses at universities and colleges while also working extraordinarily long hours in various menial and often backbreaking jobs in order to support themselves financially here in the United States and other family members back in Africa. Having had the fortune of coming to the United States, and with other family members back home depending on their success, failure is not an option for these students or the thousands of other African immigrants coming to the United States annually.

117

The desire to succeed at all costs is also evident in the increasing number of African-owned businesses that have mushroomed in many large cities like Chicago, New York City, Atlanta, Los Angeles, and Philadelphia in the last two decades or so. For many of these business owners, a fourteen-hour, seven-days-a-week work schedule is not unusual. However, while the immigration literature is replete with studies on business engagement by various immigrant groups including Cubans, Mexicans, Koreans, Vietnamese, Iranians, Japanese, and even Caribbean immigrants (see for example, Portes, 1987; Bonacich and Modell, 1980; Raijman and Tienda, 2003; Min and Bozorgmehr, 2000), very little study has been done on African immigrant businesses (see for example, Stoller, 1999 and 2002; Yeboah, 2008). For instance, a recent article in the national daily, *USA TODAY* on immigrant businesses in the United States mentioned the percentage of businesses owned by many immigrant groups including Guatemalans, Columbians and those from the Dominican Republic (Keen, 2009), but was silent on businesses owned by African immigrants as a whole or even by Nigerians, the largest and one of the most entrepreneurial African immigrant groups in the United States estimated at about 139,000 (Grieco, 2004). Indeed, the nascent literature on African immigrants to the United States still focuses largely on the push-pull factors of immigration or on some of the social, psychological and cultural impact of immigration (Takougang, 2003; Konadu-Agyemang and Takyi 2006; Apraku, 1991; Arthur, 2000; Kamya, 2007) on these immigrants.

Perhaps the absence of any significant studies on African immigrant business in the United States may be attributed to the fact that for a long time African immigrants saw themselves simply as "temporary sojourners" in the United States, more interested in returning to their respective countries after attaining their American education in order to contribute in the task of nation-building than in staying permanently in the United States. Consequently, they did not establish any permanent settlements or significant enclaves in cities that could provide the nucleus for the different types of businesses that they are currently creating throughout the United States. To the contrary, the settlement of Latinos and Asians businesses started a long time ago (Waldinger and Aldrich, 1990) because these groups had established large enclaves in major cities around the country.

Today, however, most African immigrants no longer have the sojourner mentality. Even though many of them continue to maintain a strong relationship with relatives back in Africa and still dream of one day returning home, they have reconciled themselves to the fact that America is home. The common belief among many African immigrants is that they can be Americans while also remaining Ghanaians, Nigerians, Cameroonians, or Senegalese. In other words, many of these immigrants have learned to straddle the old (African) and their new (U.S.) worlds by making frequent visits back to Africa. As we will discuss later in this chapter, this change in mentality has contributed to the growing involvement by African immigrants in various business ventures in the United States.

Specifically, this chapter will focus on the growing number of small business ownership by African immigrant in Greater Cincinnati, Ohio.[2] The choice of Cincinnati for the study is because of its familiarity to the authors, who are both residents of the city and the fact that the involvement in business by African immigrants in this mid-sized city in the American heartland represents a similar trend in larger cities across the United States including Houston, Dallas, Los Angeles, New York, Washington, D.C., Chicago, and Atlanta. We will discuss the types of businesses that African immigrants in Cincinnati are involved in, the reasons for their involvement in such small businesses, how they acquired the initial capital for the business, the customer base of these businesses, and some of the problems that they face as businessmen and women. These issues are not new, but they have not been fully addressed as far as African businesses are concerned. In the debate on immigrant businesses, it is believed that the latter are most successful when owners rely on their own communities for initial capital (Raijman and Tienda, 2003). The issue is more complex because communities and individuals behave differently when facing identical challenges.

Business owners can take advantage of opportunities that are beyond their control (i.e. institutional arrangements), rely on "specific cultural resources" existing in their communities, or make individual choices (Putz, 2002; Krogstad, 2004). Arguments on this issue has led to two research approaches (the opportunities and resources approaches) and to the critique of Putz (2002) who, using Granovetter's logic (1985), suggests that an overemphasis on opportunities and specific cultural resources leads to oversocialization and mechanical conceptions of owners' individual decisions and behaviors.

In his study of Cuban owners in the United States, for example, Portes (1987) identifies both inter-ethnic differences (that is, differences between communities) in managerial processes, and intra-ethnic variations within the Cuban business community itself. This is a key debate among Africans given their collective or community-oriented cultures (Hofstede, 1987).[3] However, regardless of the strength of ethnic cultures, mixed embeddedness is unavoidable (Kloosterman and Rath, 2001; Rath and Kloosterman, 2000; Portes and Sensenbrenner, 1993). In effect, the processes of business creation and management by foreigners in the United States will always be determined by both ethnic cultures and American cultures and institutions. How these cultures co-exist (conflict or/and compromise) is a contingent and empirical question.

Much of the data for the chapter was gathered between the spring of 2009 and the fall of 2010, during visits to eleven African-owned businesses during which we observed, interacted and talked with many of the customers and business owners. These businesses were selected for diversity (grocery, auto repair, arts and crafts, and restaurants) and their location on the I-75/I-275 loop. It is worth noting here that a high level of discomfort with researchers is another possible contributing factor in the lack of significant study of African communities in general and African businesses in particular. For instance, the fact that the authors are also African immigrants in the community who know many of the customers and have also done business with some of the owners did not necessarily make it any easier to get information from the business owners. For instance, even though the business owners were assured that we were not agents working for the U.S. government, they were reluctant to divulge information related to financial matters or what they considered to be business secrets.

We begin by examining why Cincinnati has become an important destination for many African immigrants in the last two decades and how that immigration base has led to the establishment of African immigrant businesses in the city.

Cincinnati as an Important Destination for African Immigrants

Shortly after the independence of many African nations in the 1960s and 1970s, young Africans, often with the financial support of the new post-colonial administration, the American government and private organizations, came to the United States in pursuit of higher education and other skills that were essential in building the political, social and economic institutions of the newly independent states that had largely been ignored by the colonial governments. Because many of the new African immigrants were students, they were located mostly in cities along the Eastern United States like New York, Boston, Washington, D.C., Chicago, Baltimore, and Philadelphia (Yeboah, 2008), where most of the colleges and universities that they attended were located. It wasn't until the late 1970s that the first significant group of African students from Ghana, Nigeria, Senegal, and Cameroon arrived in colleges in Cincinnati and the surrounding areas. While many of these students returned to their respective countries after completing their program of studies, a few remained in various parts of the city, forming what would eventually become the nucleus of an African immigrant population in Greater Cincinnati. The city has also experienced a significant number of new immigrants in the last two decades. It is estimated that by the early 1980s there were only about fifty African immigrants, most of whom were students in Cincinnati.[4] According to the U.S. Census figures there were only 339 African immigrants in Cincinnati in 1990, but by 2000 that number had increased to 8,500 (cited in Yeboah, 2009). Today, the population of documented and undocumented Africans in the city is estimated at over 10,000. These African immigrants come from different countries, including Ghana, Nigeria, Senegal, Cameroon, Mauritania, Ethiopia, Zambia, Kenya, Eritrea, and Uganda.[5]

However, unlike some of the students of the late 1970s and early 1980s who might have remained in Cincinnati after their education, the recent wave of African immigrants to the city come from two groups: the first group consists mostly of secondary immigrants whose initial destination when they came to the United States was not Cincinnati. Rather, these new immigrants have relocated to Cincinnati from cities like New York, Chicago, Washington, D.C., Baltimore, Columbus, Cleveland, and Los Angeles. These immigrants are attracted to the city because of employment opportunities and a more affordable and less hectic lifestyle than in the larger cities (Yeboah, 2008; Takougang and Tidjani, 2009). This view was also expressed in a recent article in the *Cincinnati Enquirer* (July 18, 2010), by an immigrant from Mauritania who noted that Cincinnati was a more favorable destination because unlike New York City, you did not have to sell sunglasses on the sidewalk in order to make a living.[6] Similarly, one of the business owners interviewed for this project noted that his decision to leave the East Coast where he had first settled when he came to the United States and come to Cincinnati was because the only jobs that he could find in the Washington D.C. and Maryland area were white-collar office jobs that he was neither interested in nor qualified for.

The second group of new immigrants to the city are mostly made up of new arrivals coming directly to Cincinnati from Africa since the early 1990s. As the political and economic situation in many African countries grew worse, especially during the prodemocracy movements of the early 1990s, so too did the number of African immigrants to the United States in general and Cincinnati in particular. The omnipresent repressive state institutions that were used to suffocate free speech, the economic malaise, and the corruption and ineptitude of the political elites since independence all facilitated the decisions by many young people to leave their countries. This was especially true in Rwanda, Sierra Leone, Sudan, and Liberia, where the situation had led to civil wars. Because of the deplorable conditions in their home countries, many of these new African immigrants are determined at all coasts to seek their fortunes in the United States or elsewhere. Indeed one of the catch phrases among many African immigrants today is "anywhere but home."

This attitude has spurred a new wave of interregional and intercontinental migration by Africans. For instance, despite the high crime rate and increased anti-immigrant sentiment in South Africa since the collapse of apartheid[7] the country remains an economic haven for many immigrants from other African nations (see for example various chapters in Handmaker, de la Hunt and Klaaren, 2008). In other words, many African migrants see a better future anywhere else except their own country. And they are willing to do whatever it takes to realize that dream. For those who can afford the cost and risk of transcontinental migration, the United States is the ultimate destination. Often, these immigrants, whether the secondary immigrants from other American cities or the new immigrants coming directly from Africa, come to Cincinnati because they have friends or relatives who are able to provide them with temporary residence and information on employment opportunities and various social safety networks in the city. Once these new immigrants acquire the knowledge and resources to become independent, they may decide to move to other cities or remain in Cincinnati where they in turn can provide migration networks and opportunity to other friends and relatives from other cities in the United States or to prospective immigrants in Africa who are interested in coming to the United States.

Apart from the deteriorating economic and political conditions in many African states, another important contributing factor that has fueled the population of African immigrants in the United States and in Cincinnati in particular may be a change in U.S. immigration policy, especially the passage of the 1990 Diversity Lottery Visa Program (DLP). Unlike the 1965 Hart-Cellar Immigration Act, which allowed only potential immigrants with relatives who already had legal status in the United States the opportunity to bring them to the country (Johnson, 1995: 62), or the 1986 Immigration Reform and Control Act (IRCA) which allowed only immigrants already in the country illegally to become permanent residents, the 1990 DLP provided thousands of Africans still on the continent and who might otherwise not have had the opportunity under the two previous laws a fair chance of coming to the United States. In fact, the goal of the DLVP is aimed at promoting immigration to the United States from hitherto unrepresented countries and regions of the world.

Additionally, the narrowing of the global divide through advances in technology and the wide use of the internet have also increased the opportunity for potential immigrants who might not have had a real chance of coming to the United States without the help of friends or relatives already in the country (Okome, 2006). In other words, the fact that many of these potential immigrants can now fill out the DLP form on the internet has given them a fair chance of winning the lottery and ultimately coming to the United States. Lobo (cited in Yeboah, 2008: 29) notes that as a result of the 1990 DLP, the number of legal African immigrants to the United States increased dramatically, from 15,466 annually between 1978 and 1998 to 35,080 annually between 1990 and 2000. And according to Terrazas (2009), more than 75 percent of the 1.4 million African foreign born in the United States in 2007 arrived since 1990.

Although the DLP requires strict educational criteria for potential immigrants, it has nevertheless provided opportunity for many unskilled and less educated people to enter the country. And since many of the immigrants under this program also include those from countries where English is not spoken, some of these immigrants are reluctant to acquire new skills and education that would allow them to be hired in skilled positions once they enter the country. As a result, many of them often seek employment as unskilled workers in factory jobs and service industry. Those interested in business might eventually do so once they have accumulated enough capital to start the business. Perhaps the success story of El Hassan Mohamed, an African immigrant from Mauritania, a French-speaking country in West Africa, is evident of this group of African immigrants. Having arrived in Cincinnati nine years ago without even owning a car, he now owns a fleet of seventy-one taxi cabs (see the full story in the *Cincinnati Enquirer*, July 18, 2010). This influx of African immigrants into many American cities including Cincinnati has provided a viable market environment where African immigrant businesses can flourish.

Factors Influencing the Growth of African Businesses in Cincinnati

A combination of factors, including the growth of a large African immigrant population in the last two decades, a change in the mentality and perspective among African immigrants, perceived opportunities, and perceived employment discrimination are all factors that have contributed to the growth of African immigrant businesses in Cincinnati. In fact, Waldinger, Aldrich, Ward (1990) and others have noted that the initial market environment for immigrant entrepreneurs usually emerges from the immigrant community itself since these entrepreneurs understand and are best equipped to serve the special needs and demands of their community.[8] For instance, Halter (1995: 161) points out that the influx of Haitian immigrants from Haiti and other cities in the United States and Canada to Boston in the 1980s led to the proliferation of small business ventures ostensibly aimed at serving the needs of Haitians. Similarly, in his study of Senegalese entrepreneurs in the United States, Tidjani (2007: 42) makes the same argument when he points out that:

> . . . as citizens from a given country increase in a number of given area of a foreign country, they bring with them more trades, skills and competencies, try to reconstruct their home environment, and, thus, stimulate the creation of

businesses whose mission is generally and primarily, at least at their inception, to respond to the needs of these citizens.

As the number of African immigrants in Cincinnati has grown in the last two decade or so, so has the number of African-owned businesses that have emerged in an effort to meet the needs of that population. For example, this is how the owner of one the most popular African restaurant in the Cincinnati area explains his decision to enter this business:

> I was working in the computer department of a large American food company. One day, my wife and I thought that it would be a good and fun idea to cook and sell Senegalese food to our growing community, because it did not exist anywhere else in the city. This is how it started.

Also important is the change in the mentality and psychology of most African immigrants. For decades, African immigrants were less interested in establishing any kind of business because of what Li (1976) has described as the "sojourner orientation," which did not allow them to see the United States as home. In other words, these early post-independence immigrants were more interested in obtaining an American education and perhaps working for a brief period in order to make some money before returning home to contribute in the task of nation building or opening a business with the capital that they might have accumulated while working in the United States. Even though some of these immigrants eventually became American citizens or acquired permanent residence status, which allowed them to legally remain in the country for as long as they wanted, the sojourner mentality still did not allow them to engage in any form of business. They were still straddled with what Johnson (1995), in her discussion of British West Indian immigrants in Boston, has described as the colonial mentality, whereby many of them believed that social mobility and prestige could only be attained by obtaining a higher education and a white collar, stable and respectable salaried employment within a government structure. Therefore, for many of these early African immigrants who had made the decision to remain in the United States after completing their program of study, opening a business was only supposed to be for those who wanted to remain in the United States forever or did not have the educational credentials to gain other forms of employment. Many of these educated and skilled African immigrants preferred working in various government and private organizations, universities or international organizations like the United Nations, the World Bank, and the International Monetary Fund rather than engage in business. At the same time, the dream of building that "retirement home" in Africa, where they could eventually return and live happily ever after, remained strong. However, as the political and economic situation in many African countries have worsened in the last two decades or so, so has the desire by a significant number of African immigrants to remain permanently in the United States and to engage in business. Indeed, while many African immigrants, especially those who are able to do so, continue to support other family members back home and still believe in building that dream vacation or "retirement home" in Nigeria, Ghana, Cameroon, Kenya, or Zambia, the new reality is that many consider the United States a permanent home. Hence, their involvement in business is no longer seen as either unwise or unrealistic.

Other African immigrants have gone into business because of perceived racism and discrimination in employment. Like their Chinese and Japanese counterparts on the West coast in the late nineteenth and early twentieth centuries, or more recently Cuban immigrants in Miami who were often forced into entrepreneurial activities because of discriminatory practices and exclusion from the economic mainstream (Light, 1972; Portes and Sensenbrenner, 1993; Rath, 2000; Rath 2000b; Olson, 1979), many African immigrants have also been forced into business for many of the same reasons. They argue that they often have to work harder than their American counterparts. Even so, their effort is almost never appreciated by their bosses, nor are they given the opportunity to be promoted to higher positions. According to Arthur (2010), African immigrants often face an additional stigma of being cast into the racial stereotype that has often dogged black Americans. And regardless of their educational attainment and skill levels, African immigrants are often cast as lazy and more likely than other immigrant groups to need social welfare assistance. Some of the business owners interviewed for the study noted that they had decided to go into business because they had either lost their jobs, felt discriminated against by their American supervisors or simply felt that they could succeed on their own rather than continue working for somebody else. They want to be their own bosses and not be pushed around or made fun of by their native-born American superiors who may even be less qualified or less skilled than they are.

Taking the Leap: African Immigrant Businesses

As in many other American cities, a major focus of African immigrant business in Cincinnati is in the retail grocery store business that provides a wide variety of African food products such as garri, cocoyams, smoked fish, palm oil, and other exotic food items. In the early 1990s, the only grocery store that carried many of these items was owned by a Filipino along the I-74/I75 intersection. Thus it was not surprising to see African immigrants from Ghana, Senegal, Nigeria, Cameroon and many other African countries lined up, usually on Fridays when the store had fresh supply of fish and other produce, or on weekends when many of these African immigrants were off from work and had the opportunity to do their grocery. The second option for African immigrants during this period was "Jungle Jim's," a grocery store known to many immigrants around the tri-state area (Cincinnati, Northern Kentucky, and Southern Indiana) that carried a wide variety of ethnic foods to the diverse group of immigrants in the area. However, because the prices of food at "Jungle Jim's" were often prohibitive to many of the African immigrants, they preferred shopping at the Filipino-owned store. Today, however, there are at least six African-owned grocery stores in Cincinnati, most of them in the Northern suburbs along the I-75 and I-275 nexus. The location of these businesses is very much influenced by the settlement patterns of African immigrants in the city. Unlike in some major American cities where there may be a large concentration of African immigrant population in specific parts of the city, the geography of Greater Cincinnati does not lend itself to that opportunity. Instead the African population in Cincinnati is spread out, and can be found in suburbs like Forest Park, Wyoming, Springdale, West Chester, Lockland, Westwood, Mason, and College Hill. In his study of Ghanaian immigrant experience in Cincinnati, for example, Yeboah (2008: 36) noted that only two of the thirty-seven Ghanaians interviewed actually lived in the city of Cincinnati, while the rest lived in the various suburbs that make up Greater Cincinnati. The dispersed nature of the population clearly explains why many of these stores are located in the Northern suburbs with easy access from the I-75 and I-275 nexus.

Despite the fact that the grocery store owners interviewed in the study were either Ghanaians or Senegalese (and even though many Ghanaians and Senegalese tend to shop in a particular store because it is owned by their co-nationals or because of family or personal loyalty to the owners), they all indicated that they had started the business in order to meet the needs of the growing African population in the city and not necessarily only those of their nationals.[9] There are also a significant number of Caribbean and Latin American immigrants who are regular customers. In addition to the different variety of foods that they carry, these stores also sell African CDs, DVDs, phone cards, and also serve as agents for Western Union and other financial agencies used by Africans to send money to relatives back in Africa.

In addition to the grocery store business, African immigrants also own auto-repair shops, medical supply and home healthcare agencies, gas stations, restaurants, taxi cabs, arts and crafts stores, and are flea market vendors. While it appears that most of the businesses are owned by men, there are a few cases where the wives are also very active in running the business.[10] Unlike the grocery stores whose main client-base are African immigrants, the other businesses do not necessarily focus on Africans as their main group of clientele. For instance, the two restaurant owners in the study noted that they were interested in the restaurant business because they wanted to bring a taste of the African cuisine to Americans just as the Japanese, Indians, Vietnamese, Thai and other immigrant groups had done in the past. The owner of *Kilman-jaro*, the arts and crafts store who has been in the United States for decades indicated that he had carved out this area of business because he had seen a desire among Americans for African arts and crafts. That is why he chose the location of his business near the University of Cincinnati where there is a more diverse and educated population that is open-minded and appreciate different cultures. Although many clients of the auto repair businesses are African immigrants, there are also many Americans and immigrants from the Caribbean, Latin America, Middle East, and Asia who use their services. These clients initially come to them as a result of referral by other customers, the low cost of repairing their vehicles compared to the traditional auto repair shops, and because of the trust and personal relationship that they have developed with their clients.[11] In addition to serving its customers, many of these businesses also function as centers of social networking where new friend are often made, information on the latest political news back in the home country is disseminated, and fliers about the latest parties and other social events in the different African communities in the city could be found.

While a few of the business owners have been involved in some form of family business back home, many of them indicated that they had no business experience before coming to the United States or even starting their business. Like many African immigrants, they had initially come to the United States either to study or to pursue their American dream in other ways—which often meant getting a job. The decision to go into business on their own was because they had lost their jobs and were unable to find work in their area of expertise. Others indicated that they had planned on opening the business once they had enough capital to do so, and that losing their jobs was just another motivation to get into business. As one of the grocery store owners put it "I wanted to be my own boss and quit chasing a corporate American position."

Perhaps not surprisingly, none of the business owners had even bothered to seek a bank loan to start their business. They indicated that they were not sure that banks would bother to give loans for such small start-ups, particularly since they also did not have the resources that could serve as collateral for a bank loan. Some of them did not want to be burdened with the paperwork involved in getting a loan or be saddled with paying bank loans with a high interest rate. That is why they either had to save enough money until they had enough to start the business or borrowed money from friends and family members in order to come up with the start-up capital for the business. One of the business owners noted that the desire to save money by most Africans is strong and is something that we learn growing back in Africa. And because of that spirit of saving, I did not have to "eat steak or pizza every time that I had a hundred dollars."[12] In other words, it was necessary to make the sacrifice and avoid such frivolities in order to save the money that enabled him to start his business. In order to minimize the risks involved in any business, some have combined factory job and business, seeking help running the business from relatives or close friends when they are at their factory jobs.

All the businesses are still family-owned, with the husband, wife, and a few employees. While many of the businesses were reluctant to give the exact number of nonfamily members who worked for them, an educated guess from observation is that there were no more than three nonfamily employees (mostly co-ethnics) in any of the businesses. In a few cases, one of the spouses still had a full-time job elsewhere and only worked in the business whenever they were able to do so. The reason for such an arrangement is so that the family can still afford healthcare insurance and other benefits since the cost of buying it on their own could be very prohibitive.

A major problem faced by most of the business owners was the lack of financial capital. In fact, most of them indicated that they would like to expand their business if they had the capital to do so. The grocery store owners also face strong competition from each other. Therefore in order to maintain their customer base, they must not only maintain competitive prices, but they also have to maintain the good old-fashioned African culture of respect and politeness towards their customers. In his discussion of Ghanaian immigrant entrepreneurs, for example, (Yeboah, 2008: 119) notes that in order to be successful or survive these business owners have to also maintain social networks within the ethnic community or within the general host society. For example, over the last few years, the owner of ASAFO African Market has routinely made phone calls to mothers who shop at her store wishing them A HAPPY MOTHERS' DAY. In other words, the lack of financial capital is somehow compensated by a social capital which, when carefully managed, provides stability and even opportunity for growth (through word of mouth) to businesses.

It appears from all indications that these businesses are a realization of the American dream to many of the owners. Not only are these businesses providing them with the financial resources to sustain themselves and their families here in the United States, but they have also given them the opportunity to help other family members back home in Africa. Each business owner interviewed indicated that the business has provided him with the financial resources to be able to pay the tuition for relatives in colleges and universities back home or to take care of other family problems on a regular basis.

Most of them also indicated that they had either completed or still planned on building that "retirement home" back in their countries, where they hope to retire once they are done with the hectic business life in America. Along with these achievements, a culture of success, in rupture with experiences of failure at Home, has emerged in many African communities in the United States. During interviews, two statements made by business owners best characterized this culture: "in the US, when you work hard, you make it" and "in the US, if you want to be rich you must open a business, not work for factories." By contrast, in African countries, most people are convinced that hard work does not bring success and that salaried jobs are keys to prosperity.

CONCLUSION

It is clear from our discussion that like other immigrant groups before them, African immigrants are definitely making inroads in the United States economy as a whole and Cincinnati in particular. Although they may not be as established as other immigrant businesses such as the Mexicans, Indians, or other Asian groups, they are certainly making strides in this area. While the increase in the African population in Cincinnati and a change in mentality have provided important foundations for the emergence and growth of African-run businesses, it is evident from the narrative that these businesses are also geared towards serving multiple populations in the city. African immigrants no longer see themselves as sojourners, or helpless and hapless souls who have nothing to offer (Okome, 2006: 32), but as an important piece in the ever-growing economic engine of the United States. Unlike twenty or so years ago, an increasing number of Africans are trying to carve a niche in the business environment rather than relying on being employed by others. They want to be their own bosses.

Needless to say this process of African businesses is not unfolding without problems. One of the problems is related to the way emerging contexts may affect the growth of African businesses in the diaspora. Others are related to the general U.S. economic and social context. Some come from individual choices made by African business owners. Elaborating briefly on these different issues allows us to open new avenues for research on businesses in the diaspora and to more or less speculate on their future.

African owners have all growth objectives essentially based on two strategies: an extension of their customer base to all Africans and to non-Africans and/or a diversification of their activities. However, our observation of some of them, food stores and auto repair, for example, during this period shows that the success of their activities continues to depend largely on the ethnic/

African customer niche that constituted their market base during their emerging phase.

Meeting growth objectives requires changes in quality and quantity. At the quality level, most owners understand the need to improve their managerial and organizational processes, in order to attract the larger community. But, because their businesses have been designed (especially from a sociocultural viewpoint, as mentioned earlier) to satisfy primarily the needs of their ethnic community, they need the capacity to manage the paradox between their desire to do things differently and their obligation to continue to satisfy this community, which constitutes a niche and an almost risk-free market leading to financial stability.

However, to avoid overgeneralization, it is worth mentioning that some activities, because of their nature, are easier than others to be sold to the larger community, and cannot actually limit themselves to an ethnic market (this is the case of a taxi business compared to an ethnic restaurant, for example). Thus, many African owners, despite their discourse on growth, still have to make the necessary steps leading to it. In fact, this slow move towards the creation of the needed conditions for growth is also related to the general social and economic American context that we consider as the second problem facing African businesses in the diaspora. This is a structural/institutional issue that involves several potential risks for African businesses.

First, in a context where race and ethnicity still matter, the adoption of a growth strategy focusing on the larger community may end in fact in a customer base largely composed of the so-called minority population. This has been the experience of a large number of African-American or Hispanic businesses (if not most of them) despite changes in attitudes on the part of the so-called majority. Second, a growth strategy requires not only changes in managerial and organizational processes as mentioned earlier, but also the capabilities to face a tough and merciless competitive environment, for which few African owners are prepared for, based on our investigations.

This leads us to yet another problem faced by these businesses; the growth and development in the U.S. market makes the construction of a relationship of power in favor of African businesses indispensable. Among others, collective ownership is one way towards that. Our interviews reveal that few African owners are involved in strategic partnerships, although they talk to each others. Also, generally, besides the construction of their retirement house at Home, they do not seem to have business objectives for their country of origin. The failure and disappointment that led to their coming to the United States may be an explanation to their attitudes and decisions.

Although it may be too early to draw a final conclusion given the relative newness of the African experience, we must underline the fact that this is where the latter differs from the Chinese experience, for example. The creation of businesses by Chinese, whether in the United States, in Europe, or today in Africa, systematically leads to solid networking in families and beyond, and to a significant business and economic impact on the villages and small towns where business owners are from.[13] In the case of Africans, the economic impact on relatives at Home has been underlined in this chapter, but it seems to be limited to that.

In a competitive environment, it is in the nature of business to evolve in quality by improving their internal processes and/or in quantity through activity growth. Nevertheless, the business orientation that has taken place in the African diaspora in the United States during the past ten to twenty years, the success culture that has come with it, and the discourse on growth on the part of business owners, are a clear sign that the above mentioned evolution is taking place. However, a good understanding of this evolution is beyond the scope of this preliminary investigation and requires future research.

NOTES

1. This quote by Dan Danilov, an immigration lawyer in Seattle, Washington is cited in a July 13, 1992 article in *Business Week* magazine.

2. In this study, Cincinnati will also include the suburbs of Mason, Forest Park, College Hill, Lockland, Springdale, Wyoming, and West Chester.

3. Although we see the importance of this issue, we tend in this chapter to consider the African community in the United States as one culture. Thus, we emphasize more opportunities and community resources than individual choices in the decision made by Africans to start and develop a business. Further studies ought to look for more specific processes of business creation and management among Africans.

4. Interview with Christopher Che on August 23, 2010. Che is one of the few African immigrants who came to the United States in the early 1980s to attend the University of Wilmington, about thirty miles from Cincinnati.

5. In his 2007 study on Senegalese immigrants in Cincinnati, Tidjani estimates that there are at least 4,000 Senegalese immigrants in the Cincinnati.

6. For a fascinating discussion of life among African immigrants in New York City, see Paul Stoller, *Money has no Smell: The Africanization of New York City.* Chicago: The University of Chicago Press. 2002.

7. According to a report by the African Union, more than fifty people were killed and thousands more were displaced during anti-immigrant disturbances in May 2008.

8. For a similar opinion see, Joseph P. Ferrie and Joel Mokyr "Immigration and Entrepreneurship in the Nineteenth-Century U.S." in Herber Giersch, ed. *Economic Aspects of International Migration.* New York: Springer-Verlag, 1994: 115-138.

9. An African immigrant who has lived in the city for over two decades noted that living in Cincinnati today is almost like living back home in Africa. Not only are there

many more Africans in the city than when he first arrived here, but also one can get any kind of African food that would not have been possible to get at that time. And if someone has a taste for African food but is too busy of tired to cook it, then he/she could get it from one of the African restaurants in the city.

10. A few women we spoke to indicated that they also did hair braiding or were seamstresses on part-time basis because they needed to have full-time employment elsewhere in order to pay the bills. Others described themselves as independent home healthcare providers. However, because they were sub-contractors working for a larger healthcare agency and did not actually own a home healthcare agency, they were not included in the study.

11. During one of several visits to one of the auto repair businesses this author met a client from Dayton, about an hour's drive from Cincinnati, who had brought his vehicle to be checked by the mechanic. When asked why he had driven all the way just to this shop, he said he had been referred there by a friend who said that the price that he would be charged was worth the drive and that the owner could be trusted to do the work well.

12. Interview, October 12, 2010.

13. In Senegal where the largest avenue of the capital city, Dakar, looks like a Chinatown today, Chinese merchants, through their association have even been able to obtain the support of the Chinese Embassy, when they felt threatened by Senegalese business owners and some politicians.

REFERENCES

African Union. May 5–7, 2008. Special summit on refugees, returnees and displaced persons in Africa. Addis Ababa, Ethiopia.

Apraku, K. K. 1991. *African Émigrés in the United States*. New York: Praeger Publishers.

Arthur, J. A. 2010. *African diaspora identities: negotiating culture in transnational migration*. Lanham, MD: Lexington Books.

———. 2000. *Invisible sojourners: African immigrant diaspora in the United States*. Westport, CT: Praeger Publishers.

Bonacich, E, Ivan L. and Charles C. W. 1980. "Korean immigrant small business in Los Angeles." In Bryce-Leporte, R. S., assisted by Delores M. M. and Stephen R. C. *Sourcebook on the new immigration: implications for the United States and the International Community* (ed.). New Brunswick, NJ: Transaction Books , 167–84.

Bonacich, E. 1987. "Making it" in America: A social evaluation of the ethics of immigrant entrepreneurship." *Sociological Perspectives*. Volume 30 (4): 446–66.

Bonacich, E. and Modell, J. 1980. *The economic basis of ethnic solidarity: small business in the Japanese American Community*. Berkeley and Los Angeles: University of California Press.

Danilove, D. 1992. "The immigrants: how they're helping to revitalize the U.S. economy." *Business Week*: 114–22.

Granovetter, M. 1985. "Economic action and social structure: the problem of embed-dedness." *The American Journal of Sociology.* Volume 91 (3): 481–510.

Grieco E. 2004. "The African Foreign-Born in the United States." *Migration Policy Institute.*

Ferrrie, P. J. and Joel M. 1994. "Immigration and Entrepreneurship in the Nineteenth-Century U.S." In Herbert G. *Economic Aspects of International Migration* (ed.). New York: Springer-Verlag, 115–38.

Halter, M. 1995. "Staying close to Haitian culture: ethnic enterprise in the immigrant community." In Halter, M. *New immigrants in the market place: Boston's ethnic entrepreneurs* (ed.). Amherst: University of Massachusetts Press, 161–73.

Handmaker, J. L. and Jonathan, K. 2008. *Advancing refugee protection in South Africa* (eds.) New York: Berghahn Books.

Hannah, J. 2010. "Mauritanians find home here." *Cincinnati Enquirer.*

Hofstede, G. 1987. "Relativite culturelle des practiques et des theories de l'organisation." *Revue Francaised Gestion*: 10–21.

Johnson, V. 1995. "Culture, economic stability, and entrepreneurship: the case of British West Indians in Boston." In Marilyn, H. *New Immigrants in the Market Place: Boston's Ethnic Entrepreneurs* (ed.). Amherst: University of Massachusetts Press, 59–80.

Kamya, H. 2007. "The stress of migration and the mental health of African immi-grants." In Marilyn, H., Yoku, S-T and Steven A. T. *The other African Americans: contemporary African and Caribbean immigrants in the United States* (eds.). Lan-ham, Maryland.: Rowman and Littlefield Publishers, Inc., 255–80.

Keen, J. 2009. "For immigrants, living the dream getting tougher." *USA TODAY.*

Kloosterman, R. and Jan R. 2001. "Immigrant entrepreneurs in advanced economies: mixed embedddedness further explored." *Journal of Ethnic and Migration Studies.* Volume. 27 (2): 189–201.

Konadu-Agyemang, K. and Baffour K. T. 2006. "An overview of African immigra-tion to the US and Canada." In Kwado K-A, Baffour K. T. and John Arthur. *The New African Dispora in North America* (eds.). Lanham, MD: Lexington Books, 2–12.

Krogstat, A. 2004. "From chop suey to sushi, champagne, and VIP lounge." *Social Analysis.* Volume 48 (1): 196–217.

Li, P. S. 1976. "Ethnic businesses among Chinese in the USA." *Journal of Ethnic Studies.* Volume 4: 35–41.

Light, I. H. 1972. *Ethnic enterprise in America: business and welfare among Chinese, Japanese and Blacks.* Berkeley: University of California Press.

Min, P. G. and Mehdi B. 2000. "Immigrant entrepreneurship and business patterns: a comparison of Koreans and Iranians in Los Angeles." *International Migration Review.* Volume 34 (3): 707–38.

Okome, M. O. 2006. "The contradictions of globalization: causes of contemporary African immigrants to the United States of America." In Kwadwo K-A, Baffour K. T. and John Arthur. *The new African dispora in North America* (eds.). Lanham, MD: Lexington Books, 29–48.

Olson, J. S. 1979. *The ethnic dimension in American history*. New York: St. Martin's Press.

Portes, A.1987. "The social origins of the Cuban enclave economy of Miami." *Sociological Perspectives*. Volume 30 (4): 340–72.

Portes, A.and Julia S. 1993. "Embeddedness and immigration: notes on the social determinants of economic action." *American Journal of Sociology*. Volume 98 (6): 1320–50.

Putz, R. 2002. "Culture and entrepreneurship-remarks on transculturality as practice," *Tijdschrift voor Economische en Sociale Geografic*. Volume 94 (5): 554–63.

Raijman, R. and Tienda, M. 2003. "Ethnic foundations of economic and transactions: Mexican and Korean immigrant entrepreneurs in Chicago." *Ethnic and Racial Studies*. Volume 26 (5): 783–801.

Rath, J. and Robert K. 2000. "Outsiders" business: A critical review of research on immigrant entrepreneurship." *The International Migration Review,* Volume 34 (3): 657–81.

Stoller, P. 2002. *Money has no smell: the Africanization of New York City*. Chicago: The University of Chicago Press.

———. 1999. *Jaguar: a story of Africans in America*. Chicago: The University of Chicago Press.

———. 2000b. "Introduction: immigrant businesses and their economic, politico-institutional and social environment." In Jan R. *Immigrant businesses: the economic, political and social environment* (ed.). New York: St. Martin's Press, 1–20.

Staring, R. 2000). "International Migration, Undocumented Immigrants and Immigrant Entrepreneurship." In Jan R. *Immigrant businesses: the economic, political and social environment* (ed.). New York: St. Martin's Press, 182–98.

Takougang, J. 1995. "Recent African immigrants to the United States: A historical perspective." *The Western Journal of Black Studies* . Volume19 (1): 50–57.

Terrazas, A. 2009. African immigrants in the United States. *Migration Information Source*.

Tesi, M. 2008. "Africans in Tennessee." In Wornie R. *Africans in Tennessee: past and present* (ed.). Dubuque, Iowa: Kendall/Hunt Publishing Company, 259–83.

Tidjani, B. 2007. "Senegalese entrepreneurs in the USA and managerial decision making: a pilot study." *Africa Development*. Volume 32 (2): 41–65.

Waldinger, R., Howard A. and Robin W. 1990. "Opportunities, group characteristics, and strategies." In Waldinger, et. al. *Ethnic entrepreneurs: immigrant business in industrial societies* (eds.). Newbury Park, CA.: Sage Publications, 13–48.

———. 1990). "Trends in ethnic business in the United States." In Waldinger, et. al. *Ethnic entrepreneurs: immigrant business in industrial societies* (eds.). Newbury Park, CA.: Sage Publications, 49–78.

Yeboah, I.E.A. 2009. "Globalization and Ghanaian immigrant trajectories to Cincinnati: who benefits?" In John W. F., Joe T. D. and Norah F. H. *The African Diaspora in the United States and Canada at the Dawn of the 21st Century* (eds.). Binghampton University: Global Academic Publishing, 287–305.

———. 2008. *Black African Neo-Diaspora: Ghanaian Immigrant Experiences in the Greater Cincinnati, Ohio Area*. New York: Lexington Books.

Chapter Seven

Geography of a Globalized Labor Market: Zimbabwean Migrant Nurse Trajectory and Work Experiences in the UK

INTRODUCTION

International migration of health care workers has been on the agenda of academics and practitioners alike (Eastwood, 2005) as part of a globalized labor market (Sassen, 1991; Dwyer, 1999; Light, 2004; Yeboah, 2008). Attention in this field has focused on the costs and benefits of such globalized migration of physicians, nurses and pharmacist from the global periphery to the global core, especially physicians. Very limited attention has focused on first, the geography of migration of nurses and second, the work experience of immigrant nurses in their host society. This is despite the fact that the UK for example, employs international nurses from over thirty countries (NMC 2008) because its nurse industry is plagued with severe shortages of more than 30,000 nurses (Batata 2005). This chapter therefore contributes to our understanding of the geography of international migration of nurses and their work experience, using the case of Zimbabweans in the United Kingdom.

Immigrants to a new society have varied experience in their efforts to acculturate and assimilate (Likupe, 2005; Alexis et al., 2007; O'Brien, 2007; Gough, 2004; Lipley, 2005; Allen and Larsen, 2003) and this affects their life chances in their host society as well as their relationship with their source society. For Zimbabwean nurses in the UK, their experiences include working long hours, dislike of certain aspects of their work, limited opportunities for promotion and training, low status in the work place, underutilization of their skills and racism. Yet, they make a lot more money in the UK than they did in Zimbabwe and are able to contribute (through remittances) toward the well being of family and friends they have left in Zimbabwe.

Conceptual Framework

We contextualize Zimbabwean nurse immigrants as part of a globalized nurse migration that illustrates a geographical relationship between the source and destination of nurses. This offers an opportunity to assess their work experience in their host society as a part of brain drain migration (Akokpari 2006; Clark, Stewart, Clark 2006; El-Khawas 2004; Getahun 2000). Fundamentally, international migration is a geographical phenomenon that depends upon opportunity gradients between places of origin and destination of migrants. Particular place attributes in destinations attract specific immigrants to them and particular place attributes in origins propel people to emigrate out of their source countries (Yeboah, 2008; Saravia and Miranda, 2004).

Our argument is that global labor migration, and for that matter nurse migration, is based on a geography between places of origin and destination of migrants (Yeboah, 2008; Saravia and Miranda, 2004). These place-differences are manifest in two ways. On one hand, a shortage of nurses in the UK due to changing demographic factors (Gerrish and Griffith 2004) and the relative low status of nursing as a female profession to British-born citizens (Batata 2005; Buchan 1999; O'Brien, 2007) have led to polices that emphasize a reliance on foreign-born and foreign-trained nurses in the UK. These policies have made nurse training easy for foreigners and provided a path to legalize their stay in the UK. On the other hand, the economic and political milieu in Zimbabwe (under Mugabe's dictatorship) has made life to medical professionals (amongst other occupations) unbearable (Akokpari, 2006; Chikanda, 2006; Marquette 1997; Potts and Mutambirwa 1998; Skalnes 1993; Mhone 1995, Potts and Mutambirwa 1998). Because of the colonial legacy, nurses trained in Zimbabwe are trained using standards that are acceptable in the UK. In addition, networks that facilitate migration from Zimbabwe to the UK exist. The net effect of these place differences is that Zimbabweans have emigrated either as professional nurses or as people willing and able to train as nurses once they arrive in the UK. Thus, this geography of this migration is bound in the trajectory and experiences of the migration process.

By trajectory, we mean the process of migration to the UK. In this case, the demographic attributes of migrants underlie this migration. Young and able-bodied (Buchan et at., 2004) females (because of the construction of nursing a female occupation) rather than men (Mansuri, 2007; Dannecker, 2005; Da, 2004, Massey et al., 1998) as well as persons from other occupations who see the UK as an alternative to the harsh economic and political conditions in Zimbabwe are the ones who migrate. Because nursing has become a way to legalize their stay in the UK, they have migrated with their families rather than alone. To a large extent they rely upon networks (Hermanu, 2006; Mohan, 2006; Herring et al., 2004; Kandel and Massey, 2002) of previously migrated Zimbabweans in order to migrate to the UK. Because of its cosmopolitan nature, the majority of these migrants settle in the Greater London area. Not only is this the place with the greatest demand for nurses (so they will find jobs) but also it is the place where they perceive they will minimize racist experiences.

By experience, we mean how migrants acculturate to the work environment of their host society. Even though nurse immigrants from Zimbabwe may benefit in terms of improved economic conditions, their work experience in the UK indicates they tend to sacrifice their dignity for cash (Carter 2003; Likupe 2005; Alexis et al., 2007, Gerrish and Griffith, 2004; Beishon et al., 1995). In an economic sense, Zimbabwean immigrants benefit from migration yet, in a social sense, they sacrifice dignity for cash. Migrants therefore make social sacrifices to enjoy economic benefits. Often, their work experience has to do with existing historical relationships and racial differences between source and destination and this influences the kinds of nursing they engage in, their relationships with their patients and even their attitude towards promotion and personal advancement.

Countries of the global periphery have complained of the brain drain and poaching of their medical professionals (McGregor, 2007) so countries of the global core, such as the UK, are changing some of their migration policies and this has recently slowed Zimbabwe's nurse migrations but the economic costs to Zimbabwe of this brain drain are germane since this migration continues.

Within this conceptual framework, this chapter addresses three research questions. First, what is the trajectory of Zimbabwean nurse migrants to the UK, (who are they demographically and occupationally, how do they migrate, what are their settlement patterns in the UK and what are their future plans)? Second, what place attributes of both the UK and Zimbabwe have facilitated this geography of Zimbabwean emigration to the UK? Third, what work place experiences do Zimbabwean nurses have in the UK?

METHODOLOGY

Findings presented in this chapter are based on data collect in the summer of 2007 in the UK using three methods. First, secondary data from the UK's Nursing and Midwifery Council (NMC 1999–2007) provides aggregate data pertaining to each nurses' country of training amongst others. These data are used to determine the changing scale of Zimbabwean nurse migration to the UK.

Second, a survey instrument was used to gather information about Zimbabwean nurses in the UK. In this case, snowballing was utilized to acquire respondents. The emphasis of this data is not representative of Zimbabwean nurses in the UK (Kitchin and Tate 2000; Salganik 2004) but rather a cross-section of these nurses' migration experience. Out of fifty-two surveys distributed, thirty-six responded. Questions asked in the survey were closed in nature, making their analyses amenable to quantification.

Third, because survey data collected is not necessarily representative, ethnographic methods were used to provide depth of knowledge of respondents. An insufficient amount of attention has been paid to, "migration as cultural events rich in meaning for individuals, families, social groups, communities and nations" (McHugh, 2000). A deeper understanding of subtleties that pertain to the migration experience can be enhanced by ethnography as it is able to capture varying tempos and rhythms of movement and connection. Twelve of the thirty-six respondents to the survey participated in semi-structured interviews. The basis of this selection was whether they were trained as nurses in Zimbabwe or the UK, whether they were recruited as nurses in Zimbabwe before coming to the UK and their gender and age attributes. Three other nurses now living in Zimbabwe were added to the twelve who participated in semi-structured interviews to provide insights into their migrant experiences.

Migration of Zimbabweans in the UK

Migration trajectory of Zimbabweans in the UK is part of a globalized labor market that we explain by their demography, occupation and human capital, how they migrate, their participation in UK's nursing industry and their settlement patterns in the UK.

DEMOGRAPHY OF ZIMBABWEAN MIGRANTS IN THE UK

Although men historically dominate international migration (Mansuri 2007), women's participation in migration has increased. Massey et al. (1998) argue increase in female labor work force; increase in divorce rates, falling birth rates and extension of formal education to women account for increasing participation of women in migration. Table 7.1 shows females dominate the group of nurse migrants from Zimbabwe in the UK. Despite Massey et al.'s (1998) arguments, the dominance of women in this case is also because of the particular economic activity in question: nursing. The occurrence of male nurses in the global periphery is rare (Buchan et al., 2006). Even when men join the nursing field in the UK they all tend to go into mental health nursing since it requires physical strength in addition to skills. It is therefore not surprising that all male participants in the study were in mental health nursing.

Table 7.1. Demographic Attributes of Zimbabwean Nurses

Attribute	Number				
Gender	Male	Female			
	5	31			
Age (years)	20-29	30-39	40-49	50 and over	
	9	20	5	2	
Marital status	Single	Married	Widowed		
	9	26	1		
Married to	Zimbabwean in the UK	Other in UK	Zimbabwean in Zimbabwe		
	20	4	1		
Moved to UK with spouse	Yes	No			
	21	12			
Number of children	None	One	Two	Three	Four
	7	12	10	4	2

Zimbabwean nurses in the UK tended to be middle aged with the majority falling within the thirty to thirty-nine years age cohort (Table 7.1). Buchan et al. (2006) argue that international nurses in London from Subsaharan Africa tend to be older or middle aged. Yet, in this sample there is a significant number in the twenty to twenty-nine age group. This suggest two things, increasingly younger immigrants are coming to the UK as nurses or many younger immigrants turn to nursing once they arrive in the UK.

Table 7.1 also shows that the majority of participants are married. Given that the respondents can generally be characterized as middle aged it is no surprise that most of them are married. Of the married participants, predominantly most live in the UK with a Zimbabwean spouse. A small number have a non-Zimbabwean spouse living with them in the UK. To a large extent this seems to suggest that this is a migration of established people who are attempting to reestablish their lives in the UK and this involves their family members.

Only a small number of participants have no children with the majority having one or two children (Table 7.1). Only a few of migrants have three or more children. This trend suggests that migration in this context is a family activity or decision (Yeboah, 2008) where the family is seeking to start new lives outside Zimbabwe. This stands in stark contrast to migration patterns where the breadwinner migrates and supports the family through remittances

creating a sojourner family (Gonzales 1990). One explanation for this difference is that nursing in the UK provides a pathway for naturalization so
participants tend to include their family members in their decision to move.

HOW DO ZIMBABWEAN MIGRANTS GET TO THE UK?

For economic migrants the manner by which they immigrate is largely determined by their skills (human capital) and resources (cultural capital). For
highly skilled immigrants, recruitment is more likely the manner by which
they end up in the destination country (Khadria 2001). The need for highly
skilled labor in a country is typically accompanied by immigration policies
and incentives to attract this skilled labor (Lobo, 2007; Yeboah, 2008). Other
researchers argue the greatest determinate for economic migrants are social
networks or cultural capital available to them in the destination country rather
than identifiable skills (Beaverstock and Boardwell 2000). Raghuram (2004)
notes the importance of skill levels are dependent of the particular sector in
question. For example, the medical sector requires specific skills and in this
case, skills become more important in immigration.
      Among the respondents only a very small number of them found their way
to the UK by virtue of recruitment: only two were recruited. This low number
is not surprising given that all respondents in this study work for the NHS
which is not allowed to recruit nurses from Zimbabwe (Department of Health
2004). By and large, the majority of respondents came to the UK on their
own accord and the majority came to the UK not as nurses but have turned to
nursing as a coping strategy (as will be shown soon). Even though the law in
the UK is designed to prevent poaching of nurses from the global periphery,
McGregor (2007) notes there is indirect neglect of the law since once persons
arrive in the UK they can work using their nursing training from their course
country or become nurses in the UK.

Changing Occupation and Human Capital
of Zimbabwean Migrants in the UK

Human capital and occupational status of migrants is the basis of brain drain
or gain assessments (Akokpari 2006; Clark, Stewart, Clark 2006; El-Khawas
2004; Getahun 2000). The theoretical basis of brain drain migration lies in the
historical-structural approach of world systems theory (Arango 2000). Table
7.2 shows that respondents were predominantly employed in Zimbabwe before they emigrated since only eight were unemployed but of those employed
only eleven were employed as nurses in Zimbabwe. The rest were employed

Table 7.2. Occupational and Human Capital Attributes of Zimbabwean Nurses

Attribute	Number		
Employed in Zimbabwe	Yes	No	
	28	8	
		Skilled	Non-skilled
Occupation in Zimbabwe	Nurse	non-Nurse	non-Nurse
	11	9	7
Educational attainment in Zimbabwe	'O' Level	'A' Level	
	14	9	
Education acquired outside Zimbabwe	Yes	No	
	33	2	
Type of terminal education	Diploma	Degree	
	19	10	
Country of terminal degree	Zimbabwe	UK	
	1	28	

in both skilled professions (such as accountants, pharmacy technicians, teachers and computer technicians) and unskilled occupations (such as secretaries, factory workers and retail assistants).

Prior to leaving Zimbabwe, the majority of respondents did not have a college education since most had attained either an Ordinary or Advanced level education (Table 7.2). Yet, since leaving Zimbabwe, most of respondents have acquired an education in nursing, especially in the UK. They have therefore improved the educational attainment to college degrees and diplomas. Professions and educational attainment they held before emigrating from Zimbabwe suggests both a brain and skill drain have occurred. Their improved human capital in UK, however, is an indication that they have resorted to nursing as a coping mechanism to live in the UK. The eleven nurses and nine skilled emigrants are all examples of the "Professional, Technical and Managerial" workers that Logan (1999) refers to in his definition of who comprises the brain drain. Zimbabwe has borne the cost of educating these professionals (Eastwood, 2005). The nine non-nurse skilled migrants represent a skill drain and a loss as they are now working in the nursing field and not working in the original fields of specialization (Lianos, 2007).

Why do these immigrants resort to nursing instead of embarking upon human capital development in their original occupations? DW_C0030 notes that he had attempted to purse his accounting career in the UK but had been unsuccessful:

> "It is difficult here because these are the kinds of jobs (*e.g., accounting*) that locals here would do, so to break through in that area it takes a lot of effort and patience. It's not a no-no area but it's not easy. Nursing is basically a dirty job and this is why they have shortages here . . . foreigner I was looking to the future and what would let me stay in this country."

For the group of emigrants who became nurses upon arriving in the UK an added reason they entered into the field was that their tuition would be waived and they would receive a bursary. When asked why they entered the nursing field in the UK, ten stated that they did so because it entailed no financial investment on their part and they actually received money for going to nursing school. The UK's policy under which foreigners who wish to be nurses do not pay tuition means these Zimbabweans essentially found the nursing option to be the easiest, given their limited ability to raise money for tuition. This point of view is expressed by DW_C0014: "Initially I wanted to study computers but then you had to pay all these fees and my aunt could not afford it. The second best option was nursing because I had no fees to pay and I would get a bursary." Yet, entry into the nursing field gives foreigners the ability to legally live in the UK on a long term basis, although this rule has change recently. This is why we argue that the fee waiver was an additional reason. DW_B0003 exemplifies this point: "To be honest the only reason was that was the only course I could do without paying first. Also being a nurse would give me a path by which to stay in the country."

ZIMBABWEAN PARTICIPATION IN THE UK NURSING INDUSTRY AND THEIR SETTLEMENT PATTERNS

Figure 7.1 shows that starting in the late 1990s there were relatively small numbers of Zimbabwean nurses immigrating to the UK. Nurse migration from Zimbabwe to the UK is a recent phenomenon that has occurred under globalization. Overall, a total number of 2,566 nurses have immigrated to the UK from Zimbabwe (NMC 1998–2007). There is strong evidence to suggest that there are many Zimbabwean nurses who are now working in the private sector (McGregor 2007) and are unaccounted for in the NMC data. Based on the MNC data over this nine year period; an average of 285 nurses have immigrated to the UK annually. The majority of participants arrived between 1999 and 2005 but the peak years were 2002 and 2003. Since 2005, there has been a decline because of changes in migration policies in the UK that are designed to ostensibly check poaching from the global periphery. Despite the

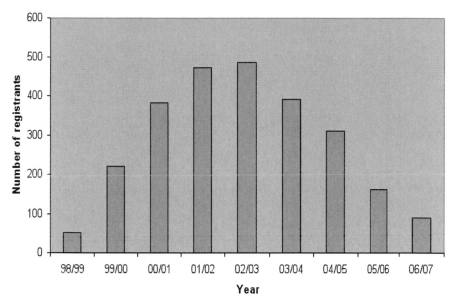

Figure 7.1. Immigration of Zimbabwe Nurses to the NMC registry

change of policies in the UK, recent evidence suggests Zimbabwean nurses are involved in a global hierarchy of migration of nurses. South African nurses see to be filling nurse positions in the UK, Australia and New Zealand (Buchan et al 2006) and Zimbabwean nurses are filling shortages in South Africa (de Castella 2003; Crush 2002).

Respondents in this study have mostly worked at only one hospital since arriving in the UK. Given the relative short amount of time that the participants have been in the UK this comes as no surprise but new policies introduced in 2004 under the Agenda for Change (Dept. of Health) within the NHS no longer allows nurses to negotiate pay. As a result, they can only get pay increases through time served and further education rather than move to another hospital. The implication is that these nurses have worked at their current hospital for between two and six years as shown in Table 7.3. They probably will continue to work at the current hospitals. As a result of this policy change, therefore, the majority of Zimbabwean nurse respondents have no intention of moving from their current hospital.

Foreign nurses are typically found in London (Batata 2005; Gough 2004). Respondents in this study were mostly taken from London and the surrounding area (with only three resident in Portsmouth). Though the respondents in this study mostly reside in London Table 7.4 shows London is not the only place they have lived since coming to the UK. Almost all respondents have lived in other places before coming to London with the number of places ranging up

Table 7.3.   Zimbabwean Nurse Participation in UK Nursing Industry

Attribute		Number	
Country of nurse training	UK 25	Zimbabwe 10	Other 1
Number of years as nurse in UK	Less than Three 4	Three-Eight 27	More than Eight 2
Country of nurse training	UK 25	Zimbabwe 10	Other 1
Length of adaptation course in UK (years)	One 8	Two-Fours 2	1
Number of years at current hospital	Less than Two 4	Two-Six 21	Six-Eight 6
Plan to move?	Yes 6	No 28	Maybe 1

Table 7.4.   Settlement Patterns of Zimbabwean Nurses within the UK

Attribute		Number		
Length of stay in UK (years)	Less than Six 21	Six-Eleven 32	More than Eleven 3	
Lived in London only?	Yes 14	No 20		
No. of places lived before London	One 8	Two 4	Three-Five 5	
Current city of residence	London 34	Other 3		
Number of years lived in London	Less than 2 3	Two-Eight 27	More than 8 4	
Attraction to residence in London	Job Related 17	Housing/School 21	Family/Friends 10	Peaceful 10

to five. Zimbabwean nurses in the UK are recent migrants with the majority lived in the UK between six and eleven years. The majority have however been in London between two to eight years. Thus, although their initial points of settlement may not be London, they quickly settle in London. The leading reasons for migrants being attracted to London are favorable cost of living, it being a peaceful place, demand for their services and its cosmopolitan character. Predominantly, migrants showed no interest in moving from London. Those who have no intention of moving from London give psychological reasons such as feeling settled, being happy in their current location, feeling content, feeling comfortable and wanting to avoid the hustle of moving.

CAUSES OF ZIMBABWEAN NURSE MIGRATION TO THE UK

Four factors account for this emerging geography of nurse migrations from Zimbabwe to the UK. First, the UK nurse shortage and polices to address it have facilitated flows of nurses from all over the global periphery to the UK, as part of a globalized nurse market. Second, dire economic, social, political and work conditions in Zimbabwe have implied that Zimbabweans with skills can participate in a globalized labor market. Third, Zimbabwe's colonial legacy has ensured that education of nurses in Zimbabwe and the UK are compatible in standards and practices. The second and third factors have provided a supply of nurses (and other professionals who are willing to become nurses) trained in Zimbabwe, ready to work in the UK. Fourth, this supply of nurses has been facilitated by the historic existence of social networks (cultural capital) that reduce migration "costs" for potential migrants from Zimbabwe to the UK. These four factors work together to create place attributes specific to the nurse migrations from Zimbabwe to the UK, within the context of a globalized nurse market.

UK Nurse Shortage and Policies to Combat the Shortage

Five reasons underlie the UK's nurse shortage. First, the field of nursing in the UK has traditionally been seen as a female-oriented labor activity with poor remuneration for British citizens. In recent times when women have more career options, fewer of them have entered the field (Batata 2005; Buchan 1999; O'Brien, 2007). It is therefore not surprising that there is gap between the supply and the demand for nurses in the UK. Second, the UK is experiencing a demographic shift, where a falling birthrate greatly reduces the potential for new female recruits from the UK becoming nurses (Gerrish and Griffith 2004). With fewer nurses entering the field, the average age of nurses has increased. The higher average age of nurses increases the propensity for retirement (Clark, Stewart, and Clark 2006). Thus, the nurse shortage has lead to higher nurse patient ratios, making work more stressful and increasing the propensity for burnout (Aiken et al., 2001).

A third cause for nurse shortages in the UK comes from general dissatisfaction with the profession. The NHS has been plagued with a reputation of being a bad employer in terms of conditions of service and wages. As such it is not able to compete with employers in other sectors and even the private nursing sector (Batata 2005; Gough 2004). Batata (2005) notes that though nurse wages in the UK have risen in real terms over the last twenty years, compared to other careers nurse wages have actually fallen. This has led to other careers being more attractive. Fourth, Batata (2005) notes the failure of the NHS to have greater geographical variation in its wage structure so as to reflect higher costs of living (in areas such as London and the South East) has resulted in many British nurses shying away from working n the London area.

A fifth reason for the nurse shortage in the UK has been poor labor force planning, particularly in the early 1990s. The early 1990s saw the number of training schools reduced (Batata 2005; Buchan 1999). Nurse administrator respondents are of the view that there was a failure on the part of the government to strategically deal with the nurse shortages on a long term basis rather than focus on short term goals which tended to lead to cycles of shortages (Steele 2008).

Place Attributes of Zimbabwe

A new immigration path, created by nurse shortages in the UK, has made the UK an attractive destination for Zimbabweans (both nurses and nonnurses). This however has been the case because of unfavorable economic, political, social and workplace and living conditions present in Zimbabwe. Migration occurs because of place-differences that manifest uneven geographical distribution of resources and opportunities between source and destination places (Yeboah, 2008; Saravia and Miranda, 2004; Arango 2000).

Zimbabwe's Economic Structural Adjustment Program (ESAP) has made the country an unattractive place to live and work, just as Okome (2007) argues for Subsaharan Africa. Increases in the cost of living occurred as government subsidies were removed from basic commodities such as corn (Marquette 1997). Fees for social services (like health and education) were introduced and increased (Marquette 1997; Potts and Mutambirwa 1998; Skalnes 1993). Government safety nets disappeared as subsidies and programs were cut in an effort to reduce government spending (Mhone 1995). Devaluation of the Zimbabwe dollar resulted in cost increases for essential economic products like petrol, resulting in inflation (Potts and Mutambirwa 1998). Zimbabwe's legendary hyper-inflation is well noted and in 2008 it stood at 11,200,000 percent (BBC 2008). Prices of commodities have increased so much that the government allows some businesses to formally sell their good in US dollars (BBC 2008). In addition, Zimbabwe's unemployment rate conservatively stands at 80 percent (BBC 2008; CIA 2006).

Economic factors are most important in emigration since 41 of 100 responses given by respondents in our survey relate to declining Zimbabwean economy, to get better remuneration, to find better work conditions, and find new opportunities for income. Yet, social reasons that center on family reunion, trying to find better living conditions, fleeing the increase in violence and seeing no future in Zimbabwe are also important (31 of the 100 responses). A third important factor involves opportunities for study and self improvement that were limited in Zimbabwe (19 responses). For these respondents, their desire for further education in their original occupations was important in leaving Zimbabwe. Yet they ended up in nursing because of the ease of entry into nursing and their desire to settle in the UK.

The experience of the three nursing candidates who have returned to Zimbabwe is revealing in terms of the role of economic and social factors in emigration. All three nurses currently practicing in Zimbabwe complained about their inability to live off their salaries alone. Many Zimbabweans, if they can find work, are forced to moon light or engage in additional income generating activities in order to be able to take care of their families. DW_D0031 moonlighted by selling snacks and vegetable in order the make enough money to take care of her family. Her monthly nursing salary barely covered her travel cost to work. This sentiment is also expressed by DW_A0034: "As a nurse in Zimbabwe you can't afford good education, a good house . . . I just do other things other than nursing to get extra income just to make sure that my family survives."

Such economic and social desperation is shared by BW_0023 but this translates into unfavorable working conditions in Zimbabwe. Upon completion of her nurse training and midwifery in the UK, Zimbabwe had just gained independence, so BW_0023 returned home: ". . . it was 1980, independence had come and obviously when I was here (UK) everybody spoke about when we had finished, when we think we have done enough we will go home. Our aim was to go back home (Zimbabwe) and work and that is what I thought."

However, the good times were to be short lived. By the early 1990's things began to take a negative turn.

The hospitals when I started in Zimbabwe were very clean, very efficient. The matrons were matrons. I don't know how, but somehow things began to break down and were not replaced. Patients increased and yet the staffing establishment was not increased. By then the salaries were not going up. And that does not help because when someone is used to a certain way of life and then it starts to diminish they start to lose interest in their job, because I have to look for other ways of making money. I am not going to put 100 percent in a job that does not pay me much. And of course people's attitudes, I don't know how you would describe it, the respect we had for matrons got lost somewhere along the line . . . people would say who is the matron, she is just an employee . . . if she is talking about doing work let her come and do it. Yet, at the same time, they cannot fire anybody. So things just went down and down and down.(BW_B0023)

Within the context of unfavorable economic, social work place attitudes, and BW_B0023 eventually decided to return to the UK as a second-time emigrant:

The overall conditions were not good. Our salaries were not rising relative to inflation. I had to consider my children who were about to go to university and their fees were going up and I would not be able to pay for them. Before, if the child had gotten into the university they would have received a grant. But now they had introduced fees. I know I could not afford them so I thought it was time for me to do something so that they could go to a foreign university. England appeared to be the easiest way for me as I had been here before.

Not only the reality of conditions in Zimbabwe but the perception of future conditions also contributed to their emigration. Most respondents rated the Zimbabwean economy as average (nineteen) or good (eleven) and only a few rated it as bad (five) when they left the country. However, when asked how the Zimbabwean economy is today all thirty-five respondents stated it is worse than they left. Thus, a combination of personal development, economic and social insecurity and a bleak future seem to have propelled emigration of these Zimbabweans. Even though DW_C0006 was "doing okay in Zimbabwe . . . things were beginning to get tough."

Despite economic woes, politics in Zimbabwe was a fourth factor in emigration decisions between 1994 and 2000. Invasion of farms in 1997, by war veterans from the liberation struggle, created a heighted sense of anxiety (Chaumba 2003) with its associated violence, lawlessness and insecurity (Hellum 2004; Laakso 2002). The 2000 parliamentary elections by far were the biggest contributor to political instability and an enormous sense of insecurity as supporters of the governing ZANU-PF intimidated, beat, terrorized, raped and allegedly killed supporters of Movement for Democratic Change (MDC) supporters. During the campaign economic production in the country worsened. These political-economic factors further damaged the already fragile economy which saw a decrease in productivity, increases in unemployment and increases in inflation (Laakso 2002).

For nurse migrants (those who were nurses prior to leaving Zimbabwe) working conditions in nursing in Zimbabwe were a paramount and fifth factor in their emigration decisions. The nursing industry in Zimbabwe is plagued with severe shortages, resulting in deteriorated working conditions (Chikanda, 2006). In 1991, there were 8,663 nurses in Zimbabwe. By 2000 that number had dropped to 7,795 (Chikanda 2006) with especially private sector nurses emigrating. This resulted in increases in patient-to-nurse ratios, especially in rural areas. As DW_D0031 (an intensive unit nurse) argues: ". . . there was a shortage of staff. . . . I would say its 50 percent short. At times when there are meant to be four nurses on duty you will find there are only two."

In terms of deteriorated work conditions, DW_A0034 also spoke of "shortages that has been a main problem. You have to put in treble (three times) the effort. Compared to when I started, you really have to put in more time . . . there has just been a mass exodus. Maybe after a month or two someone is leaving again." Deteriorated nurse work conditions in Zimbabwe have been made worse by the lack of equipment and basic provisions in Zimbabwe's hospitals. Nurses express fears of contracting HIV because they are not provided basic inputs like surgical gloves (Chikanda, 2006), a situation similar to what Feeley (2006) reports for Zambia.

The Colonial Legacy

Despite current tense relations between the Mugabe-led ZANUPF government and the UK, the colonial legacy between the two countries has facilitated migration out of Zimbabwe to the UK. Under colonial rule, Zimbabwe adopted the British system with Zimbabweans taking both "O" and "A" level examinations that are set in Cambridge. Compatibility of educational systems has made it possible for Zimbabweans to fit into nurse training in the UK. Yet, nurse training in Zimbabwe and Southern Rhodesia differed in some respect by race. Black nurses, especially in rural areas were trained to meet the needs of the communities they lived in.

In those days DW_C0021 (who started her nurse training in 1969 in Southern Rhodesia) said nurses in rural areas were trained to be able to deal with whatever situation may come up because there was limited access to doctors. Although DW_C0021 notes that such training in Zimbabwe still continues to meet the needs of remote areas, she however argues that the arrival of independence saw an upgrading of nurse training (for blacks) go meet the standards of other countries, especially Britain. Upgrading initially started with training blacks as medical assistants, followed by maternity assistants and then registered nurses (RNs). DW_C0021 believe that had the Zimbabwean government not upgraded nurse training after independence, Zimbabwean trained nurses will not be able to work in the UK. This argument is echoed by Levy (2003) who laments that efforts to bring medical training of Zimbabweans to international standards have contributed to their emigration out of the country.

Despite independence, Zimbabweans still have close ties to the UK. Information links that were setup during the colonial era have been strengthened through business, social and other activities which continue to link the two places. There are also multiple direct flights between London and Harare each week and these have made it easy for emigrants to be in Harare one day and London the next.

Social Networks between the Colony and Metropole

The last way by which Zimbabwean nurses have been able to fit in the UK is through social networks that have been established over the long relationship between the two countries. One would be hard pressed to find a Zimbabwean who does not have a relative in the UK. Nowadays London is commonly referred to as "Harare North" by Zimbabweans. Social networks fall under the micro-structures of migration within the context of "chain migration" (Price 1963) highlights the vital role social networks play in migration flows. Migrant groups employ beliefs, practices and social resources to develop strategies that enable them to deal with the struggles of migration and settling in new locations (Castles and Miller 2003).

Social capital, also known as cultural capital—i.e. "knowledge of other countries, capabilities for organizing travel, finding work and adapting to a new environment" (Castles and Miller 2003: 27)—effectively reduces the "costs" of migration and increases potential for subsequent successful migrations (Hermanu 2006). As more migrants from a particular locale successfully immigrate to a new country, cultural capital only gets richer, increasing the potential for more successful emigrants to the particular destination, from the source country. Vital links between source and destination countries that keep migrants connected to their home countries result in new dynamics and complexities that make the destination country more welcoming to immigrants (Kandel and Massey 2002).

Networks of Zimbabweans in the UK have been important in helping nurses find their way to the UK in two ways. The first is through the dissemination of information. Participants note that they came to the UK because family in the UK had told them that there were many opportunities they could pursue. It is quite different reading about opportunities from a newspaper versus hearing about it from a relative who lives in the locale. The second way that social networks play a role is through providing financial and establishment support. The prospect of going to a place where one does not know and has no contacts makes it a daunting task. Table 7.5 shows the significance of social networks in immigrating to the UK.

The importance of cultural capital is highlighted by the informal networks that migrants have developed to address their needs of shelter, employment, emotional support and assistance toward legal residency as can also be seen among Mexican immigrants to the USA (Kandel and Massy, 2002). Within the context of cultural capital it is clear that the respondents' decisions were influenced by networks of relatives or friends who were already in the UK. The majority received help to enable them to travel outside Zimbabwe, especially

Table 7.5.   Role of Networks in Immigration of Zimbabwean Nurses to the UK

Attribute			Number		
Recruited in Zimbabwe	Yes	No			
	2	20			
Help in leaving Zimbabwe	Yes	No			
	27	9			
Type of help received	Ticket	Visa	Passport	Place to Stay	Job Search
	13	5	2	20	8
Help others move to UK	Yes	No			
	24	10			
Relationship to those helped	Friends	Relatives	Both		
	3	18	4		
Number of people helped move to UK	One-Four	Five-Seven			
	17	5			
Type of help given others	Ticket	Visa	Passport	Place to Stay	Job Search
	25	13	0	13	14

through paying for their airfare, providing them with a place to stay in the UK and helping with job-search upon arrival in the UK. Settlement issues, especially the provision of a place to stay and assisting in finding employment are clear signs of the advantages of having a network to tap into when migrating.

Once respondents move to the UK they also tend to serve as networks for other migrants, resulting in chain migration (Table 7.5). So, the value of cultural capital is not simply expressed in the help migrants receive in settling in the UK but also in terms of the help they offer future immigrants to settle in the UK. The ability to tap into this cultural capital is therefore a significant factor as to whether or not Zimbabweans choose to immigrate to the UK:

DW_C004: "I had relatives here so it was easier."

DW_C0026: "The UK was easiest to come and we had family and friends here. They were the ones who encouraged us to come."

DW_C0028: ". . . well it was my dream and it is where my cousin was. If he had been in America I would have tried to go to America. I wanted to go outside."

DW_C0029: ". . . it was a bit of both. Finishing my 'A' levels I wanted to go study out of Zimbabwe, be it Botswana, South Africa but the fact that my brother had come here it meant that settling down would be easier for me here."

Work Experiences of Zimbabwean Nurses in the UK: Trading Dignity for Cash

Work experience of Zimbabwean nurses in the UK suggests they trade dignity for cash. Issues brought up include racism from patients, coworkers and their superiors, difficulty of communicating with patients and superiors because of differences in accent, deskilling and unemployment, limited opportunities for training and promotion, job dissatisfaction and working long hours. Yet, all participants in the survey are happy at the amount of money they make and the opportunity nursing offers them to live legally in the UK. Effectively, Zimbabwean nurses trade aspects of their dignity for cash and the opportunity to continue making money legally in the UK.

By far the issue that came up most from our respondents was racism. Beishon et al. (1995) find that foreign nurses are often subjected to racism from both their colleagues and patients (Carter 2003; Likupe 2005; Alexis et al., 2007). Gerrish and Griffith (2004) also find that 40 percent of ethnic minority nurses report experiencing racial harassment from colleagues and more than 64 percent suffer racial harassment from patients. Racism against ethnic minorities in the NHS is sometimes manifest through reduced access to promotion and training opportunities, disregard for foreign nurses' prior experience and underutilization of skills (Likupe 2005).

Respondents spoke about racism mostly originating from patients and co-workers. They note that many patients would rather be attended to by white nurses. Respondents often made it clear that patients rather listen to a white medical assistant instead of a black registered nurse. A theme that ran across all the interviews was that black nurses in the UK had to be very patient in order to succeed. Foreign nurses are often ignored and evaded by patients and co-workers (Alexis et al., 2007). One respondent noted that her patients are always keen to find out whether she will be going back to her country. She said she never feels like she is treated the same as her white coworkers by the patients. One of the nurses working in mental health nursing mentioned that patients tended to have a loose tongue and that they always tried to make you feel alien. As DW_C0006 states: ". . . especially when you come across racist patients. You find that you put your all into caring for them and they are not even grateful. Some do it in a clever way and are curious in finding out whether you will be going back. Others are very open about it which is very demoralizing." DW_C0021 supports this assertion of racism not only from patients but form colleagues as well:

> The patients look at the color of your skin and do not believe that you have the ability to be a nurse and don't expect you to know what you are doing. At times you get the same reaction from subordinates and colleagues. As a result you have to be very vigilant on the job. There can also be very awkward behavior among the staff which is racially motivated.

Apart from racism from patients, racism from within the institution is a significant topic among the respondents. Almost all of them had complaints about the way their coworkers treat them. Racism that comes from co-workers surprisingly did not only come from whites. It also originates from foreign nurses from other regions of the world who have prejudice against Black Africans. It seems to be a situation where people from similar ethnic groups looked out for each other. Given the diversity in the NHS nurse staff, there are likely to be difficulties working with people from different cultures. This point is echoed by Gough (2004) who notes that investment in recruiting foreign nurses should also be followed with investments to ensure proper integration and retention of these nurses. Likupe (2005); Lipley (2005); Allen and Larsen (2003) all note that very little has been done to cater to the needs of foreign nurses to ensure their integration, success and satisfaction in the NHS. It is therefore not surprising that DW_C0030 had this to say about racism from both patients and colleagues: ". . . you can be racially abused. Many a time you could be trying to help someone and you get a lot of 'F' words. There are challenges working with both patients and colleagues as cultures differ; Indians, Africans, Filipinos, etc. It takes a lot to get through to patients and nurses."

On the issue of difficulties with coworkers DW_C0029 points out that: "Another problem could be if you encounter someone who is ignorant or racist. It is difficult and quite a challenge to work with people like that because they take you being black as a weakness. You have to be strong to work with those kinds of people."

A second issue respondents raised is difficulty in communication with coworkers, patients and supervisors because of the variety of dialects and accents in the UK, especially in their initial settlement in the UK. Nurses in Allen and Larsen's (2003) study of foreign nurses often find themselves frustrated and in some cases they could not give reports because their British colleagues laughed and giggled when they spoke. As DW_C0026 states, Zimbabwean nurses in the UK have similar experiences: "Being a foreigner, English is our second language. The accent really, for me it was a challenge. I had to listen very carefully. I had to understand the English and the accent. At times people had to interpret for me."

A third experiential issue raised by respondents is deskilling and underemployment. Foreign nurses in the UK undergo a process of deskilling or under utilization when they immigrate to the UK (O'Brien, 2007). The fundamental cause of this phenomenon is that the NHS is recruiting qualified and experienced nurses to do repetitive and uninteresting tasks such as patient-toileting, -washing and -feeding (O'Brien, 2007) that British citizens shy away from. This is exactly what is transpiring with the nurses trained in Zimbabwe who now work in the NHS. Even though foreign nurses may be highly trained, they often find themselves in frustrating situations where they are not allowed to use their technical skills simply because they may not have been trained in the UK.

In order for a foreign nurse to perform more technical duties and attain a higher nursing grade they have to take additional courses in the UK, irrespective of the skills they arrive with. These courses are typically delayed due to red tape (O'Brien, 2007). The NHS is therefore missing an opportunity in taking advantage of the skills, experience and decision-making of foreign nurses. Respondents trained in Zimbabwe expressed frustrations at not being able to perform certain tasks which they typically performed when in Zimbabwe. Some mentioned that there are a variety of skills they used to perform as nurses in Zimbabwe which can only be done by doctors in the UK. They also complained that they were not given opportunities to take initiative or work independently. They always have to wait for direct orders from doctors or ward managers. A common complaint they had was that anything technical always had to be done under supervision and there is always some paper work involved. DW_C0021 states this frustration with deskilling:

> I had more job satisfaction in Zimbabwe. In Zimbabwe nurses have greater latitude to practice their profession. There are many things here that only a doctor can do and no one will do anything about the situation until a doctor comes to do it whereas in Zimbabwe the nurses are able to do a lot more. In the UK there is a specialist for everything and that can kill some moral at the work place. Even putting in an IV, here a nurse cannot do it. Yet in Zimbabwe we did everything.

According to DW_C0021, deskilling is a moral killer. Alexis, et al., (2007) note that the lack of trust from superiors in the abilities of foreign nurses, who tend to constantly watch over them, results in many losing confidence thus lowering their self-esteem. The process of deskilling seems more telling on Zimbabwean trained as nurses in the UK. For these nurses, the low skill duties they perform have taken them by surprise as their view of the nursing profession was shaped by what they saw of nurses in Zimbabwe. As DW_C0006 stresses: "I knew about giving medication, however, this thing of washing and feeding patients, I do not like at all. It is just so different from what I used to think. . ."

A fourth experiential issue raised (by both Zimbabwe trained and UK trained) is restricted opportunities for further training and promotion, compared to their white counterparts. This is especially for younger nurses trained in the UK. DW_C004 stresses this point:

I have been working as an ophthalmic nurse for three years and I have not been given much opportunity to take further training courses and as a result I do not expect any promotion . . . they tell us that there is no funding, however, others are being given the opportunity to take courses . . . it may have to do with me being from Zimbabwe and others being born here. I don't really know.

DW_C0006 put it quite bluntly when she argues: ". . . as for whites, a new one comes today and tomorrow they are training. A new black hire comes and it will take two years for them to get a training course. . . . It is not officially written but it is how things work. The whites look out for each other." These echo findings by Alexis et al. (2007) and O'Brien (2007) that foreign trained nurses are therefore seen as cheap labor expected to fill positions in low grade nursing. Yet, some respondents have had positive experiences with respect to promotion. As BW_B0023 states:

. . . usually black people don't get much opportunity to rise. The post I am now took me six months to rise to it where normally it would be two years. I had a lot of experience behind me and since I had gotten my training here, they counted me to have twenty years of experience. The reason I did not want to raise is that I had seen what had happened to the other black girls who rise. As soon as you get up there they (Whites) don't like you anymore. They only like you when you are rising or when you are at the bottom.

Even though a perception exists among the Zimbabwean nurses that they are intentionally being kept out of higher positions, when some get an opportunity for promotion, there is a general sense of pessimism that they will not be successful and a promotion will translate to an elimination of overtime and will equal a pay cut. These nurses will continue to do menial nursing work because of the financial gains. This is BW_B0023's experience:

I was just recently due for a promotion which I turned down. For that position it is a non nursing management position, it is an 8-4 job and I can't afford it. My salary goes up yes for my basic pay, but I can't do any extra work. With all the extra work I do, it would be a 20,000 per year cut if I took the job. I am paying my children's university fees and I simply can't afford it.

Perceptions of UK nurse administrators who participated in this research shed more light on the experiences of Zimbabwean nurses. They argue that lack of training and promotion opportunities for foreign-trained nurses is due to the financial problems facing the NHS. They also state that there is a communication gap between the nurses and their supervisors about the process and selection criteria. However, the nurse administrators note they are aware of prejudice on the part of some ward managers. One of the administrators admits that some of the ward managers view foreign nurses as transient therefore there is no point in investing in them if they are only going to leave.

A fifth issue of concern to Zimbabwean nurses relates to job satisfaction. There is a general consensus amongst respondents that the money is good and helps them solve many problems in Zimbabwe. As DW_C0030 states: "the money is good . . . when you send it back home it is helping a lot of people." Nurses trained in Zimbabwe were happy to get a lot more money for the same job. Yet, they are not happy being deskilled or underemployed. Thus, they are split as to whether the overall job satisfaction is good or bad.

A sixth issue of concern that many respondents have is that they worked really long hours. A typical shift in the UK is normally twelve hours. The typical nurse shift in Zimbabwe is eight hours. Despite this concern over long working hours, many respondents take on extra hours to make overtime pay. Overall, though, respondents were generally pleased that nursing gave them a legal path to stay in the UK. As DW_C0030 points out: ". . . as a foreigner I was looking to the future and what would let me stay in this country. The ability to get papers is what drives me in working as a nurse." So, though respondents have complaints about their work experience, on the whole they are happy with their financial circumstances. After all, they are economic migrants who will put up with non-economic interferences that infringe upon their dignity, so far as they achieve their economic objectives.

CONCLUSION

Globalization has generated a geography of healthcare migrants emigrating from the global periphery to the global; core. Attention in the literature has focused on the developmental impacts of this migration on economies and societies of the global periphery, such as Sub-Saharan Africa. Not much attention has been paid to the immigrant work experiences of specialized labor like healthcare immigrants. This chapter has presented the experiences of nurse emigrants from Zimbabwe to the UK by teasing out the specific geography of this globalized labor migration.

Our conclusion is that these immigrants to the UK are economic migrants who are willing to trade their dignity for cash. For the majority of them, they see nursing as the only way to regularize their stay in the UK and make a living for both they and their families. They are therefore willing to put up with the indignity of racism, discrimination for both institutions and patients associated with being a nurse in the UK. They are also willing to put up with being passed over for promotion and further education so as to escape the economic and political turmoil in Zimbabwe. Place differences between Zimbabwe and the UK (captured by the shortage of nurses in the UK, the colonial legacy between the two countries and socio-economic gradients between the two countries) have facilitated this migration as part of a globalized labor market for health care workers.

This chapter raises questions as to the impacts of these nurse experiences on both the UK health sector and on Zimbabwe. Will these transnational migrants continue to trade their dignity for cash in the UK or will they switch their occupations, with time? Will they ever return to Zimbabwe and will they work as nurses once they return? Will Zimbabwe need nurses upon their return or will it need people trained in other occupations such as accountants, teachers and economists? What are the implications of these experiences for nurses for brain gain or brain circulation in Zimbabwe? These questions should guide development policy and migration policy for brain drain migration from the global periphery to the global core.

REFERENCES

Aiken, L. H., Clarke, S. P., Sloane, D. M., Sochalski, J. A., Busse, R., Clarke, H., Giovannetti, P., Hunt, J., Rafferty, A.M. and. Shamian, J. 2001. "Nurses' Reports on Hospital Care in Five Countries." *Health Affairs*, Volume 20(3): 43-53.

Akokpari, J. 2006. "Globalization, Migration, and the Challenges of Development in Africa." *Perspectives on Global Development & Technology,* Volume 5(3): 125–53.

Alexis, O., Vydelingum, V., and Robbins, I. 2007. "Engaging with a New Reality: Experiences of Overseas Minority Ethnic Nurses in the NHS." *Journal of Clinical Nursing,*Volume 16(12): 2221–28.

Allen, H. and Larsen, J.A. 2003. "We Need Respect': Experiences of Internationally Recruited Nurses in the UK." *Royal College of Nurses Press Association Ltd*, www.rcn.org.uk.

Arango, J. 2000. "Explaining Migration: A Critical View." *International Social Science Journal,* Volume 52(165): 283-296.

Batata, A.S. 2005. "International Nurse Recruitment and NHS Vacancies: A Cross-Sectional Analysis." *Globalization & Health*, Volume 1: 7–10.

BBC. 2008. "Zimbabwe Inflation hits new high," www.news.bbc.co.uk, accessed 10/09/2008.

BBC. 2007. "Zimbabwe Inflation nears 1,600%," www.news.bbc.co.uk, accessed 02/12/2007.

BBC. 2006. "IRN Clampdown by NHS", www.news.bbc.co.uk, accessed 07/03/2006.

Beaverstock, J.V. and Boardwell, J.T. 2000. "Negotiating Globalization, Transnational Corporations and Global City Financial Centres in Transient Migration Studies." *Applied Geography,* Volume 20(3): 227–304.

Buchan, J. 1999. The 'Greying' of the United Kingdom Nursing Workforce: Implications for Employment Policy and Practice. *Journal of Advanced Nursing,* Volume 30(4): 818–26. Jobanputra, R.; Gough; P. and Hutt, R. 2006. "Internationally Recruited Nurses in London: A Survey of Career Paths and Plans." *Human Resources for Health*, Volume 4: 1–10.

Castles, S. and Miller, M. J. 2003. *The Age of Migration: International Population Movements in the Modern World.* New York: Guilford Press.

Chaumba, J., Scoones, I., and Wolmer, W. 2003. "From Jambanja to Planning: The Reassertion of Technocracy in Land Reform in South-Eastern Zimbabwe?" *Journal of Modern African Studies,* Volume 41(4): 533–54.

Chikanda, A. 2006. "Skilled Health Professionals' Migration and its Impact on Health Delivery in Zimbabwe." *Journal of Ethnic & Migration Studies,* 32(4): 667–80.

Clark, P. F., Stewart, J, B. and Clark, D. A. 2006. The Globalization of the Labor Market for Health-care Professionals. *International Labor Review*, 125 (1–2): 41–70.

Crush, J. 2002. "The Global Raiders: Nationalism, Globalization and the South African Brain Drain." *Journal of International Affairs*, Volume 56(1): 147-172.

Central Statistical Office. 2000. *Zimbabwe: Facts and Figures*. CSO: Harare.

CNN. 2008. "Zimbabwe Inflation hits 11,200,000 percent," www.cnn.com, accessed 08/19/2008.

Da. W. 2004. "A Regional Tradition of Gender Equity; Shanghai Men in Sydney, Australia." *The Journal of Men's Studies*, Volume 12(2):133-49.

Dannecker, P. 2005, "Transnational Migration and the Transformation of Gender Relations: The case of Bangladesh Labor Migrants." *Current Sociology*, Volume 53(4): 655–74.

de Castella, T. 2003. "Health Workers Struggle to Provide Care in Zimbabwe." *Lancet,* Volume 362(9377): 46-47.

Department of Health. 2004. *Agenda for Change*. London: UK Department of Health.

Department of Health. 2004. *Code of Practice for the International Recruitment of Healthcare Professionals.* London: UK Department of Health.

Dwyer, C. 1999. "Migrations and Diasporas". In *Introducing Human Geographies,* edited by Paul Cloke, Philip Crang and Mark Goodwin. London: Arnold.

Eastwood, J. B., Conroy, R. E., Naicker, S. S., West, P. A., Tutt, R. C., and Plange-Rhule, J. J. 2005. "Loss of Health Professionals from Sub-Saharan Africa: the Pivotal Role of the UK." *Lancet*, Volume 365(9474): 1893–1900.

El-Khawas, M.A. 2004. "Brain Drain: Putting Africa between a Rock and a Hard Place." *Mediterranean Quarterly*, Volume 15(4): 37-56.

Feeley, F. 2006. "Fight AIDS as well as the Brain Drain." *Lancet*, Volume 368(9534): 435–36.

Gerrish K. and Griffith, V. 2004. Integration of Overseas Registered Nurses: Evaluation of an Adaptation Programme. *Journal of Advanced Nursing*, Volume 45: 579–87.

Getahun, S.A. 2006. "Brain Drain and Its Impact on Ethiopia's Higher Learning Institutions: Medical Establishments and the Military Academies between 1970s and 2000". *Perspectives on Global Development & Technology,* Volume 5(3): 257–75.

Gonzales, J.L. 1990. *Racial and Ethnic Groups in America.* Iowa: Kendall-Hunt.

Gough, P. 2004. "Nurses from Overseas: Making a World of Difference." *Nursing Management,* Volume 11(5): 16–17.

Hellum, A. and Derman, B. 2004. "Land Reform and Human Rights in Contemporary Zimbabwe: Balancing Individual and Social Justice Through an Integrated Human Rights Framework." *World Development,* Volume 10: 1785–1805.

Hermanu, E. 2006. "Migration as a Family Business: The Role of Personal Networks in the Mobility Phase of Migration." *International Migration,* Volume 44(4): 191–230.

Herring. L., van der Erf, R. and Wilson, L. 2004. "The Role of Family Networks and Migration Culture in the Continuation of Moroccan Emigration. A Gender Perspective." *Journal of Ethnic and Migration Studies,* Volume 30(2): 323–37.

Kandel, W., and Massey, D.S. 2002. "The Culture of Mexican Migration: A Theoretical and Empirical Analysis." *Social Forces,* Volume 80(3): 981–1004.

Khadria, B. 2001. "Shifting Paradigms of Globalization: The Twenty-First Century Transition Towards Generics in Skilled Migration from India." *International Migration,* 39(5): 45–71.

Kitchin, R and Tate, N.J. 2000. *Conducting Research in Human Geography: Theory, Methodology and Practice.* Harlow, NY: Prentice Hall.

Laakso, L. 2002. "The Politics of International Election Observation: The case of Zimbabwe in 2000. "*Journal of Modern African Studies,* Volume 40(3): 437–64.

Levy, L.F. 2003 The First World's Role in the Third World Brain Drain. *British Medical Journal,* Volume 327(7407): 170.

Lianos, T.P. 2007. "Brain Drain and Brain Loss: Immigrants to Greece." *Journal of Ethnic & Migration Studies,* Volume 33(1): 129-140.

Light, I. 2004. "Immigration and Ethnic Communities in Giant Cities." *UNESCO*: 385–98.

Likupe, G. 2006. "Experiences of African Nurses in the UK National Health Service: A Literature Review." *Journal of Clinical Nursing,* Volume 15(10): 1213–20.

Lipley, N. 2005. "Call to Meet Individual Needs of Overseas Nurse Recruits." *Nursing Management—UK*, Volume 12(6): 5.

Lobo, P. A. 2007. "Unintended Consequences: Liberalized U.S. Immigration Law and the African Brain Drain." In. *The New African Diaspora in North America: Trends, Community Building and Adaptation,* edited by Kwadwo Konadu-Agyemang, Baffour K. Takyi, and John A. Arthur. Lanham, MD: Lexington Books.

Logan, B.I. 1999. "The Reserve Transfer of Technology from Sub-Saharan Africa: The Case of Zimbabwe." *International Migration,* Volume 37(2): 437–63.

Mansuri, G. 2007. "Does Work Migration Spur Investment in Origin Communities? Entrepreneurship, Schooling, and Child Health in Rural Pakistan." In *International Migration, Economic Development & Policy* edited by Özden, Çaglar and Schiff, Maurice. Washington, DC: World Bank.

Marquette, C.M. 1997. "Current Poverty, Structural Adjustment, and Drought in Zimbabwe. *World Development*, Volume 25(7): 1141–40.

Massey, D.S., Arango, J., Hugo, G., Kouaouci, A., Pellegrino, A., Taylor, J.E., 1988. *Worlds in Motion : Understanding International Migration at the end of the Millennium*. New York: Oxford University Press.

McGregor, J. 2007. "Joining the BBC (British Bottom Cleaners): Zimbabwean Migrants and the UK Care Industry." *Journal of Ethnic and Migration Studies*, Volume 33(5): 801–24.

McHugh, K. E. 2000. "Inside, Outside, Upside Down, Backward, Forward, Round and Round: A Case for Ethnographic Studies in Migration." *Progress in Human Geography*, Volume 24(1): 71-89.

Mhone, G.C.Z. 1995. "The Social Dimensions of Adjustment (SDA) Programme in Zimbabwe: A Critical Review and Assessment." In *Adjustment and Social Sector Restructuring*, edited by Jessica Vivian. London: Frank Cass.

Mohan, G. 2006. "Embedded Cosmopolitanism and the Politics of Obligation: The Ghanaian Diaspora and Development." *Environment and Planning A*, Volume 38(5): 867–83.

Nursing and Midwifery Council. 2008. "Statistical Analysis of the Register: 1 April 2007 to 31 March 2008." www,.nmc-uk.org, accessed March 31, 2008.

Nursing and Midwifery Council. "Statistical Analysis of the Register, 1 April 2001 to 31 March 2002". www.nmc-uk.org, accessed March 31, 2008.

O'Brien, T. 2007. "Overseas Nurses in the National Health Service: a Process of Deskilling." *Journal of Clinical Nursing*, Volume 16: 2229–36.

Okome, M.O. 2007. The Contradictions of Globalization: Causes of Contemporary African Immigration to the United States of America. In *The New African Diaspora in North America: Trends, Community Building and Adaptation*, edited by Kwadwo Konadu-Agyemang, Baffour K. Takyi, and John A. Arthur. Lanham, MD: Lexington Books.

Raghuram, P. 2004. "The Difference that Skills Make: Gender, Family Migration Strategies and Regulated Labour Markets." *Journal of Ethnic and Migration Studies*, Volume 30(2): 303–21.

Salganik, M.J. and Heckathorn, D.D. 2004. "Sampling and Estimation in Hidden Populations Using Respondent-Driven Sampling." *Sociological Methodology*, Volume 34: 193–239.

Saravia, N.G. and Miranda, J.F. 2004. "Plumbing the Brain Drain." *Bulletin of the World Health Organization*, Volume 82(8): 608–15.

Sassen, S. 1991. *The Global City: New York, London, Tokyo*. Princeton, N.J.: Princeton University Press.

Steele, R. 2007. "UK: No Quick Fix to Workforce Shortage." *Australian Nursing Journal*, Volume 15(6): 18.

Yeboah, I.E.A. 2008. "Immigrant Trajectories and Settlement Patterns." *Black African Neo-Diaspora. Ghanaian Immigrant Experiences in the Greater Cincinnati, Ohio, Area*. Lanham, MD: Lexington Books.

Chapter Eight

Relationship among Blacks in the Diaspora: African, and Caribbean Immigrants and American-Born Blacks

In a January 1915 letter to the *Washington Post*, the African American Booker T. Washington, head of Tuskegee Institute, made an "appeal to the American Congress and to the people of the United States in favor of fair play and justice in connection with the immigration bill now pending before the United States Senate which by amendment excludes from coming into this country any person of African descent" (Washington, 1915). He went on to emphatically state that the bill was "unjust, unreasonable, and unnecessary. It is unnecessary because only a few thousand people of African descent enter this country annually. Practically all of these that do come are mainly from the West Indies and almost none from the continent of Africa" (Washington, 1915). Washington went on to cite the 1910 census, claiming that in that year only 40,319 blacks in the United States were foreign born, out of which 473 were from Africa. He further noted that the immigration bill "puts an unnecessary slight upon colored people by classing them with alien criminals" (Washington, 1915). Washington argued that the bill put "unnecessary hardship" on countries like Liberia, Cuba, and Haiti by restricting the entry of citizens from those countries. Those blacks that had immigrated to the United States from the Caribbean and Africa, in his view, had "proved as a whole to be a law-abiding intelligent, industrious class" (Washington, 1915).

Recent narratives exploring the relationship between blacks from Africa and the Caribbean with native-born black Americans have constructed it as characterized by friction, tension, rivalries, and sometimes hostility. Blacks from the Caribbean and Africa had been arriving as immigrants to the United States long before Washington commented on their presence in 1915. Although the large African presence in the United States resulted from the involuntary migration of men and women enslaved on the continent since

161

the seveneenth century, beginning in the nineteenth century West Indians and Africans from the continent came in small numbers to the United States.

During the era of slavery blacks from the Caribbean were a large component of the black population in the United States. Many Africans brought to the early American colonies in the early eighteenth century came from the West Indies. (Hine and Hine, 2000). At the beginning of the twentieth century a significant voluntary migration of Caribbean blacks to the United States occurred. Despite the fact that restrictive legislation such as The Immigration Act of 1924 limited the number of non-European immigrants, black West Indian immigrants continued to come to the United States. Although the number of immigrants dropped from 10,630 in 1924 to 321 in 1925, after World War II, Caribbean immigration increased and continued to rise. Economic and political conditions in the various Caribbean islands, and increasing economic opportunities for Blacks in the United States, stimulated increased migration (*In Motion*, 2011). These Caribbean immigrants were professional and skilled workers, who settled in states with large urban populations, like New York and Florida. New York City received a steady flow of Caribbean immigrants over the course of the twentieth century. They founded social, cultural, and religious institutions, and were active in political movements. According to the 2000 census, 60 percent of foreign-born blacks were from the Caribbean, making up 10 percent of the foreign born population in the United States. Today there are an estimated 3 million Caribbean born immigrants in the United States (McKinnon and Bennett, 2005). Perceived as black by the larger society, Caribbean immigrants often found common cause with native-born blacks, rallying around social and political causes.

Although West Indian immigrants were some of the earliest black immigrants to come to the United States, a small number of Africans also came. Throughout the late nineteenth century Africans trickled into the United States, largely interacting with African Americans, and the small Caribbean population already there. One of the earliest groups from Africa came as students in the late nineteenth, and early twentieth century. Many of them attended black institutions of higher learning, and frequent interaction with black Americans allowed for exchanges on various levels. Africans often came to study in the United States with hopes of returning to their homeland upon completion of their studies. At institutions like Fisk, Howard, Lincoln, and Livingstone colleges, African students interacted with their native-born American counterparts (Williams, 1980). These interactions were often guided by prevailing stereotypes of Africa held by Americans in general.

The predominant view held by most Americans, including black Americans, was of Africa as the "Dark Continent." Images and representations were largely negative, portraying the continent as a savage, barbaric land, needing uplift from those more civilized. American churches and missions, in the hopes of producing missionaries to serve in Africa, had, in fact, sponsored many of the black students in American colleges in this era. By the late nineteenth century major black churches were sending African-American missionaries to serve in Africa. Because of the difficulties of adjusting to the African climate, like their white counterparts, black churches began training native-born Africans to serve as missionaries in their native land. African students came to study in the United States under the auspices of African American missions. These early students offered African Americans the first opportunity to see that the prevailing stereotypes about Africa and Africans were wrong. Most Africans coming to the United States in that era, particularly those from British colonies would have been educated within colonial systems or missionary schools. They would have been westernized, largely Christian, with some knowledge of the society they were entering. In fact, in 1899, Bishop Henry McNeill Turner of the African Methodist Episcopal (AME) Zion church noted, "everybody appears to be amazed at their learning, refinement, and general intelligence. So many of our people in this country believe all Africans are mere heathens, that they are paralyzed with surprise to find such boys coming" (Turner cited in Williams, 1980:239).

James Kwegyir Agyeman Aggrey was perhaps the most famous African to arrive in the United States in that era. Born in the Gold Coast (later Ghana), Aggrey attended mission and colonial schools in that British colony, excelling in his studies. He soon came to the notice of missionaries and colonial officials. In 1898 he was sponsored by Bishop Bryan Small of the AME Zion church, arriving in the United States that year to study at Livingstone College in North Carolina. Aggrey completed his studies at Livingstone, later becoming a member of faculty and administrator in the college. Together with his wife, Rose Douglass, an African American woman from Virginia they settled in North Carolina where he lived until his death in 1927. Clearly, his relationship with African Americans was characterized by mutual respect, as is evident from the many outpourings of grief from African Americans after his death. The bibliophile Arthur Schaumburg, in remembering Aggrey, pointed out his influence and legacy in the United States, describing his contributions to black Americans: "At a native American school, Livingston [sic] College, set in the panoramic mountains of Salisbury, N.C., he received the milk of kindness and remained with his own people, later his loved joined that of an American Rose and made his stay permanent among us" (*Aggrey Papers*).

Like Aggrey, Orishatukeh Faduma came to the United States as a student. Born William Davis in Sierra Leone, Faduma came to the United States in 1890 to study at Yale Divinity School in New Haven Connecticut. After completing his degree in 1894 he took a position in the American South.

He married Henrietta Adams, a black American woman from Georgia. He taught at the Peabody Academy, a black institution in Troy, North Carolina for seventeen years, and serving as a missionary and educator to African Americans in North Carolina for more than fifty years. In 1913, Faduma worked closely with the African American Chief Alfred Sam and his Back to Africa movement, encouraging African Americans to return to Africa (Okonkwo, 1983:26). Faduma himself never returned. He was naturalized in 1902, spending the rest of his life in the United States. He died in North Carolina in 1946 (Moore, 1987:260). Both Faduma and Aggrey, like many Africans in that era, lived in a segregated south, and operated within a world in which, by virtue of the color of their skin, they were thought to be inferior. Both men adapted to their lives as black men in a racially segregated nation, at a time when discrimination and racism were leveled at men and women of African descent. Both men lived and worked among less privileged African Americans and saw it as their responsibility and duty to enhance their lives and improve their condition, with Faduma referring to them as "kith and kin." Faduma's contributions among African Americans were recognized in a 1904 publication. In an article profiling him, Faduma was lauded for his contributions to African Americans and for his missionary work. The article noted: "We question if this native African could have made a better investment of his powers had he remained in Africa. Africa is here" (*The American Missionary*, 1904:16). Although Aggrey and Faduma settled in the South, a few Africans lived in northern cities like New York.

Over the years, blacks from Africa continued to migrate to the United States for various reasons. While relations with African Americans were not always positive, Africans found more commonalities with blacks from the Caribbean and African Americans, than with the larger white society. For the most part, in these early years, Africans faced the same discrimination from white Americans as their native born counterparts. Although some blacks from the Caribbean and Africa sought to highlight their difference and distinctiveness from black Americans, what white Americans saw was their black skin. On the other hand, African Americans, not infrequently, welcomed them as brethren. In a 1971 interview, Bishop William Jacob Walls, an alumnus of Livingstone College remembered that "Africans were not looked down upon as inferior by this campus" (Williams, 1980:239).

Many years after Aggrey and Faduma came to the United States as students, Kwame Nkrumah and Nnamdi Azikiwe, future leaders of newly independent African nations, came as students to Lincoln University, a black college in Pennsylvania. Long an institution welcoming to Africans students, both men noted the great influence the college and its black American students exerted on them. Black colleges in the period before African nations gained their independence served to politicize young Africans coming to the United States. During the 1920s African American and Caribbean leaders influenced Africans like John Dube, Solomon Plaatje, and D.D.T. Jabavu. All these men, who later played a role in the growth of the South African Native National Congress (SANNC), had studied in the United States and been influenced by African Americans like Carter G. Woodson, W.E.B. Dubois, and Booker T. Washington (She person, 1960:304).

Likewise Alfred Xuma, later to become a prominent leader in the (SANNC), which had changed its name into the African National Congress (ANC) in 1923, came as a student to Tuskegee, a college in a county with a significant black American population. (Ralston 1973:72-93). In the 1920s when the Jamaican born Marcs Garvey formed his Universal Negro Improvement Association (UNIA), the black nationalist organization, Caribbean-born, African-born, and native-born blacks were all drawn to this movement, for he spoke out not only against racial segregation and discrimination in the United States, but against colonialism in Africa and the Caribbean, calling for blacks around the world to rally around Africa and unite. Garvey urged blacks in the Western Hemisphere to consider a return to the motherland Africa. While this call was unrealistic for many, and his mission of sending large numbers of blacks to Africa failed, Garvey succeeded in politicizing blacks from Africa, The Caribbean and the United States and had significant influence on members of these groups (James, 1998:136-137).

Many Africans who had come to study in the United States also had tremendous influence among the African American population. For example, as early as the 1920s there is evidence of the many influences African Americans exerted on Africans, but also the inspiration Africans in the United States gave to black Americans. Simbini Mamba Nkomo, from the British colony of Rhodesia, was a professor of African history at Tuskegee, having received his degree from a University in Ohio. While a student Nkomo had formed an African student organization in an attempt to rally African students in the United States to help with Africa's uplift. At Tuskegee, Nkomo also succeeded in creating strong ties with black Americans, and had tremendous influence on his black American students (King, 1970:24). Likewise, James Aggrey was well regarded by his African-American students. Aggrey graduated from Livingstone in 1902, continuing to work on campus as a professor and administrator. As a teacher he was popular among the students he taught, and had a "great reputation." W. J. Trent, a classmate of Aggrey, who later became the president of Livingstone College observed that Aggrey's influence "was very precious and had a great deal to do with the improvement of the moral and spiritual conditions of the whole college life" (*Aggrey papers*, 1942). Aggrey also spent many years working among rural African-American farmers in Salisbury, North Carolina, pastoring two black churches in that state. His parishioners, mostly poor illiterate rural farmers and laborers, had a high regard for him, and his work in the community. Working with these communities was one of the most fulfilling aspects of Aggrey's work in the United States, for "it took him out of an academic atmosphere and introduced him to the actualities of life led by the American Negro" (Smith, 1930:85).

The reality of being black in the United States was a discovery many Africans made on arrival. For example, a young African woman living in New York City in the 1930s commented on the disparity between white and black life in America. Describing her first visit to Harlem she observed: "To me it was a strange Negro world filled with Negroes, no longer African, but with the definite stamp of Western civilization. What an over-crowded place! How inferior to those other areas I learned were for whites!" (Reid 1939:190). Indeed, black immigrants coming to the United States in the late nineteenth and early twentieth century, soon came to understand how the racial hierarchy operated. Ira Reid discusses at great length the social adjustment problems for black immigrants. They were alien by law, but also part of a racial minority, with a cultural heritage "vastly different from that of the American Negro" (Reid, 1939:35). The black immigrant had to "adjust in a three-fold way from the point of view of *nationality, mores,* and the *social role played by his racial group"* (Reid, 1939:36). Describing the position of new black immigrants in the 1930s Reid maintains that:

> The Negro immigrant enters the United States in the dual role of Negro and immigrant. Moving into a few centers of Negro population in large numbers, threatening the existing order of Negro adjustments he brings the bases for intra-racial conflict. One factor prevents the conflict from becoming intense, the visibility of the Negro immigrant is low. The external characteristics of Negroes, native and foreign, are the same. Looking alike, they are not inherently estranged; differing in mores they are isolated (Reid, 1939:215).

In the wake of World War II, as nationalist movements in Africa took root, so too did calls for change in the United States from black Americans. African and African-American war veterans returned to their respective homelands, calling for change and more equality, whether in Birmingham, Alabama, or the Gold Coast, West Africa. Africans in American colleges often engaged in activities with their African American classmates, which, more often than not, led to solidarity. In his autobiography Kwame Nkrumah noted the strong bonds he created with Caribbean and African-American students at Lincoln University. Recognizing their commonalities, and the status assigned them by white America, they sought each other out, seeking assistance when needed.

Nkrumah goes on to tell the story of how he was helped by a fellow student from the Caribbean during a break from college, with no place to stay:

> I was wandering down Seventh Avenue in Harlem wondering where I could turn next when I suddenly ran into a fellow student from Lincoln who came from Demerara in British Guiana. I told him of my difficulties; no money, no job and nowhere to go. "Don't worry old chap," he said encouragingly, "I think I can solve the accommodation problem as a start." He explained that he knew a West Indian family who were extremely kind and sympathetic and that if he went along and put my case before them, he felt they might help me out. Sure enough, by the time I had told my story tears were in the eyes of the womenfolk who offered me their small spare room, and added that I was not to worry about payment until I managed to find a job (cited by Tolbert 2001:344).

Nkrumah also had the opportunity of mixing with African Americans outside academic settings. While a student at Lincoln, and the University of Pennsylvania he worked in segregated shipyards in Pennsylvania (*Penn Digital Exhibition*). Many of his coworkers were black Americans, and like Aggrey before him, Nkrumah saw the disparities between black and white in America.

For many Africans, the issues facing African Americans came to be theirs while they were living in the United States. In the period before the 1960s, perhaps because their numbers were small, and because of the hostile environment in which they often found themselves, Africans in the United States found themselves living mostly alongside, and among, black Americans. Although they may have held particular views and stereotypes of African Americans before arriving, as they lived in the United States for extended periods, they relied on them for an understanding of the society into which they had come. Furthermore, many Africans in this era had no intention of staying in the United States. They saw themselves as sojourners, their stay as temporary, and the discomfort of living in a racially stratified society was often seen as a cross they had to bear in order to receive the benefits of the education for which they had come. The goal of these early Africans in America was to use the skills they had acquired to develop their homelands in Africa.

The 1965 Hart Cellar immigration bill would change the size, composition, and demographic profile of the African population in the United States. This act, which liberalized American immigration laws, by removing national origin restrictions, would change, to some extent, the nature of the relationship between Africans and African Americans. Significantly more liberal than earlier immigration laws, the 1965 law with its quota system, allowed more black immigrants to enter the United States. Citizens of newly African independent states eschewed the nations of their former colonizers, choosing to seek educational and other opportunities in the United States. Coming at the height of the Civil Rights movement, Africans who came to study in American colleges often found themselves in the midst of agitation, civil rights protests and marches, sit-ins, and other attempts by African Americans, particularly in the South, to desegregate public spaces and institutions. As the United States increasingly became a desegregated society, and one that was more open to foreigners, Africans continued to arrive on its shores in larger numbers. The 1970s and particularly the 1980s, following the 1980 Refugee Act, saw the African population in America grow to numbers never before seen. The composition of African immigrants also changed. Africans coming to the United States in earlier years had come mainly from English speaking African colonies. Newer immigrants following 1965 came from all over the continent. Francophone Africans came in larger numbers, as did Africans from other non-speaking countries in Africa. Following the 1980 Refugee Act the composition of African immigrants has also changed. Where earlier immigrants were likely to be highly skilled and educated the large refugee populations, from places like Somalia, were largely rural, often lacking skills and formal education.

As the number and composition of African immigrants has grown, so have the perceptions that they, like immigrants from the Caribbean, are different from African Americans. While during the era of segregation black immigrants were often forced to live alongside black Americans, the new liberal and relatively tolerable post-civil rights America has given more recent immigrants the opportunity to live apart from, and distance themselves from African-American populations. These black immigrants are no longer settling in traditional gateway cities like New York or Miami, but more and more are attracted to suburban areas, or in rural areas as in the case of Somalis in Maine. Yet even amidst the racial stereotypes and views held by some whites, some black immigrants prefer settling among mixed or largely white populations, believing that assimilating with African Americans would hinder their socioeconomic advancement (Obiakor and Grant, 2002). African immigrants also fear the loss of ethnic identity, highlighting their distinctive heritage and noting that as immigrants they have no understanding of, and therefore are less likely to identify with post-slavery issues than, native-born American blacks (Freeman, 2002). As one young immigrant, interviewed for an Arizona news article stated "I don't associate myself with slavery" (*Scottsdale Tribune*, 2005). The article notes that "these new African-Americans lack ties to American slavery and the inner city culture frequently associated with black America. Many grew up in middle–class, two-parent families and have access to social networks that include doctors, nurses, engineers, professors and business executives" (*Scottsdale Tribune*, 2005). Nonetheless, urban areas remain important destinations for black immigrants. In fact, black immigrants often choose to settle in areas with significant black populations because they recognize their status as a minority, and understand the consequences of ethnicity and race.

African immigrants recognize the struggles of African Americans in providing the world into which they came. One immigrant remarked: "We feel that those African-Americans who were here before were the pioneers. . . . If it wasn't for Martin Luther King, Jr. and the civil rights movement, we wouldn't be here in the first place" (*Scottsdale Tribune*, 2005). The recognition of that fact is something African immigrants often come to as they spend more years in the United States, and as they become more than sojourners. As one scholar has noted, in their bid to acculturate to a racially stratified society, "black migrants, unlike light-skinned migrants, also face an entirely different set of issues directly related to fitting in with American society—they must reconstruct and redefine their identity in terms of the American society's system of race relations and hierarchy" (Benson, 2006:221) This they find difficult to do. While black immigrants, in their attempt to cope with the racial hierarchy in the United States have frequently claimed a "foreign status," as Arthur has noted, they find it hard to "insulate themselves from white racial stereotypes and discrimination" (Arthur, 2000:4).

More recent African immigrants unlike their predecessors have traditionally been "disconnected from civic engagements and more importantly remain divided from their black American counterparts on issues of race solidarity" (Lenoir and Kidane, 2007:50) As one immigrant noted "African immigrants sometimes struggle to fit into black American culture that has been shaped by civil disobedience and peaceful protests. He said African immigrants contribute financially to these efforts when they can, but many hesitate to speak out on race issues because they fear deportation or showing disrespect to their adopted homeland" (*Scottsdale Tribune*, 2005). They have, largely, not integrated themselves into African American institutions and organizations, often creating separate ethnic, hometown, or country associations. This reluctance to identify fully with African Americans has sometimes led to tensions between African Americans and black immigrants. For example, at the turn of the twenty first century several incidents in New York City and Atlanta, Georgia, highlight the differences between the two groups. In Harlem, an Ivorian street vendor frequently harassed by black Americans lashed out in return, resulting in a street brawl (Cunningham, 2005). While these kinds of incidents are infrequent, they nevertheless point at continued misunderstandings between African Americans and black immigrants. Stereotypical views and representations of Africa continue to be shown in mainstream media. Negative images and ideas about Africa still persist among African Americans, largely because African American students still are not taught much about Africa, and when exposed to Africans fall back on old stereotypes of Africa as the "Dark Continent" (Walker and Rasamimanana, 1993). A need to distance, and feelings of shame often characterize African-American attitudes toward the continent. Also at the heart of African-American suspicion of black immigrants is the belief that they are competing for jobs and other opportunities and resources with them. Interviewed by Jennifer Cunningham, John Bracey, professor of African-American studies at the University of Massachusetts, remarked, "Africans are seen as another immigrant group that is pushing past African Americans" (Cunningham, 2005), A survey done in 2006 showed that 34 percent African Americans, compared to 25 percent of whites believe that immigrants take jobs from American citizens. This is particularly true of black immigrants who some African Americans believe are given preference for employment by white employers. In an article in the February 18, 2007 edition of the *Los Angeles Times*, titled *"Redefining 'black': Obama's Candidacy Spotlight Divide between Native Black Culture and African Immigrants,"* Louis Chude-Sokei (2007) points out that "whites have historically tended to regard black immigrants as a model minority within a troublesome native-born black population. A good proportion of immigrants tend to be better educated than African Americans, don't have the 'chip' or racial resentment on their shoulder and exhibit the classic immigrant optimism about assimilation into the mainstream culture." He further notes that many whites "exploit these differences to magnify the problems of African Americans while avoiding charges of racism. And because these differences often result in greater employment and more educational opportunities for immigrants and their descendants, they also feed tensions between native and immigrant blacks."

On the other hand, misconceptions about African Americans remain among Africans in the United States as well. The belief perpetuated by the media and other sources that African Americans are not hardworking, and frequently fall back on the history of racism in America to make excuses still persists among some Africans. As Bill Fletcher, president of Trans-Africa Forum commented "Many African Americans are embarrassed or ambivalent about Africa…and many Africans have misconceptions about the opportunities available to African-Americans. They often fail to appreciate what the African-Americans have gone through" (Cunningham, 2005). The attempt by black immigrants to maintain a distinct identity from traditional African Americans allows them the hope of protecting their children from racialization in American society. They do this by settling in particular neighborhoods and cities as they recognize that an important factor hurting a chance of success is residence in residential concentrations of one's ethnic group or race.

Some Africans make an effort to assimilate into American society, involving themselves in local politics, business, and professional sports. Africans settling in urban areas are more likely to be in closer to African Americans, resulting in some tensions but also providing the opportunity for the groups to learn about each other, and in some instances, to work together in both social and political causes, and also on an individual level. While misunderstandings persist between black immigrants and African Americans, in recent years, as in years past these groups have cooperated with each other rather than highlighting their differences. Arguably, this is due to the increasing visibility of Africans and Caribbean immigrants. In most major metropolitan areas, and even in smaller suburbs, African businesses and organizations can now be found as established institutions. Whether the hair braiding salons or Senegalese restaurants in Harlem, New York, or the many African grocery stores in Woodbridge, Virginia, these businesses run by black immigrants have become familiar part of the landscape. They are patronized not only by other Africans, but also by African Americans, Caribbean Americans, and black immigrants from other parts of the diaspora. In other words, the relationship between black immigrants and American born blacks is not always characterized by tension. In her fascinating study on intermarriage among Haitian immigrants, Regina Jackson (2007: 219-220) cautions us not to overstate the tensions by putting too much "emphasis on conflict, competition, or antagonism between immigrant blacks and native Americans," noting that the often "pronounced ethnic boundaries that divide black Americans are permeable." By looking at intermarriage between these communities, she illustrates that social interactions between African Americans and black immigrants is ongoing. Like Aggrey and Faduma, black immigrants are also intermarrying in greater numbers with African Americans. The children of these unions frequently identify with both parts of their heritage. Furthermore, children of black immigrants born in the United States, or brought here as young children, more often than not, think of themselves as African Americans, identifying with that culture, often with some resistance from their parents. However, the American born children of African immigrants have often been more successful at understanding American society than their parents have, as evident in their increased participation in civic and political issues.

More formal ties and connections are also being created between African Americans and black migrants. Just as Booker T. Washington spoke out against the 1915 immigration bill, in 2006 a group of black American and black immigrants came together in Oakland, California to form the Black Alliance for Just Immigration (BAJI) to "support the demands of the immigrant rights movement and to engage African Americas in a dialogue about the underlying issues of race and economic status that frame U.S. immigration policy" (Lenoir and Kidane, 2007:50). Recent events illustrate attempts by African immigrants and African Americans to recognize their commonalities, as they come together for mutual benefit and advancement. In June 2005 the

African Catholic Ministry of the Roman Catholic Archdiocese in Indianapolis sponsored an event that brought together African Americans and Africans. "A Celebration of the African Family Tree" allowed both groups to learn about elements of each other's cultures and to recognize their common ancestry (Perry, 2005). Perhaps the most high profile and visible face of this solidarity came on February 5, 1999, when Amadou Diallo, a Guinean immigrant was shot to death by New York City policemen. African Americans joined Africans in rallying and protesting the injustice. In March of that year several prominent African Americans were arrested at a New York City demonstration as they demanded accountability in the Diallo shooting. Among them was Kweisi Mfume, then-president of the NAACP, State Senator David Patterson, and some members of the New York City Council (*Chicago Citizen*, 1999). After his death Diallo's mother Kadiatou Diallo formed a foundation in October 1999 called the Ahmadou Diallo Foundation to promote racial healing, with several African Americans on its board. Wheeler street, the street in the Bronx where Diallo was killed has been renamed Amadou Diallo Place, and African Americans now have an increasing awareness of the African immigrant experience.

The relationship between blacks from Africa and the Caribbean with native-born blacks has been long and continuous. Since the late nineteenth and early twentieth century, black immigrants have been arriving in the United States. Although at times they may have seemed invisible to the larger society, black immigrants were never invisible to African Americans among whom they settled, worked with, married, and who were often their entry point into the society. Since the mid-twentieth century the increasing number of black immigrants has changed the demographic profile of black America. Coming from a broader socioeconomic background, and from wider regions, African immigrants can be found living in all parts of the United States, from Portland, Maine to Cincinnati, Ohio, to Laurel, Maryland. Although in adjusting to American society, they have experienced difficulty in assimilating, the presence of established native-born black populations has been beneficial to black immigrants. The relationship between the two groups, though sometimes fraught with tension, has largely been positive. As more black immigrants arrive in the United States the definition of African American will expand as black immigrants and native-born blacks find common cause.

REFERENCES

Arthur, J. A. 2000. *Invisible sojourners: African immigrant diaspora in the United States.* Westport, CT: Praeger.

Benson, J. E. 2006. "Exploring the racial identities of black immigrants in the United States," *Sociological Forum.* Volume 21 (2): 219–47.

Clark H. D., William C. H. and Stanley H. 2000. *The African-American Odyssey.* Upper Saddle River, N.J.: Pearson Prentice Hall.

Cunningham, J. 2005. "Tension between Africans and African Americans surface again." *New York Amsterdam News.* Volume 96 (6).

Freeman, L. 2002. "Does spatial assimilation work for black immigrants in the U.S."? *Urban Studies.* Volume 39(11): 1983–2003.

Jackson, R. O. 2007. "Beyond social distancing: Intermarriage and ethnic boundaries among black Americans in Boston." In Shaw-Taylor, Y. and Steven A. T. *The other African Americans: Contemporary African and Caribbean immigrants in the United States* (eds.). Lanham, MD: Rowman and Littlefield Publishers, 217–53.

James, W. 1999. *Holding aloft the banner of Ethiopia: Caribbean radicalism in early twentieth century America.* London and New York: Verso.

King, K. J. 1970. "African students in Negro American colleges: Notes on the good African." *Phylon.* Volume 31 (1):16–30.

Lenoir, G. and Nunu, K. 2007. "African Americans and immigrants: Shall we hang together or hang separately." *The Black Scholar.* Volume 37: 50–52.

Moses , N. M. Jr. 1987. *Orishatukeh Faduma: An intellectual biography of a liberal evangelical pan-Africanist, 1857-1946*, Ph.D. dissertation, Union Theological Seminary.

Obiakor, F. E. and Patrick A. G. 2002. *Foreign-Born African Americans: Silenced voices in the discourse on race* (eds.). New York: Nova Science Publishers, Inc.

Okonkwo, R. 1983. "Orishatukeh Faduma: A man of two worlds." *The Journal of Negro History.* Volume 68(1): 24–36.

Ralston, R. D. 1973. "American episodes in the making of an African leader: A case study of Alfred B. Xuma (1893-1962)." *The International Journal of African Historical Studies.* Volume. 6 (1): 72–93.

Reid, I. deAugustine. 1939. *The Negro immigrant: His background, characteristics and social adjustment, 1899-1937.* New York: Columbia University Press.

She person, G. 1960. "Notes on Negro American influences on the emergence of African nationalism." *The Journal of African History.* Volume 1 (2): 299–312.

Smith, E. W. 1930. *Aggrey of Africa: A study in Black and White.* New York: Richard R. Smith, Inc.

Tolbert, Emory J. 2001. Extract from the autobiography of Kwame Nkrumah quoted in *Perspectives on the African Diaspora. Volume Two, since 1800* (ed.). Boston: Houghton Mifflin.

Walker, S. S. and Jennifer R. 1993. "Tarzan in the classroom: How 'educational' films mythologize Africa and miseducate Americans." *The Journal of Negro Education.* Volume 62 (1): 3–23.

Williams, W. L. 1980. "Ethnic relations of African students in United States, with Black Americans, 1870–1900." *The Journal of Negro History.* Volume 65 (3): 228–49.

DIGITAL AND ARCHIVAL SOURCES

Aggrey papers, Box 147-1, Folder 15. Howard University, Moorland-Spingarn Research Center (Washington, D.C.) NIDS Fiche #: 4.72.131 NUCMC Number: DCLV96-A502. Pamphlet. "Know This of Aggrey": 1942 commemoration of Aggrey, celebrating the fortieth year of his graduation from Livingstone and twentieth of MA from Columbia. By West African students union of Great Britain and African students association of USA.

Chude-Sokei, L. February 18, 2007. Redefining black, Obama's candidacy spotlights the divide between native black culture and African immigrants in *Los Angeles Times*. http://www.latimes.com/news/printedition/opinion/la-op-chude-sokei18feb18,0,1047776.story. Accessed January 28, 2011.

Daryl, J. September 17, 2005. Immigrants and new U.S citizens question race -category label. *Scottsdale Tribune.* Accessed December 2010.

In Motion. The African American migration experience. http://www.inmotionaame.org/migrations/. Accessed February 11, 2011.

Kwame Nkrumah at Penn: A Digital Exhibition, http://www.archives.upenn.edu/people/notables/nkrumah/nkrumah_exhibit.htm. Accessed February 13, 2011.

McKinnon, J. D. and Claudette E. B. n.d. We the People: Blacks in the United States (www.census.gov/prod/2005pubs/censr-25.pdf). Accessed February 3, 2011 *Chicago Citizen*. March 25, 1999. NAACP's Mfume and 58 activists arrested at New York City police protest. http://www.highbeam.com/doc/1P1-23661867.html. Accessed January 28, 2011.

Perry, B. A. June 3, 2005. Historic celebration to build bridges among local residents and African immigrants. *Indianapolis Recorder*. http://www.highbeam.com/doc/1P1-112091845.html. Accessed January 28, 2011.

Washington Post. January 17, 1915. *Protests Alien Bill; Booker T. Washington Says It Is Unfair to His Race. Few African Immigrants*, accessed through Proquest Historical Newspapers, March 17, 2011. Accessed March 2, 2011. Rev. Orishatukeh Faduma. *The American Missionary*. Vol. LVIII (1): 13-16. Accessed September 2010 in Google Books.

Chapter Nine

Contextualizing the Attitudes of African Americans Toward U.S. Immigration Policies: Some Preliminary Findings

INTRODUCTION

African migration is a growing feature of the new migration to the United States. A number of factors have spurred this trend. Among these are the end of colonization and the agitation for political independence, the proliferation of geo-political conflicts in the region often causing population displacement, economic malaise, the gradual incorporation of Africa into the global economy, the surge in family reunifications, and the growth in the size of Africa's educated middle class (Arthur, 2000; Okpewho and Nzegwu, 2009; Takougang, 1995; Gordon, 1998; Yeboah, 2008; and Apraku, 1991). The Africans are arriving from Nigeria, Ghana, Kenya, South Africa, Sudan, Senegal, and Liberia. Others are coming as refugees from war-torn Somalia.

Upon their entry to the United States, the African émigrés encounter not only the white majority society, but also black Americans with whom their share physical traits and varying degrees of cultural institutions. Together with immigrants coming to the United States from Latin America and Asia, the African immigrants become part of the national discourse and debate about the importance and impact of immigration in American society. The central question forming this debate is whether the country can continue to accept more immigrants. Another issue is what to do with the 12 million or so undocumented persons already living in the country, working, and paying taxes with children some of whom are American citizens.

Immigration has become a hotly contested and nationally polarizing issue. The issues forming this debate are as varied as the different groups representing a broad spectrum of the American body polity. Of central concern is the impact of large-scale immigration on poorly-educated, low-waged, unskilled workers in America, particularly urban blacks. As more and more immigrants

175

enter the country (legally and illegally), competition over scarce jobs, housing, healthcare, and education intensifies. In major cities across the United
States, Latinos, Asians, and African immigrants continue to displace blacks
in once black-held sectors such as beauty parlors, taxi driving, janitorial and
custodial services, parking ramp attendants, meat packaging, tax preparation
services, and community family-owned grocery stores. For inner-city and
poorly-educated whites in particular, these concerns are expressed and felt as
more immigrants compete and are successful in carving economic niche for
themselves in fields such as landscape, home remodeling, construction, and
hospitality services. Some of the consternations about immigrant (as Portes
and Rumbaut, 1990 had long noted) is based on xenophobia and irrational
fear that immigrants take-away jobs from American citizens. The public antipathy toward both legal and illegal immigration is not just confined to the
United States (see for example, Cohen, 2006; Huntington, 2004).

On their part, blacks perceive that centuries of economic racism, coupled
with institutionalized denial of access to opportunities, further aggravates their
economic disadvantages in the United States as new immigrant groups flood
labor markets to compete for dwindling jobs. The economic displacement of
African Americans by newly-arriving immigrants has been noted by a number
of researchers such as Bouvier and Grant (1994), Brimelow (1995); Fairchild
and Fairchild, 1994; Beck (1996); Cose (1992). This economic displacement
and erosion of black economic status reached its zenith and coincided with the
mass migration of Europeans to the United States. The strain on black community resources stemming from international migration were noticeable in
the larger metropolitan cities in the Northeast and Midwest where blacks had
migrated to following emancipation from slavery. As black resentments grew
over the inundation of their communities by immigrants, so did their displacement in sectors of the economy in which they had exercised some control
(Hellwig, 1974; Shankman, 1982; and Massey and Denton, 1993).

According to Bowser (2007), black America's middle and lower classes
are still reeling from deindustrialization and the outsourcing of jobs to
suburban communities and even outside the United States. The impact of
deindustrialization on America's urban and inner-city poor was noted by
Wilson (1987; 1996). As the processes associated with economic dislocation
persist, a disproportionate number of blacks from both lower and middle
class backgrounds continue to suffer relative to their white suburban middle
class counterparts. Of particular concern is the growth in the size of the black
underclass poor whose unemployment rate is three to four times that of the
national average of 8.3 percent. The economic dislocation of the black underclass was noted by Moynihan (1965; 1986). Today, social scientists continue
to explain the pervasiveness of entrenched black urban underclass poor and

their worsening economic plight (see for example, Phil, 2003; Pinkney, 2000; Schaefer, 2000; Ross and Yinger, 2002).

The inability of blacks to pool their capital sources to mount an economic challenge to immigrant "invasion" of their economic spaces is a major source of consternation for many blacks, particularly those finishing high school with no plans to pursue post-secondary education. The concern about the penetration of immigrant-owned businesses in their communities is further aggravated by the gap in financial resources between immigrants and American-born blacks. Immigrant enclaves and co-ethnics often combine their resources to set up small businesses. Many American blacks do not have the resources to compete on equal footing with the new immigrants. Social scientists have investigated the comparative advantages that immigrants settling in black American and minority communities generally have over the native population in terms of human, social, and economic capital (see for example, Waldinger, 2008; Portes and Bach, 1985; Portes and Zhou, 1993; Waters and Eschbach, 1995; Valdez, 2009; Bonacich and Modell, 1980). On his part, Owusu (2000) attributes the economic and social inroads of foreign-born immigrant families to the immigrant ethnic, national, and tribal associations that immigrants form to provide them economic leverage and cultural resources to enable them establish businesses in largely African American communities.

Of equal consternation to Americans is whether to allow taxpayers money to be spent in providing social services for undocumented immigrants and their children. Among urban, poorly-educated, and low-income blacks, America's continued immigration debacle continue to affect many households who are experiencing a job-market squeeze. As the recessionary downturn of 2008 persist, young blacks under age fifty years without a college education are finding it very difficult to transition from a manufacturing to a service-based economy. According to U.S. Census data for 2010, the urban unemployment for black youth is currently estimated at over 30 percent or at least four times the national average. When they are able to find work, urban black youths in high immigrant concentration destinations often face stiff competition from Latino and Asian American youths. For those without basic skills and high school education, the economic consequences for job displacement are very high. These groups of black youths stand a good chance of being chronically employed (U.S. Census, 2010). Despite the protests by organized labor to protect American jobs for blacks and other minority union employees under the b*racero* program, ultimately the program also caused the displacement and job loss for many urban blacks as waves of Mexicans came to the United States to compete in sectors of the economy where blacks had historically held the upper hand. And as the rate of acquisition of naturalization and citizenship and political activism expanded among Mexicans, so did their economic clout, particularly in states such as Texas, California, Illinois, Nevada, and California (Pachon, H. and DeSipio, 1994).

A related aspect of the public debate is whether the United States should allow guest workers from its southern neighbors to enter the country to work in the agricultural and food production sector performing jobs which the proponents of this measure argue that many Americans, including blacks are not willing to perform. Closely paralleling the guest worker initiative is whether to grant amnesty and a path to citizenship to the more than 12 million illegal persons living in the country. This heated national discussion has its proponents and detractors. Under former President George W. Bush, attempts were made to regularize the status of undocumented workers in the country. To center the issue of amnesty to the political forefront, the leaders of both political parties, the Catholic Church, and labor union groups supported a combination of the guest workers program, pathways to citizenship, the deportation of illegal aliens who have committed felony violations, and securing the Southern borders of the country to stop illegal immigrant crossings into the country. Some in President Bush's own party considered this a form of amnesty and a reward for those who have violated United States immigration laws. The debate reignited and swirled around the 1986 Simpson-Mazzolli Act (sometimes also referred to as the Immigration Reform Control Act or IRCA) which legalized the status of illegal aliens and imposed fines on employers who knowingly hire illegal immigrants. Lou Dobbs, a former Cable News Network (CNN) business show host called it an amnesty and a misguided policy designed to benefit corporate America. He chastised Republican and Democratic supporters of the proposed legislation for trying to use the amnesty to depress the wages and salaries of the middle class. Few agreed with Lou Dobbs about his perennial assertions that the new wave of immigration into the country is behind increases in violent crimes. Conservative radio talk show hosts spearheaded by Laura Ingraham and Rush Limbaugh, among others lambasted the conservative and liberal proponents of the bill, including the Bush White House, Senators McCain of Arizona and Ted Kennedy of Massachusetts for the proposed legislation. The House members were even more recalcitrant. Representatives from the immigrant-rich states (California, Florida, and Texas) all voted against the measure. Ultimately, the measure was defeated in Congress. Under the current Obama administration, the debate about immigration has become even fiercer though the issues remain the same: how to tackle the problem of children of illegal immigrants born in the United States whose parents are undocumented. Coupled with this is whether or not to grant them legal resident status and eventual citizenship.

For African Americans, there is ambivalence about national policies on immigration. African Americans witness first-hand the transformative impacts of immigration in their communities. Most of the new immigrants arriving in the United States follow residential patterns similar to American blacks with a preference to live in cities and towns with a large minority population concentration. Over time, the new immigrants begin to establish their low capitalization ethnic businesses in or near to predominantly black communities. The results have been the gradual economic displacement and dislocation of blacks in ethnic-owned businesses. Politically, massive Hispanic and Asian migration into predominantly black communities are also changing the political and economic culture and representations at every jurisdiction of governance, be they local, state, and national. A salient aspect of this impact is the ascension of Hispanics as the largest minority group now surpassing blacks.

While most black Americans believe that immigrants are hard-working with strong family values, a growing number of blacks also believe that they typically end up losing service-related and manufacturing jobs to Latinos, Asian, African, and Caribbean immigrants. These loses continue to devastate their communities, causing chronic unemployment and underemployment, dwindled the tax base of cities with a large presence of African Americans, nearly crippled investment and infrastructural improvements, and resulted in the flight of middle income earners and businesses to the suburbs or to other countries (see for example, Braverman, 1974; Bluestone and Harrison, 1982). Combined with systemic racism, decades of urban economic neglect, globalization, and the outsourcing of middle class paying jobs overseas, African Americans continue to bear the brunt of harsh economic times. As more immigrants from all over the world continue to flock to the United States in search of better economic opportunities, African Americans are left wondering what the future holds for them, whether or not they have a place in the making of the American economic miracle.

A majority of the new immigrants who are entering the United States do settle in major urban centers such as Atlanta, Washington, D. C., San Francisco, Houston, New York, Chicago, Miami, Charlotte, Minneapolis, and Los Angeles. The destinations of immigrant are also places with a high concentration of blacks. The destinations of immigrant arrivals are also communities where there is intense competition among minority owned small businesses catering to the minority community. And frequently, the new immigrants are able to utilize their strong social networks to family resources to compete favorably and even in most cases outperform black American-owned small businesses (Raijiman and Tienda, 2003; Yeboah, 2008). These communities were the same cities in the North and West where thousands of blacks flocked to during the Great Migration of rural blacks from the South to the urban and industrial North. Diamond (1998) cited studies conducted by Miles, 1994; Fairchild and Fairchild, 1994; Myers, 1994; and Mohl, 1995 (among others), to show that the migration and settlements of new immigrants to these cities created opportunities for blacks to build coalitions to express and agitate for common issues such as better housing, livable wages, benefits, and improved conditions of employment. Certainly, uncontrolled migration has created an intense competition over jobs and other scarce economic resources. It has also ignited ethnic conflicts and tensions in the inner cities between poor blacks and Asian and Hispanic merchants.

The segmentation of labor and the social and cultural construction of race and ethnic identities within the broader context of immigration hold significant outcomes for blacks. As more and more immigrants enter the United States, the intersections of race, gender, ethnicity, labor force, and economic participation in distinct sectors of the economy (for example, tertiary and service) become occupied by specific immigrant groups. For black America, the selection of immigrants into those sectors of employment that blacks had previously had an upper hand continue to have devastating results on the employment prospects of blacks (Boswell, 1986; Lee, 1996; Castles and Miller, 1998). According to Ryan (2002), employer-preference for immigrant labor to reduce cost of production may also affect blacks by pushing them out of the labor market.

Over time, some aspects of the labor force may become segmented due to immigrant self-selection into specific sectors and employer favoritisms regarding preference for certain immigrant groups (Kelson and DeLaet, 1999; Boyd, 1995). For example, the continued dominance of recent African immigrants in the custodial and cleaning services in the hospitality industries in Minneapolis-St. Paul metropolitan areas and the dislocation of American-born blacks from these sectors has intensified the debate in that community over the impact of immigration on minority communities. Among African migrants to the United States, there is a tendency for networks of immigrant families to join together to set up or purchase small businesses that were once owned by blacks (Arthur, 2010). The hair care beauty shops and salon are typical examples in central Minnesota where bands of African immigrant families and their social networks have completely displaced native-born blacks. For these groups (including immigrants from other parts of the world), the opportunities offered by international migration are to insert family units into the global market and at the same time ensure that the family's economic standing is maintained (Arthur, 2010; Findley, 1993; Abella, 1993 and 1994; Cohen, 2006). In New York City (particularly in the borough of Queens and Harlem), African immigrants and Afro-Caribbean immigrants have monopolized the black hair products business sector including a near monopoly of household consumer items. These sectors were once controlled by thriving African-American middle class families. In the process of acculturation to the United States, African and Caribbean black immigrants structure their diaspora communities in such a way that the lines between economic and social (religious) institutions are somewhat blurred. Social, cultural, and economic assets from one sector can easily be transferred to shore up the other (see Schmidt, 2008).

Today, simmering conflicts and minimal cooperation continue to dominate the relationship between blacks and the new immigrants. For black Americans, continued immigration into the country means among other things, the loss of the economic position blacks have occupied for centuries as America's dominant minority group. With this also comes the loss of economic, political, and cultural power. Changes in the foreign-born composition of the American population also portend to alter the ethnic and racial landscapes of the country (See, for example Obiakor and Grant; Cunningham, 2005, and Lenoir and Kidane's 2007 characterizations of the tensions between immigrants and the black American community.) On its part, the Congressional Black Caucus (CBC) has yet to propose or formulate any concerted legislative proposals to deal with this mounting problems and social changes being brought about by both legal and legal immigration. Meanwhile, the problems posed by legal and illegal immigration continue to form.

PURPOSE OF STUDY

The purpose of this chapter is to contextualize the attitudinal perspectives of blacks regarding United States immigration policies. Emphasis is given to the factors that account for the formation of attitudinal perspectives that African Americans bring to their perceptions of U.S. immigration policies. Mapping the attitudinal perspectives of blacks toward U.S. immigration policies is significant because as a group, and due to their lower socioeconomic status relative to whites, African Americans are disproportionately affected by the cumulative social, cultural, economic, as well as the political impact of both regulated and unregulated immigration into the United States. The impact of immigration on African Americans can be seen in economic competition with new immigrants for scarce urban jobs, housing, and formation of immigrant-family-owned enterprises in the urban and suburban areas of the country. The continued relegation and economic dislocation of blacks as a result of massive immigration affects the overall quality of life of blacks. Politically, if current projections of Latino immigration persist, these groups of immigrants alone will overshadow the once enviable political power and capital that blacks historically had as a core political constituent whose voting behavior can alter the balance of congressional and Presidential elections.

DATA SOURCES

Data for this study were drawn from the General Social Survey (GSS) for the cumulative years 1972–2008. The GSS is based on a representative cross-sectional survey of the non-institutionalized adult population who are eighteen years old or older and residing in the United States. The surveys are designed to give each household the same statistical probability for selection and inclusion in the sample of respondents. For some years, the GSS had to include an oversampling of black Americans. The goal is to ensure that there is a nationally sizable pool of black respondents. Repeating some of their questions each survey period provides the opportunity to examine longitudinal trends in the data. More significantly, attitudinal patterns in key areas of social, political, and economic affairs can be delineated and changes in public opinions measured across time.

The GSS data were supplemented with a focus group survey of a nonrandom sample of 85 African Americans residing in Minneapolis-St. Paul, Minnesota. The purpose of the focus group survey was to gather baseline data and narratives about the perspectives of blacks regarding the economic, cultural, political, and social issues emanating from immigration and the manifest and latent outcomes of migration policies on African-American communities. Due to nonrandom nature of the focus group participants, the findings cannot be generalized. At best, the findings are intended to provide preliminary insights into the perspectives of African Americans upon which subsequent hypotheses can be formulated and tested.

PERSPECTIVES OF BLACKS ON UNITED STATES IMMIGRATION POLICIES: EVIDENCE FROM NATIONAL

Survey Data

Empirical evidence suggests that as a group, blacks bear the brunt of mass immigration relative to white Americans. Particularly for the urban and unskilled blacks, service and manufacturing jobs that previously hired blacks have all but disappeared. The structural re-alignments in the American economy; the transformation from a manufacturing and industrial-based economy to a service economy; the migration of middle-class income jobs in urban America to peripheral countries in Latin America and the Pacific Rim; the failure of inner-city schools in fulfilling the economic and cultural aspirations of urban blacks; relatively higher rates of black poverty and chronic unemployment; and dwindling jobs that pay livable wages have disproportionately impacted African Americans more than any other racial and ethnic group in the United

States. As they continue to suffer and lose economic ground due to uncontrolled immigration, black America's stance on the issue of immigration has hardened. As a group, black Americans favor decreased immigration into the country. Slightly more than one-half (52 percent) of blacks are in favor of curbing the pace of immigration and immigrant admissions.

During the 1980s and 1990s when the American economy was at full throttle and the national unemployment rate was less than 5 percent, black America's attitude toward immigration was more liberal and embracing of immigrants, particularly those coming from Africa and the Caribbean. However, the recent downturn in the economy, the housing crisis, job losses, and the slow down in credit availability has contributed to the hardening of black America's position on immigration. Like the rest of America, black Americans support government crackdown and raids on companies that knowingly hire illegal aliens. They are also opposed to providing driver's licenses to illegal aliens. Blacks' weak socioeconomic status and position in American society makes it rather difficult for them to fully support uncontrolled immigration policies (Diamond, 1998). Fears regarding job losses and the erosion of the economic institutions in their communities have persisted over the decades. For black America, the migration of African, Caribbean, Hispanic, and Asian immigrants to the United States are equally significant because they allow for economic coalition building to contest unfair labor practices and the poor conditions of employment that blacks and these other groups often confront.

For several of America's blacks, the continued economic recession of 2008 means that attitudes regarding immigration become more hardened. Nearly 55 percent of blacks who responded to the GSS believe that "immigrants take jobs away" from Americans. An even greater percentage of blacks (67 percent) indicated that "immigrants cause Americans to lose jobs." At the same time, blacks are cognizant of the economic potential of immigrants to America. Nearly one half of blacks responded that increased immigration has the potential to lead to economic growth in the United States.

As indicated earlier, America is a polarized nation when it comes to public sentiments about immigration. Black American perspective on immigration is a reflection of how the rest of the nation feels about legal and illegal immigration into the country. Over one-half (54 percent) of black Americans see immigrants as a burden to American society (Time, February 19, 2007: 44). Only 28 percent of blacks agreed that "Immigrants are good for America," as opposed to 25 percent who disagreed. Regarding government expenditures to assist immigrants, more than one-half (53 percent) of blacks agreed with the statement that the government is spending too much money on immigrants as a group. Black America's sentiments on the associated costs of immigration resonate with the views held by the rest of the country. At all levels of political governance (federal, state, county, and city in particular), there is public perception that both legal and illegal immigrants costs tax payers millions of dollars in unfunded mandates. These costs are incurred primarily in social services, including education, welfare, subsidized housing, and health care benefits to illegal immigrants and their dependents. The perceived high costs incurred by social services in providing assistance to immigrants correlate with mainstream belief that immigrants should not be eligible for any government assistance. In general, a plurality of blacks (70 percent) believes that "immigrants should not be eligible for government assistance." Only 30 percent of blacks indicated that immigrants should be eligible for government assistance. When the issue is whether "legal immigrants should have the same rights as Americans," blacks are divided with an equal number of blacks (40 percent) in favor of immigrant rights and a similar number in opposition. This sentiment is a reflection of the general mood of the country as a whole regarding anti-immigration sentiments. Part of the public antipathy toward immigrants is revealed in the believe held by 40 percent of blacks (and by extension the majority of Americans) that immigrants increase crime rates even though many recognize also that legal immigrants as a group are hardworking

Evidence from the GSS suggests that black Americans are supportive of refugees fleeing from political turmoil, wars, and displacement who seek a safer haven in the United States. Nearly 50 percent indicated that refugees should be allowed to stay in the country with approximately a third of blacks ambivalent about whether or not refugees should be given safe protection in the country. This ambivalence about immigration is contrasted with black America's perception that overall, immigrants help improve American society.

Blacks value the contributions immigrants make to the cultural development of the country. Nearly 77 percent of blacks believe that the presence of immigrants open up American society by fostering new cultural ideas and promoting diversity. And once they arrive in the United States, black Americans believe that immigrants should be encouraged to seek citizenship and naturalization. Though they feel that immigrants are "demanding too many rights" in the United States (according to 63 percent of blacks in the national survey), blacks believe that immigrants can overcome the social biases Americans have come to associate with them without relying on help from the government. In spite of their overwhelming believe that immigrants contribute to the social, cultural, and economic development of the country, immigration (according to 70 percent of blacks), "will make it difficult to achieve national unity" and integration.

PERSPECTIVES OF BLACKS ON U.S. IMMIGRATION POLICIES: EVIDENCE FROM FOCUS

Group Data

The focus group interview sessions with black Americans offered valuable opportunity to gauge the sentiments of blacks regarding immigrants more specifically, and U.S. immigration policies more generally. The focus group sessions enabled the researcher to probe for depth and content in respondent's answers to topical issues related to immigrants and immigration. This is in sharp contrast to the standardized and structured or closed-ended questions respondents had to answer in the GSS.

A number of findings emerged from the focus group study. First, the anti-immigration stance of blacks reported in the GSS was softened considerably among the black focus group study participants. While focus group study participants decried the harmful social, economic, and cultural consequences of illegal immigration on the future of the United States and the inability of the government to secure the borders, most of the study participants did not blame immigrants for unemployment and joblessness; neither do they blame immigrants for the worsening economic problems facing the middle class. The focus group participants represented immigrants as hardworking, frugal, risk-takers, ambitious, and agents of economic and social changes not only in the United States but also in the immigrant home countries as these immigrants share their assets and incomes with extended relatives at home. By straddling the cultures of their host and home societies simultaneously, immigrants are generally seen as altruistic often willing to sacrifice for the well-being of their family members.

A second finding from the focus group was respondents' attribution of blame for the middle class economic squeeze and the decline in manufacturing sector employment. Focus group participants attributed the 2008 economic squeeze of the middle class to the failure of America to invest in core sectors of the economy, particularly manufacturing production, including dwindling government resources for education. They also decried government and private investments in the urban core and predominantly minority communities. The lack of investment in education and infrastructure (not immigration) were cited as major causes for the current economic decline and the public anti-immigration fervor. Rather than address these issues, politically and economically powerless immigrants are used as scapegoats to divert attention away from important and fundamental structural economic deficiencies in the economy.

Focus Group Narratives of African American
Perspectives on U.S. Immigration Policies

In this section, we use specific narratives of focus group participants to contextualize the structural as well as individualistic perspectives of blacks regarding the impact of immigration on their lives. We found significant variations among blacks in terms of how they structure their perspectives regarding American immigration policies. The examples of the participant narratives that we draw upon to frame blacks' perspectives on immigration are certainly not meant to represent the perspectives of the entire focus group. The selected narratives are intended to provide a lens for evaluating the processes involved in structuring blacks' attitudes towards immigration.

We highlight the case of a college-educated African-American woman who works for a major sales and marketing company in twin cities of Minneapolis and St. Paul. She discounts the claim often made by government officials that immigrants (documented and undocumented) put a strain on social services and that promulgating laws to prohibit undocumented immigrants from receiving social services (as some states and cities have recently done) is a panacea for rolling back taxpayers subsidies of undocumented persons. According to this focus group participant, the growing anti-immigrant fervor is just "a ploy by state, and national political power brokers to arouse the anti-immigrant sentiments and furor among middle-class suburbanites whose economic fortunes continue to rapidly deteriorate due to declining home values, rising costs of living, huge personal indebtedness, and the fragility and insecurities of their jobs." In an economy that is characterized by dwindling expenditures for social services and crumbling infrastructure, Bernice indicated, "The poor, immigrants, and minorities often become the targets of discriminatory practices and economic scape-goating of a group that contributes than they take out of social services. These anti-immigrant legislations (this respondent rationalized) and their proponents are intended to whip citizens into frenzy by "fanning the flames of immigrant-baiting and promoting consciously or unconsciously the use of racially tainted codes to register angst towards the poor and immigrants in particular." This refrain and narrative, according to this respondent, is not new. "Past immigrants (especially those from Southern and Eastern Europe) and today, immigrants from Latin America, Asia, and Africa, all have to endure the anti-immigrant bashing," this study participant concluded.

In response to the question whether immigrants are to blame for the economic strains on welfare, social services, and drug crimes, including the violence often associated with it, one of the study participants pointed out that as a group, the claim that immigrants rely on and are often a drain on social services is "patently incorrect." This respondent described the elaborate familial-based networks of support that immigrants often create to buffer them from the uncertainties of the labor market. These networks often rely on kin assistance and the elaborate mutual aid services that immigrants often provide for their members. For those immigrants without valid working documents, tapping into government social services and economic safety net is out of the question. They nonetheless have to depend on school districts for the education of their children. Restrictive immigration and school policies that targets the children of illegal immigrants is seen as counterproductive to the imperative of providing education for children who are bona fide citizens of the United States by birth notwithstanding the undocumented status of their parents.

Public discourse in the United States has also focused on the economic and cultural contributions of immigrants in building America. Among focus group participants, there was unanimity that immigrants spur economic activities in the United States and often contribute more than they take out of the system. Nearly 80 percent of the respondents have had regular contacts and interactions with immigrants. More than one-half cited the strong work ethics and the strong family bonds that many new immigrants form to link their cultural communities to the United States. Of greater significance was the finding among the focus group study participants that policies at the national level to promote immigrant economic and cultural integration into the mainstream society have failed due to the cultural politicization of immigration and public antipathy toward immigrants, particularly those of color from the relatively poorer regions of the world. To this end, the respondents agreed that opening up American society to grant immigrants structural access to opportunities to ensure their full participation in every institutional fabric of American society is imperative if the country is to harness the human resources of its immigrant population.

The generally positive outlook on immigration among the study participants was punctuated by skepticism and an anti-immigrant stance among a small number of focus group participants (mainly youth and unemployed). Among this group, uncontrolled immigration is identified as a major reason behind the economic deterioration and the loss of black-owned small business enterprises that are located in predominantly African-American communities. Several mentioned the economic transitions that have taken place in their communities with the collapse or near takeover of black-owned businesses by Hispanic, African, Caribbean, and Asian immigrants who have settled in once all-black neighborhoods and communities. The perception is that black communities are being overrun by recent immigrants. For some inner-city blacks, the economic displacement resulting in joblessness brought about by the immigration of Hispanic, Asian, and African immigrants have forced low-skilled and poorly educated blacks to search for other service-related jobs most often far away from their places of residence.

Study participants referenced the Minneapolis-St. Paul airport where African and Hispanic service workers have virtually replaced American-born blacks as kiosk and retail attendants at the shops and food courts located at the airport. In that same city, Somali, Sudanese, Eritrean, Liberian, and Eastern Europeans have also replaced American blacks as taxi drivers in the counties forming the Twin Cities of Minneapolis and St. Paul. Other areas of economic activity (construction and landscaping) have also seen a dramatic shift in terms of displaced native blacks. A similar transformation is evident by the large presence of immigrants in the housekeeping and custodial services in the hotels and restaurant establishments surrounding the Mall of America (MOA) near Bloomington and Edina in Minneapolis-St. Paul. The economic impact on native-born blacks in the Twin Cities is telling. While Minnesota as a whole enjoys stable and relatively low unemployment rate of about 5 percent which is well below the national average of nearly 9 per cent, the same cannot be said for African Americans in that state. Average unemployment for adult blacks in the counties forming the Twin Cities is in excess of 15 percent. Black youth unemployment is nearly three times that of their white counterparts (20 percent and 8 percent respectively.)

In the Rondo district of St. Paul, an African-American historical enclave, scores of black youth continue to decry the lack of employment in their community, including the lack of after school literacy and cultural programs. This once-thriving historical community with black-owned stores and businesses has lost ground to Hispanic and Asian-owned business establishments in the metro areas of Minneapolis and St. Paul. Asians have cornered the restaurant and service businesses on University Drive, Lake, and making inroads in acquiring businesses on Grand Avenue. The vicinity of Cedar Avenue, parts of Franklin Street and Riverside have witnessed a transition to East African, Somali, Ethiopian, and Sudanese immigrant infiltration. With this transition has come the establishment of African immigrant businesses as well, often displacing African American-owned small business organizations.

Focus group participants pointed out that the bulk of the new immigrants are willing to work for lower wages and less likely to agitate for unionization and collective bargaining. Employers are willing to hire the new immigrants because of their excellent work ethic and strong familial and kin networks. Employer-preference in hiring immigrants (documented and undocumented) has resulted intergenerational cohorts of family members all working in the same establishment or organization. A third of unemployed blacks in the focus group study believe that undocumented immigration into the country has had a deleterious effect on their families as well. These blacks believe that employers favor immigrants for jobs and are often less likely to consider American blacks for jobs. This cohort of respondents perceive that even when they are hired, it is often at the entry level where wages are low and fringe benefits are hard to come by.

It was noted that inner-city blacks with or without high school diploma have also not fared well when they have to take and pass employer required tests with new immigrants competing for the same entry-level jobs. According to one study participant who is an African American, employer's preference to hire Eastern Europeans, Hispanics, and Asians in his community have decimated the economic standing of black families. Reflecting on the devastating economic impact of immigration on her community, this respondent stated thus: "The construction company I worked with is now almost entirely Hispanics. Two decades ago, this was not so. Blacks were able to find jobs in construction and able to earn $20-30 per hour depending on their skill level. For those who were masons, carpenters, or certified electricians, the pay was more than $30 an hour, enough to support a middle class lifestyle, including the ability to purchase a home and pay for the educational expenses of college-age dependent children. Now, the bulk of these jobs have gone to Hispanic immigrants. Several of my friends in their thirties and forties are in and out of the labor market, often the first to be laid off as more and more Latino immigrants come to Minnesota."

Another respondent echoed the above sentiments. She stated that "New immigrants from every corner of the globe are streaming into my community. Their presence has had a visible economic impact on my family already. Landlords raise the rent exorbitantly hoping you will leave. When you do leave, they rent individual rooms to several immigrants who cramp in rooms meant to be inhabited by one person. My brother lost his job with the landscape company because the manager decided to hire more Hispanics and African émigrés. He was laid off several months ago." Similarly, an African American male in his thirties who lives on the north side of Minneapolis argues that "Mass immigration into the United States diminishes the political and economic power of blacks. Employers hold up the work ethic of immigrants as desirable and therefore willing to lay off their black employees in favor of Latinos, Asians, and some Africans. But we were here first; doing all the work; never earned any respect and dignity; we have being diminished economically by these employers."

A middle-aged respondent focus group participant also decried the impact of immigration on her once thriving business. According to her, immigration from Africa and the Caribbean Islands caused the downfall of her family-owned hair-weaving and braiding business. "When the African and Caribbean women came here, I lost more than one-half of my clients. They (the immigrants) were willing to braid hair for $8 rather than the $30 that most of us were charging before. I saw this coming. So I diversified and started selling wigs, black hair and cosmetic products. But the Asians and the Africans kept coming, eventually forcing me to close for good," she said.

It was evident among the black respondents that though progress is being made in the United States in terms of protecting the gender and civil rights of vulnerable segments of the society, there is no doubt that public-led legislative initiatives to fully incorporate both immigrant and native-born black into highly-compensated sectors of the economy have met with minimal success. Despite their ability and flexibility in being able to adapt to the low wage-based global economy as it continues to take hold in every sector of the U.S. economy, immigrants continue to find themselves almost relegated to sectors of the global economy where they are subjected to economic exploitation and their skills undervalued and therefore inadequately compensated. Countering this is proving insurmountable due to the gutting of labor's rights and the lack of oversight in promoting affirmative action hires during the eight years of President Bush's administration.

For some of the focus group participants who described their status as lower class to lower middle class, the need for American immigration policies to more accurately reflect the labor needs of the country is imperative. Most feel a sense of economic abandonment by their own government. Meanwhile, both legal and illegal migrants continue to make significant economic inroads in the minority communities. To address this problem, study participants called for and advocated for better employment and job-training programs funded by the government to assist in training inner-city blacks for gainful employment in manufacturing and production. Even where these programs are available, many urban black youths and some adults do not have access to other social services such as transportation, childcare, and the informal employment networks to provide information about existing jobs. Some of the respondents expressed concern about the economic impact of stymied intergenerational mobility first on them, and secondly, on their families as they continue to bear the burden of massive unemployment and underemployment in their respective families.

The African Americans in the focus group sessions expect that continued mass and unregulated immigration will make it very difficult for them to gain full integration into America's labor force at every level of skilled and unskilled occupational participation. This problem will persist due to the educational achievement gap currently facing blacks relative to other racial, ethnic, or minority groups. For blacks who do not pursue postsecondary education, competition for scarce jobs with a growing immigrant population is expected to intensify. New immigrants have a competitive edge over blacks because of their strong educational credentials relative to blacks. The potential exist for competition for scarce jobs and dwindling economic resources to heighten social conflict and tension not only between blacks and immigrants but also between immigrants and the white majority. Commenting on this fractious possibility, one of the focus group participants reasoned that though immigration may change the ethnic fabric and national identity of the country, it is in America's interest to have a diverse and multicultural workforce or society where different groups are able to define and find expression for their ethnic and racial identities while at the same time engaging the economic system. America's diverse groups of immigrants and nonimmigrants alike must mobilize, according to one respondent, to take steps to promote coalition building and co-empowerment for problem-solving and agitation of the political structure to create ample jobs that provide livable wages and fringe benefits. But as this respondent indicated, steps to harness the human capital resources of every segment of the American labor force (immigrant and nonimmigrant) will be hard fought and may not materialize in the current atmosphere of job losses and economic depressions coupled with dwindling fringe benefits, the lack of access to healthcare, and structural deficit problems.

For many of the black respondents who participated in the focus group sessions, the issues of immigration and the decline of jobs in the inner-cities resonates as several of them have difficulty fending for themselves economically as well as providing opportunities for their children. While they recognize the cultural, political, and economic tolls that legal and illegal immigration into the country has had on their lives, some of the respondents are reluctant to fully blame immigrants and immigration policies for the worsening economic plight of black Americans in general. Many believe government rather than immigrants ought to be blamed for the deterioration in the standard of living of blacks in general, specifically urban blacks. One study participant captured the sentiments of the group thus: "The government has failed to rein in corporations and businesses that have shipped jobs outside the country devastating the economic life-blood of small and large towns alike. As the de-industrialization of the country goes on, blacks and the working poor in general are left feeling the economic pinch. These companies are given incentives by foreign countries to relocate. Meanwhile, the U.S. government does not do anything about jobs that are being lost to overseas competitors. When times are good, black folks are always the last to enjoy the fruits of prosperity. And as the economy tanks, blacks are persistently the first group to feel the pinch via layoffs and joblessness."

Another African-American respondent who participated in the focus group interviews adopted a cultural approach to the problem of legal and illegal immigration and the effects it has on working class and inner-city poor blacks.

According to this respondent, immigrants rely on the vitality of their cultural institutions to make it in America. They live frugal and know how to save their money. Blacks, according to this respondent, have yet to learn about the economic benefits of savings and investments. The immigrants often support one another and are willing to bat for their relatives by sharing their meager means. They (the immigrants) are yearning to become successful because they come from very poor countries. From this focus group partici-pant perspective, black Americans are sometimes unwilling to perform the low-paying jobs that these immigrants do: Too much pride to soil our hands; and that is why we are being left behind. I think we have become consumers rather than producers. We do not educate our children properly. The immi-grant children are very smart. Their parents also like to go to the community colleges to acquire more skills, often relying on grants to educate themselves for a changing labor market."

A black American woman raising three children believes that part of the solution to ease chronic urban black male and youth unemployment is for black communities to emulate the examples of Latino and Asian immigrant business proprietors to create jobs requiring low capitalization. The lack of jobs continues to economically have destabilizing effect among adult black males. Even the black cosmetic and hair products business have been taken over by the Asians, as one study participant alluded: "You only see fast foods, mainly fried chicken joints, pawn shops, and liquor stores. In the suburbs, you have organic grocery stores, banks and financial institutions, shopping centers, better roads, and many more. The same cannot be said for predomi-nantly black areas." Study participants cited the need for public and private sector start-up funds, management oversight, and support for minority small businesses to enable them compete with immigrant family-based enterprises. In addition, there is need for quality and affordable housing to ensure com-munity sustainability and economic viability. Policies to arrest the invest-ment neglect of the urban black poor must be implemented with urgency. The burden of renewing these communities has fallen mainly on state, local, and private agencies and organizations. For those communities experiencing migratory influx, stiff competition for dwindling job opportunities continue to erode any gains blacks made before the recession.

Coupled with this is the problem of institutional racism. Financial institu-tions, in particular, continue to show a disinterest in investing in some of the predominantly black communities. Some of these communities do not have grocery stores, pharmacies, banks, and other essential social and cultural services. Banks and financial institutions may steer investments away from the predominantly black areas in favor of white suburban communities. The few remaining businesses that are left behind in the black communities are the ones owned and operated by Latino, Asian, African, and Caribbean immigrants. According to this focus group study participant, "This is a testimony of the effects of unchecked immigration. We (blacks) have allowed Korean and other Asian merchants to come to our neighborhoods to open small-scale businesses which we patronized very well. They are able to raise the capital needed to start these businesses, but blacks usually encounter problems tapping into existing investment loans.

One respondent elucidated the new reality of migration and globalization on black economic standing. Noting that both processes promotes the free movement of people, goods and services, there is, they rationalized, a slow response among blacks in America in recognizing the net implications of how these forces are altering the economic aspects of their lives. To regain and map their own economic trajectories to confront these issues, study participants (once again) reiterated the imperative of education if black America is to become a part of the unfolding globalized migratory circulation of labor. As one participant opined, "Our people (blacks) do not stay in school; we do not push our children to excel in school; the foreigners who are here do; and eventually they get hired because of their skills and work ethic. Everyone must learn to adapt to the forces of economic globalization and labor migration because it is going to dominate our lives for decades to come. Recognizing the impact of immigration and globalization means that blacks will have to seek more job and educational skills to render them more marketable. This is proving difficult for many blacks," this respondent stressed.

CONCLUSION

In a sense, the economic interests of immigrants and American blacks intersect and converge in multiple domains. Both groups are minorities and a subordinate class. Their collective economic destinies are shaped by class, gender, ethnic, national, and racial identities transcending the geographic and spatial boundaries of their communities. Their minority, class, racial or ethnic status, while social and cultural markers, straddles geopolitical and cultural worlds, one foreign, immigrant, and the other native, citizen, but not fully integrated. When immigrants and black Americans collectively assert their subordinate economic and class relationships, they express and find meaning and fulfillment in the notion and belief that as marginalized and alienated as some of them are, they can still find meaning in the common pursuit of economic goals designed to give them empowerment and full citizenship. Their differences, which are several, and sometimes caused by the perceived threats posed by new immigrants; and at times caused by breakdown in economic structures, only serve to provide a new prism for rationalizing and interpreting different constructions of minority identities and how the expectations associated with these constructed identities can facilitate or enhance access to better economic opportunities and better quality of life. Core to their sense of community (irrespective of their historical or migratory legacies in the United States) is the assertion and contention that they (immigrants and blacks alike) are an integral part of America and its collective stories. And whether they embrace an immigrant ethos and normative system, or one that is black in all its cultural forms, several of the study participants desire to carve positive and rewarding niches for themselves in the American experience to facilitate and broaden their cultural prisms and at the same time open up new vistas of opportunities not only for themselves, but also for their posterity.

As a group (and irrespective of their cultural and normative beliefs about immigrants and immigration policies), blacks generally recognize that economic forces (globalization, changing patterns of immigration, and access to employment) are pivotal in shaping or defining the complex cultural and economic relationships between them and immigrants in general. Ultimately, both groups (blacks and immigrants) will have to confront their economically and culturally marginalized statuses. For both groups, it is acknowledged that the intersections of immigration, race, ethnicity, and class statuses will converge in mapping out the framework of exchange and dialogue critically needed in efforts to promote the advancement and overall well-being of blacks and immigrants as a whole. Increased scholarly attention is needed to position blacks to take advantage of the increasing economic and cultural opportunities in Latino, African, Caribbean, and Asian immigrant communities. Existing structural impediments (unemployment, unchecked immigration, lack of education) and nonstructural problems (xenophobic anxieties about immigrants, immigrant antipathy) are important considerations in reshaping and reformulating the new immigration policies that will ensure or protect the economic competitiveness of black job-seekers and promote effective labor force integration and participation. For black America, therefore, such an approach will have to include a holistic understanding of the transformative impact of the system of global labor mobility. Such an awareness will assist blacks in restructuring their institutions (with government backing) to take full advantage of the global dispersion of labor via the mechanisms of international migration.

Acknowledgement of the social, economic, and cultural consequences of mass immigration on minority communities is imperative. Concerted efforts are warranted to mount an effective grassroots mobilization and coalition building to tackle some of the economic dislocations in the urban minority communities across the nation brought upon by mass immigration. As they forge ahead and struggle to eliminate or reduce the material and structured inequalities that they persistently encounter in American society, blacks are aware that they will have to join with other protected classes and groups to agitate for broader social changes to revitalize economic institutions in the urban centers with the goal of creating jobs and providing better access to economic opportunities. Streamlining legal immigration and controlling illegal immigration in general should form an integral component of this process. As indicated, such an approach may also require an effective grassroots mobilization to center the growing economic disparities between America's black and minority population and immigrant populations. Current social, cultural, and economic conditions in America are ripe for the sort of activism and mass collective mobilization akin to the 1960s and 1970s era to address key and fundamental problems affecting those at the lower rungs of society, including lower class whites who are also faced with similar social and economic problems.

REFERENCES

Abella, Manolo. 1993. "Labor Mobility, Trade, and Structural Change: The Philippine Experience." *Asian and Pacific Migration Journal*. Volume 2 (3): 249–68.
———. 1994. "Introduction to Special Issue on Turning Points in Labor Migration." *Asian and Pacific Migration Journal*. Volume 3 (1): 1–8.
Apraku, Kofi. 1991. *African Émigrés in the United States. A Missing Link in Africa's Social and Economic Development*. New York: Praeger.
Arthur, John. 2010. *African Diaspora Identities. Negotiating Culture in Transnational Migration*. Lanham, MD: Lexington Books.
———. 2000. *Invisible Sojourners. African Immigrant Diaspora in the United States*. Westport, CT.: Praeger.
Beck, R. 1996. *The Case Against Immigrants: The Moral, Economic, Social, and Environmental Reasons for Reducing U.S. Immigration Back to Traditional Levels*. New York: W. W. Norton and Co.
Bluestone, B. and Harrison, B. 1982. *The Deindustrialization of America*. New York: Basic Books.
Bonacich, Edna and Modell, John. 1980. *The Economic Basis of Ethnic Solidarity. Small Business in the Japanese American Community*. Berkeley, CA: University of California Press.
Bouvier, L. F. and Grant, L. 1994. *How Many Americans? Population, Immigration, and the Environment*. San Francisco, CA: Sierra Club.
Bowser, Benjamin. 2007. *The Black Middle Class. Social Mobility and Vulnerability*. Boulder, CO: Lynne Rienner Publishers.
Boyd, M. 1995. "International Migration Policies and the Status of Female Migrants." *Proceedings of the UN Expert Group Meeting on International Migration Policies and the Status of Female Migrants*. Rome: United Nations.

Braverman, H. 1974. *Labor and Monopoly Capital: The Degradation of Work in the Twentieth Century*. New York: Monthly Review Press.

Brimelow, P. 1995. *Alien Nation: Common Sense About America's Immigration Disaster*. New York: Random House.

Castles, S. and Miller, M 1998. *The Age of Migration: International Population Movements in the Modern World*. London: MacMillan.

Cohen, Robin. 2006. *Migration and its Enemies. Global Capital, Migrant Labour and the Nation-State*. London: Ashgate.

Cose, E. 1992. *A Nation of Strangers: Prejudice, Politics, and the Populating of America*. New York: William Morrow and Co.

Cunningham, J. 2005. "Tensions Between African and African Americans Surface Again." *New York Amsterdam News*. Volume 96 (6).

Diamond, Jeff. 1998. "African-American Attitudes Towards United States Immigration Policy." *International Migration Review*. Volume 32 (2): 451–70.

Fairchild, H. and Fairchild, D. G. 1994. "African-Americans and Korean-Americans: Cultures in Conflict." In Myers, E. R. (ed.). *Challenges of a Changing America: Perspectives on Immigration and Multiculturalism in the United States*. San Francisco, CA.: Austin and Winfield, 167–74.

Findley, Sally. 1993. *Choosing Between African and French Destinations. The Role of Family and Community Factors in Migration From the Senegal River Valley*. Working Paper Number 5. CERPOD, BP 1530, Bamako, Mali.

Gordon, April. 1998. "The New African Diaspora. African Immigration to the United States." *Journal of Third World Studies*. Volume 15 (1): 79–103.

Hellwig, D. 1974. *The Afro-American and the Immigrant, 1800-1930*. Ph.D. Thesis, Syracuse University, New York.

Huntington, Samuel. 2004. *Who are We? America's Great Debate*. London: Simon and Schuster.

Kelson, G. and DeLaet. 1999. *Gender and Immigration*. London: MacMillan.

Lee, S. 1996. "Issues in Research on Women, international Migration and Labour." In Battistella, G. and Paganoni, A. (eds.). *Asian Women in Migration*. Scalabrini Migration Center, Quezon City: Phillopines.

Lenior, G. and Kidane, N. 2007: "African Americans and Immigrants. Shall we Hang Together or Separately?" *The Black Scholar*. Volume 37: 50–52.

Massey, D. S. and Denton, N. A. 1993. *American Apartheid: Segregation and the Making of an Underclass*. Cambridge, MA.: Harvard University Press.

Mohl, R. 1995. "Blacks and Hispanics in Multicultural America. A Case Study." *Amerikastudien*, 40.

Moynihan, Patrick. 1965. *The Negro Family. The Case for National Action*. Washington, D.C.: Superintendent of Documents, United States Government Printing Office.

———. 1986. *Family and Nation*. San Diego, California: Harcourt Brace Jovanovich.

Miles, J. 1994. "Blacks vs Browns." In Mills, N. (ed.). *Arguing Immigration*. New York: Simon and Schuster, 101–42.

Myers, E. R. 1994. "Korean-American Marketing in the African-American Community: An Exploratory Study in the Nation's Capital City." In Myers, E. R. (ed.).

Challenges of a Changing America: perspectives on Immigration and Multiculturalism in the United States. San Francisco, CA.: Austin and Winfield, 175–215.

Obiakor, F. E. and Grant, P. 2002. *Foreign-Born African Americans: Silenced Voices in the Discourse on Race (ed.).* New York: Nova Science Publishers.

Okpewho, Isidore and Nzegwu, Nkiru. 2009. *The New African Diaspora* (ed.). Bloomington: Indiana University Press.

Owusu, Thomas. 2000. "The Role of Ghanaian Immigrant Associations in Toronto, Canada." *International Migration Review.* Volume 34 (4): 1155–81.

Pachon, Harry and DeSipio, Louis. 1994. *New Americans by Choice. Political Perspectives of Latino Immigrants.* Boulder, CO.: Westview Press.

Phil, S. 2003. "African Americans and Mortgage Lending Discrimination." *Western Journal of Black Studies.* Volume 27 (2): 65–80.

Pinkney, Alphonso. 2000. *Black Americans.* Upper Saddle River, NJ: Prentice-Hall.

Portes, Alejandro and Rumbaut, Ruben. 1990. *Immigrant America.* Berkeley: University of California Press.

Portes, Alejandro and Zhou, M. 1993. "The New Second Generation: Segmented Assimilation and its Variants." *The Annals of the American Academy of Political and Social Science.* Volume 530: 74–96.

Portes, Alejandro and Bach, Robert. 1985. *Latin Journey. Cuban and Mexican Immigration in the United States.* Berkeley: University of California Press.

Raijiman, R. and Tienda, M. 2003. "Ethnic Foundations of Economic Transactions: Mexican and Korean Immigrant Entrepreneurs in Chicago." *Ethnic and Racial Studies.* Volume 26 (5): 783–801.

Ross, S. and Yinger, J. 2002. *The Color of Credit: Mortgage Discrimination, Research Methodology, and Fair-Lending Enforcement.* Cambridge, MA: MIT Press.

Ryan, Jan. 2002. "Chinese Women as Transnational Migrants: Gender and Class in Global Migration Narratives." *International Migration.* Volume 40 (2): 93–114.

Schaefer, Richard. 2000. *Racial and Ethnic Groups.* Upper Saddle River, New Jersey: Prentice-Hall.

Schmidt, Bettina. 2008. *Caribbean Diaspora in the USA.* Aldershot, England: Ashgate.

Shankman, A. 1982. *Ambivalent Friend: African-Americans View of the Immigrant.* Westport, CT.: Greenwood Press.

Takougang, Joseph. 1995. "Black Immigrants to the United States." *Western Journal of Black Studies.*" Volume 19 (1): 50–57.

Time Magazine. 2007. February 19: p. 44.

United States Bureau of the Census. 2010. *Current Population Survey.* Washington, D. C.: Government Printing Press.

Valdez, Zulema. 2007. "Beyond the Ethnic Enclave. The Effect of Ethnic Solidarity and Market Opportunity on White, Korean, Mexican, and Black Enterprise." In Brettell, Caroline (ed.). *In Constructing Borders. Crossing Boundaries.* Lanham, MD: Lexington Books, 243–71.

Waldinger, Roger. 2008. "Immigrant Transnationalism and the Presence of the Past." In Barkan, E.; Hasia Diner, and Alan Kraud (ed.). *From Arrival to Incorporation. Migrants to the U. S. in a Global Era.* New York and London: New York University Press, 267–85.

Waters, Mary and Eschbach, Karl. 1995. "Immigration and ethnic and Racial Inequality in the United States." *Annual Review of Sociology*. Volume 21: 419–46.

Wilson, Julius. 1987. *The Truly Disadvantaged. The Inner City, the Underclass and Public Policy*. Chicago: University of Chicago Press.

———. 1996. *When Work Disappears*. New York: Random House.

Yeboah, Ian. 2008. *Black African neo-Diaspora: Ghanaian Immigrant Experiences in the Greater Cincinnati, Ohio Area*. New York: Lexington Books.

Chapter Ten

African Immigrant Relationships with Homeland Countries

Although there are no accurate statistics, approximately 30 million Africans are migrants both within and outside the continent. This constitutes an estimated 3 percent of all Africans, and includes refugees, exiles, and people who migrate by choice. Paradoxically, most migration occurs in the smallest countries, with Cape Verde leading with a rate of migration almost reaching 40 percent in 2010 (Ratha, 2011). A significant proportion of African migration occurs within the African continent. There are, however regional variations, for example, in Southern Africa, 66 percent of the migration is intra-regional, with majority flocking to South Africa; in West Africa, an estimated 70 percent, migrate within the same region but approximately 90 percent of migrants from North African go outside the continent (Ratha, 2011). Approximately half of all African migration goes outside the continent, with majority of the flows from the continent going to Europe. France attracts 9 percent; Saudi Arabia, 5 percent; and both the United States and the United Kingdom have 4 percent (Ratha, 2011: 9). These migrations involve the movement of refugees, traders, workers, and exiles from less to more politically, economically, environmentally and socially secure areas, according to the primary needs that propel their movement (Okome, 2007). The International Labor Organization estimates that there were over 16 million African migrants in 2005, and 5.4 million of them were migrant workers (Okome, 2007: 152). It is also estimated that there are about 140 million people of African descent outside the continent, and that most of them live in the Western Hemisphere (Ratha, 2011: 13).

As a result of historical and contemporary migrations, African immigrants are now part of the transnational communities that can be found in virtually all regions of the world. Glick, Basch, and Blanc (1995) consider such people transmigrants, that is, "immigrants whose daily lives depend on multiple and constant interconnections across international borders and whose public identities are configured in relation to more than one nation state." They differ from sojourners to the extent that they do not cut ties with their countries of origin and just settle and "become incorporated into the economic and political institutions, localities and patterns of daily life in their country of settlement, but also simultaneously remain connected, build institutions, conduct transactions, and influence local and national events in the countries from which they emigrated."

If migration is nothing but the expression of a labor supply system in operation, each area of the world responds to the forces that propel its incorporation into the world capitalist system. For sociologist Saskia Sassen-Koob, a region's role in the world economy determines the nature of its labor supply systems. Traditionally, the labor supply systems include many methods that attract or compel foreign workers to enter the world capitalist system. Foreign workers have always been used, particularly to solve the problem of labor shortages and to increase productivity. Immigrant connections with home countries can in this sense be seen as encouraging chain migrations by people who seek similar economic opportunities (Sassen-Koob, 1981). As part of chain immigrant flows, earlier sojourners or immigrants provide information, assistance to secure jobs, housing and other services as well as living examples of the possibilities and limits of immigration as a move to the promised land.

But globalization has a Janus-face that both creates the incentive to move and stay; as well as the tendency to embrace and rebuff immigrants. Globalization has both negative and positive consequences that vary by national and international region, nationality, gender, race, and class. Thus, according to Okome (2007a: 154):

> Today's imperialism does not require the physical presence of imperialists within their empire. Instead, neo-colonial relations of power maintain imperialistic domination by extracting economic and financial resources and labor, using them in new ways in the peripheries of the empire. Today's imperialism is driven by transnational capital, especially multinational corporations in the global north. It is supported by state policies in both the north and the newly liberalized global south, which is compelled to integrate into the global economy.

Instead, imperialism has morphed, wearing the face of transnational capital, and doing its bidding. The continent of Africa attracts those variants of transnational capital that have an interest in mining, including those in the petroleum business; most other involvement is in raw materials that are taken away from the continent without any value added.

This chapter will critically analyze the major themes that have shaped post-war African migratory patterns, focusing attention on dominant themes such as religion, remittances, civic engagement, cultural practices, language, memory, foodways, entrepreneurship, and philanthropy. The chapter also reveals the complexities of African migration during a moment of great social, economic, and political transformation, revealing the resilience and resourcefulness of African communities.

AFRICAN IMMIGRANTS' DEEP AND ENDURING TIES TO THEIR HOME COUNTRIES

Given that the twentieth and twenty-first century communities of African immigrants are transnational, there are many possibilities in terms of engagement with African immigrants' home countries. Arthur (2000) contends that the connections between African immigrants and their home countries, is deep and enduring. In his study of African immigrants in the United States, Arthur (2000: 80) contends that many African immigrants see themselves as sojourners in their countries of settlement, and insist that they will return to their home countries when economic and political conditions improve. They live their lives and engage in activities that affirm their commitment to this goal. And according to Arthur,

> Fiercely kinship oriented in their world view, the Africans who come here share the economic benefits of their migratory experience with their entire extended families. In doing so, these African immigrants become agents of social change in their home countries—sharing pieces of the material and non-material culture of this nation with people living in both peripherally and centrally located towns, cities, and villages all over Africa. They are active in the social, cultural, economic and political development of their home countries, sojourning in America, waiting patiently for conditions to improve at home, and then repatriating (viii-ix).

Similarly, Owusu (1998), in a study of the home ownership patterns of Ghanaian immigrants in Toronto argues among that the ties to their home countries and desire for home ownership there lead to their ownership of fewer homes than Canadian-born populations. These studies confirm a 2011 World Bank study edited by Ratha (2011: 10) which makes the claim that highly skilled African immigrants could be a source of:

> increasing direct investments, improving access to foreign capital markets through investment funds and diaspora bonds, providing grants for development, establishing contacts to promote trade and investment, increasing demand for a country's exports, and transferring technology (through, for example, professional associations that provide expertise to origin-country firms,

temporary assignments of skilled expatriates in origin countries, and the return of emigrants with enhanced skills).

RELIGIOUS MOVEMENTS

African religious traditions have thrived among its diaspora populations and are one of the most visible, enduring demonstrations of the maintenance of strong connections between these diasporas and the continent. *Orisa* worship derived from Yoruba religious tradition, *Lucumi* in Cuba, *Shango* cult in Trinidad, *Santeria* in Puerto Rico and the mainland United States, from the Yoruba religious tradition; *Cadomble* and *Kumbanda* in Brazil, also from Yoruba and Congo traditions as well as *Voodoo* in Haiti, from Dahomey (contemporary Republic of Benin); are New World expressions that combined elements from the African religions with other traditions. These religions continue to the present day and also have had profound influences on the arts and philosophy of people of African descent in the continent's diasporas in Europe, the Americas and the Caribbean (Olupona, 1993). Some contemporary members are new African immigrants but majority are from the old diasporas.

Research on African New Religious Movements (ANRM) in Europe and to a lesser extent, North America indicate that whether the expressions are within Christianity or Islam, these ANRMs are proliferating robustly in all parts of the world, including the African continent. In the first place, religion offers immigrants avenues to re-create home in a strange land, and to negotiate integration and forestall total assimilation and consequent anonymity in the country of settlement (Adogame, 2003). Deep immersion with religious practice also offers solace, hope in the face of adversity, information, opportunities for leadership, social interaction, and mutual support to immigrants. According to Adogame (2003: 25), "Most African immigrants to Europe and elsewhere carried their religions with them" and have contributed to transforming the world's religious landscape. He estimates that Nigerians and Ghanaians have established most of the ANRM churches in Europe and gives a history of these churches that began in the 1920s and continues today in the African Initiated Churches (AICs) and Pentecostal Charismatic churches that have sprung up throughout Europe. Although founded in Africa, many of these churches have now become transnational (Adogame, 2003: 28).

The AICs in Europe have their origins in the 1960s, when Nigerian immigrants in the United Kingdom established churches that belong in the *Aladura* movement, the first documented one in London being in 1964, as the Church of the Lord—*Aladura* (CLA), followed in 1965 by the Cherubim and Seraphim (C&S), and in 1967 by the Celestial Church of Christ (CCC). The Christ Apostolic Church (CAC) and the Evangelical Church of Yahweh (ECY), also part of the *Aladura* movement were established later. Contemporarily, many more churches have sprung up. Some are branches of churches back home, others are founded by breakaway groups from churches in the diaspora, and yet others, such as the *Aladura* International Church founded by Olu Abiola, in London, are entirely new churches that emerged in the diaspora (Adogame, 2003: 28-29). At the same time, the mainline churches like the Anglican, Catholic and Lutheran churches, also have African congregations who sometimes have worship services in their indigenous languages, and even facilitate the hire of clergy from Africa to provide pastoral care and leadership in more culturally relevant and familiar ways (Okome, 2007b).

In the case of the *Aladura* churches in the U.K., Nigerian students, businesspeople and people in diplomatic service who thought of themselves as temporary sojourners set in motion a gradual process of establishing first, prayer groups, and then small churches. From these modest beginnings, AICs have now grown in size and spread all over Europe (Adogame, 2003: 28). From the Pentecostal/Charismatic movement, the Redeemed Christian Church of God (RCCG), which spread from its original source in Nigeria, and the Church of Pentecost International which was first established in Ghana, are just two of the now dizzying array of AICs. There are also other Pentecostal churches, such as the Christian Church Outreach Mission in Hamburg, Germany and the Kingsway International Christian Centre in London. These and other interdenominational prayer groups and African Christian organizations provide communities within which African immigrants can connect with people of like mind for spiritual empowerment in arena that serve as home away from home (Adogame, 2003: 29). Branch churches send financial support back to their mother churches in Africa. They also offer international platforms for the churches' Africa-based leaders to proselytize and evangelize. Increasingly, many AICs based in Africa have mobilized what amounts to a "reverse mission" in the sense of bringing Christianity from Africa to the West (Olupona and Gemignani, 2007). There is constant interaction between these reverse missionaries and their mother churches in the African continent. The liturgy, hermeneutics, and praxis of Christianity at home and abroad are identical. Many African immigrant Christians find these connections with home so valuable that they flock to AICs in significant numbers. Another factor that makes the churches attractive is the desire to escape xenophobia, racism and ethnocentric bias in the mainline churches. Many want to connect with those with similar ethnicity, nationality and religious identity, they seek support, sanctuary, camaraderie, information on approaches that are likely to produce success in their new environments (Adogame, 2003: 30-32).

MUSLIMS IN THE UNITED STATES:
THE MURIDS OF HARLEM, NEW YORK

The desire to maintain connectedness with their home countries can also be observed in Harlem, New York, where for over two decades, the Murid Sufi community has celebrated Cheikh Ahmadu Bamba day with a parade on 7th Avenue from 110th-125th Street. The parade honors the memory of Cheikh Ahmadu Bamba Mbacké (1853-1927), who founded the brotherhood in the city of Touba in Senegal in 1895. Cheikh Ahmadu is revered as a *marabout* (revered religious authority and leader), saint and sage. The parade in Harlem is indicative of pious, reverent and dedicated commemoration of Cheikh Ahmadu's contributions. His followers carry banners with his image, that of his mother, that of the great mosque in Touba and many sayings in English, French, and Arabic that affirm commitment and allegiance to Sufi identity. Cheikh Ahmadu was buried in the mosque in Touba, which has become a pilgrimage site. The images borne and displayed during the parade express connections between the Murids of Harlem and their home country, particularly Touba, the foundational source of their religion, and Cheikh Ahmadu, the founder (Abdullah, 2009). The paraders wear mostly African garb, even young children wear boubous (long flowing gowns), people carry their prayer beads, Cheikh Ahmadu's *khassaïd* poems and Muslim prayers are recited in the procession. Senegalese and American flags are waved. Particularly in the post 9/11 New York City, Murid Sufi Muslims have found it necessary to project a positive image of Islam and Muslims. In an America where black identity is still discreditable (stemming from an assumption that black people are bad, and the onus is on them to prove that they are good, they also affirm a positive African identity, and also to demonstrate some visible allegiance to both Senegal and the United States in the case of the American flags, in a style that has become de rigueur in post-9/11 America (Abdullah, 2009: 211). The American flag is also indicative of respect and deference to the host country (Abdullah, 2009: 212).

That there is a connection with home is even more evident because the Murids display images of Cheikh Ahmadu and Touba at their places of worship. In addition, as Abdullah aptly puts it: "National flags are more than colorful pieces of cloth waving in the wind. They capture, in a brief moment, the heritage of a homeland—historic victories, bitter defeats, popular dishes, the national anthem, and an idyllic landscape instantly conjured up in the mind's eye" (Abdullah, 2009: 212). Abdullah also reports that the parade is recorded by a Senegalese television crew, and is aired for weeks in Senegalese cities, including Touba, as well as in other U.S. and Western cities where there is substantial Murid presence (Abdullah, 2009: 211). What's more, the reverence for Cheikh Ahmadu extends to Touba in a way that fuses the identity of the saint, contemporary Murid marabouts and the holy city, in expressions of adoration, submission, and connectedness to Allah through the agency of the Murid saints.

LANGUAGE

African societies are steeped in oral traditions that pervade the ethos and philosophy of life and express the essence of the people's worldview. Proverbs, oratory, stories, poetry, and all manner of verbal communication are vehicles through which traditions, social practices, aesthetics, and meaning are transmitted, interpreted, re-created, and otherwise articulated (Mugambi, 1994). The various genres encompassed by oral expressions and traditions are an integral part of everyday life. During important rites of passage, the best of such expressions are used to better commemorate the events. Orally-transmitted folklore has also comfortably co-existed with writing and electronic modes of transmission, and tradition co-exists with modernity in the continuities embraced in social practices devoted to ensuring the longevity of inherited customs and practices (Oyegoke, 1994). Through the use of signs and symbols, language conveys meaning in even non-verbal communication.

Immigrants from the same or similar ethnic, religious, language and cultural roots tend to congregate in the same countries, regions and communities (Ratha, 2011: 19–21). People also tend to migrate to regions, countries and communities where they are able to communicate with people with whom they share common languages and values, thus, much migration in the African continent tends to be of the cross-border variety, or to replicate patterns of earlier migrations (ibid). Immigrants' longing for connectedness with their home countries and culture drive the reproduction of traditional practices, and the use of familiar languages and linguistic art forms enrich celebrations and make them more meaningful. Many African immigrants speak their indigenous languages at home, teach their children these languages and some sponsor the establishment of language classes to ensure that their languages continue to thrive and their children are connected to their cultural roots.

Technological tools have been useful in the preservation of language in music, poetry, plays, films, and in the written/literary form. In areas with sizeable African immigrant populations, live performances by artistes who are skilled in the use of indigenous art forms are sponsored. Those who have attained international acclaim give these performances to huge audiences. One prominent example is Youssou N'dour, the Senegalese musician who gives live performances at Lincoln Center in New York. Another is the Nigerian musician, Sunny Ade. Both artistes sing in their indigenous languages, in the case of Youssou N'dour, Wolof (and French, with the occasional song in English), and Yoruba in the case of Sunny Ade, with some smattering of English. Films, music videos and newspapers are other means through which immigrants can get entertainment as well as maintenance of contact with their culture.

Commemoration of rites of passage is a way in which Africans maintain connectedness with their countries of origin, language and culture. However, modernity, the spread of Christianity and Islam, lack of will, and consequent changes in the trends have contributed to most African families slack observance of indigenous rites of passage rituals and rites in their originally forms. However, birthdays, weddings, graduations, particularly from college and professional schools; and advanced degrees are acknowledged as important and observed. There is great joyfulness in the celebration of births among Africans both in the continent and its diaspora. These occasions bring together friends and family for ceremonies to name newborn children. The naming and the rituals and practices that accompany it present opportunities to use indigenous language in socially acceptable and prescribed ways, and the practices in the diaspora closely follow those in the home country. The music played at the parties and clothes worn also follow current trends.

Most African immigrant families celebrate weddings with sumptuous parties that combine religious ceremonies with indigenous ceremonies. Funerals tend to be sad when a young person dies. Among some ethnic groups such as the Yoruba, it is traditionally taboo for parents and those older than the departed to be present at funerals for those younger than them. This has proved to be impossible given modern realities, and both young and old attend such funerals. African immigrant communities support their bereaved members by giving monetary gifts to assist with expenses. Some transport the body back to their home countries for burial and have memorial services in the United States, but others have burials in their countries of settlement. For the death of parents in their home countries, African immigrant Christians have services of songs, and Muslims have *fidau* prayers. Funerals of the elderly are considered celebrations of life by Nigerian immigrants, who believe that these are lives well-lived. At most of these celebrations, people dress in what Yorubas call *aso-ebí* (uniform) colors or clothing. Dancing to contemporary music from the given home country of the immigrants, and also to other African music that are popular at the given time, national and ethnic delicacies are important elements in the celebrations. When people mourn, they also follow ethnic, national and indigenous practices. Children who participate and observe learn about the traditions and practices and have the opportunity to choose to maintain and preserve them. Language is the medium through which the communications are transmitted, and although it is extremely difficult to maintain pristine linguistic integrity, some language is passed on to succeeding generations. Many immigrant groups want to be more systematic and they have language classes for young people. Some want to maintain connectedness to their language and attend exclusively African churches and mosques where there are significant members with whom they share common cultural practices.

CONNECTIONS THROUGH CREATIVE EXPRESSIONS, IMAGINATION, PSYCHIC, AND CULTURAL LINKAGES

Hargreaves (1997: 1), in a study of Beur literature in France, shows that these second generation Maghrebian immigrants maintain connections with their heritage through various activities in their daily lives, particularly in their imagination and creative expressions:

> In their daily lives the Beurs have . . . been compelled to migrate constantly between the secular culture of France and the traditions carried with them by their Muslim parents from across the Mediterranean. These experiences have been explored by Beur writers in poems, plays and, above all, prose fiction.

Beur identity and the sensibilities that flow from it have been shaped by larger sociopolitical forces, such as the circumstances of immigration, as there are differences between the *harkis* (the Algerian soldiers that fought on the French side during the war of independence who were repartriated to France as exiles) and immigrés who migrated to France for economic reasons. The *harkis* are traditionally conservative, while the émigrés tend to be leftist. But the sameness of the two communities in terms of socio-economic status, as the least educated in France, and the disadvantages that flow from this, has made for equality in lack of access to housing and employment, making their children less wedded to these distinctions, and more united in affirming the same identity as part of a subordinate ethnic minority (Hargreaves, 1997:5–6). Hargreaves (1997:12–13), in the biographies of the Beur writers, reveals a very important factor that keeps the connection between African immigrant and their home countries—leaving their families behind (12–13). Arthur (2000:96) also affirms that many African immigrants in the United States send their American-born children home "to be raised by extended family members" for economic reasons such as extraordinarily high cost of child care, the responsibilities of work and education. In addition, it is very difficult to secure visas for family members such as grandmothers, who could come to lend a hand in child-rearing (Arthur, 2000: 96–97). This could spur the flow of remittances, family reunification, and travel back home to visit.

REMITTANCES

The World Bank expressed a fact of life that has become widely acknowledged when it introduced a 2011 study which confirms that "international migration has profound implications for human welfare" (Ratha, 2011: 1). Challenging the near-universal embrace of migration as brain drain, the Bank considers remittances the most significant source of development financing, and potential source of increased trade, investment and technology; but also assesses African governments as heretofore unable to harness and appropriate such benefits (Ratha, 2011: 1). It also raises the issue of the low proportion of tertiary educated Africans compared with the general population, and the grave effects on human capital, of the migration of too many in this category (Ratha, 2011: 110–42).

Is international migration to be considered an unproblematic cash cow? Is brain gain more appropriate than brain drain as the catchphrase that describes the flow of skilled, technical and professional Africans as well as African youth of all stripes from the continent? No doubt, remittances have become some of the most significant capital flows to African countries, second only to foreign direct investment, and more significant than official development assistance (Sander and Maimbo 2003; Ratha, 2011: 112). They are predominantly in the form of altruistic financial and material flows that connect family members who are separated by long distances (Chami, Fullenkamp and Jahjah, 2005). Africa received approximately 15 percent of the world's total remittances in 2002, of which, $8 billion went to North Africa, and $4 billion to Sub-Saharan Africa (Sander and Maimbo, 2003: 7).

The volume of remittances have grown exponentially and will continue to increase, as evidenced by the World Bank's statistics, which show that these flows have increased fourfold between 1990 and 2010, an estimated $40 billion and approximately 2.6 percent of the continent's GDP in 2009 (Ratha, 2011: 47). People who send remittances home do so more regularly than any other financial flows that go into the African continent. Especially during times of economic privation, these flows are a reliable recourse for those left behind that help mostly to fund survival needs (Sander and Maimbo, 2003:17; Loup, 2005; Puri and Ritzema n.d.; Baruah, 2006:8). An underappreciated effect of remittances is that they make the countries that receive them more creditworthy since they boost the volume, magnitude and constant flows of foreign exchange. Economists have also claimed that remittances contribute to poverty reduction and increases the spending ability of families in the continent that receive them by providing them with the resources to take care of health and educational needs of family members. These households also are protected from wild economic swings because they have a steady source of support from remittance sending relatives abroad. Thus, such families do not have to resort to economically desperate measures such as selling off or pawning property, including land and other valuables when they are in dire straits (Ratha, 2011). Since most remittances to Africa fund the survival, welfare and subsistence needs of family members, migrants tend to send money and staples as well as some luxury goods, including electronics. Some migrants also put money in bank accounts in their home countries to cover the cost of children's education and "future migration by children and other family members" (Puri and Ritzema, n.d.).

According to Sander and Maimbo (2003), 70 to 90 percent of remittances go toward everyday necessities and expenses that guarantee subsistence and contribute to better living standards to those who receive them. Often emergency and routine health care needs and more predictable and planned education expenses are also funded (Ratha, 2011: 65-68). Remittances also go toward the purchase of consumer goods such as household electronics, renovation or construction of housing, land or livestock acquisition, contributions toward the celebration or commemoration of birth, marriage, pilgrimage, burial, assistance, with the repayment of loans, cost of migration, savings; and investments (Sander and Maimbo, 2003: 17).

A study of remittances by migrants to France from Senegal, Mali, Guinea-Bissau, and the Comoros show that most mainly finance the acquisition of housing either through building, rent or purchase; entrepreneurial ventures, and community development. Community development projects tend to privilege the construction of health and educational institutions. Ghanaian migrants also reported that up to 70 percent of the funds they remit home went toward assisting kinfolk for subsistence, school fees, medical well-being, and urgent situations where immediate disbursement is called for. Thirty percent of remittances were devoted to entrepreneurial ventures. Malian migrants sent 80 to 90 percent of their remittances to help their families with subsistence expenses (Loup, 2005).

Due to the long-term economic crisis experienced by African countries, African migrants tend to prioritize the survival and welfare requirements of their kinfolk and they send less remittances for entrepreneurial ventures and loan repayments than is the case for migrants from other regions (Loup, 2005: 12). Although the World Economic Meltdown/Great Recession has affected these flows, since most African immigrants who send the largest of these remittances are in Europe and North America, regions that were devastated by the breadth and depth of the recession, African immigrants continue to make substantial remittances (Ratha, 2011: 1, 47).

In the aftermath of natural disasters and in the midst of adverse economic conditions in their countries of origin, African immigrants send assistance to their families. This was the case during Botswana and Ethiopia's droughts when immigrants made substantial remittances to family members; the same was true of East African pastoral communities, as well as for Mali, Senegal, and Ghana when those countries experienced economic adversity (Ratha, 2011: 69).

The data on remittances point to their importance in contributing to economic development, particularly in the context of the long term economic downturn experienced by many African countries after the Arab-Israeli war and consequent oil shocks of the 1970s. However, these data are incomplete, because many of the remittances are made in informal transfers that cannot be accurately and completely documented. As has become customary in development analysis, the World Bank has led the research on remittances. It has also aggressively pushed for a laudatory assessment of the impact of remittances, for example, saying:

> After foreign direct investment (FDI), remittances are the continent's largest source of foreign inflows. Migrant remittances contribute to international reserves, help finance imports, and improve the current account position of recipient countries. They are associated with reductions in poverty, improved health and education outcomes, and increased business investments. Although the limited reach of intermediaries in rural areas, lack of effective competition, and inadequate financial and regulatory infrastructure contribute to high remittance costs and the prevalence of informal channels (especially for intra-African remittances), the rapid adoption of innovative money transfer and branchless banking technologies are increasing access to remittances and broader financial services for the poor (Ratha, 2011: 47).

Experience from Egypt, Ghana, Nigeria, and some non-African developing countries show that future remittances could be securitized in the sense of being used as collateral for borrowing for development projects. Doing this enables the countries in question to borrow at a cheaper rate and from more diverse pool of creditors (Ratha, 2011: 56-57). This assessment makes it seem as though the brain drain has instantly been transformed into unqualified gain, but it may be prudent to ask: if the remittances continue to fund survival needs, and encourage governments not to be proactive in embracing their responsibilities for the welfare of the citizens in their countries, should remittances be considered benevolent in all respects?

There is no doubt that remittances yield contributions to personal, community and national well being, but given the huge development challenges faced by African countries, do remittances really make up for the losses suffered by source countries of immigrants? Some believe that especially skilled and technical personnel from the African continent could be a source of considerable remittance flows. They also could help connect their home countries with foreign markets, could facilitate technology transfer, when they return to their countries of origin, could contribute to introducing improved skills and knowledge, and could also contribute to higher demand for education in their countries of birth or origin (Ratha, 2011).

There is also the possibility of adverse effects from remittances, as the World Bank study indicates, for example, huge remittance flows could contribute to unfavorable decline in the exchange rate of the remittance receiving country, a situation that benefits the individuals, families and businesses that receive remittances, but unfavorably impacts those whose earnings are exclusively in the currency of the receiving country, and the economy at large. Further, huge remittances may make it unprofitable to produce tradable goods, and also negatively impact on the prices of domestic nontradeable goods (goods that cannot be easily exchanged internationally like prepared perishable foods; and goods that cannot be easily or cheaply transported). There are also possible effects on labor supply, because it may be more profitable to rely on remittances than to seek employment that does not enable people to cover their expenses (Ratha, 2011). Other negative effects include the propensity for diasporas to participate in conflicts, and to engage in money laundering in their home countries by proxy through the cash and in-kind remittances they send (Ratha, 2011: 6).

The most significant of the negative ramifications of migration to developing countries, particularly in the African continent, is the brain drain. Africa needs skilled, professional, and technical workers in virtually all fields of human endeavor, yet there is a high incentive for the emigration of these categories of people from the continent in ever larger numbers. This contributes to the weakening of development because important skills and services are lost. The ability of such highly skilled workers to positively influence productivity in obvious and more covert ways is considerably weakened or even invalidated, as are the possibilities that they can contribute to "innovative and creative activities that are at the core of long-term growth" (ibid); and possible impact on society, politics, economy and community. Also, when the skilled workers have been trained with government funding, the country loses tremendously, and the receiving country to which immigrants flock gain from something they did not invest in. The matter is further complicated because many African immigrants may have excellent education and skills but may not be able to secure employment in their fields of expertise due to lack of proper documentation or additional certification, and thus, take on menial jobs for the purposes of survival. They are able to make remittances, but the practical measures they take "in high-income destination countries represent a lost investment in human capital (a recent study of the U.S. job market finds that immigrants with bachelor's degrees from 7 of 15 African countries surveyed have less than a 40 percent chance of ending up in a skilled job)" (ibid).

Africa, particularly its smallest and lowest income countries have lost significant numbers of skilled workers, and according to 2000 statistics, the losses suffered by the continent to OECD countries where one out of every eight Africans with a university education resides," is second only to the Caribbean, Central America, and Mexico region (Ratha, 2011: 6–7). According to World Bank statistics on Ghana, people with the best education tend to be the ones that migrate at the highest rate. Measures taken to discourage skilled migration, such as attempts to recover the cost of scholarships given by governments have sometimes recovered the cost without generating return migration, as also documented by the Ghana example (Ratha, 2011: 8).

Regardless of the possible negative ramifications of remittances, African immigrants make cash and in-kind remittances to their home countries and other countries in the continent to which they are connected through organizational, religious, and other affiliations. From a purely economic perspective, these remittances are very tangible, quantifiable measures of deep and enduring commitment to immigrants' countries of origin. Some of these contributions are also invaluable in the sense that they constitute intangible but nonetheless significant social and human capital that has extraordinary impact on community and nation building.

It is widely acknowledged that accurate data does not exist on the size, frequency and impact of remittances by Africans (Ratha, 2011: 51–52). According to a 2006 study, two-thirds of sub-Saharan African countries do not have data or have inaccurate statistics on remittances (Baruah, 2006: 7; Ratha, 2011). Many assessments claim that there are more clandestine and informal remittances than those documented as part of formal transactions. For example, Egyptian migrants were said to have transferred up to 33 percent of remittances made from 1985 to 1986 through informal means; and in 1984, up to 85 percent of remittances by Sudanese migrants were not transferred through official channels (Puri and Ritzema, n.d.). From 1983–1984 Sudanese migrants were believed to have sent 39 percent of adjusted GNP through informal transfers (Puri and Ritzema, n.d.).

IMMIGRANT TRANSNATIONAL ENTREPRENEURSHIP

Portes et al. (2002) analyzed the phenomenon of immigrant transnational entrepreneurship and point out that immigrants engage in entrepreneurship in a manner that makes them bridges between the economies of their home countries and countries of settlement (Portes et al). Sassen-Koob (1981) went further and described migrants as a labor system created by the consolidation of the world economic system. For her, the penetration of capitalism into the periphery of the world economy, and not abstract push and pull factors, connect migrants, their home countries, and the countries in which they settle. The actions of states in response to the reproduction of capitalist relations at the center of the world economy create the dynamics that cause migrants to be treated as commodities. Migration is not caused by economic backwardness and stagnation, and the individual responses of migrants (Sassen-Koob, 1981: 65). If one accepts Sassen-Koob's conceptualization, the fact that transnational immigrants travel back and forth contributes to the development of the world economy through the commercial relations that develop between countries of origin and countries of settlement.

Newland and Tanaka (2010) agree with Portes, et. al (2002), and Ratha, 2011) in the assessment that diaspora entrepreneurs can become bridges to development, particularly in the establishment of businesses in their countries of origin. They are aware of the possibilities to profit from investments, they can both invest their own funds and encourage others to do so, consequently creating employment and generating profits. Newland and Tanaka's (2010) USAID-sponsored study also agrees with Ratha's (2011) evaluation of the efforts of sending countries to track and increase diaspora engagement. Despite the propensity of diasporas to seek direct investment and entrepreneurial opportunities back home, and despite their desire to increase investment in businesses; create jobs; encourage innovation; build social capital; direct more favorable political attention from their countries of settlement to their home countries, many developing countries do not have the ability and resources to foster increased diaspora engagement.

Newland and Tanaka (2010) distinguish between those kinds of entrepreneurship that are likely to generate positive returns to economic development and those that have limited to no effects. "Necessity entrepreneurs" establish small enterprises due to lack of alternative means of generating income. While they create subsistence type employment for themselves, these efforts do not yield much in the way of economic development. Those that engage in "opportunity" entrepreneurship may also be small or medium size in scale, but they see and grasp opportunities more readily and also tend to contribute to increased economic development. The interest in investment most directly derives from desire to maintain enduring ties, give something back, increase economic wellbeing, and also entrepreneurial profit in a way that could be immensely beneficial for countries that have high levels of opportunity entrepreneurship. Ratha is in agreement with Newland and Tanaka in advising states to collect data on their diasporas, provide services, information and incentives to them to encourage entrepreneurship (Newland and Tanaka, 2010: 1).

The fears that investment could be mismanaged in the absence of the fund's owner, and also fears of devaluation causing substantial reduction in the capital and less value from profits make many migrants reluctant to invest. A study by Baruah (2006) shows that Malian migrants tend to be wary of even small-scale entrepreneurial ventures in their country of origin because of the belief that if they are not there, lack of appropriate and adequate oversight will cause the business to fail. When investments are made "livestock and petty trade sectors are preferred over transport or import/export businesses" (Okome, 2007: 158).

A more recent study that conducted household surveys in several African countries shows that:

> a significant portion of international remittances are spent on land purchases, building a house, business, improving a farm, agricultural equipment, and other investments (as a share of total remittances, investment in these items represented 36.4 percent in Burkina Faso, 55.3 percent in Kenya, 57.0 percent in Nigeria, 15.5 percent in Senegal, and 20.2 percent in Uganda ... A substantial share of within-Africa remittances was also used for these purposes in Burkina Faso, Kenya, Nigeria, and Uganda (Ratha, 2011: 65).

The businesses established by African immigrants are not only in their countries of origin. There are also immigrant stores and businesses that provide products from various African countries. The tendency to cluster such businesses in neighborhoods with significant numbers of people from the countries that consume them, for the businesses to be owned and serviced by people from these same countries has been described as evidence of the operation of a niche economy. Both choice and perceived lack thereof motivates the establishment of such businesses. Food, clothing, music, film products and items considered essential are sold by them and used by immigrants in everyday life as well as for weddings, birthdays, festivals and other celebrations. The establishment of these businesses builds commercial bridges between the home and host country. Other businesses provide services tailored to the needs of immigrants. The media in its various manifestations is one kind of business geared to serve immigrants. Newspapers that serve African immigrants publish news, records of social events, and advertisements of services, restaurants, staple foods, religious services, travel and shipping services.

PHILANTHROPIC FLOWS

Given the deep enduring connections between immigrants and their home countries, there is concern about the well-being of communities and nations left behind, and especially in times of natural disasters, there are philanthropic flows from immigrants to their home countries. These flows are however, not limited to times of distress, but tend to be continuous. One particularly noticeable form of philanthropic flows is by Hometown Associations that levy members in order to contribute to community development projects, which are often geared at providing services that governments have become either unwilling or unable to provide, especially after the onset of what has become long-term economic crisis in African countries. Some of these funds are raised to cover the cost of building roads, health care facilities and equipment, schools, boreholes, and rural electrification projects. Some fund scholarships and books. Some are in the form of in-kind contributions, and involve volunteer drives to provide medical services during vacation periods. Apart from individual entrepreneurial efforts, there are also networks geared at social cum economic entrepreneurship. The African Network (TAN) was established in Silicon Valley in 2004 as a nonprofit organization, to alleviate poverty by encouraging the establishment of businesses and offering employment opportunities to people of African descent. Through monthly networking dinners; a biennial TAN Conference (TANCon) in Africa and the United States that brings together budding and successful entrepreneurs, "venture capitalists, investors, business leaders, community leaders, and policymakers" to confer on investment opportunities; and TAN Empowerment (TEP), which raises funds from the diaspora to assist and "develop low-income, needy, and underserved communities in Africa" (Newland and Tanaka, 2010: 16). While African migrants tend to prioritize family survival expenses, they send money back home for construction of noncommercial housing to dominate (Ratha, 2011: 63). Some African countries, including Mali and Burundi both match the contributions of migrants toward local development projects (Baruah, 2006: 19-21). Mali also has a matching fund to finance housing. Uganda is one of the few African countries that offer treasury bills and bonds to migrants as investment opportunities. The Ugandan government also gives its diaspora an idea of possible individual and collaborative entrepreneurial ventures (Okome, 2007a: 159).

Philanthropic remittances could take the form of in-kind donations, such as clothes; educational materials; equipment; information; communication infrastructure and know-how. Some nongovernmental organizations are similar to the TAN, but could direct their efforts at purely social aspects of philanthropy, or political endeavors. Nigerian medical doctors in North America for example, supported the pro-democracy movement in their country of origin to fight against dictatorial regimes led by Generals Ibrahim Babangida, and more concertedly, General Sani Abacha. Kudirat Initiative for Democracy (KIND) was founded by Hafsat Abiola, the daughter of the woman for which it was named, who was a Nigerian in the diaspora. It joined the Nigerian pro-democracy and human rights coalitions to campaign in Nigeria, Europe and North America to challenge the Nigerian dictatorships during the 1990s. Supported by international donors, KIND and its coalition partners were able to transmit Radio Kudirat broadcasts into Nigeria from abroad to provide alternatives to government controlled media reports (Sykes, 1999: 6-7).

Some remittances are in the form of services, and include religious proselytization combined with donations of clothing, books, medicine and equipment, free medical care, and teaching (Sander and Maimbo, 2003: 20). Hometown Associations (HTAs), migrant ethnic associations, and professional organizations also do fundraising to send similar assistance to their home communities and countries. Many also volunteer to personally offer free or highly subsidized medical care, teaching, mentoring and other specialized services.

Somalia's diaspora has undertaken some extraordinary philanthropic efforts that demonstrate continued engagement with their home country. Through the diaspora's efforts, six universities were founded, two in Somalia, and four in Somaliland, which is "a self-declared independent state that is not recognized by any other states" (Okome, 2007a: 159). In 2000, The Somaliland Forum, a group of Somali diaspora scholars, in partnership with Californian Friends of Hargeisa University collaborated to create the University of Hargeisa. They were supported by the UNDP and other UN affiliated agencies, and by Somali entrepreneurs and other migrants (University of Hargeisa, 2006). As a result of collaboration by the World Bank, UNDP and African Virtual University, Hargeisa University offered courses on-site and virtually (World Bank Institute, 2005). Similarly, University of Burao was founded in 2004 by a public-private partnership, set up with funding from Germany, but damaged as a result of the 1980s and 1990s conflicts, individual Somali in the diaspora, and organizations such as the Somaliland Forum, Somaliland Welfare Organisation in Oslo (University of Burao, 2004; afrol News, 2004).

Patrick Awuah, a Ghanaian immigrant to the United States who was educated at Swarthmore College, and employed by Microsoft, returned to his country of origin after fifteen years in the United States to establish Ashesi University College in Accra, Ghana. Swarthmore College, University of California, Berkeley, University of Washington, Seattle, Microsoft, the World Bank and other investors partnered with Awuah to execute this project. The institution is also supported by the Ashesi University Foundation, a nonprofit organization headquartered in Seattle, Washington (The Ashesi University Foundation, n.d.; Ashesi University College, n.d.).

Increasingly, in countries that are relatively peaceful and economically viable, there is temporary/short-term teaching at the tertiary level by diasporan Africans in institutions in their home countries as well as longer term teaching by return migrants. One prominent recent example is Professor Abiola Irele, who began his career in the African continent as a professor of at the University of Ghana, University of Ife (now Obafemi Awolowo University), and the University of Ibadan. He later emigrated to the United States as a professor of African, French, and Comparative Literature at Ohio State University, Columbus. He also founded the journal, *Research in African Literatures*, and was a visiting professor of African and African American Studies at Harvard University and general editor, with Simon Gikandi, of the Cambridge Studies in African and Caribbean Literature series before he returned to Nigeria as the first provost of the College of Humanities Management and Social Sciences at Kwara State University. Irele also donated his library, transported to Nigeria with funding from the W.E.B. DuBois Institutes at Harvard, to Kwara State University, and established a new journal, *Savannah Review* at the University (Irele, n.d.).

FOLKWAYS AND FOODWAYS

In addition, there are linkages in folkways and foodways. In a myriad of ways, immigrants demonstrate their desire to preserve their folkways and foodways. The Beur case is an example of efforts to hold on to cultural practices and their expressions. Most immigrants long for familiar tastes, foods and practices. This is more possible in areas where there is a critical mass of immigrants with similar cultural practices and traditions, but even where this is not the case, great pains are taken to travel to locations that provide access and opportunities to participate. In terms of folkways, dress and aesthetics can be observed in places like Harlem, New York where there are numerous Francophone West Africans, many of whom don clothing made of African print as everyday wear, and more elaborate and expensive clothing for special ceremonies like child naming ceremonies, birthday celebrations, weddings, funerals and the like.

Many African immigrants commemorate their countries' independence annually. Such celebrations are occasions for parades by larger groups, parties and sometimes scholarly events that consider the given country's historical legacy. African Muslims celebrate *Eid el Fitr* at the completion of Ramadan, the thirty-day period of prescribed fasting, reflection, and abstinence from pleasurable activities. For *Eid el Fitr*, alms are given to the poor, presents to children, and there's feasting and celebration by friends and family. *Eid el-Adha*, the Feast of the Sacrifice, celebrates the memory of Prophet Moham-med's return to Mecca. In African countries, rams are slaughtered by Muslims, then cooked and served with festive foods for friends, kith, kin, and neighbors. Muslims go to the mosques and prayer grounds to pray for Allah's blessings. In the United States, Muslims purchase slaughtered (*halal*) rams from farms. Others buy affordable portions from African or Muslim grocery stores for the celebration feast. People also go to the mosques for prayers. In many ways, what is done in the diaspora is identical to what was done at home, with varia-tions due to lack of wherewithal to maintain strict observance.

African immigrant Christians celebrate Christmas and Easter, and predomi-nantly African immigrant churches have annual harvest ceremonies with danc-ing and prayers. Instead of the harvest ceremonies, *Aladura* churches celebrate annual Adoption Services during which fruits and foodstuff are presented as offerings in the church and distributed among worshippers when the ceremo-nies are over. There are also banquets. *Orisa* worship preceded post-World War II African immigrants' presence in the Americas. Puerto Rican Santeria, African-American Yoruba religion, Ocha, Haitian Vodun, Cuban Lucumi, and Brazilian Cadomble and Umbanda sometimes mingle Yoruba religion with Christianity and other religions. Some contemporary African immigrants wor-ship ancestral deities, but this aspect of religious observance has not been suf-ficiently studied. Where these worship services occur, they are accompanied by prayers, chanting, singing, and drumming that continue indigenous practices in ways that are influenced by what is possible in the new environment.

Food is one of the fundamental human needs. It also serves a social func-tion because it is like the grease that oils social relations. There is a dizzying array of African foods, which is a function of the huge range of ethnic and national traditions and customs, the historical linkages and combinations of ethnic groups over time, colonial history, migration of Africans from the slave-created diaspora back to the continent, and the experience of slavery in the new world. Brazilian returnees influenced Nigerian food, Recaptives from the high seas after the abolition of the Transatlantic Slave Trade in Sierra Leone, African Americans who returned to Liberia all had an impact on the foods of Africa, and these have in turn influenced African immigrant foods and foodways. African food has profoundly influenced the Americas and Ca-ribbean due to the cultural retention by enslaved peoples of African descent. Hopping John (black-eyed peas) and chitterlings resemble foods traditionally eaten in the continent. Archeological studies in the United States as well as the foodways of African-American and African-Caribbean people provide evidence of African influences (Samford, 1996).

Africans in the diaspora often long to eat food from their home countries. One of the ways in which African immigrant entrepreneurship is manifested gratifies this longing through the establishment of grocery food stores, eateries, party planning and catering services. In many metropolitan areas where there is a critical mass of African immigrants, wholesale markets advertise and sell staple ingredients and foods. Africans in New York City go to the Bronx and Brooklyn Terminal Markets for their bulk food needs.

CIVIC ENGAGEMENT

Civic engagement with the politics of the home country demonstrates connections between immigrants and their country of origin. Some African immigrants campaign for voting rights. The Ghanaians in North America did this successfully. Others seek dual citizenship. Currently (June 2011) twenty-five African countries permit dual citizenship (Ratha, 2011: 10). The African countries that have dual citizenship with the United States include Benin, Burkina Faso, Cape Verde, Egypt, Ghana, Lesotho, Nigeria, and South Africa (Renshon, 2001: 45; Ionescu and IOM, 2010: 123–33). Being dual citizens enable immigrants to maintain contact with their home country more easily, as they do not have to obtain visas when they visit, can more easily purchase land, access temporary employment, and legally own businesses. The status also has the additional emotional and psychological benefits of helping people feel that they are still part of their countries of origin (Ratha, 2011: 10). To return to civic engagement, the ease of ability to vote, and to run in elections, the recognition of the skill and expertise of immigrants demonstrated when their countries of origin recruit them for high level political appointments, both enable them to contribute and encourage them to maintain keen interest. Increasingly, such interest is actively cultivated by some African countries through government agencies that call upon "diasporas to invest, assist local communities, and provide policy advice" (Ratha, 2011: 11). But given the potential huge benefits to African countries from diaspora contributions, it is remarkable that there is yet inadequate data-gathering on diasporas and poor coordination between the foreign representatives of African countries and domestic ministries on the kinds of information they need from their diasporas, as well as poor provision of information and services by African consulates and embassies to their diasporas (Ratha, 2011: 11). Some of the services that consulates and embassies can provide that could devolve into diaspora contributions to development in their countries of origin include support for professional associations and cultural organizations through sponsoring events, supporting private sector networks, investments in modern information and communications technology, information on possible private and public investments, despite the impact of currency devaluation.

Some countries for example, offer "diaspora bonds"; some permit emigrants to be eligible for social security coverage and benefit from savings schemes to which all citizens are entitled. Some African countries with considerable numbers of emigrants, such as Ghana, Nigeria, Senegal, and South Africa, have come up with schemes to encourage their diasporas in development programs as "partners in development" (Ratha, 2011: 11).

DESIRE FOR RETURN MIGRATION/MYTH OF RETURN

Many immigrants maintain an interest in return migration, but the elusiveness of this desire has made scholars conceptualize the often unrequited desire as the myth of return. Although the data is not comprehensive enough to warrant categorical conclusions, a study of Ghanaian immigrants in Canada shows that the men were more interested in returning home because they would return to a patriarchal society, while women were more reluctant because they relished the freedom gained from patriarchy in their country of settlement (Ratha 2011, 31). Since fewer than 10 percent of emigrants from Nigeria and Senegal were return immigrants, available statistics also point to the likelihood for the longing to return home to remain mythical (Ratha, 2011: 14). In addition, there may be differences in the desire of men and women to return to the home country. The myth of return serves a psychological purpose because it helps to assuage the helplessness that could accompany long-term exile, sojourn, refugee status and immigration. The desire to return expresses dogged connectedness to the idea of home, the status and comforts left behind, and it also enables immigrants/refugees/exiles to manage the existential problems and challenges wrapped up in their new status.

VIRTUAL COMMUNITIES

Increasingly, the availability of the tools of information and communication technology has propelled the establishment of online communities around areas of common interest. The communities formed include those by hometown associations, ethnic, national, religious, professional and other groups. Belonging to, and participating in these groups has given African immigrants the opportunity to establish and groom more robust connections with their home countries through the pursuit of conversations, debates information exchange, signature drives, fundraising and other activities in these groups. Although USAfricaDialogue was established as an international discussion group (the group was established by a Nigerian, Professor Toyin Falola, a historian at the University of Texas, Austin it is and also dominated by Nigerians.) There is a myriad of other groups that enable participants to keep up-to-date with current developments in the issue and areas that interest them. I have argued that some of these online communities could also be epistemic, in the sense that they bring together experts who are interested in, and have the highest levels of expertise on the same issue(s), causing them to become the "go-to" group in all matters related to such issues, such that they can give sound advice, recommendations and opinions. In the case of Africa, I suggest that such groups are one possible way in which the continent can reverse some of the problems arising from the brain drain (Okome, 2010).

Virtual communication has also reduced the cost of keeping in touch with kith and kin in far-flung areas, and enables the easier bonding of transnational families (Ratha, 2011: 31). As well, virtual and mobile telephone services have increased the ease and decreased the cost of transmitting and accessing remittances and saving money. M-pesa, which was set up in 2007 in Kenya is one of the first African examples but since then, more have been established (Ratha, 2011: 80-84). Traditionally, banks connected with money transfer firms like Western Union and Money Gram dominated this business but post offices are also increasingly getting into the money transfer businesses (Ratha, 2011). African immigrants' remittances are clearly an essential part of tangible transactions that denote concern for and connectedness to their home countries. These transactions generate funding for kith and kin as well as for international and African money transfer businesses, mobile phone companies, post offices and even informal transfer networks. To the extent that African migrations increase over time, such transfers will continue and are even likely to increase substantially. Businesses that profit from them will also proliferate both internationally and in the African countries that have large numbers of immigrants.

CONCLUSION

Immigration and diasporization are often challenging experiences. Those who become immigrants either through volition or compulsion devise many coping mechanisms, and maintenance of connectedness to the homeland is an important tool. However, although not discussed in this chapter, it is important that those whose exit from their countries of origin is traumatic may want to forget, and may take great pains to accomplish the erasure of their connections to their countries of origin. However, the evidence from observation and studies of African immigrants and diasporas attest to the accuracy of the conclusion that they have deep and enduring ties to their countries of origin. Even for the old diasporas where the break was violent and entirely nonvolitional, psychic, literary, religious, customary, and linguistic connections are maintained. For the post-1945 African immigrants, connections with their home countries can similarly be found in connections through language, creative expressions, imagination, psychic and cultural linkages, remittances, folkways, foodways, philanthropic flows, civic engagement, desire for return migration/myth of return, and the formation of online communities. These are ongoing processes that are highly dynamic and in flux. Understanding them requires consistent study and scholarly engagement.

REFERENCES

Abdullah, Z. 2009. "Sufis on parade: The performance of Black, African and Muslim identities." *Journal of the American Academy of Religion. Volume.* 77 (2): 199–237.

Adogame, A. 2003. "Betwixt identity and security: African new religious movements and the politics of religious networking in Europe." *Nova Religio: The Journal of Alternative and Emergent Religions* 7 (2): 24–41.

afrol News. 2004. Somaliland now counts on four universities. *afrol News.* http://www.afrol.com/articles/13763.

Arthur, J. A. 2000. *Invisible sojourners: African immigrant diaspora in the United States.* Westport, CT: Praeger Publishers.

Ashesi University College . Ashesi University College News. *Ashesi University College.* http://www.ashesi.edu.gh/

Baruah, N. February 2006. Remittances to least developed countries (LDCs): Issues, policies, practices and enhancing development impact. Presented at the Ministerial Conference of the Least Developed Countries on Enhancing the Development Impact of Remittances, Cotonou, Benin. *International Office of Migration.* http://www.iom.int/en/PDF_Files/benin/Remittances_to_LDCs_Background_Paper_English.pdf

Chami, R., Connel F., and Samir J. 2005. Are immigrant remittance flows a source of capital for development? *International Monetary Fund Staff Papers.* 2005. http://dukespace.lib.duke.edu/dspace/bitstream/handle/10161/2030/Fullenkamp_are_immigrant_remittance.pdf?sequence=1.

Hargreaves, A. G. 1997. *Immigration and identity in beur fiction: Voices from the North African community in France.* Oxford: Berg Publishers.

Ionescu, D. and IOM. February 2005. Engaging diasporas as development partners, for home and destination countries in workshop on the national strategy on migration, selected papers. *IOM Tirana.* September 2010. http://www.iomtirana.org.al/en/ELibrary/Brochures+/Nat%20Strat%20WSH%20Selected%20papers.pdf#page=124.

Irele, A. 2010. Abiola Irele. *Abiola Irele.* http://abiolairele.blogspot.com/2010/11/journeys-of-scholarprofessor-abiola.html.

Loup, J. June. 2005. "Economy of solidarity: Expatriate workers remittances to Sub Saharan Africa." *Fondation L'Innovation Politique, Paris, France.* http://www .fondapol.org/pdf/Fondapol-Loup-VA-210605.pdf (accessed July 15, 2006).

Mugambi, H. N. 1994. "Intersections: Gender, orality, text, and female space in contemporary Kiganda radio songs." *Research in African Literatures.* Volume 25 (3): 47–70.

Newland, K. and Hiroyuki T. 2010. "Mobilizing diaspora entrepreneurship for development." *Migrationpolicy.org.* http://www.migrationpolicy.org/pubs/diasporas -entrepreneurship.pdf (accessed June 25, 2011).

Okome, M. O. 2007a. "African diasporas." In Barbara, M., Lincoln, C. and Peter, G. *Diasporas and development* (eds.). Cambridge, MA: Harvard University Press, 151-184.

Okome, M. O. 2007b. "African immigrant churches and the new christian right." In Olupona, J. K. and Regina, G. *African immigrant religions in America* (eds.). New York: New York University Press, 394 431.

Okome, M. O. 2004. "Emergent African immigrant philanthropy in New York City." In Jerry and Ray Hutchinson Krase. *Race and Ethnicity in New York City* (eds.). Volume 7, Research in Urban Sociology. New York: Elsevier/JAI Press, 179 92.

Okome, M. O. 2010. "Immigrant voices in cyberspace: Spinning continental and diasporan Africans into the world-wide web." In Byfield, J.A., LaRay, D. and Anthea, M. *Gendering the African Diaspora: Women, Culture, and Historical Change in the Cariand Nigerian Hinterland* (eds.). Indianapolis: Indiana University Press, 285-312.

Okome, M. O. 2006. "Spinning an African academy into the world wide web: the liberatory and democratic potential of African scholarship in cyberspace." *The Bridging the North-South Divide in Scholarly Communication on Africa: Threats and Opportunities in the Digital era Conference Conference.* Leiden: The Netherlands Online. 2008-10-31. http://www.ascleiden.nl/Pdf/elecpublconfokome.pdf, 2006.

Okome, M. O. 2006. "The contradictions of globalization: causes and consequences of African immigration to the United States." In Kwado, K-A, Baffour, K.T. and John Arthur. *The New African Diaspora in North America: Trends, Community Building and Adaptation* (eds.) Lanham: Lexington Books, 29–48.

Okome, M. O. 2006. "The dividends of Democracy: The Nigeria experience." In Olayiwola and Olusoji A. *Nigeria in Global Politics: Twentieth Century and Beyond* (eds.). New York: Nova Publishers, 47-62.

Okpewho, I., Carole B. D. and Ali A. M. 1999. *The African diaspora: African origins and New World identities.* Bloomington: Indiana University Press.

Olupona, J. K. 1993. "The study of Yoruba religious tradition in historical perspective." *Numen.* Volume 40 (3): 240–73.

Olupona, J. K. and Regina G. 2007. *African Immigrant Religions in America .* New York: New York University Press.

Owusu, T. 1998. "To buy or not to by: determinants of home ownership among ghanaian immigrants in Toronto." *Canadian Geographer / Le Géographe canadien.* Vo. 42 (1): 40–52.

Oyegoke, Lekan. 1994. "Sade's testimony: a new autobiography in African folklore." *Research in African Literatures.* Volume 25 (3) : 131–41.

Portes, A., Luis E. G. and William J. H. 2002. "Transnational entrepreneurs: an alternative form of immigrant economic adaptation." *American Sociological Review.* Volume 67 (2): 278–98.

Puri, S. and Tineke, R. 2006. "Migrant worker remittances micro-finance and the informal economy: prospects and issues." *Working Paper No. 21, International Labor Organization.* n.d. http://www.ilo.org/public/english/employment/finance/papers/wpap21.htm (accessed August 3, 2006).

Ratha, D. 2011. "Leveraging migration for Africa: remittances, skills, and investments." *The International Bank for Reconstruction and Development / The World Bank* (ed.). http://siteresources.worldbank.org/EXTDECPROSPECTS/Resources/476882-1157133580628/AfricaStudyEntireBook.pdf (accessed June 22, 2011).

Renshon, S. A. October, 2001. "Dual citizenship and American national identity." *Center for Immigration Studies.* October 2001. http://cis.org/articles/2001/paper20/renshondual.pdf (accessed June 15, 2011).

Samford, P. 1996. "The archaeology of African American slavery and material culture."*The William and Mary Quarterly.* Volume 53 (1): 87–114.

Sander, C. and Samuel M. M. 2003. "Migrant labor remittances in Africa: reducing obstacles to developmental contributions." *World Bank Africa Region Working Paper Series No. 64.* http://www.worldbank.org/afr/wps/wp64.pdf (accessed April 30, 2011).

Sassen-Koob, S. 1981. "Towards a conceptualization of immigrant labor." *Social Problems.* Volume 29 (1): 65–85.

Schiller, N. G., Linda B. and Szanton B. C. 1995. "From immigrant to transmigrant: Theorizing transnational migration." *Anthropological Quarterly.* Volume 68 (1): 48-63.

Sykes, R. Spring 1999. "Alumna speaks out for freedom." *The Andover Bulletin*: 6–7.

Temple, C. N. 2006. "Strategies for cultural renewal in an American-based version of African globalism." *Journal of Black Studies. Volume* 36 (3): 301–17.

The Ashesi University Foundation. 2011. "Ethical leadership • Innovative thinking • A new Africa." *The Ashesi University Foundation.* http://www.ashesi.org/ (accessed June 27, 2011).

University of Burao. 2004. "Update: A major meeting in Oslo discussed ways to contribute to Burao's young university." November 21, 2004. http://www.burao university.com/news/archive/21Nov2004.htm (accessed July 24, 2006).

University of Hargeisa. 2006. "About University of Hargeisa." http://www.hargeisa university.net/AboutUS.htm (accessed July 23, 2006).

World Bank Institute. 2005. "Somali universities enter the world of distance learning. 2005." (http://web.worldbank.org/WBSITE/EXTERNAL/WBI/0,,contentMDK:20 852653~pagePK:209023~piPK:207535~theSitePK:213799,00.html (accessed 23 2006, July).

Zeleza, P. T. n.d. "African Labor and International Migrations to the North: Building New TransAtlantic Bridges." *Department of African Studies, University of Illinois, Chicago.* http://www.afrst.uiuc.edu/SEMINAR/AfricanLabor.doc (accessed May 5, 2005).

Chapter Eleven

African Women in the New Diaspora: Transnationalism and the (Re)Creation of Home[1]

INTRODUCTION: ISSUES AND OBJECTIVES

With the growth in African and Caribbean immigration to the United States over the past twenty-five years, we are witnessing the development of a New African diaspora. Changes in immigration legislation beginning with the Hart-Cellar Immigration Act of 1965, the Immigration Reform and Control Act of 1986, the Immigration Reform Act of 1990, which included the establishment of the Diversity Lottery among other laws, have made it possible for immigrants to enter the United States from Africa, especially during the 1990s, as well as from other regions in the Global South.[2]

In addition to the changes in U.S. immigration law, the United States became an increasingly attractive option for Africans seeking to leave the continent due to the prospects for enhanced socio-economic mobility and the U.S. position as a technological leader in the past few decades. From the late 1980s to the present, political and socioeconomic conditions on the African continent have also served as major "push" factors for increased migration to the United States. Included among these factors are: the current phase of globalization (and the related consequences of economic crisis and adjustment), political instability and corruption, wars, civil unrest and natural disasters. As a result, some Africans have migrated to the United States in an effort to further their education, to escape poverty and to seek asylum. Most have legally entered the US under provisions in immigration law for family reunification, to meet the demand for highly-trained specialists or in the status of refugees, asylum seekers, or students. Since the terrorist attacks on September 11, 2001, however, it has become increasingly difficult for Africans to visit or settle in the United States (Boyce Davies, 2007).[3] Throughout the peak years of African migration to the United States and beyond, both women and men from a range of educational and occupational backgrounds have participated in the immigration streams.

This chapter will explore one small segment of this new African diaspora—African women entrepreneurs and/or leaders of community organizations in two major metropolitan areas—Philadelphia and Boston. Drawing on in-depth interviews with fifteen women entrepreneurs and/or leaders of African organizations, this exploratory study will examine how their development of transnational identities is leading to successful efforts in the revitalization of parts of major cities and civil society. This sample is part of a larger, ongoing study of African immigrants, whose ties on both sides of the Atlantic are strengthening the development of their businesses and some urban neighborhoods, contributing to development in their "home" nations and reinvigorating civil society in the process. Their activities can perhaps be best seen in these neighborhoods, which served as sites in my study: West Philadelphia, Dorchester and Hyde Park in Boston, and Worcester, a city south of Boston. This chapter, will not present a comprehensive overview of the operation of their enterprises and their many contributions to the revitalization of commercial areas in these cities, but focuses on the transnational ties and the general contributions that these women are making to the maintenance of communities on both sides of the Atlantic. This work will situate the experiences of these immigrants within the context of the literature in migration studies, interrogate how these migrants define themselves and discuss some of their experiences with race/race relations in the United States. In many ways, they have forged a new Pan-African identity. In addition, this paper will discuss the role of intersectionality in their lives—how the factors of race, class, and gender affect their professional and personal experiences. While these women are clearly transnationals who are making very valuable contributions to the maintenance of their extended families in their nations of origin, they are especially committed to building and improving life for their families and communities in the United States. In fact, when compared to their male counterparts, these women have demonstrated a stronger commitment to building civil society organizations in the United States, while their male peers have been more concerned with development in their nations of origin. The roles and responsibilities of these respondents as women and mothers explain in large part their stronger commitments to community building in the United States as opposed to their countries of birth. Several of them have (or had) school-aged children who encountered problems in the educational system in the United States, and their commitment to the educational and occupational success of their children often led them to start and/or join organizations that could advance their children's achievement. In the absence of extended family ties from home, several women also found that community organizations in the United States could assist them in addressing their personal and professional needs as women, particularly when one considers the ways in which race, gender, and sometimes class intersected in their lives and limited their mobility. Further, for some African women, life in the US afforded them greater freedom from the so-called "traditional" values in their nations of origin, which further limited socioeconomic opportunities and their overall empowerment. As women of color, they face many challenges in the Greater Philadelphia and Boston areas, but most of them argue that life has been better for them in the United States. In the next section of the chapter I embark on an analysis of those theoretical and empirical perspectives that are most useful in making sense of their lives.

MIGRATION STUDIES: MAPPING A NEW TERRAIN OF THEORETICAL AND EMPIRICAL PERSPECTIVES

Over the past twenty years, the current phase of globalization characterized by the substantial movements of capital, populations, and ideas suggests that a new body of theory is needed to account for the experiences of populations of color who have recently migrated to the United States or elsewhere.[4] The assimilation theories of the past are no longer tenable in making sense of the experiences and positions in the social hierarchy that newer, post-1965 immigrant groups encounter in the United States.[5] It is at this point where the field of migration studies enters the equation complementing the old field of race and ethnic relations in providing greater breadth and specificity in understanding the experiences of migrants around the world. Migration studies enables us to acknowledge and accord agency to the global movements of populations involved in multiple sites/stages in the process of immigration. They also provide us with the tools to comprehend how the current phase of globalization presents new "push" and "pull" factors for migrants linked to economic crisis/insecurity, wars and political instability in their home countries. While some of these factors might resemble the reasons why many immigrants came to the United States in the past, this phase of globalization facilitates transportation and the spread of technology in ways that make information about, communication with, and travel to, foreign shores easier and to some extent more affordable. Of course, this stage of capitalist development in the North has demands for migrant labor that is both similar to and different from earlier periods (Sassen, 1988; Hu-Dehart, 2007).[6]

It is precisely in the field of migration studies where we can begin to understand the experiences of New African diaspora immigrants. African immigrants to the United States, as well as those migrating elsewhere, are perhaps best understood through the concept of transnationalism. Transnationals maintain "identities that extend across national borders and involve participation in both their home countries and new societies of settlement" (Swigart, 2001: 3). These immigrants engage in "transnational practices" that involve:

> multi-stranded social relations along family, economic and political lines that link together migrants' societies of origin and settlement. In this way, migrants are said to build transnational social fields that crosses geographic, cultural and political borders (Basch, 2001 as cited in Foner, 2001: 9).

These multi-stranded social relations involve African immigrants sending remittances back to relatives in their home countries, which are often the critical means of support for many poor families on the continent and indeed, are major contributors to the economies of these nations.[7] These remittances are a major source of money for food, education for the young and health care for families in Africa. However, these transnational ties are also maintained by migrants' abilities to frequently visit home, to maintain ties via the telephone and the internet and by sponsoring relatives from abroad (Arthur, 2000). Further, Stoller (2002) noted in his work that West African traders in New York City maintained strong allegiances with trading cartels and their families in Niger, Mali, and other West African states. While earlier European immigrants to the United States were also likely to maintain ties to their homelands, I argue that the ties of contemporary immigrants of color are far deeper, stronger and likely to be very current, and therefore of longer duration than the ties of old. This is partly due to the changes in technology and economic development (or the lack thereof) linked to globalization and to the issue of "race" and exclusion in the United States, which often leads immigrants of color to maintain close ties to home and to their national identities. As Vickerman (2001:220) observed, "transnationalism, by orienting immigrants back to their homelands, strengthens ethnicity and slows the process of assimilation."

Portes (1996) also discussed the increased importance of transnational communities in the United States, especially in relation to immigrant entrepreneurship. In their travels back and forth between their home and host nations, transnationals carry both their cultural and political attitudes in both directions. In the case of African immigrants, they share information, develop contacts and establish trust on both sides of the Atlantic, which contributes to the development of their businesses and other ventures in their host societies, as well as the establishment of enterprises in their home nations. As Stoller (2002) observed for many traders from Francophone West Africa, they maintained strong ties to their communities of origin, which facilitated their access to West African crafts and other goods to sell in the United States.

This leads us to the question of how Africans are treated by and respond to the "host" society. What ties do Africans develop on this side of the Atlantic?

As opposed to older models of assimilation posited by early U.S. sociologists, Portes and Rumbaut (2001) have developed a new, more complex term known as "segmented assimilation." They define segmented assimilation as a situation "where outcomes vary across immigrant minorities and where rapid integration and acceptance into the American mainstream represent just one possible alternative" (Portes and Rumbaut, 2001: 45). This theory maintains that assimilation is not a uniform process that all groups experience equally and not a desirable process on the part of all migrants, especially those who see their stay as temporary. Further, segmented assimilation allows us to see the pivotal role that "race" plays in the processes of incorporation in the United States. Even if they so desire, not all groups will be able to assimilate. Other possible outcomes in their experiences are remaining part of an immigrant enclave or as also noted by Ogbu becoming part of a minority oppositional culture (Ogbu, 1978; Portes and Zhou,1993; Portes and Rumbaut, 2001).

Moreover, in this theory and in other contemporary empirical works, race and ethnicity play critical roles in the processes of incorporation as well as in socio-economic mobility for immigrants in the United States (Portes and Zhou, 1993; Waters, 1999; Glick Schiller and Fouron, 2001; Stepick et al, 2003). In this regard, are first-generation African immigrants likely to be viewed as African Americans by mainstream society or as Africans? How might their association with African Americans and/or Caribbean immigrants in major cities affect how they are treated by European Americans and in turn, lead to upward or downward mobility?

Bryce-Laporte (1993:40) discussed the development of a Pan-African identity among Caribbean immigrants to the United States. He argued that much of this Pan-African identity stems from the way that black immigrants "find themselves branded and thus bond along racial, regional, or pan-ethnic lines." This view of Pan-Africanism has relevance for contemporary African immigrants but this analysis demands that we first distinguish between the various forms of Pan-Africanism. First, there was political Pan-Africanism launched at the Pan-African Congress held in Ghana in 1919. Political Pan-Africanism focused on the liberation of all African peoples from oppression, the independence of African states, and the unity of all black peoples and was spearheaded by many African continental and diasporic scholars and activists including Nkrumah, DuBois, Garvey, and Padmore. Second, during the U.S. Civil Rights Movement and the Black Power Movements from the 1950s through the 1970s, which overlapped the period of the independence movements in many African states, cultural Pan-Africanism flourished in the Diaspora as African Americans and Afro-Caribbeans adopted forms of African arts and culture for inclusion in their daily lives. This cultural Pan-Africanism was perhaps most evident in the styles of hair and clothing, musical and dance forms, and in the "taking of African names" that prevailed among many in the African diaspora.

Today, a new Pan-Africanism exists among immigrants in this study which is linked to Bryce-Laporte's (1993) earlier research and the work of the African Union. With its establishment in 2001-02, the African Union called for "the unity, solidarity, cohesion and cooperation among the peoples of Africa and the African states" (Boyce Davies and M'Bow 2007:15). In subsequent years, the African Union pushed for unity of all African populations and other specific goals including the creation of a Diaspora Fund for investment and development in Africa and the development of a diaspora database to facilitate collaboration between those on the continent and those in the diaspora in science and technology as well as in other areas (Boyce Davies and M'Bow, 2007). Thus, the African Union sees a pivotal role to be played by those in the diaspora for the development of the continent (Reddock, 2007).

As demonstrated by their transnational ties, most African migrants around the globe remain dedicated to assisting in the development of their homelands regardless of the magnitude of their efforts. In this sense, these migrants, sometimes united with African American and Caribbean populations in their host societies and Africans on the continent, embody the new Pan-Africanism. This new Pan-Africanism differs from the earlier political and cultural forms that flourished during the freedom struggles of black peoples on both sides of the Atlantic. However, as noted by Bryce-Laporte (1993), it is also the experience of racism and to some extent classism that leads some African immigrants, such as those in my study, to bond with other Africans, African Americans and Afro-Caribbeans in order to achieve the access to educational, income and occupational resources that are vital to their mobility in the United States. As this study will show, such bonds were mainly evident among African women migrants as opposed to their male peers. This expression of the "new Pan-Africanism," though, is not without conflict. As indicated below, in the competition over resources in the current phase of globalization, relations between African immigrants and others in the diaspora are sometimes strained.

On the other hand, do most African immigrants experience "favored treatment" in gaining access to resources in the United States, as many scholars have observed for first generation Caribbean immigrants, or are they likely to be viewed as African Americans, in keeping with the treatment of second-generation Caribbean immigrants and experience downward mobility (Apraku, 1996; Portes and Zhou, 1993; Waters, 1999). Research by sociologists and others has revealed that African immigrants do not experience the returns to education that are realized by Caribbean immigrants, namely they earn lower salaries than one would expect given their educational attainment (Dodoo, 1997; Yesufu, 2003).

In addition to the variable of race, gender, and class further complicate the lives of women of color and more specifically the lives of African immigrant women. Feminist researchers have noted that migration is a gendered process (Kibria, 1994; Purkayastha et al, 1997; Yesufu, 2003; Boyce Davies, 2007; Reddock, 2007). Intersectionality plays a critical role in the returns that African women receive for their level of educational attainment. A study in Edmonton, Canada, revealed that they received lower salaries and were more likely to be located in lower-status service occupations than other recent immigrant groups (Yesufu, 2003). These women also faced discrimination in the labor market since many of them held foreign degrees (earned in their nations of origin), had employers who held stereotypical views of black women and had low levels of social capital in their host societies which resulted in their lack of information about jobs and overall life in Canada (Yesufu, 2003). Thus, black women migrants often experience the intersection of gender, race, and class in their lives, which affects their life chances and is likely to have an impact on the development of their communities. However, immigrant women of color have also demonstrated their agency in establishing organizations to facilitate their entry/immersion into a community and to shield them from the effects of the larger society (Purkayastha et al, 1997). Such organizations often provide support in areas such as domestic abuse previously provided by extended family members at home. By "giving voice" to the experiences of immigrant women of color these groups further empower these women.

Although many African women migrate with their husbands and/or children in an effort to improve their economic well-being, not all African women migrate specifically for material gain. Some women of color leave their home countries in an effort to escape unsatisfying relationships and to increase their autonomy. They hope to gain greater control over their labor, their lives and often those of their children (Boyce Davies, 2007). Even when women of color migrate along with their families, life in the host society usually involves some renegotiation of gender roles that often benefits women (Kibria, 1994).

While this chapter does not intend to answer all of the questions surrounding African women and their position in the broader socioeconomic system, it will explore African immigrant women's transnationalism, other notions of identity and their assessment of and experience with race relations. Paradigms that explore transnationalism, segmented assimilation and intersectionality appear to be the best starting points for such analyses.

DEMOGRAPHIC BACKGROUND: AFRICAN IMMIGRANTS IN THE UNITED STATES, PHILADELPHIA, AND BOSTON

While Africans have been migrating to the United States since the Hart-Cellar Act of 1965, the New African diaspora really emerged with the significant increase in African (and Caribbean) migration from the 1980s to the present—a change from about 30,000 African immigrants arriving in the mid-late 1960s to over 350,000 in the decade of the 1990s. As stated above, this increase is specifically linked to the current phase of globalization which has created the largely economic and political "push" and "pull" factors leading Africans to leave the continent.

In the 1960s and 1970s, many Africans came for higher education—to attend university to attain bachelors' or graduate degrees or both. At that time, African governments and some U.S. universities sponsored students to study abroad to develop the human capital believed necessary for development and to lead the newly independent states on the continent. Upon completion of their degrees, some African students returned to the continent while others settled in the US. For many, the decision to return after graduation was based in large part on the economic and political conditions that prevailed in their home countries at the time.[8] The decision of some Africans to return to their nations of origin or to stay in the United States was also conditioned by the type of visa they obtained to study in the United States. From the 1980s to the present, economic and political crises, such as the imposition of structural adjustment programs, civil wars, and ethnic and religious conflicts have led many Africans to migrate to the United States.

Today, Africans still constitute a very small percentage of the overall number of immigrants who come to the United States each year—they are about 6 percent of all immigrants. According to the 2000 Census, 881,300 Africans resided in the United States, comprising about 3 percent of the foreign-born population. Today, it is estimated that about one million Africans reside in the United States. Half of the African population currently residing in the United States arrived between 1990 and 2000. It is important to note, however, that these are official statistics for those who enter from such categories as: refugees, relatives of U.S. citizens/permanent residents and those receiving visas through diversity programs. The total number of Africans who enter the country may exceed these approximately 50,000 legal migrants who have been arriving every year over the past decade. (*People's Weekly World*).

The largest number of African-born populations in the US comes from West Africa, constituting about 36 percent of this population in 2000, followed by East Africans with 24 percent, and North Africa with 22 percent of the African-born population (www.migrationinformation.org). Among the most significant sending countries in Africa are: Nigeria, Ghana, Ethiopia, Sierra Leone, Egypt, South Africa, Kenya, and Liberia. By the end of the 1990s, Nigerians were the largest population of migrants from the region constituting about 17 percent of all African immigrants, followed by Ethiopians at about 13 percent (Arthur, 2000).

African-born populations are somewhat scattered throughout the United States, with the greatest concentrations found near large cities and in the northeast. Although Philadelphia has been an understudied area in the literature on immigration, it is becoming an increasingly important location for Africans, ranking among the top ten metropolitan areas with respect to the percentage of the African-born population. According to the 2000 Census, over 2 percent of all African-born populations in the United States reside in Greater Philadelphia—about 20,392 persons.[9] They constitute about 6–7 percent of the foreign-born in Philadelphia (Welcoming Center for New Pennsylvanians 2004; www.migrationinformation.org). Migrants from just about every African country reside in the Delaware Valley with the largest number coming from Liberia. Many also come from Nigeria, Ethiopia, and Ghana (Swigart, 2001; Welcoming Center for New Pennsylvanians, 2004). This region has also been an important site for resettlement of refugees from Sierra Leone, Ethiopia, Sudan, and Liberia (Swigart, 2001).

An African presence can be found in several areas of the city. West Philadelphia has become the most important commercial district for African-owned businesses, with several dotting the Baltimore Avenue corridor. Several other communities are now home to Africans—a small Kenyan population lives in Norristown; the Sudanese tend to concentrate in West or Northeast Philadelphia while Sierra Leoneans, Liberians, and Ethiopians tend to live in Southwest Philadelphia. Nigerians and Ghanaians tend to be scattered throughout many parts of the Delaware Valley (Welcoming Center for New Pennsylvanians, 2004). The region is also home to at least three African mosques and eleven churches, several of which are located in West Philadelphia. The Greater Philadelphia area has also been an important locale for African community organizations and annual events, such as the Odunde Festival. The Coalition of African Communities (AFRICOM), an umbrella group representing African and Caribbean immigrant organizations, is a model association in the city and nationwide. It facilitates African immigrants' access to many vital city services.

In recent years, Massachusetts and the city of Boston have also witnessed important growth in their African-born populations. In 2005, the foreign-born population in Massachusetts was 14.4 percent of the total state population, with Africans constituting the second-fastest growing immigrant group in the state (after immigrants from Latin America). The African immigrant population grew by 26.7 percent in the 2000–2005 period totaling 59,322 in 2005. Boston also experienced substantial growth in the African population, which now numbers 15,975 and constitutes 27.2 percent of the foreign-born population in the city (American Community Survey, 2006). Boston, like Philadelphia is an understudied area of immigration but yet is also among the top ten cities in the nation having the largest share of the African-born population, with the former having slightly over 3 percent of the total African-born population in the United States (Migration Policy Institute 2003). The number of Africans in Boston is quite substantial when one considers that it is a much smaller city than Philadelphia (Boston—approximately 590,763 persons in 2006; compared to about 1.5 million in Philadelphia) and that these numbers are for the city of Boston and not for the Greater Boston area. However, Africans living in Philadelphia encounter a more "black" city than is the case for those in Boston since the black population in the former is 44 percent of the urban population versus about 25 percent of the Boston population.

While African immigrants live in many areas of the city and their surrounding suburbs, African entrepreneurs in Boston, like those in Philadelphia, are making their presence known in neighborhoods that have historically been home to the African American community: Roxbury, Dorchester, and Mattapan. Cape Verdeans, Nigerians, and Ethiopians are some of the largest populations of the African-born in Boston, as well as in the Greater Boston area.

Although tensions have been noted between some African Americans and black immigrant populations particularly over access to scarce resources such as employment and education (Waters, 1999; Glick Schiller and Fouron, 2001; Stepick et al, 2003), my study reveals that in many cases, African women have joined with their African-American sisters in working for improved life chances for those in their communities. These encounters have not always been without tensions, but my study indicates that such tensions were few compared to the bridge-building that occurred between these groups of women to address community needs.

RESEARCH METHODOLOGY

During the summer of 2006, I, along with a few student-research assistants, began interviewing African entrepreneurs and civic leaders in the Greater Philadelphia and Boston areas. Six of the twenty-five interviews conducted in Phase One of this study were with women.[10] Phase Two began in the summer of 2007 and included interviews with ten women in these areas.

Respondents were interviewed using an in-depth interview schedule including about 150 open-ended and fixed-choice questions on such issues as: the personal backgrounds of the respondents and their connections to home; their educational, family and occupational histories; their residential history and reasons for migrating to the United States; their identity characteristics; the operation of their firms; the establishment of their organizations and their ethnic celebrations. Interviews lasted about 1.5–2.5 hours and were held in the offices or homes of the respondents.

Snowball sampling was largely used to obtain the names of possible participants in this study. Names of businesses and organizations were also obtained from the books, *Extended Lives: The African Immigrant Experience in Philadelphia* (Swigart, 2001) and *Immigrant Philadelphia: From Cobblestone Streets to Korean Soap-Operas* (Welcoming Center, 2004). Informants from Nigerian communities in Greater Boston provided lists of members of civic organizations and churches and thus, Nigerians are oversampled in this segment of the study.

The identity of the interviewers can also contribute to bias in the study and thus, it is important to acknowledge who the interviewers are. I, an African-American woman, conducted some of the interviews along with advanced undergraduate students, a graduate student, and an alumna of Bryn Mawr College. A Haitian-American undergraduate student worked with me to interview participants in Boston while an African-American alumna, an African-American graduate student, and a European-American male rising senior and I conducted the interviews in Philadelphia. Our identities might have affected the responses that we received to various questions particularly those involving race, ethnicity and gender. I also have connections to the Nigerian communities in these cities through my husband, who was born in Nigeria.

AFRICAN WOMEN ENTREPRENEURS AND CIVIC LEADERS—WHO ARE THEY?

Of the fifteen women who will be considered in this study, eight of them reside in the Greater Boston area and seven in metropolitan Philadelphia. Those women interviewed in the Boston area include women working and/or living in Lowell, Brockton, Cambridge, and Worcester as well as in the city of Boston itself. East Cambridge and Brockton are important areas of settlement for Cape Verdeans in Massachusetts, while Worcester and Lowell are former industrial cities. With respect to the Philadelphia area, the majority of the respondents worked in the city of Philadelphia, with one participant each living and/or working in Upper Darby (a suburb immediately adjacent to West Philadelphia) and Paulsboro, NJ. Due largely to the identities of my informants in the Boston area, the interviews there were very clustered with respect to nation of origin of the respondents. Six of the interviewees were born in Nigeria, while one was from Ethiopia and another was a Cape Verdean born in Senegal. The Philadelphia sample contained a much broader distribution of respondents—two from Nigeria and one each from the following nations: Guinea (but raised in Senegal), Sierra Leone, Eritrea, Liberia, and Cote d'Ivoire. Like the national statistics, however, Nigerians were most highly represented in this study and overall, most immigrants were from West Africa.

The Boston sample consisted of a younger group of African immigrants than their Philadelphia counterparts. The mean age of respondents in the Greater Boston area was forty-four, with a median age of forty-two, compared to an average age of fifty-two and a median age of fifty-three in Philadelphia.

African immigrants are among the most highly educated migrants to the United States with at least half of their population holding four-year college degrees (Yetman, 1999; Arthur, 2000; Swigart, 2001). Although they possess somewhat lower levels of educational attainment than their male peers in the larger sample, women in this study were strongly committed to education. Four of the participants in the Philadelphia area attained Bachelor's degrees, with two of these women holding graduate degrees as well. One of these women earned her Bachelor's degree in Nigeria and a Doctorate in Education in the United States. Boston area participants generally had higher levels of educational attainment than their Philadelphia peers in this study (which is borne out in the larger city statistics), with six of the women holding Bachelors' degrees. Four of these women pursued graduate studies and three of them earned Masters' degrees. Two Bachelors' and one Master's degree achieved by these Boston-area immigrants were awarded in Nigeria. Generally, all participants in these two major metropolitan areas demonstrated significant dedication to educational pursuits throughout their lives. The owner of an African market in Boston earned her Associate's degree in the United States, a seamstress received a three-year certificate in dressmaking in London, an entrepreneur completed a three month computer course in the Boston area, a minister pursued studies in theology as an adult in Lagos and a care worker from Francophone Africa earned her GED (General Equivalency Degree)[11] in the United States. Women who migrated to the United States as adults generally worked in their home countries before leaving. They held a range of gendered-occupations including: teachers, salespersons, seamstresses and secretaries.

Each city's sample contained five women who were community leaders, with three entrepreneurs in Boston and two in Philadelphia. The Boston businesswomen were involved in the following activities: a real estate broker, a sales director for Mary Kay Cosmetics, and the owner of an African market. The Philadelphia entrepreneurs consisted of a restaurant owner and the owner of a beauty supply shop. In four cases, (three in Boston and one in Philadelphia), the African immigrants were employed as directors of the major community organization in which they were engaged: the African Family Health Organization in Philadelphia, the Ethiopian Women's Alliance, the African

Assistance Center of Greater Lowell and the Association des Caboverdians de Brockton, the latter three in the Boston area. In some cases, although less frequently found among this sample than one would expect to find in their home nations, some of the women were engaged in another line of work along with their major activity. For example, the owner of the beauty supply shop also worked as a seamstress for individual clients and a state administrator in Child Welfare is starting a travel agency.

Why did these women migrate to the United States? Although five women initially came to join their husbands in their quest for higher education and/ or better employment opportunities, two women came in an effort to escape bad marriages, a finding also noted by Boyce Davies (2007) in her work on Caribbean immigrant women. Most women who joined their husbands also seized the opportunity to advance their education and earned Bachelor's, Master's and a Doctoral degree in the United States. Two women came with their husbands in the diversity lottery, while one entrepreneur was an asylum seeker as a result of the war between Ethiopia and Eritrea. Two current African community leaders, one in Boston and one in Philadelphia, migrated to the United States as children—one of these a Cape Verdean from Senegal under provisions for family reunification and the other, a Liberian, who was adopted by an African-American family.

These women all migrated to the United States in the period of the late 1970s to the beginning of the new millennium with most immigrants coming in the 1980s and 1990s. Most of them came to the United States when they were in their twenties and early thirties, with the exception of two women who were leaving bad marriages, and arrived in their late thirties and forties. Two women migrated as minors—one came specifically for higher education and another came to join her husband.

Slightly over half of these respondents are currently married—four in Philadelphia and four in Boston (of the latter group, one has filed for an annulment). The intersection of class and gender in the lives of two women noted above led them to leave difficult marital situations in Africa in the hopes of improving their lives in the United States. Problems posed by patriarchy, polygyny and so-called "traditional" values in their nations of origin led two women to leave bad relationships. One woman, the leader of The African Family Health Organization, left Senegal after a divorce. It was discovered that she could not have children with her husband and as she noted: "If I stayed there, it would be depressing." She further commented:

> I quit this marriage. I had everything . . . a car, a modern home. I decided that I was not for him. I am not a woman who would have a child with another man for him. I came here, left my job as an administrative assistant. When I was leaving, I emptied my home. When I divorced, to go back to the same country would be embarrassing for me (Interview, community leader, Philadelphia, July 2007).

A Boston seamstress also came to the United States after she encountered difficulties with her husband's second wife. She had a daughter in the United States who urged her to come over for a while. After a three month visit, the entrepreneur became sick and had to be hospitalized. When she had only a few weeks left on her visitor's visa, her daughter, then a citizen, hired an attorney and applied for permanent residency for her mother. Within six weeks, she was approved and later filed to bring her other children to join her. Within a year, she was able to bring her remaining four children to the United States. Her migration and that of her family occurred in the late 1980s.

In addition to the four immigrants in the Philadelphia area who are currently married, two are divorced and one is widowed. With one exception, these women were all married to Africans, generally from their country, although not always from their ethnic group. The one exception was a Liberian who migrated as a child, was raised by an African-American family and married an African American. The latter woman is divorced.

With respect to Boston, three immigrants are divorced and one has never been married. One of the married entrepreneurs is currently seeking an annulment, after experiencing both physical and psychological abuse from her husband, a Nigerian that she married in the United States.

All of the Philadelphia area participants had children. The mean and median number of children they had was three. Given the older ages of these interviewees, most of them had adult children (eighteen years of age or older) with two exceptions: the Liberian-born woman with a thirteen-year-old son, and the Guinean woman from Senegal, who divorced since she did not have children with her first husband, but who now has a sixteen-year-old biological son in the United States.

The mean and median number of children for Boston area participants was also three. Given the younger ages of these businesswomen and community leaders, five of them had at least one child under the age of eighteen. One unmarried respondent did not have children.

TRANSNATIONAL IDENTITIES: CONNECTIONS ON BOTH SIDES OF THE ATLANTIC

Entrepreneurs and community leaders in this study were clearly transnationals. They had maintained close ties to their kin in their home countries through the sending of remittances, building/purchasing and maintaining homes, making frequent visits, and in some cases, purchasing inputs for their U.S. businesses. On the other hand, most of these African immigrants were leaders of community organizations which were strongly committed to enhancing the quality of life and specifically, providing social services for many of their communities in the United States. Unlike their male counterparts in these two metropolitan areas who were largely involved with organizations seeking to foster economic and political development in their nations of origin, these women's gaze was quite firmly fixed on enhancing the quality of life for their families and communities in the United States. Although they certainly contributed to development on the continent, I would argue that more of their efforts were focused on the well-being of their families and other members of theirs and other African communities in the United States.

Building and/or purchasing a home in one's country of origin is one way of maintaining ties to the continent, contributing to the well-being of one's extended family and to development. Six of the seven participants from the Greater Philadelphia area owned homes in their nations of origin. The one exception to this was the entrepreneur from Eritrea, who left her country due to the war with Ethiopia. The younger ages of the Boston participants help explain why only four of the respondents owned homes in their birthplaces. As this sample ages, it is highly likely that more of these women will build homes in Africa. Extended family members generally resided in these homes although in some cases, these and other properties were leased to non-relatives.

Every participant in this study was involved in the sending of remittances to their home countries. Such financial contributions are a key source of support for many extended family members, as well as a major source of revenues for several African states. In many nations, remittances continue to be an important source of foreign exchange. These payments contribute to community and national development and demonstrate an immigrant's dedication to fulfilling responsibilities to family and community, to maintaining ties and earning respect at home.

Entrepreneurs and community leaders in this study largely sent these payments to assist their families in the payment of school fees, medical costs, particularly for elderly relatives and to generally supplement family incomes. Some participants sent remittances on a regular basis, while others sent money in response to requests from family members. In some cases, the women sent remittances every month to their parents. Yearly payments to family members ranged from $500 to over $6,000. Most respondents sent a few thousand dollars per year. There is no doubt that these cash payments whether for $1,000 or for several thousand dollars per year were an important source of support for families and community development on the continent.

In a few cases, women were donating money to their nations of origin to promote development. The case that stood out was a Liberian diplomat who sent over $10,000 per year:

> I send money to Liberia—for humanitarian and educational assistance. Send money generally for the rebuilding of primary schools, money for the collegiate

level and for clothing for women and children. I've been doing this for about 12 years. I also send money periodically, according to requests (Interview, community leader, Philadelphia, July 2007).

Respondents in this study also demonstrated their close ties to their nations of birth through their visits home. The frequency with which interviewees traveled home is one of those variables that is quite gendered. Very few African women immigrants in this study visited their nations of origin as often as every year—in fact only two women, one each from Boston and Philadelphia were found in this category. Male respondents, on the other hand, were much more likely to visit home once a year. In addition to the fact that women's incomes in this study were generally less than their male counterparts, childcare responsibilities and the school calendar made it more difficult for women to visit home on a more regular basis, thus illustrating the critical role that the intersection of gender and class played in their lives. In fact, those women who visited home most often both had grown children. Women from areas that had experienced substantial destabilization due to wars and other political crises were also unlikely to have regular visits home, such as those from Ethiopia, Eritrea, Sierra Leone, and Liberia.

In addition to maintaining ties through visits and the sending of remittances, women in this study maintained contact with relatives and close associates abroad which enhanced their businesses. As noted by Portes (1996) for immigrant entrepreneurs, African immigrants share information, develop contacts and establish trust on both sides of the Atlantic, which strengthens their businesses and other ventures in sub-Saharan Africa. Further, as noted by Stoller (2002), maintaining strong ties to one's community of origin can facilitate access to goods to sell in the United States. This was certainly the case for the owner of the African Market in Boston's Hyde Park, who is playing an important role in urban renewal and whose business has become quite successful:

I own the shopping strip—a commercial and residential strip, which includes my business (and another Nigerian-owned business, tha includes Western Union) . . . Only two businesses in this street are African owned, another is Puerto Rican owned, another is white owned. If I locked this place for one day, people would cry. They know that if they need something, I have it. They can get several services/goods from this shopping area . . . I have a sister who is helping me in Nigeria. When I go home, she tells me where to get the goods and she carries me around. When I am here, I order the goods through her. I get some food from Nigeria. Cassava flour is shipped to me as well as yam flour, Ijebu gari, etc. (Interview with business owner, Boston, August 2007).

Women in this study, however, did not only establish, build and maintain strong relationships with those in their home nations, but they also established strong ties in the United States. When compared with their male peers in this study who led African organizations that were largely concerned with development in their homelands, women's efforts as community leaders were very focused on improving the lives of their families and other African and diasporic populations on this side of the Atlantic. They accomplished this through their leadership of service-oriented organizations in the Boston and Philadelphia areas as well as by building personal ties with others in the diaspora. These women not only enhanced their communities in the United States, but they also contributed to the revitalization of historically African American neighborhoods, the reinvigoration of civil society and the formation of a new Pan-Africanism.

Before discussing some of the contributions to urban renewal and civil society more broadly, let's consider the relationships that these women established and how they identified themselves in the United States. The majority of women in this study stated that most of their friends and close associates were Africans, followed closely by African Americans and Afro-Caribbeans. One-third (5) of the women counted European Americans, as well as the other black populations in the United States in their circle of close friends. When asked how they would describe their identity, most women (6) discussed this in national terms—they stated that they were Nigerian or Ivorian, for example. Three of the women described themselves as a hyphenated American—as Nigerian-American, Ethiopian-American, or Eritrean-American, while a few others simply stated that they are Africans. It was also interesting to note that three women described themselves as African-American. None of the participants described themselves as a member of a particular ethnic group from their nations. Such descriptions of identity are quite distinctive from the ways in which African women (and men) typically describe themselves on the continent where they generally use several variables to indicate the complexities of who they are. As Beoku-Betts and Njambi (2005) note in quoting the Nigerian feminist scholar, Ogundipe-Leslie:

> Until she went abroad, she had never viewed herself as black or used this language to describe other African women. In her culture of origin, the question of one's identity and representation involved multiple and complex signifiers such as that of age, kinship, clan, ethnicity, class and marital status among other things, but never skin color (Beoku-Betts and Njambi, 2005).

While the vast majority of women in this study had not considered the issue of race nor race relations in the United States before migrating here, several of the women in this study had encountered discrimination and racism at both the institutional and individual levels. As noted by several scholars (Bryce-Laporte, 1993; Vickerman, 2001; Portes and Rumbaut, 2001), race does play a key role in the social placement and everyday experiences of African immigrants and other members of the African Diaspora. Further, as Yesufu (2003) discovered for African migrant women in Canada, not only their race, but also their gender and class (or perceived class) clearly played a role in the treatment that African women received from the broader society. A similar finding is observed for women in this study in their roles as mothers, students, wives and workers:

> It was my husband's birthday. I had made reservations for dinner at a local restaurant. Then, a white couple came and stood behind us. The maitre'd went and helped the white couple. I decided the establishment did not need my money and I said this. I didn't play the race card, but it is there (Interview with community leader, Philadelphia July, 2006).

For this respondent, the institutional racism in a suburban Pennsylvania school district led her to start an organization to protect the rights of her children and those of other black parents:

> My daughter was in the 99th percentile. North Penn had a two year accelerated math program in middle school. My daughter came home and cried when she told me what was happening in school. The teachers had to screen (test) the children in order for them to be accepted into an accelerated program. The teacher said that since my daughter wanted to become a medical doctor, she did not need to be tested further. She was then told that she draws so well and she does not need this. I went to look at my daughter's folder with 99th percentile scores. Why was she not screened? The Principal said that he did not want to set my daughter up to fail. He made me sign a form—I was not working then, so I was at the school every day . . . Due to a racial incident in the North Penn School District, I organized 'Concerned Parents for Equity in Education,' from 1989-1996. Parents had many issues as black parents living in the suburbs. Our children were the only black children in their classes. We would initiate meetings with the superintendent. We would have building administrative meetings each month. Many children were assigned to Special Education classes. Parents would ask me to go with them to their children's classes and to their parents' meetings. (Interview with community leader, Philadelphia, July, 2006).

A woman pastor from Worcester, MA also discusses the discrimination that African immigrants experience from institutions:

> There are still pockets of discrimination here and there. Even in the schools, black children are having a lot of difficulties. They're being taught by white teachers and the way they are being taught, such as in Worcester, immigrants from Africa who are new residents, the teachers teach the bare minimum. They have already pre-judged them. They discriminate based on their accents. Yes,

going to a restaurant, for example, you want a chair that is visible, but they put you in a dark corner. Even in doctor's offices, they want to put others before you, so I had to change doctors. (Interview with community leader, Boston, August 2007).

Another woman from Philadelphia admits that her opinion about race relations changed once she was in the United States, given incidents she experienced, such as the following:

Ah well . . . of course, I had experienced racism when I came to the US. I had a personal experience at St. Joseph's University. I fell victim to racism at St. Joseph's, but I fought with it. My professor gave me a "C" which was racially motivated, but gave my white partner a "B" on an educational research project. He said that he thought that my white project partner did the work. (Interview with community leader, Philadelphia, September 2007).

The discrimination that women entrepreneurs have historically faced in borrowing in their home countries rears its ugly head again in the United States, where factors of race and gender intersect in the lives of women of color in trying to obtain bank loans:

In banking, we are trying to buy the new church. We were turned down even in our own bank. We bank with them . . . it is a major bank. We invited the loan officer to the property that we want to buy. We are buying it below value. (He) said I do not think this is the right building for you. There is no concrete reason why he turned us down. The lawyer recommended another bank. They gave us a loan, the interest is a bit high. They called me five times to take the loan. The interest was too high so we did not take this loan. We have gone to a Vietnamese Bank in Worcester and they gave us the loan. (Interview with community leader, Boston, August, 2007).

Entrepreneurs in this study did not just experience discrimination and racism in their business dealings from European American bankers, but also encountered these issues when dealing with other populations of color, especially those who were viewed as controlling the niche economy in such areas as black hair products.[12] As noted by a Nigerian-born entrepreneur in the Greater Philadelphia area:

In everything you do in life, there are problems. Overcoming them is what is important. This business is not supposed to be a black business. There are more Asian businesses (in this field). Many blacks come here and ask to speak to the owner. This used to be a problem. Because of this, we lose some customers to the Koreans. They think you (we) go to the Koreans, buy from them, and then raise the price. They think the Koreans are going to be cheaper. They come to this store and also think that I am not the owner. Even when we go to trade shows . . . When the Koreans come, they come with money. The Koreans have their own banks, blacks have difficulty getting loans. Often you cannot compete with the Korean-owned businesses. If you are not strong on this, they will buy you out. Many black businesses have closed . . . You can't go to the bank and get money and the Koreans have their own institutions. If I go to a bank, when you check the application line for black, they do not want to differentiate you from African Americans (Interview with an entrepreneur, Philadelphia, July 2007).

This beauty supply shop owner pointed to another source of discrimination and tension for some respondents in this sample—their relationships with African Americans. Although many interviewees have close relationships with African Americans and some even identify as African American (although in general, they are likely using this term to mean they are "Africans in America"), some participants in this sample did report discriminatory and/ or negative experiences with African Americans. In her work on African immigration to the United States, Okome (2005) noted that there is a:

conscious decision of black immigrants to distance themselves from the 'undeserving underclass,' (meaning 'African Americans') without consciously apprehending that they are necessarily part of the under-class. It takes events like the Amadou Diallo shooting by the New York City Police to send the clarion call to most African immigrants that they are part of the discreditable, undeserving underclass (Okome, 2005).

The director of a Family Health Organization in Philadelphia generally did not demonstrate the distancing attitude from African Americans that Okome (2005) observed for some African immigrants. She discussed the racism she experienced from one African-American coworker and her efforts to forgive her, while her African-American supervisor was supportive of the participant in this study:

I worked at Penn for five years as a file clerk. My African American friend trained me—she was the supervisor. The other African American woman (in the office) said she would "blow my head off" (in response to a reprimand that the respondent gave to her in the absence of the boss). I said I wanted to take this woman to lunch, and my boss, my African American friend was not here. I said we needed to protect our sister, the boss who was not there (from any conflicts that would ensue from problems in her department). I told her not to say to me again that 'I am a monkey,' etc. If you don't want me to talk, then please tell me . . . I hugged the woman before I went home and said 'don't let the devil divide us' . . . I begged my boss not to fire her. I made peace with her. (Interview with a community leader, Philadelphia, July 2007).

The owner of the African Market in Boston also has a changed attitude about race relations. As a result of a few negative encounters with African Americans, this entrepreneur more closely resembles the African immigrants that Okome (2005) discussed and tries to distance herself from African Americans, whom she sees as perpetrators of many crimes in the Boston area. In my interview with her, she discussed one of these negative experiences:

> When I came a long time ago, at Eggleston Station, someone asked for a ride. I gave the two ladies a ride—they took my money from my pocketbook, they were threatening me and said give me your money. They are asking me for directions. No one was hurt. Since that time, I do not give anyone a ride. They were both African Americans (Interview with an entrepreneur, Boston, August 2007).

Discrimination and other negative encounters with African Americans were not the norm for respondents in this sample and in fact, African women in this study overall had fewer negative experiences with all groups around race than their male counterparts (which is perhaps to be understood given the greater threat that black men supposedly pose in the broader society). However, despite the problems that African women in this study encountered, most of them were quite focused on improving the lives of their families, their communities and the broader society in the United States. While a few women discussed how they would like to return to their home countries in the near future—say in the next two years or so, all of the Boston respondents and half of the Philadelphia respondents claimed that their "lives had been better here than in their nations of origin." Of course, many factors contribute to this response including greater political and economic stability in the United States for many and the opportunity to experience greater material comforts than in their nations of origin. Most women expressed some ambivalence about whether they would like to return home in the long run—decisions that would be based on the economic and political conditions prevailing in their countries of birth, the well-being of their children and their lives at the time of retirement.

BUILDING AFRICAN IMMIGRANT COMMUNITIES IN THE UNITED STATES: WOMEN'S LEADERSHIP IN AFRICAN ORGANIZATIONS

As stated above, African immigrants are making important contributions to the rebuilding of urban communities in the United States, especially in African American neighborhoods in our major cities. This is very much the case in Boston and in Philadelphia, where businesses such as the African Market in Hyde Park in Boston and Dahlak Restaurant in University City and Germantown in Philadelphia are contributing to urban renewal in parts of these major cities. What has been more salient, however, in this sample of entrepreneurs and civic leaders in these two cities are African women's leadership of community associations that are providing vital social services to Africans and the broader community. In several cases, these relationships are strengthening their bonds with other black diasporic populations, reaffirming their transnational identities and re-invigorating aspects of urban civil society. This section will highlight the activities of some of these groups and showcase the leadership of African immigrant women.

One of the foremost groups in addressing the problems faced by African immigrants in the Greater Philadelphia area is The Coalition of African Communities (AFRICOM). AFRICOM is an important vehicle in facilitating settlement in the area and assists immigrants to access resources such as health care and education. In the process, it also helps forge strong relationships with other black diaspora populations, such as Afro Caribbeans/West Indians and African Americans. As such, they make major contributions to building a strong Pan-African, diasporic community.

AFRICOM is an umbrella organization that brings together African and Caribbean community organizations throughout the Greater Philadelphia area. According to one of the participants in my study and a founding member of the group, AFRICOM's mission is: "to empower the African and Caribbean refugee and immigrant communities by facilitating family access to health and social services with special focus on women, children and the youth; promoting economic development; facilitating resolution of inter and intra-group conflicts; advocating on issues of concern to African communities; and educating the media and the broader public on African cultures and experiences" (http://africom-philly.com and interview with community leader July 2006). In its efforts to make health care accessible to all Africans, AFRICOM encouraged the Philadelphia Health Department to hire a French-Speaking health worker to do outreach in the Francophone African immigrant community. The group also assists immigrants and refugees with immigration issues and refers individuals to appropriate legal counsel. Among the special events sponsored by AFRICOM is an Annual Health Fair, which includes on-site HIV testing and social events, such as "Echoes of Africa" to promote knowledge about the diversity and richness of African cultures to the broader Philadelphia community.

Educational initiatives around immigrant issues, especially focused on developing culturally sensitive curricula are some of AFRICOM's major goals. It is precisely in this area that a Nigerian respondent in my study has been most involved in providing very valuable expertise as a founding and current board member of the organization. She has been particularly involved in the West African Refugees Assistance Program, which addresses the issues facing children traumatized by wars, several of whom served as child soldiers on African battlefields. Her experience battling the North Penn School District for her own children in suburban Philadelphia well-equipped her to help organize workshops for teachers in the Philadelphia School District to enable them to work with these children. She also played a focal role in organizing multicultural activities within the school district and establishing group therapy for the children. She has clearly been a major leader in shaping the educational environment for many African immigrant and refugee children.

Another group which was established by a Guinean immigrant in this study was the African Family Health Organization (AFAHO). Like AFRICOM, AFAHO exists to serve and empower African and Caribbean immigrants in order to improve their access to health care and social services. It especially aims to address the needs of the underserved immigrant populations in the Greater Philadelphia area, particularly those who have major language, cultural and financial barriers preventing them from accessing mainstream institutions. A participant in my study began this organization and is responsible for all aspects of its operation. She provides vital health outreach services, particularly with reference to HIV/AIDS education, testing, and counseling. Her office provides language interpreters in several West and East African languages, as well as in Haitian Kreyol, and publishes its materials in English and French. Under her leadership, the organization also provides employment, immigration, educational referral and health services often working in tandem with AFRICOM on such issues. The director of this group is perhaps best known for the African Health Fair, a major event each year in Philadelphia which provides on-site medical tests and information for those members of the broader Philadelphia community that attend the fair. In this sense, the participant in this study has contributed not only to the health, safety, and development most especially of low-income members of the African and Caribbean communities, but is also making a vital contribution to the health and well-being of the broader populace.

An association with a somewhat narrower focus on one national immigrant group is the Adbar Ethiopian Women's Alliance in Cambridge, MA. This group is dedicated to social change and women's rights, with a particular emphasis on the conditions that African women, not just Ethiopian women, face who live in the Greater Boston area. Adbar provides a wide range of services to African immigrant women including: legal assistance with immigration issues, literacy training, orientation and acculturation for new arrivals, assistance in accessing social services, such as health care, and advocacy support for issues of domestic violence, female genital cutting, family unification and mental illness. This organization is especially committed to providing job assistance to women to help them achieve financial independence.

The Adbar Women's Alliance is the oldest Ethiopian Women's Organization in the United States. The participant who started this group fourteen years ago was determined to create a space where women could "share their stories and come to terms with common problems." From the establishment of this organization, she realized that many African women immigrants face problems of female genital cutting and domestic violence, but often accept the blame for these issues. Thus, in addition to creating an organization to provide assistance for these problems, she also organized support groups and began a newsletter as places where women could discuss the challenges that they faced in their families, their households and in the host society. In this way, the Adbar Women's Alliance resembles the South Asian women's group, SNEHA, which provides the "extended family-type" support that is missing from the daily lives of women of color immigrants in the United States and assists in their empowerment (Purkayastha et al, 1997). The leader of the Adbar Women's Alliance also identified specific needs on the part of African immigrants here and sought to address these needs by linking her efforts and expertise with local funders such as The Boston Women's Fund, the Unitarian Universalist Church, and the Cambridge Community Fund.

In an earlier interview that the Director of the Adbar Ethiopian Women's Organization shared with me, she revealed her commitment to addressing the immediate needs of the African community that I think is a major focus of many women's efforts in this study:

> After working with a few international relief organizations, I found myself disillusioned by some of the groups; their focus on larger goals that seemed to ignore everyday hardships. Lacking a political motivation (a quality that she sees as divisive), I mentioned that I 'longed to organize in a spiritual way.'

CONCLUSION

African women in this study were indeed transnationals who exhibited strong connections to their home and host societies and in the process, contributed to development on the continent and the revitalization of parts of historically African-American communities. Through sending remittances and maintaining ties to their nations of origin, these women were important sources of support for the health and well-being of their extended family members and at the same time, these linkages benefited the development of their businesses in the United States. Although these women did experience racism as well as the intersection of race, gender, and class in their lives, they also forged relationships with other black populations and in fact, contributed to the development of a new Pan-Africanism. Moreover, these African immigrant women were significantly committed to organizations that addressed the "everyday hardships" of life on this side of the Atlantic, which really distinguished them from their male peers.

This study makes an important contribution to feminist analyses of transnationalism as a gendered process, a very understudied phenomenon especially with respect to African immigrant women. This work reveals that these women established and/or led organizations which facilitated the settlement of African and Caribbean immigrants in the Philadelphia and Boston areas, lending support to Purkayastha et al's (1997) thesis about the valuable roles that support networks play in the lives of immigrant women of color. Such networks enabled women to navigate the often difficult terrain of educational, employment, and health care institutions as workers, mothers and sometimes wives, a social landscape that was more problematic for them as black women immigrants (Yesufu, 2003; Boyce Davies, 2007). These networks often replaced the roles historically occupied by extended families in one's nation of origin. Groups such as the Adbar Women's Alliance further illustrated the agency and empowerment of African women, who developed support groups to address the problems they encountered with domestic violence, female genital cutting and other issues. Through their many activities, these women are assisting in the rebuilding of the urban social landscape, saving lives and re-creating "home."

NOTES

1. This chapter is reprinted from *African and Asian Studies*, Vol. 7, No. 4 (2008) 367–94. We wish to thank the copyright holder, E.J. Brill, Leiden, The Netherlands, for granting us permission to use the material. Although some minor editing was done in order to fit the piece in this volume, the thrust and focus of the article remain unchanged.

2. The Hart-Cellar Act opened the United States to immigrants from the Global South. The Immigration Reform and Control Act required employers to certify their employees' immigration status. It also granted amnesty to those who were out of status and who could prove they had been living in the United States for at least two consecutive years before January 1982. The Diversity Program of the Immigration Act of 1990 was instituted to increase the admission of immigrants from nations that have been underrepresented in the United States.

3. Since the attacks on the World Trade Center and the Pentagon on 9/11/01, in an effort to further secure the United States, the State Department has increased the requirements and scrutiny of those applying for visas to travel to or settle in the United States, especially for those from Global South nations.

4. I do believe that conflict theories are still important in understanding the vestiges of colonization that persist for several groups in the United States including African Americans, Native Americans, Chicanos, Puerto Ricans, and Chinese and Japanese Americans.

5. In 1965, the Hart-Cellar Immigration Act was passed which opened the United States to immigration from the Global South.

6. Therefore, the United States still has great needs for cheap agricultural labor while at the same time demands for highly skilled professionals.

7. In some cases, remittances from relatives in the North have been found on occasion to exceed the GDP in some nations in the Global South, such as Bolivia. About a decade ago in Ghana, remittances were found to be a major contributor to the Ghanaian economy.

8. Thus, many Nigerian students in the 1970s were encouraged by their families and the Oil Boom to return home after completion of their studies. On the other hand, many Ghanaian students in this period were encouraged by their parents to remain in the United States due to the presence of the military government at the time.

9. Slightly over 11 percent of the population in Philadelphia is foreign-born.

10. One of the six interviews with women was a group interview and thus only five interviews with individuals from Phase 1 will be considered in this study.

11. The General Equivalency Degree (GED) is achieved after passing a group of five tests in secondary-school level subjects. This diploma is considered the equivalent of a high school diploma in the United States.

12. In many major cities in the northeastern United States, the Korean-born own many beauty supply shops, particularly in African-American communities.

REFERENCES

Apraku, K. 1996. *Outside looking in: An African perspective on American pluralistic society*. Westport, CT: Praeger.

Arthur, J. 2000. *Invisible sojourners: African immigrant diaspora in the United States*. Westport, CT: Praeger.

Basch, L. 2001. Transnational social relations and the politics of national identity: An eastern Caribbean case study. In Foner, N. *Islands in the City: West Indian migration to New York* (ed.). Berkeley: University of California Press, 2001.

Beoku-Betts, J. and Wairimu N. N. 2005. African feminist scholars in women's studies: Negotiating spaces of dislocation and transformation in the study of women. *Meridians*. Vol. 6 (1) http://muse.jhu/.edu/journals/meridians/v006/6.1_beoku_betts.html

Boyce Davies, C. 2007. Caribbean women, domestic labor and the politics of transnational migration. In Harley, S. *Women's labor in the global economy: speaking in multiple voices* (ed.). New Brunswick, NJ: Rutgers University Press.

Boyce Davies, C. 2007. Towards African diaspora citizenship: Politicizing and existing global geography. In McKittrick and Woods. *Black geographies and the politics of place* (eds.). Boston: SouthEnd Press, 2007.

Bryce-Laporte, Roy S. 1993. Voluntary immigration and continuing encounters between blacks: Post-quincentenary challenge. *Annals of the American Academy of Political and Social Science*, Vol. 530 (1).

Dodoo, F. N. 1997. Assimilation differences among Africans in America." *Social Forces*. Vol. 76 (2).

Foner, N. 2001. *New immigrants in New York.* New York: Columbia University Press.

Glick Schiller, N. and Georges F. 2001. *Georges woke up laughing: Long-Distance nationalism and the search for home.* Durham, NC: Duke University Press.

Hu-Dehart, E. 1997. Surviving globalization: Immigrant women workers in late capitalist America. In Harley, S. *Women's Labor in the Global Economy: Speaking in Multiple Voices* (ed.). New Brunswick, NJ: Rutgers University Press.

Kibria, N. 1994. Migration and Vietnamese American women: Remaking ethnicity. In Zinn and Dill. *Women of Color in US Society* (eds.). Philadelphia: Temple University Press.

Ogbu, J. 1978. *Minority Education and Caste.* New York: Academic Press.

Okome, M. 2005. The antinomies of globalization: Causes and consequences of contemporary African immigration to the United States of America. In Vaughn, et al, *Globalization and its discontents* (eds.). Ibadan Nigeria; Sefer Academic Press. http://www.africamigration.com/archive_01m_okome_globalization_02 .htm

People's Weekly World: http://www.pww.org/article/view/7085/1/270.

Portes, A. and Min Z. 1993. The new second generation: Segmented assimilation and its variants. *Annals of the American Academy of Political and Social Science.* Vol. 530 (1).

Portes, A. 1996. Global villagers: The rise of transnational communities *The American Prospect*, Vol. 7 (25).

Portes, A. and Ruben R. 2001. *Legacies: The story of the immigrant second generation.* Berkeley: University of California Press.

Purkayastha, B., Shyamala, R. and Kshiteeja, B. 1997. Empowering women: SNEHA's multifaceted cctivism. In Shah. *Dragon Ladies: Asian American Feminists Breathe Fire* (ed.). Boston: South End Press.

Reddock, R. Editorial: Diaspora Voices. *Feminist Africa*, Issue 7. http://www.feminis tafrica.org/index.php/editorial-6

Sassen, S. 1988. *The mobility of labor and capital: A study in international investment and labor flow.* New York: Cambridge University Press.

Stepick, A., Guillermo, G., Max C., and Marvin D. 2003. *This land is our land: Immigrants and power in Miami.* Berkeley: University of California Press.

Stoller, P. 2001. West Africans: Trading places in New York. In Foner, N. *New Immigrants in New York* (ed.). New York: Columbia University Press.

———. 2002. *Money has no smell: The Africanization of New York City.* Chicago: The University of Chicago Press.

Swigart, L. 2001. *Extended lives: The African immigrant experience in Philadelphia.* Philadelphia: The Balch Institute of Ethnic Studies.

Vickerman, M. 2001. Jamaicans: Balancing race and ethnicity. In Foner, N. *New immigrants in New York* (ed.). New York: Columbia University Press.

Waters, M. 1999. *Black identities: West Indian immigrant dreams and American realities.* New York: Russell Sage Foundation.

Welcoming Center for New Pennsylvanians. 2004. *Immigrant Philadelphia: From cobblestone streets to Korean soap operas.* Philadelphia: The Welcoming Center for New Pennsylvanians and the Historical Society of Pennsylvania.

Yesufu, A. 2005. The gender dimensions of the immigrant experience: The case of African-Canadian women in Edmonton. In Tettey and Puplampu. *The African diaspora in Canada: Negotiating identity and belonging* (eds.). Calgary: The University of Calgary Press, 2005.

Yetman, N. 1999. *Majority and Minority: The Dynamics of Race and Ethnicity in American Life* (ed.). Boston: Allyn and Bacon.

Chapter Twelve

Border Questions in African Diaspora Literature

What is the state of the African diaspora now that the Jim Crow segregation is ostensibly behind us? Institutionalized borders of race, class, and gender have created an exilic condition in the diaspora. The vices of racial injustice and economic inequality continue to breed displacement, dispossession, and second class citizenship among diasporic Africans, indicating a long way from the promised land. Considering the persistence of systemic poverty and racial injustice, diasporic Africans cannot help but lament together with the black subjects captured in W.E.B. Du Bois's *The Souls of Black Folk*; that the lamentation is directed at God shows the gravity of the situation, "Why did God make me an outcast and a stranger in mine own house?" (38). In this quotation we educe the ongoing experiences of hostility and marginalization among diasporic Africans. To appreciate the diasporic Africans' claim to America, the Caribbean, France, Britain, etc. as home, one has to trace how slavery developed the mentioned regions through the infamous exploitation of labor, and how diasporic Africans have culturally enriched the Americas. It is on this basis that Du Bois calls for a space in which diasporic Africans can thrive "without being cursed and spit upon by [their] fellows, without having the doors of Opportunity closed roughly in [their] face[s]" (39). This paper draws on literary analysis not only to further our understanding of the systemic inequalities that have reduced the dream to a nightmare for so many diasporic Africans, but also to imagine ways of crossing these oppressive borders. These ways would include making decent education a right of every child regardless of residential location, building more schools instead of prisons, and practicing gender equality. To borrow the words of Manning Marable in *Beyond Boundaries,* this chapter calls for "the shattering of barriers that divide people into social hierarchies, that condemn human beings to lives of inequality due to their color, class, or gender. Another way of life is possible and critical reconstructions of the past are essential in creating such futures" (vii). Here, then, is literature's role.

A number of literary texts critically engage the political and racial economy of diasporic Africans, making an intricate link between racism and poverty. Three among many examples are Derek Walcott's *Dream on Monkey Mountain,* Langston Hughes *The Big Sea,* and James Baldwin's *Another Country.* These texts give voice to the voiceless, and in turn challenge readers to (re)commit to the cause of the marginalized. More importantly, they show how the borders of race and class continue to isolate many ordinary diasporic Africans. This is the case for Derek Walcott's Makak in *Dream on Monkey Mountain* who has to leave like a hermit largely because of his racial and economic station. His isolated shanty reminds one of colonially institutionalized reservation camps that we have witnessed in Apartheid South Africa among other places. Makak entertains the thought of returning to his roots, only to find that such a return is more complicated than it appears. Some may read his determination to return to Africa as a rebellion against oppressive forces on the Caribbean while others may view it as a cartographic necessity for, and political imperative of, mourning lost worlds. Either reading puts pressure on the unqualified celebration of movement that we have become used to in the age of postmodernism. Makak's nostalgic references to Africa is in some ways an exilic melancholia attempting to make a connection between the past and the present, between Africa and the Caribbean; the resultant connection in turn rewrites the story of exile. Our focus is to read Makak's nostalgia as a protest against the diasporic condition, as an indictment of the African diaspora as a dream deferred.

It is this type of condition that Manning Marable, in *How Capitalism Underdeveloped Black America*, alludes to when he calls black poverty "the highest stage of underdevelopment" (53). Marable goes further, "Black families throughout the United States, in every region and city assume the unequal burden of poverty. In suburban districts outside the ghetto, 21.3 percent of all black families are poor, vs. only 5.9 percent of white families" (56). What is tragically striking is that Marable's analysis is as largely relevant to blacks in the United States as it is to the blacks in the Caribbean, and indeed to nearly all the people of African descent. For example, as Marable observes, "the hub of international financial markets, Wall Street, is only blocks from some of the worst urban slums in the world. Atlanta's Omni and glittering convention center is walking distance from dilapidated shanties that are mirror images of eighteenth and nineteenth century slave quarters" (53). These urban slums and shanties are occupied by the poor. Everywhere one goes, affluent residential areas are almost always located across a valley of shanties, as the former can neither be nor do without the poor. To be sure, "Poverty must be understood properly as a comparative relationship between those segments of classes who are deprived of basic human needs (for example, food shelter, clothing, medical care) vs. the most secure and affluent classes within a social and economic order" (Marable 54). The poor have to be near enough to allow for the convenient exploitation of their labor, but not too near to interfere with the extravagant lifestyle of the affluent. God forbid if what is left of the affluent's conscience and ethics is awakened by the suffering poor because their affluence is inextricably linked to the former's abject poverty. Of course, this is not to say that all affluent people are unethical; it is just a way of saying that ethics and affluence are typically strange bedfellows. In fact, looking at the sacrifices of white abolitionist John Brown and white civil rights icon Viola Liuzzo, great strides are made when whites and nonwhites cross borders of race and stand up together to defend justice for all. Let us hope that there will be many more *Browns* and *Liuzzos*, as the work of justice cannot be the sole burden of the direct victims of injustice. After all, as Martin Luther King Jr. has observed in "Letter from Birmingham Jail," located in his book *Why We Can't Wait,* we have to work as one beloved community because, "Injustice anywhere is a threat to justice everywhere. We are caught in an inescapable network of mutuality, tied in a single garment of destiny. Whatever affects one directly, affects all indirectly" (87).

In Ama Ata Aidoo's *The Dilemma of a Ghost*, we encounter characters, for example Eulalie, who *return to the source.* Aidoo's play is based on two major characters: Ato, a Ghanaian, and Eulalie, an African American. Both of them are university students in America. They meet at the university and develop an intimate relationship which leads to their marriage. The play starts off with a conflict between the old and new. We are told, "The action takes place in the courtyard of the newest wing of the Odumna Clan house. It is enclosed on the right by a wall of the old building and both at the centre and on the left by the walls of the new wing. At the right-hand corner a door links the courtyard of the old house" (5). It becomes evident, therefore, that the play is in part concerned with the relationship between time (past and present) and home space. The play uses the newest wing of the house to symbolize new developments in the history of the clan, and how these developments re-define and extend the home space. In the play it is fashionable to embrace modernity; as such, the horn blower sings with pride, "We are moving forward, forward, forward . . ." (8). The new wing of the house is part of this forward movement. But we encounter problems right away. This forward movement is exclusionary because it leaves out almost all the residents, "[I]t is expected that they [members of Odumna clan house] should *reserve the new addition to the house for the exclusive use of the One Scholar.* Not that they expect him to make his home there. No . . . he will certainly have to live and work in the city when he arrives from the white man's land" (8; my emphasis). Many questions arise at this point.

Why is the new wing of the house exclusively reserved for Ato? One reads a divided home. The rest of the family rejects newness by not sharing the new house, and Ato rejects his past by not demanding to share the old wings of the home. But the issue is much more complex. Even though Ato does not live in the rural area, "they all expect him to come down, now and then, at the weekend and festive occasions like Christmas. And certainly, he must come home for blessings when the new yam has been harvested and Stools are sprinkled" (8). One is compelled to think that Ato does not fully identify with the rural home. Home for Ato has become a contested space. Is home the city where Ato lives everyday, or the rural area where he comes at least once a year to attend the new yam blessings? That the Odumna clan house is no longer a home to Ato in the way it was is evident in the fact that it is a space he visits because he is expected to do so. It does not come naturally to him as the city does. It is possible, therefore, that the new wing is not new enough for Ato. What his parents perceived as a half-way home, bridging his world and theirs, effectively becomes an abandoned home. One of the lessons one learns from Ato's location of home in the city is that travel widens one's cultural bearings, and thus shifts one's understanding of home. Little wonder Ato believes that his love his wife, not his family's love for her, is "what matters" (10). Ato registers his distance from the rural home when he tells his prospective wife, Eulalie, about where they would live, "There are no palms where we will live[. . .].Unless of course if I take you to see my folks at home. There are real palm trees there" (9). Ato seems to view the rural home more as his parents' home than his home, and his going there is a matter of *if* as opposed to *when*. Ato's usage of "if" casts doubts on the givenness of his family ties and originality. Indeed, his stance here deconstructs the idea of return to the source. It is as though his return stops at the outskirts of the source (in the city); it is a journey that cannot be completed, contrary to the gospel of the *returnists*.

If we look at home in terms of family and community, then we can see that home is divided at many levels. First, the forces that plucked Eulalie's grandparents from Africa into slavery not only delinked them from their ancestral home but also destroyed the homes they left behind. Their labor which was meant to build their ancestral home was now serving the slave master's interests. Walter Rodney's *How Europe Underdeveloped Africa* (1972) is relevant here because it talks about the relationship between labor exploitation and underdevelopment. Second, the system of modernity in place during Ato's time demands that he goes to the West to acquire Western education so as to be relevant in the new dispensation. If his departure was not bad enough for the cohesiveness of the family, his settlement in the city when he returns is. The alienation that afflicts Aidoo's characters must be understood as systematic rather than isolated/individual homelessness.

When we meet Eulalie, we learn that her university degree has not granted her the happiness she expected (8). We also learn that she is an orphan when she asks Ato, "Could I even point to you a beggar in the streets as my father or mother? Ato, can't your Ma be sort of my Ma too?" (9). Finally, Ato tells us "her grandfathers and grandmothers were slaves" (18). Eulalie's return and her Afro-centrism represent a form of black diaspora politics. The three instances above provide a subtext for Eulalie's homelessness. Eulalie pursued her university degree on the understanding that it would grant her happiness as it did her fellow Americans. However, upon her graduation, she realizes that her case is different. What Eulalie is alluding to here is that she has been treated differently because she is different from most Americans; that is, a university degree has not worked for her because she is black, poor, and parentless (24). Her loneliness stems not only from her parents' death, but also from her society's unwillingness (not even a beggar wants to be a parent figure for her) to give her parental care. And a society that does not care about an orphan, one is tempted to think, would not care about the conditions that made her/him an orphan. When viewed from that angle then the fact that Eulalie has no relatives comes across as a commentary on her society's calculated destruction of family unit. Eulalie's rhetorical question to her mum concurs: "There was no one left was there? And how can one make a family out of Harlem?" (24). If Harlem is not congenial for raising a family, then African Americans, to whom Harlem is home far away from home, are doomed. Eulalie adds, "Ma, I've come to the very source. I've come to Africa and I hope that where'er you are, you sort of know and approve" (24). It is her alienation in America that drives her away, lest she perish prematurely like her parents. But the issue becomes more complex when we read Eulalie as a decoy of the Biblical Ruth. Echoing the Biblical Ruth's plea to Naomi, Eulalie asks Ato, "Ato, can't your Ma be sort of my Ma too? And your Pa mine? And your gods my gods? Shall I die where you will die?" (9). Eulalie's pledge here draws on Ruth's declaration to Naomi, "Thy people shall be my people, Thy god shall be my god, Whither thou diest, I will die, and there I will be buried" (Ruth 1:17). Ironically, as soon as she arrives in Ato's home, Eulalie falls short of her *Ruthian* pledge. For example, she refuses to make Ato's food her food when she discards the food that Ato's mother gives her (31-32). What is food to Ato and Ato's people, to Eulalie, only amounts to "horrid creatures" (32). In addition, instead of embracing the rituals that Ato's people perform in order to bless the home, she reduces them to "a blasted mess" (41) of "savage customs and standards" (47), to a "rotten land"

(48). The irony is that Eulalie uses the American culture, which she strived to escape, to measure other cultures.

Eulalie also drinks Coca-cola, saying, "I was only feeling a little home-sick and I drank it for sentimental reasons. I could have had a much cooler, sweeter and more nourishing substitute in coconuts, couldn't I?" (26). Here, again, Eulalie fails to meet her *Ruthian* declaration. She is homesick not for Ato's home, but her home in America. The point here is that Eulalie finds the task of making Ato's home her home much more complex than she antici-pated. One could persuasively argue that the Biblical Ruth does a much better job of living up to the *Ruthian* pledge than Eulalie—Ruth embraces Naomi's people while Eulalie calls Ato's people "goddam people" who are "[m]ore savage than dinosaurs" (47).

When Ato uses his people's culture to put pressure on her, she vexingly asks Ato, "Who married me, you or your goddam people?" (47). Eulalie's question departs from her Ruthian pledge, and demonstrates not only that she never studied the cultural constitution of *the source* before returning, but that the ideal of a return to Africa is more difficult than the reality. In that sense, the text parodies the Afro-centrism of African Americans. If she had done so, she would have known that she was not only marrying Ato, but also Ato's people, as this is one of the basic articles of Ato's world. In any case, Ruth and Eulalie make the new places they move to more tolerant of diversity, as they undergo transformation in adjustment. Ruth is a Moabite while her mother-in-law, Naomi, is an Israelite. The two sides (Moabites and Israelites/ Bethlehemians) are enemies.

Eulalie's problem of belonging becomes clearer when she tells Ato, "To belong to somewhere again . . . Sure, this must be bliss" (9). Eulalie implies here that she does not belong anywhere, certainly not to America. Eulalie's implied unbelonging to America requires analysis. The word "again" sug-gests that Eulalie once belonged somewhere. She is metaphorically referring to the collective belongingness of African Americans to Africa, to the fact that African Americans belonged to Africa before the historic slave trade. Politically, Eulalie's claim is strategic. But, culturally and socially, it is dif-ficult to view Eulalie's belonging to Africa as wholly synonymous to the belonging (to Africa) of the very ancestors who were uprooted. Neverthe-less, Eulalie decides to *return to the source* together with Ato in an attempt to find this elusive happiness, to find a home. But the fact that she is neither grounded in America nor Africa complicates her relocation. Born in America, Eulalie does not know Africa, except through stereotypes (25). And even if she were one of the uprooted slaves from Africa, her possible return would not necessarily be "bliss" as she assumes. Upon her *return,* Eulalie finds out that *the source* is much more challenging than her romanticized view comprising "The palm trees, the azure sea, the sun and the golden beaches" (9). As soon as she arrives in Africa, she realizes that she has a lot of adjustments to make. That she is American first, then African second, becomes clear when warm Coca-cola (read America) wins over "a much cooler, sweeter and more nourishing substitute in coconuts [read Africa]" (24). Eulalie's homesickness for America undermines her attempts to abandon it.

Aidoo's play, one could argue, uses Eulalie to echo Marcus Garvey's "Return to Africa" call. Eulalie's presence in America and her identity as an African American dates back to the seventeenth through the nineteenth century when Africans were shipped out of the continent through the Middle Passage into the New World in the name of slave trade. There have been enormous cultural transformations both in the Continent and in the diaspora within that period. It is on that premise that Paul Gilroy, in *The Black Atlantic* (1993), bases his argument that the diasporic Africans share neither a similar history nor experience with the Continental Africans (23-24). Gilroy's main concern is that the similarity claims misleadingly translate to the homogenization of the differences between the two groups. Indeed, as long as culture is lived and experienced, one cannot intelligently argue that Eulalie (African Americans) and Ato (Africans) share a common culture. But even before Gilroy's book, Aidoo had documented the cultural differences; for example she exposes a clash of values to underscore "the differences between [Eulalie's] people and [Ato's]" (9). But some of the diasporic Africans who seek to *return to the source* are already aware that they do not share a common experience with Continental Africans. Homeland and belongingness need not, and should not, be solely linked to geographical locations. How then can we explain their quest to return to "the source?"

One way is through a proverb, "a toad does not run in the daytime unless something is after its life" (Achebe 138). Aidoo's Eulalie is a university graduate; we therefore expect her to secure *a good job* and to lead *a good life*. But, as she reveals in a rhetorical question, this is not the case: "Why should I have supposed that mere graduation is a passport to happiness?" (8). As a result of slavery and its legacies, Eulalie leads a fragmented life without a family. So, Eulalie's return is an attempt to fill a missing link (family), for as John Durham Peters has so convincingly argued, "The shock, disruption, or loss accompanying exile together with the distance from the home's mundane realities, can invite the project of restoring the 'original'—the original home, the original state of being. Idealization often goes with mourning" (19). The play does not tell us what exactly happened to Eulalie's parents—they could have succumbed to the very system that Eulalie is trying to run away from. The point is that Eulalie and, by extension, diasporic Africans, would not be so determined to return to the source if American state ideological apparatuses had fully accommodated them. If African Americans and other minorities are *looking back*, it is partly because the state apparatus "feeds at a prissy distance on the wild glamour of minorities while neither alleviating their hardships nor recognizing their autonomy. People of color thus have real reasons for suspecting a whiteness that joins—and effaces, all colors" (Peters 35). Indeed, "[v]ery often it is when we feel deeply dissatisfied with market-place pluralism and its unwillingness to confront and correct the injustices of dominant racism that we turn our diasporan gaze back to the home country. Often, the gaze is uncritical and nostalgic [. . .] half-truths, stereotypes, so-called traditions, rituals, and so-forth" (Radhakrishman 128). Aidoo's return, therefore, can be read as a search for belonging.

It is, admittedly, hopelessness and the thought that slavery is still alive except in a subtle form, that makes some diasporic Africans "look back, even at the risk of being mutated into pillars of salt" (Rushdie 10). Eulalie's muta-tion, for instance, is marked by her frustration in Ghana. Writing on the same issue of diaspora, but addressing the Caribbean people, Hall makes a long statement that in my opinion applies to all diasporic Africans:

> Black, brown, mulatto, white—all must look *Présence Africaine* in the face, speak its name. But whether it is, in this sense an *origin* of our identities, unchanged by four hundred years of displacement, dismemberment, transpor-tation, to which we could in any final or literal sense return, is more open to doubt. The original "Africa" is no longer there. It too has been transformed. History is, in that sense, irreversible. We must not collude with the West which, precisely, normalizes and appropriates Africa by freezing it into some timeless zone of the primitive, unchanging past. Africa must at last be reckoned with by Caribbean [African American] people, but it cannot in any simple sense be recovered. (241)

Hall's argument that diasporic Africans ought to accept the *Africanness* and *exileness* in them is persuasive. A return to pre-slavery Africa would be atavistic. But Hall does not seem to provide a clear alternative—the fact that diasporic Africans cannot return does not mean that they are at home. One needs to go beyond stating where people cannot go, because the problem of the diaspora is not so much a place to return to, but a place and space to be-long to. Echoing Hall, Caren Kaplan reminds us that people in the diaspora have "no possibility of staying at home in the conventional sense—that is, the world has changed to the point that those domestic, national, or marked spaces no longer exist" (7). Kaplan is right in observing that "marked spaces no longer exist" but she does not address the imaginary or the discourse of origins that operates regardless of the changes she talks about. She also does not give an alternative space in which racial others of the world like Eulalie can have a sense of belonging. Undoubtedly, cultural identity and belonging are more problematic than they seem.

Worth noting is the question of hierarchy. By placing a premium on returning to "the source," Eulalie unwittingly reinforces the general misconception that Africa (homeland) is superior to diaspora (America). She says, "Ma, I've come to the very source. I've come to Africa and I hope that where'er you are, you sort of know and approve" (24). Like *The Dilemma of a Ghost*, Lorraine Hansberry's *A Raisin in the Sun* draws on Garvey's political clarion, "Back to Africa." Beneatha's relationship with Joseph Asegai, like Eulalie and Ato's, is partly motivated by Beneatha's search for African identity. Asegai is a Nigerian (African), so Beneatha sees him as a gateway to African heritage. Not even the knowledge that she is studying to be a medical doctor—a well paying and respected profession—can appease her. It is this notion that the diasporic Africans' home is in Africa that makes many of them associate their sense of belonging with Africa without critically assessing other factors that affect one's belonging. Braziel and Mannur rightly view "belonging as a process always in change and always mediated by issues of class, ethnicity, gender, and sexuality" (14). For example, *The Dilemma of a Ghost* has two classes—the rich/ upper class which consists of those who "have arrived" and the poor/ lower class which is made up of those who "have not arrived." In the words of Esi to Ato: "My knees are callous with bending before the rich . . . How my friends must be laughing behind me now. 'After all the fuss, she is poorer than ever before'" (35). The existence of these two classes—the poor and the rich—means that one could belong or not belong depending on one's class. The same is true of gender and race. For instance, "Eulalie is objectified and her identity is gendered, racialized, and contested as an 'other'" (Eke 76). In the play the second woman refers to her as "black-white woman" (22). Note Esi's speech to her son when Eulalie throws away the snails: "Do you not know how to eat them now? What kind of man are you growing into? Are your wife's taboos yours? *Rather your taboos should be hers*" (33; my emphasis). This could be read as gender inequality or patriarchal tyranny, affirmed and perpetuated by women, but it could also be read as the norm or culture of Ato's people. Still on gender inequality, Ato gives the men chairs while the women sit on the ground (42). Interestingly, the women have internalized the inequality so much that when Ato later gives Eulalie his chair and offers to sit on the ground, the women condemn him (43). That women have internalized their oppression is also evident in Nana's utterance when Eulalie leaves the gathering of men and women: "I have not heard the like of this before. Is the woman for whom *stalwart men* have assembled herself leaving the place of assembly?" (43; my emphasis). Why, one is tempted to ask, doesn't Nana acknowledge the women's presence in this summit? The issue of belonging, as we have seen, becomes more problematic when stretched along the lines of gender, class, and sexuality.

In an attempt to configure a plausible home for characters like Eulalie, Peters considers nomadism. According to Peters, "Nomadism [. . .] denies the dream of a homeland, with the result that home, being portable, is available everywhere" (31). Nomads laudably don't subscribe to the notion of a fixed home, a position that would perhaps solve the diasporic people's endless desire to return home. Defying settlement, the proponents of nomadism like Deleuze readily embrace change. But nomadism does not simply refer to people in motion. As Braidotti would say, "It is the subversion of set conventions that defines the nomadic state, not the literal act of traveling" (Peters 33). That said, nomadism does not adequately address the crisis of diasporic identity, especially among African Americans. One needs to recognize that there is a world of difference between being forced into exile and going to exile voluntarily. The African Americans like Eulalie "did not choose to lose their homes and homelands; mourning is not their fault but a fate" (Peters 34). Moreover, and perhaps more importantly, as Bourgeot argues, "[t]hough nomadism may inspire theorists, actual nomads arouse disdain and disgust from nation-states and their citizens" (qtd. in Peters 36). Nomads generally live in miserable conditions, and, thanks to racism and bigotry, are associated with backwardness. We risk undermining their political struggles for change when we romanticize nomadism. Looked at in that context, we ought to declare where we stand before we celebrate nomadism, even if it is only a metaphor. Even so, one must still recall that diasporic peoples and *original* homelands "are not naturally and organically connected" (Boyarin and Boyarin 723).

In the words of Karen Chapman, "The American Black has been removed from Africa for a long time. Contrary to what many romantically inclined Garveyites would like to believe, to return to the 'source' is a much more difficult task than its fascination may suggest, for it would mean returning to a culture never experienced" (30). Sharing a similar view, but in a different context, Kenneth Harrow rightly argues that diasporic return to the source can be "realized only as a dream, as [. . .] fantasy, in the spaces outside of harsh reality and its dilemmas" (172). Paradoxically, it is precisely these dreams and fantasies that feed the actions of individuals and even the political movements of return. In other words, it might be delusive to think that diasporic Africans' identity is lying somewhere in Africa, waiting to be embraced; however, that does not stop the dreams. In brief, even though we can never feel at home anywhere, it is imperative to negotiate identity and home wherever we are, and to recognize that they are bound to undergo constant change with time and with new situations and experiences (given their fluidity). Glissant makes a similar point in his argument about poetics of relations.

As Hall so persuasively argues in a different context, homelands "are subject to the continuous 'play' of history, culture, and power" (236). To understand the complexity of this notion of *return to the source,* one has to follow the conversation between the old man, Medouze, and the little boy, Jose, in Euzhan Palcy's film, *Sugar Cane Alley* (1983). The film is set in the Martinique of 1930s, and depicts the lives of "former" slaves and their descendants who work on sugar cane plantations. They live in shacks, and live on "pig tails." In other words, poverty is their daily bread. When Palcy's Jose asks Medouze to take him with him when he returns to Africa, the old man wisely educates him on what returning to Africa entails. Calling Africa his "dad's country," Medouze explains to Jose thus,

> Alas, my child . . .
> Medouze will never go to Africa
> Medouze has no one left in Africa
> When I will be dead . . .
> When my old body is buried . . .
> then I'll go to Africa
> But I can't take you along.
> We'll all go to Africa one day.

It is important to analyze Medouze's subtlety here: I'll never go to Africa, I'll go to Africa when I am dead, and we'll all go to Africa one day. What exactly does Medouze mean? Medouze tells Jose that he would never return to Africa except in death, meaning that he would only *return to the source* in spirit. He realizes that his return in life is not practical without dismissing the concept of return. This education is critical and timely. It is an education that Aidoo's Eulalie could learn from. Palcy does not in any way suggest that Medouze has a happy home in Martinique. In fact, what Medouze calls home is nothing but a Black Shack, an equivalent of slums, where black sugar cane plantation workers are forced to live by the oppressive socioeconomic conditions. Even though slavery has formally ended, Medouze says, "Nothing has changed, son. The whites own all the land. The law forbids their beating us, but it doesn't force them to pay us a decent wage." This, of course, is well before workers' unions and labor organizations. His bed is a hard pile of bamboo. His body reveals penury and hardship. While his younger life was reduced to slavery, his old age involves servitude. He has to work the plantations for wages that can only buy alcohol to help him sleep through the hard-labor and age related aches. He has no family because all his family were scattered by "The white men [who] hunted us. They caught us with lassos. Then . . . They took us to the edge of the big water. One day we were unloaded here. We were sold to cut cane for the whites." Why, then, does Medouze, who has a much closer relationship with Africa, and a vivid memory of the capture and subsequent enslavement across the Atlantic, reject a physical *return to the source?* What are we to make of his position? And what are we to make of this charcter who actually provides a historical link to Africa for Jose? Medouze recognizes that Africa is not spared from the oppressive forces that have subjected him to servitude.

Kane's *Ambivalent Adventure* (1963), like its title, is more ambivalent than Aidoo's *The Dilemma of a Ghost*. It is set in the period of new independence, and explores the challenges arising from locating the source in the shadow of empire. It shows that Samba Diallo's exposure to western culture has cost him his faith and spirituality, which is why he no longer wants to pray. The novel seems to echo a common belief toward the end of the nineteenth century that "western material progress had amounted to spiritual and artistic decadence" (Snead 236). At the same time, the novel presents the Most Royal Lady's case positively, implying that there is another way of locating home— beyond the source. To that end, the novel is a dialogue about whether to return to the source or form an alternative community beyond the source. For example, Samba Diallo completely refuses to pray upon his return, a refusal which leads the fool to kill him. His refusal to pray and to reach the teacher's grave, symbolically suggests that his *return to the source* is incomplete. Of course, one could argue that his death is in keeping with *return to the source,* that a seed must die in order to bring new life. But that argument is debatable because if it were the case, then Samba Diallo's spiritual death in France would have sufficed. It seems here that a narrative of *return* has burst its seams, thus indicating the difficulty, even impossibility, of a complete return.

Aidoo's *source* also ruptures, even if to a lesser degree. At the time of Ato's return, *the source* is a shadow of its past. According to the Second Woman, "[T]hose days are over When it was expedient for two deer To walk together, Since anyone can see and remove The beam in his eye with a mirror" (22). By shifting from a community in which people care for one another to an individualistic arena in which everyone is for herself/himself, *the source* yields to the forces that made Eulalie leave America. What, then, is the point of returning? On a similar note, women without children are not at home (23). That is, to be barren in this space is a misfortune.

The questions of race weaves through the three major narratives discussed here. Note, for example, the racial tension in Eulalie's "conversation" with her late mum,

> And I had it all, Ma, even graduation. "You'll be swank enough to look a white trash in the eye and tell him to go to hell." Ma, ain't I telling the whole of the States to go swing! Congress, Jew and white trash, from Manhattan to Harlem . . . "Sugar, don't let them do you in." Ma, I didn't. "Sugar, don't sort of curse

me and your Pa every morning you look your face in the mirror and see your-self black. Kill the sort of dreams silly girls that they are going to wake up one morning and find their skins milk white and their hairs soft blonde like the Hol-lywood tarts. Sugar, the dear God made you just that black and you canna do nothing about it." Ma, it was hard not to dream but I tried . . .only I wish you were not dead. . . . I wish you were right here, not even in the States, but here in this country where there will be no washing for you no more and where. . . . (24)

Eulalie makes it clear that she is disappointed with the white American state apparatus, led by the Congress. She says that her mum's hands are "chapped with washing to keep [her] in college" (24). The dreams reveal that blacks are under media pressure to conform to white/ Hollywood beauty standards. The black girls' daily dreams for white skins and blonde hair remind us of Derek Walcott's *Dream on Monkey Mountain* (1971), especially the part where Walcott's Moustique says, "And that is what they teach me since I small. To be black like coal, and dream of milk. To love God, and obey the white man" (290). Milk, in this play, symbolizes whiteness. So, Moustique, like many blacks growing up in the colonial system, is trained to yearn for that which he cannot be, right from his childhood. It is not accident that Makak has been taught to dream of milk and to obey the white man. Dreaming of milk and obeying the white man perpetuates the supposed supremacy of the white race, and systematizes oppression. Manning Marable, in *Beyond Boundaries,* makes an argument that reinforces my thinking here, "To be white is not a sign of culture, or a statement of biology or genetics: it is essentially a power relationship, a statement of authority, social construct which is perpetuated by systems of privilege, the consolidation of property and status" (7).

Walcott's *Dream on Monkey Mountain* examines the problem of locating home among Afro-Caribbeans; that is, it plays out a conflict between return-ing to Africa and remaining in the West Indies. The ambivalent and multi-layered play employs both dream and parody to demonstrate the agony of being what Patrick Colm Hogan, in *Colonialism and Cultural Identity* (2000), calls a "white in self-perception and black in self-image" (48). It is predicated on an ambiguous dream, a dream that simultaneously passes as a vision and as an illusion. Walcott warns us that the dream is "illogical, derivative, con-tradictory" (208). And, one may add, destructive and unattainable. Yet, the characters need these dreams to navigate a Caribbean world defined by the black and white tropes, a world that constantly marginalizes them, a world that they perpetuate by internalizing the dehumanizing labels they are given. As Hogan elaborates, "[T]here is dissociation in virtually all the characters, dissociation that results from the denigratory identities projected onto Afro-Caribbeans by colonialist racism, identities partially accepted by those men and women themselves" (46). One example of such dissociation is seen in

Makak's self-hatred. He hates his visual image the same way the colonizer hates it; Lacan would say that he sees himself as others (the colonizer) see him. Nowhere is this Lacanian self-hatred more conspicuously seen than in Makak's confession: "Not a pool of cold water, when I must drink, / I stir my hands first, to break up my image" (226). While one could read his action of stirring the water to break his image as a symbol of his fragmented mind, it especially reveals his determination to avoid coming face to face with his image (which he perceives as ugly). He is clearly denying himself. That reading is reinforced by his revelation, "Is thirty years now I have look in no mirror" (226). Makak avoids the mirror because he has wrongly subscribed to the notion that he is ugly. He cannot stand what he sees when he looks at the mirror. There is much more to the image question. Makak apprises Corporal Lestrade, "Sir, I am sixty years old. I have live all my life/ Like a wild beast in hiding. Without child, without wife" (226). One's child is essentially one's image, and, since Makak is already ashamed of his image, he does not want a child. Both the wife and child would act as mirrors (he will see himself in them), which he has avoided all his life. He hides because he does not fit into the norm. In order to avoid further humiliation, Makak and his fellow Afro-Caribbeans try to become white.

Upon realizing that the goal of becoming white is unattainable, they begin to search for blackness through reactionary nativism/ reverse racism and the original moment or source. Walcott's "What the Twilight Says: An Overture" notes the process: "Once we have lost our wish to be white we develop a longing to become black, and those two may be different, but are still careers" (20). Even the retrieval of the *original moment,* which the characters in the play, led by Makak, attempt to do is ultimately futile for several reasons, one of which is the realization that their ancestry is multi-rooted. If Makak fails in his bid to liberate his people, it is because, as Cornel West says in a different context, his dream "remained captive to the supremacy game—a game mastered by the white racists he opposed and imitated with his black supremacy doctrine" (142). In a similar vein, as Fanon would say, "the assertion of pure, essential blackness is a reaction, still imprisoned within the dualism [Manicheanism] of colonial discourse. With the destruction of the myth of white superiority, the need for that reaction disappears as well" (Breslin 130).

Following his dream and experiences, Makak realizes that any meaningful liberation must recognize that the two races (whites and blacks) are intricately tied together, they are not Manichean in relationship: "I wanted to leave this world. But if the moon is earth's friend, eh, Tigre, how can we leave the earth" (304). In other words, Walcott is challenging the colonized to acknowledge their *Africanness* as well as their *Caribbeanness,* hence hybridity. He illuminates his position in his paper, "Necessity of Negritude."

For us, whose tribal memories have died, and who have begun again in a New World, Negritude offers an assertion of pride, but not of our complete identity, since that is mixed and shared by other races, whose writers are East Indian, white, mixed, whose best painters are Chinese, and in whom the process of racial assimilation goes on with every other marriage. (23)

"For Walcott," argues Paula Burnett, "the task is to demonstrate the incorporation of multiple traditions in the Caribbean location, mythified as the site of hybridity" (35). Granted, hybridity is the pragmatic way forward. After all, as Werbner and Modood put it, "cultures evolve historically through unreflective borrowings, mimetic appropriations, exchanges and inventions. There is no culture in and of itself" (4-5). That previously opposing camps (whiteness and blackness) can question their supposed purity and coexist in the subject is encouraging.

Walcott expects his characters to move from "the *expressive,* with its rigid claims and oftentimes unexamined ethnocentric biases" to "the *performative,* a self-critical model that conceives identity as open, interculturally negotiable, and always in the making—a process" (Olaniyan, Scars 4). Walcott's objective in this play, to borrow from West, is to make his characters "affirm themselves as human beings, no longer viewing their bodies, minds and souls through white lenses, and believing themselves capable of taking control of their own destinies" (136). That is why his main character, "Makak (monkey) begins as the exemplary victim of the colonial hegemonic discourse, living fully his constitution—his subjection, as 'black, ugly, poor [and so] worse than nothing' (237), then gradually negotiating his way towards self-definition" (Olaniyan, "Corporeal" 156). Olaniyan's observation is echoed by Brown, who rightly says that the Makak we see at the end of the play marks "a new Black self-definition" (20). Like Makak, the colonized in West Indies ought to accept that they are Afro-Caribbeans, and that their home is the West Indies. If Walcott's Makak realizes the need to find home in the diaspora, Aidoo's Eulalie does not. In any case, his acceptance of Afro-Caribbean culture and West Indies notwithstanding, Makak's living condition remains at best squalid. What would cultural hybridity mean to Makak if does not have sustainable access to basic human dignity (decent housing, food, and companionship)? At the end of the play, the trans-cultural Makak still resides at the very reservation camp where his journey began, which erroneously suggests that diasporic Africans' recognition of their cultural hybridity (race) guarantees their economic empowerment (class). Nothing could be further from the truth. An answer to Makak's problem of the color line does not necessarily address his problem of poverty. Makak will continue to search for a place to call home as long as he is economically exploited. Diasporic Africans' liberation must be simultaneously anchored on decolonization of the mind, cultural diversity, education, health, and equal economic opportunity.

REFERENCES

Ahmad, Aijaz. 1994. *In Theory: Nations, Classes, Literature.* San Francisco: Analytical Pyschology Club of San Francisco.

Aidoo, Ama Ata. 1985. *The Dilemma of a Ghost and Anowa.* Essex: Longman.

———. 1979. *Our Sister Killjoy: Or, Reflections from a Black-eyed Squint.* New York: NOK.

Anderson, Benedict. 1983. *Imagined Communities: Reflections on the Origin and Spread of Nationalism.* London: Verso.

Anzaldua, Gloria. 1987. *Borderlands/La Frontera: The New Mestiza.* San Francisco: Aunt Lute.

Appadurai, Arjun. 2000. "Spectral Housing and Urban Cleansing: Notes on Millennial Mumbai." *Public Culture* 12.3:627–51.

Appiah, Kwame Antony. 1998. "The Cosmopolitan Patriot." *Cosmopolitics: Thinking and Feeling Beyond the Nation.* Ed. Pheng Cheah and Bruce Robbins. Minneapolis: University of Minnesota Press, 1998.

———. 1992. *In My Father's House: Africa in the Philosophy of Culture.* Oxford: Oxford University Press.

Baldwin, James. 1993. *Another Country.* New York: Vintage International.

Boyce Davies, Carole. 1994. *Black Women, Writing and Identity: Migrations of the Subject.* London: Routledge.

Boym, Svetlana. 2001. *The Future of Nostalgia.* New York: Basic Books.

Boyarin, Daniel, and Jonathan Boyarin. 1993. "Diaspora: Generation and the Ground of Jewish Identity." *Critical Inquiry.* 19: 693–725.

Braidotti, Rosi. 1994. *Nomadic Subjects: Embodiment and Sexual Difference in Contemporary and Sexual Difference in Contemporary Feminist Theory.* New York: Columbia University Press.

Braziel, Jana Evans, and Anita Mannur, eds. 2003. *theorizing diaspora.* Malden, MA: Blackwell Publishing.

Breslin, Paul. 2001. *Nobody's Nation.* Chicago: The University of Chicago Press.

Burnett, Paula. 2000. *Derek Walcott: Politics and Poetics.* Gainesville: University Press of Florida.

Chambers, Ian. 1990. *Border Dialogues: Journeys in Postmodernity.* London: Routledge.

———. 1994. *Migrancy, Culture, Identity.* London: Routledge.

Clifford, James. 1997. *Routes: Travel and Translation in the Twentieth Century.* Cambridge, MA: Harvard University Press.

———. 1988. *The Predicament of Culture.* Cambridge, MA: Harvard University Press.

Cohen, Robin. 1994. *Frontiers of Identity.* London: Longman.

de Lauretis, Teresa. 1987. *Technologies of Gender: Essays on Theory, Film, and Fiction.* Bloomington: Indiana University Press.

———, ed. 1987. *Feminist Studies/Critical Studies*. Bloomington: Indiana University Press.

Deleuze, Gilles and Felix Guattari. 1987. *A Thousand Plateaus: Capitalism and Schizophrenia*. Trans. Brian Massumi. Minneapolis: University of Minnesota Press.

Du Bois, W.E.B. 1997. *The Souls of Black Folk.* Ed. David W. Blight and Robert Godding-Williams. Boston: Bedford/St. Martin's.

Fanon, Frantz. 1967. *Black Skin, White Masks*. Trans. Charles Lam Markmann. New York: Grove Press.

———. 1967. *Toward the African Revolution*. Trans. Haakan Chevalier. New York: Grove Press.

———. 1963. *The Wretched of the Earth*. Trans. Constance Farrington. New York: Grove Press.

Featherstone, Mike. 1996. "Localism, Globalism, and Cultural Identity." *Global Local: Cultural Production and the Transnational Imaginery*. Ed. Rob Wilson and Wimal Dissanayake. Durham, NC: Duke University Press. 46–75.

Friedman, Susan Stanford. 1998. *Mappings: Feminisms and the Cultural Geographies of Encounter*. Princeton: Princeton University Press.

Gates, Henry L., Jr. ed. 1985. *"Race," Writing, and Difference*. Chicago: University of Chicago Press.

Gates, Henry L. Jr. and Cornel West. 1996. *The Future of the Race.* New York: Vintage Books.

Gilroy, Paul. 1993. *The Black Atlantic: Modernity and Double Consciousness*. Cambridge, MA: Harvard University Press.

———. 1991. "It Ain't Where You're From, It's Where You're At . . .: The Dialectics of Diasporic Identification." *Third Text* 13 (Winter): 3–16.

———. 2005. *Postcolonial Melancholia*. New York: Columbia University Press.

Glissant, Edouard. 1989. *Caribbean Discourse: Selected Essays*. Trans. J. Michael Dash. Charlottesville: University Press of Virginia.

———. 1997. *Poetics of Relation*. Trans. Betsy Wing. Ann Arbor: The University of Michigan Press.

Hall, Stuart. 2003. "Cultural Identity and Diaspora." *Theorizing Diaspora: A Reader*. Ed. Jana Evans Braziel and Anita Mannur. Malden, MA: Blackwell Publishing. 233–46.

———. 1997. "The Local and the Global: Globalization and Ethnicity." *Dangerous Liasons: Gender, Nation, and Postcolonial Perspectives*. Ed. Anne McClintock, Aamir Mufti, and Ella Shohat. Minneapolis: University of Minnesota Press.

———. 2002. "Political Belonging in a World of Multiple Identities." *Conceiving Cosmopolitanism: Theory, Context, and Practice*. Ed. Steven Vertovec and Robin Cohen. Oxford: Oxford University Press.

Hansberry, Lorraine. 1992. *A Raisin in the Sun*. Ed. Robert Nemiroff. New York: Penguin Books.

Harrow, Kenneth W. 1994. *Thresholds of Change in African Literature: The Emergence of a Tradition*. Portsmouth, NH: Heinemann.

———. 2001. *Less Than One and Double: A Feminist Reading of African Women's Writings.* Portsmouth, NH.: Heinemann.

———. 1999. "Of Those Who Went Before." *Emerging Perspectives on Ama Ata Aidoo.* Ed. Ada Uzoamaka Azodo and Gay Wilentz. Trenton, NJ: Africa World Press.

Hogan, Patrick Colm. 2000. *Colonialism and Cultural Identity: Crisis of Tradition in the Anglophone Literatures of India, Africa, and the Caribbean.* Albany: State University of New York Press.

hooks, bell. 1990. *Yearning: Race, Gender, and Cultural Politics.* Boston, MA: South End Press.

———. 2000. *Feminism is for Everybody.* Cambridge, MA: South End Press.

Hughes, Langston. 1964. *The Big Sea.* New York: Hill and Wang.

Kane, Cheikh Hamidou. 1963. *Ambiguous Adventure.* Trans. Katherine Woods. London: Heinemann.

Kaplan, Caren. 1996. *Questions of Travel: Postmodern Discourses of Displacement.* Durham, NC: Duke University Press.

King, Martin Luther Jr. 2000. *Why We Can't Wait.* New York: Signet Classics.

Kowash, Samira. 1998. "The Homeless Body." *Public Culture* 10.2: 319–39.

Marable, Manning. 2011. *Beyond Boundaries.* Boulder: Paradigm Publishers.

———. 2000. *How Capitalism Underdeveloped Black America.* Cambridge, MA: South End Press.

Miyoshi, Masao. 1993. "A Borderless World?: From Colonialism to Transnationalism and the Decline of the Nation-State." *Critical Inquiry* 19 (Summer): 726–51

Morrison, Toni. 1997. "Home." *The House That Race Built.* Wahneema Lubiano, ed. New York: Pantheon Books.

Olaniyan, Tejumola. 1995. *Scars of Conquest/ Masks of Resistance: The Invention of Cultural Identities in African, African American, and Caribbean Drama.* Oxford: Oxford University Press.

Palcy, Euzhan. 1993. *Sugar Cane Alley.* Film.

Peters, John Durham. 1999. "Exile, Nomadism, and Diaspora: The Stakes of Mobility in the Western canon." *Home, Exile, Homeland: Film, Media, and the Politics of Place.* ed. Hamid Naficy. New York: Routledge.

Radhakrishnan, R. 1996. *Diasporic Mediations: Between Home and Locations.* Minneapolis: University of Minnesota Press.

Read, Peter. 1996. *Returning to Nothing.* Cambridge: Cambridge University Press.

Rodney, Walter. 1981. *How Europe Underdeveloped Africa.* Washington DC: Howard University Press.

Rushdie, Salman. 1991. *Imaginary Homelands: Essays and Criticism 1981-1991.* London: Granta Books.

Said, Edward. 2000. "Reflections on Exile." *Reflections on Exile and Other Essays.* Cambridge, MA: Harvard University Press.

Stam, Robert. 2003. "Beyond Third Cinema: The Aesthetics of Hybridity." *Rethinking Third Cinema.* Ed. Anthony R. Guneratne and Wimal Dissanayake. New York: Routledge.

Walcott, Derek. 1970. *Dream on Monkey Mountain. In Dream on Monkey Mountain and Other Plays.* New York: Noonday Press.

West, Cornel. 1993. *Race Matters.* New York: Vintage Books.

Wilson, William Julius. 2009. *More Than Just Race: Being Black and Poor in the Inner City.* New York: W.W. Norton.

Wilson, Rob and Wimal Dissanayake, eds. 1996. *GlobalLocal: Cultural Production and the Transnational Imaginery.* Durham, NC: Duke University Press.

Chapter Thirteen

Modeling the Determinants of Voluntary Reverse Migration Flows and Repatriation of African Immigrants

INTRODUCTION

Scholarships on transnational African migrations to the West have been robust and comprehensive since the late 1980s as record number of Africans came to settle in the United States. To date, such studies have been successful in highlighting the push-pull factors influencing the migration of skilled and unskilled Africans to global labor and economic centers. Among these factors are mass graduate unemployment, lack of production capacity, structural adjustments, underdeveloped or private sector, political violence and economic corruption, numbing poverty, civil unrests, low remunerations, rapid urbanization, and population growth. Other factors include the pressure to earn foreign exchange and provide support to extended family members, availability of low-skilled jobs in the West, and the desire for better standards of living (Gordon, 1998; George Ayiteh, 1992; Adepoju, 1991; Takyi and Konadu-Agyemang, 2006; Peil, 1995; Takougang, 1995; and Arthur, 2000).

A significant aspect of the new African migratory process is irregular and illegal economic migrants who are driven solely by work in menial roles, including agricultural labor and meat packaging in the West. This includes the foot migration of economically displaced and impoverished African youth who walk across the Sahel with the objective of crossing into North Africa, the Mediterranean, and ultimately to the European Union (EU). Unmet and failed aspirations in Africa coupled with the yearning for global economic and cultural incorporation has given impetus to hundreds of thousands of Africans to look beyond the continent for the fulfillment of their dreams. For many Africans, international migration has become a strategy for achieving social mobility and achieved status. The result of the evolving migration of Africans to the West (particularly the United States) is the formation of

African diaspora communities and the intensification of diaspora-facilitated development projects whose goals are to link (African) immigrants to their respective homelands and at the same time play pivotal roles in the socioeconomic and cultural change of Africa (Robinson, 2002; Arthur, 2000; Konadu-Agyemang et al., 2006; Sheffer, 2007; Totoricaguena, 2007; Arthur, 2011).

The long-term social and cultural orientations of African immigrants cannot be grasped or appreciated from a scholastic point of view unless systematic attempts are made to elucidate how these immigrants define and express their post-migration intentions. Hitherto, African migrations to the United States and the West in general have been rationalized as a linear process involving the geographic movement from locations in Africa to fixed destinations in the United States. This approach treats African migration as one stream devoid of any long-term subsequent return migration. African migrations have become more complex in response to rising global economic, cultural, and social incorporation. Faster modes of transportation and communication continue to play major roles in the migratory behavior of Africans. No place is out of reach of prospective African migrants who desire to search for better opportunities outside the continent. Understanding the repatriation plans of African immigrants will lead to a clearer understanding of the continuing role and importance of international migration for Africa. More significantly, it is possible that scholarship on African migrant repatriation can lead to the development and testing of statements or hypotheses about the transformative impact of return migration and repatriation in the socioeconomic, political, and cultural developments of the African immigrant-sending countries. As the African diaspora unfolds in the United States, a systematic understanding of the planned and unplanned reverse migration of Africans is critical in shedding light on how return migration as a process is inextricably bound with Africa's emerging economic potential and development. Reverse migration continue to serve as the driving force and catalyst behind the increased economic and cultural development in the region. In some of the countries such as Ghana where the export of labor has become the chief mechanism for acquiring foreign currency and investment through remittances, return migration is fueling assets transfer to aid in the economic and cultural development of the country.

Concomitant with financial or monetary asset transfer from the West is the transfer of skills, roles, acquired norms, beliefs, and new ways of thinking that the immigrant returnees bring with them to foster change in Africa. In a recent article "Africa is Awakening, Helped by Free Trade," the *Wall Street Journal* (June 27, 2011: Page A15) noted that "Six of the ten fastest-growing economies of the last decade were in Sub-Saharan Africa. Over the next five years, the average African economy will outpace its Asian counterparts." The

African Growth and Opportunity Act (AGOA) and the Millennium Challenge Corporation are opening up the continent for business with the United States and the rest of the West. Under these programs, African goods exported to the United States will be reduced and markets previously not accessible to African-made goods will be available to the African exporters. The region is certainly being incorporated into the global economic production process similar to what the Asian "tiger economies" of Singapore, Malaysia, and South Korea experienced at the end of the World War II. Some of the African immigrants living in the United States and the West are poised to take advantage of this social change in terms of how they conceptualize and implement their repatriation and resettlement in Africa. The resources, assets, skills, and the normative beliefs acquired following their migration are ultimately transferred back home and their cumulative impact on the migrant-returning societies can be phenomenal (Arthur, 2008). The educational and income earnings of these immigrants have surpassed whites and in particularly native-born American blacks (Dodoo, 1991; Dodoo and Takyi, 2002). Their human capital resources are of tremendous significance for uplifting Africa out of its underdevelopment quagmire. As African immigrant repatriation from the West gains momentum, studies such as the current one become imperative if advancements are to be made in the current state of scholarship regarding the prospects and viability of economic development utilizing interpretative theoretical and empirical models constructed on the importance of reverse migration on diaspora national development.

The purpose of this study is to examine the macro-level (structural) and the micro-level (individualistic) components that account for how African immigrants structure the decision-making process regarding repatriation and resettlement in Africa. The goal is to identify the sociological processes involved in the formulation of the decision to return to Africa and the specification of the underlying narratives and contexts of migrant repatriation. The questions addressed include but are not limited to the following. Are there specific reverse migration trends that can be discerned among African immigrants currently domiciled in the United States? What factors in both the host country and the homeland influence the return migration decision? How is repatriation transforming the sojourner transnational immigrant identities of African émigrés? Does the migration of Africans come to an end once they arrive and become settled in the United States? What can we extrapolate from the repatriation processes of this immigrant group and what are the implications of African immigrant repatriation for the host and immigrant origination countries of Africa? The presence of well-educated African immigrants in the United States who are strikingly well-off economically than their American-born black counterparts may create the impression to the casual observer that these African immigrants are here to stay in the United States permanently. After all, one may rationalize, why go back to Africa when several of the immigrants have fared well economically relative to those they left behind in Africa to come to the United States? Even among the ranks of the new African refugees who have arrived in the country since 1980, significant strides have been made in terms of economic and cultural gains in income growth, educational attainment, home ownership, and overall standard of living comparative to pre-refugee status. Post-refugee problems such as language deficiencies, cultural shocks, racism, and discrimination, lingering psychological traumas associated with statelessness and displacement, and isolation continue to affect many of the new refugees that have fled war torn countries in Africa to find safer havens in the United States.

Theoretically, this study is informed by researches conducted in Jamaica, Puerto Rico, Egypt, and Greece. A summary of the results have revealed two findings. First, while economic and political conditions are critical in explaining the motivation for migrating to the West, the same variables are significant also in delineating return or reverse migration. Second, migrant-exporting countries have come to recognize the importance of incorporating migration policies in their development plans. In Jamaica, Thomas-Hope (1999) found that networks and linkages of support that Jamaican immigrants establish with relatives back home have been critical in accounting for return migration. The returning Jamaicans set up small businesses, boost the country's foreign and domestic savings, set up schools and literacy programs, and worked with Non-Governmental Organizations (NGOs) to organize rural villagers into marketing cooperatives to facilitate the distribution and marketing of food supplies. What emerged from the Jamaican study was that macro-economic variables (increased global trade, the spread of international capital, growth of subsidiaries of major corporations in the developing countries, and the rise in the demand for tertiary education) have created the propensity for people to move around more liberally, often transferring with them their human and natural capital. Some of these same macro-structural and global economic issues are also central in influencing decisions migrants subsequently make to repatriate.

A study of Puerto Rican returnees revealed that economic and political concerns in the country of origination and the country of immigrant destinations serve as mediating factors in determining return migration (Muschkin, 1999). This study revealed that the desire to return home or the chance to participate in social and political affairs in the country of immigrant origination are significant influential or motivational factors influencing the decision to return home. The returning Puerto Rican immigrants from the United States and Canada opened cottage industries, taught English classes to fellow Puerto

Ricans, and launched export-driven initiatives in areas such as tourism and hospitality management.

In their study of returned immigrants from Egypt, Kandil and Metwally (1998) reported that return migration is inexorably linked to the remittances or the cash transfers that immigrants send home. The study showed that the voluntary repatriation of Egyptian immigrants abroad is determined by two factors: first, the frequency and amount of money the immigrants remitted home, and second, the political environment existing at home. The remittances that Egyptian immigrants send home become a valuable source of foreign exchange for their governments. Remittance also enables the return migrants to have the capital to invest in sectors of their country's economy upon their return home. Recognizing the immense contributions of the migrant returnees, the central government of Egypt liberalized their banking laws to enable returnees from the United States and Britain to expedite the transfer of their assets and capital to Egypt. The net effect of this policy was that the returnees have been able to set up mini and large-scale enterprises that offer employment to Egyptians.

While there is a dearth of literature on the returned migration of African immigrants living in the West, Logan's (1992; 1999) study of the effects of brain drain and return migration on economic development in Zimbabwe is very informative and provides a model on which the proximate determinants of African immigrant reverse migration can be based. Despite the political and economic uncertainties that have recently engulfed the country, some Zimbabweans are returning home mainly to set up their own businesses. Logan found that in Zimbabwe, return migrants have moved to the forefront of entrepreneurial activities, political change, and technological innovations. Zimbabwe-born immigrants from the United States who returned home brought with them knowledge about political mobilization, resource management, capital formation and utilization, data creation and retrieval, and community governance. Logan established that the combined assets of the Zimbabwe returnees currently held in Western banks far exceed the amount of foreign capital that the Zimbabwe government can raise from international financial markets. For a developing nation like Zimbabwe, the task is how to develop and initiate policies that would tap the private capital of its citizens to invigorate national economic development. Equally significant for the rest of Africa is how to tap the human capital resources of her immigrant citizens living abroad as well as the development of protocols and strategies to ensure their return home (Ammassari and Black, 2001).

Research investigating the impact of return migration on migrant home countries may be approached from a number of perspectives. One perspective seeks to unravel the consequences of return migration on the socioeconomic and political as well cultural development on the returning homeland. In this perspective, emphasis is usually given to the processes whereby returnees are able to reestablish themselves and become reintegrated into the affairs of their returning societies. Studies incorporating this perspective highlight both structural and individualistic factors in the reincorporation of returns in the country of origination (Baerga and Thompson, 1999; Muschkin, 1999). The structural approach assesses the macro-level broad-based global economic factors that may spur migrants to return home. For example, business and employment opportunities, acquired assets, capital and investment dispersion, and growth in emerging economies and their relationships with advanced economies are some of the factors that may motivate migrants at the structural level to return home.

The second perspective stresses micro-level or individualistic factors such as time migrant has spent away from home, age of migrant, skills, norms, beliefs, and values acquired in the host society, family-oriented variables such as number and age of children still living at home, migrant health status, feelings of nostalgia about home, and the desire to leave close to relatives. In designing this study we, incorporate both structural and individualistic components about migrants to better understand how the return process is formed, implemented, and acted upon (Thomas-Hope, 1999). Alternate explanations of African immigrant repatriation are provided within the context of the underlying broader socioeconomic and cultural parameters of African migrations and the social systems in which migratory behaviors are given content.

DATA AND STUDY DESIGN

Data for this study were collected from a nonrandom sample of eighty-five immigrants representing six African countries currently residing in a large Midwestern city with a metropolitan population in excess of one million. The study participants were identified using a snowball purposive sampling where each respondent were asked to identify potential participants who could be contacted and included in the study. The snowball purposive sample proved valuable for identifying and collecting information from the study participants because it gave prospective respondents and the researcher the opportunity to include as many subjects as possible in the study and at the same time the opportunity to opt out. The drawback of the purposive sample is that the findings cannot be generalized and should therefore be considered tentative.

The nonrandom purposive sampling design yielded a total 134 potential respondents. Of this number, 85 respondents representing 63 percent of the respondents were selected for inclusion in the study. Some cases were excluded to protect the legal immigration status and anonymity of respondents. The countries of immigrant origination are Senegal, Ghana, Nigeria, Sudan, Somalia, and Ethiopia. Immigrants who self-identified as legal residents, naturalized citizens, or undocumented were selected for study. The interviewees were pre-selected to include only those immigrants who had indicated in the pilot survey that they had formed a short and long-term decision about their repatriation plans. The main reason for identifying respondents who had already formed their repatriation plans was based on previous research findings about immigrant repatriation in general which shows that though many immigrants in the United States contemplate repatriation, only a small number are able to successfully implement strategies to make their repatriation a reality.

A combination of structured closed-ended and unstructured open-ended interviews by mail and telephone were used to collect the data on immigrant plans for repatriation and reverse migration. The structured closed-ended questions were Likert-scale format in which study participants were asked to response to predetermined issues and measures of the intent to repatriate. The telephone interviews lasted approximately thirty minutes and were primarily intended to yield a case-by-case data source describing each participant's experiences and formulations about the intent to repatriate. The telephone survey also provided an opportunity to probe into subject's formulation of the intent to repatriate and the preparatory steps or strategies they have undertaken to implement the decision to return to Africa.

The questions were grouped thematically with attention given to demographic variables (age, marital status, type employment status, educational attainment, household size, total family income, gender, length of stay in the United States); household economic variables (amount of money saved at home and in the United States, frequency of remittance flows, amount of money remitted, immigrant sense of economic opportunities in the country of origination, home ownership, small-scale business formations at home, immigrant categorization of ease of transferability of assets, number of children or grandchildren under age twenty-one, spousal labor force participation, immigrant perception about the American economy, frequency of unemployment, sector of immigrant employment); immigrant rationalization of the political culture and environment in the country of origination (home government policies to promote smooth repatriation, immigrant sense of political insecurity, confidence in core institutions at home, fear of social incorporation and integration, fear of violence, crime, personal safety and security) and their significance in the decision-making process to repatriate.

Statements designed to measure respondent's perceptions about the short and long-term prospects of Africa's rise to global economic incorporation, including the viability of economic institutions in Africa were included in the predictive variables. In a sense, the explanatory models being proposed here to account for reverse migration are also inextricably linked with the initial impetus and cumulative forces that spur African outmigration in the first place. Their inclusion in this study is therefore significant because they can shed light on whether or not the push factors of African transnational migration to the West in general also serve as the pull factors motivating repatriation home. Ordinary least squares (OLS) regression analyses were performed with voluntary repatriation as dependent variable. We reported the standardized beta coefficients, the errors associated with the coefficients, the levels of statistical significance, and the adjusted R-squared.

Presentation of Descriptive Findings

Migrant repatriation is a complex process which involves time, cost, risk, and potential benefits for migrants and their families. Whether the decision to return is made by the individual migrant acting alone or made in concert with immediate or extended family members, the decision may often involve accessing information pertinent to implement the repatriation, effective utilization of the knowledge or information, collaboration, shared decisions, responsibilities, and known or unknown obligations.

To present a portrait of African immigrant repatriation behavior, we have selected a number of variables to use as illustrations of the patterns of immigrant repatriation decision making. We begin with educational attainment. African immigrants who have acquired significant educational and labor market credentials were more firm in their plans to repatriate compared to those immigrants who have not acquired significant educational attainment following their migration to the United States. In general, repatriation plans varied by educational attainment with highly educated immigrants more likely to formulate their repatriation plans than those who have lower educational attainment. Nearly 65 percent of the respondents with post-graduate credentials and who have worked for a minimum of nine consecutive years have made the decision to repatriate within the next two to five years. Of those with baccalaureate credentials, 40 percent have formulated plans to repatriate within the next six to eight years. Among those who hold associate degrees, 15 percent plan to repatriate within the next eight to ten years. For those immigrants who have secondary or high school credentials, only 5 percent have formulated definitive plans about their repatriation.

Variations in repatriation plans are discernible among the immigrants according to whether or not immigrants have pursued educational credentials following their arrival in the United States. Immigrants who have pursued educational credentials following their arrival in the United States are more likely to form their repatriation plans compared to those who have not continued their education following migration to the United States.

The professional and occupational category of immigrant work also factors in the decision to repatriate. Of those immigrants who described their occupational status as professional (healthcare, managerial, sales, teachers, marketing, and technical), nearly one-half (49.4 percent) have formed their repatriation plans. This compares with 25 percent of immigrants in non-professional work status (agriculture, custodial and janitorial services, parking ramp attendants, meat-packaging, and cab drivers) who have formed plans about future repatriation.

Duration of employment also affected the decision to repatriate. Immigrants with steady employment (compared to those who reported being unemployed) were more likely to have formed their plans about the prospects of repatriation. For all occupational categories (professional and nonprofessional), an overarching theme in the formulation of repatriation plans was immigrant perception about the economic and social viability of repatriation coupled with consternation about how to achieve full incorporation or reentry into the home society following protracted periods of absence. This consternation is mediated by the presence or absence of extended family members or close associates to provide information and assist in the repatriation process. A significant consideration among all occupational groups of immigrants is the prospects of gaining access to gainful employment upon return.

The descriptive statistics showed similarities and variations in immigrant repatriation plans according to gender, citizenship status, age, year and timing of immigration, number of children under eighteen living at home, and marital status. The data showed that slightly more than one-half of the male immigrants (51 percent) have formed their repatriation plans compared to the female immigrants (48 percent). Of those who have formed their repatriation plans, 53 percent are naturalized citizens of the United States compared with 45 percent who are permanent residents (green card holders), asylees, or non-immigrant visa holders. Immigrants who arrived in the United States before 2000 and have lived continuously in the United States for more than ten years were more likely to have formed their repatriation plans compared with those immigrants who have entered the country during the last decade. Of those who reported their repatriation plans, only one-third have children who are less than eighteen years old and living at home. The rest have no children living at home. Marital status of those who have formed their repatriation plans were nearly the same for those who are married (49 percent) and those who reported not being married (51 percent).

Sixty percent of the immigrants who reported a total family income greater than $65,000 have formed their repatriation plans. This compares with thirty-five per cent of those immigrants whose total family income was less than $65,000 per annum. Frequency of home visits also affected the formation of repatriation plans, with immigrants who reported frequent visits home (three or more times during the last five years) more likely to have formulated their repatriation plans compare to those who made fewer visits home (less than three home visits during the past five years). Immigrants who sent monthly remittances home (average amount remitted $500) are more likely to have formed their repatriation plans compared with immigrants who remitted once every two months (average amounted remitted less than $500). Immigrants who reported having savings and retirement investments (76 percent) are more likely to have formed their repatriation plans compared to those immigrants (23 percent) who indicated they have no savings or retirement investments.

A breakdown of immigrant subjective class membership (whether immigrants considered themselves upper, middle, or lower class) showed that of the nearly 75 percent who considered themselves middle class, 80 percent have already formed their repatriation plans. Of the remaining 25 percent who self-identified as lower class, less than a third (28 percent) had already formed their repatriation plans. No respondent self-identified as upper class.

The data also provided some insights into immigrant-identified constraints to repatriation. Primarily economic in nature, these constraints symbolize the trepidation that some of the immigrants have about the repatriation process. By far, the major economic constraint is structural and is based on the concern that despite the moderate improvements made in the economic lives of Africans, the governments of Africa are not capable of developing and implementing robust plans and policies to lift the mass of their citizens out of poverty. This structural constraint is attributed to economic mismanagement of resources and the gross inefficiencies associated with the improper utilization of domestic and foreign investments. On their part, the immigrants remain skeptical about the ability of African governments to be able to sustain continued economic growth considering the competing needs in other sectors such as healthcare, infrastructural developments, jobs, energy, and food. Following their repatriation, the majority of the immigrants expect these economic problems (which had motivated their migration) to persist over the long haul. The persistency of these problems mean that for some of the prospective returnees, there will be continued consternation about how their governments can manage the pressing economic problems and the frustration it causes without fanning political unrest and violence. The expectations on the part of the immigrants that unresolved economic problems may flare up into political problems create uncertainties in the minds of the prospective returnees about the viability of their repatriation. These problems notwithstanding, a majority of the immigrants (62 percent) believe that these problems are not insurmountable and that while they are better positioned to deal with the economic problems due to the foreign assets and human capital resources acquired abroad, a spillover of economic problems into violence will threaten and jeopardize their safe return.

Irrespective of whether they have made their repatriation plans or not, the commonly cited reasons repatriate (ranked in descending order) include immigrant preference to live closer to relatives, particularly siblings and elderly relatives (84 percent); to build a house (71 percent); to take advantage of improving economic, social, and political conditions in Africa (66 percent); to set up a business venture in Africa (60 percent); to offset the high cost of retirement in the United States relative to Africa (55 percent); the desire to be near relatives who will take care of them during old age rather than an institutional caregiver (52 percent); the desire to enable grandparents have a role in raising their grandchildren (47 percent); the desire to spend retirement years in Africa (41 percent); African government economic incentives to lure their nationals abroad to repatriate (34 percent); and ability to formulate their own unique racial, ethnic, and class identities independent of what they have experienced and how they have been defined or portrayed in the host society (21 percent).

Variations in country-specific repatriation plans were noticeable among the immigrants from the six countries that were studied. Immigrant respondents from Nigeria (74 percent) indicated the highest willingness to repatriate. This was followed by immigrants from Ghana (68 percent). Despite rumbles of political uncertainties, both Nigeria and Ghana are on a sustained path to constitutional governance and democracy. Despite persistent economic problems, the two countries (also members of the free-trade zone known as the Economic Community of West African States), are poised for growth if continued efforts are made by the governments to effectively manage their fiscal resources, expand industrial and manufacturing production, and at the same time promote private sector investments.

In the cases of Sudan and Senegal, slightly more than one-half (53 percent) of immigrants from the two countries have formed their repatriation plans. In the Sudan, the current contentious political rapture of the country which will lead to the breakup of the southern cone of the country into an autonomous self-determined country continues to cause tensions in that country.

Decades of intercultural and religious conflicts have caused the displacement of hundreds of thousands of refugees from the Sudan some of whom settled in the United States (Holtzman, 2000). The country was partitioned with the creation of South Sudan, an oil-rich region in July 2011. With its capital city of Juba, this newly independent country will be Africa's fifty-four country and will comprise of black Sudanese who are mainly Christians. To the north will be Sudan which is chiefly Arabic and Muslim. The partitioning of the country may not bring an end to the conflicts in that region. A continued climate of instability despite the partitioning of the country may affect the short and long-term relationships that Sudanese citizens living abroad establish with their homeland.

Senegal, a Francophone country in West Africa, is one of sub-Saharan Africa's stable countries with a robust economic system. Immigrants from Somalia and Ethiopia had the lowest number of immigrant respondents who had formulated their repatriation plans (20 percent for Somalia and 28 percent for Ethiopia.) These two nations are located in the Horn of Africa region where political conflicts have been rampant during the last three decades or so. Currently, Somalia does not have a civil government and the persistent conflicts in that country has brought hundreds of thousands of displaced Somali refugees to the United States and other Western nations. Decades of clan and tribal warfare waged by warlords continue to destabilize and tear the country apart resulting in Somalia being classified by the United States government as a failed state. Her refugee citizens who have been fortunate to flee for safer havens in the West are not rushing to return home anytime soon. Tensions within the nation-states of Africa will continue to be prime factors influencing immigrant resettlement and repatriation.

The African immigrants who were studied were all at various stages of the return process. The majority of the immigrants (nearly 72 percent) were definitive about their plans to repatriate and have taken a number of steps to initiate the arduous process of returning in the short and long-term. These steps include an identifiable timeline to implement the return, an understanding of the expectations following repatriation, the cost of repatriation, and whether or not the return will occur in stages. Of the remaining 28 percent, more than half stated that they have discussed the question about repatriation with immediate and extended relatives but had no specific timeline determined for the return to occur.

The descriptive results show further that of those who had made the decision to return, the process had involved the implementation of a number of steps or measures to enable them implement the move. These include acquisition of a home or in the process of building a home, starting a business, or sending money home to buy land. The data show that the process of making the decision to return involved immediate and extended family members as well as friends and associates at home and abroad. Only 4 percent of the migrants indicated that the process of making the decision to return did not involve any immediate or extended family members or close associates.

Overall, what emerged from the descriptive data was that from their perspective, African immigrants tend to consider repatriation and resettlement as a transitory phase in their global migratory lives. Repatriating home is framed in transitory terms and conditioned upon systematic reappraisal or evaluation of the short and long-term viability of resettlement in Africa. The option to return to the West should economic and political conditions in Africa deteriorate means that for some of the immigrants, repatriation will continue to remain a tentative proposition to be implemented only when structural conditions at the country of origination prove conducive or favorable to maximize the economic and social outcomes of repatriation. At a minimum, some may return be reserve the right to not settle in their home countries but instead opt to settle in other African countries where economic and political conditions are more favorable. The continued development of free trade protocols and the free movement of people intra Africa add to the choices of resettlement plans available for the prospective returnee (Adepoju, 2002). There will not be a rush to return as long as some of these immigrants are able to structure their lives in such a way as to enable them straddle between or among multiple transnational localities or sites. The opportunity to straddle multiple global and cultural domains is a major opportunity that international migration has provided for these immigrants. Repatriation as a migratory strategy is indeed an uncertain proposition with unknown or less predictable outcomes (particularly in the African, Latin American, and Caribbean migration circuits). This means that ultimately, some if not most of the immigrants do not have to return home if conditions at home in Africa do not so warrant. At the same time, these immigrants do not want to sever ties to their ancestral homelands.

RESULTS OF REGRESSION ANALYSES

A detailed analysis of the effects of the independent variables on the decision to return home can be found in the multiple regression results shown in Table 13.1. The results show that demographic variables (age, marital status, gender, time of immigration, number of years of schooling, class, and age of children currently living at home) did not contribute very significantly to the explanation of the decision to return home. Together, these variables accounted for less than 15 percent of the variance in the dependent variable. The

Table 13.1.   Results of the Multiple Regression Analyses with Repatriation as Dependent Variable

Demographic Variables	Beta	Error	T-Statistics	Significance
Respondent's age	.060	.030	1.30	2.011
Gender	.004	.042	0.11	1.219
Marital status	.024	.036	0.14	0.945
Respondent's class (SES)	.137	.086	3.33	0.009
Year of immigration	−.011	.004	−1.16	1.364
Years of schooling	−.019	.024	−3.15	2.158
Age of children	.063	.071	0.28	2.321
Citizenship status	.264	.087	4.33	0.003
Household Economic Variables				
Total family income	.082	.006	5.04	0.005
Frequency of remittances	.133	.004	3.62	0.001
Amount remitted	.056	.001	2.84	0.013
Owns a home in Africa	.074	.013	2.15	0.021
Owns a business in Africa	.310	.150	1.82	0.011
Frequency of home visits	.164	.025	7.11	0.001
Cultural Variables				
Desire to live close to relatives	.004	.001	0.01	1.311
Perceptions about Africa	.027	.016	5.60	0.002
Access to healthcare	.030	.002	0.02	0.972
Political Instability	.183	.068	6.10	0.011

coefficients revealed the direction of these relationships as well as the levels of statistical significance. For example, citizenship status affected the decision to return home in a statistically positive manner. The results show that once they have been able to acquire citizenship via naturalization, the decision to return home (even if for a temporary period) weighs significant in the minds of African immigrants. This finding is not surprising and can be attributed to the cultural, political, and maybe the economic security or protection that citizenship and naturalization confers on immigrants.

As expected, economic variables (total family income, savings and retirement investments, frequency and amount of money remitted, including owning a home and a business in Africa) all proved to be the major determinants of the decision to return home. Together, these variables accounted for 24 percent of the explained variance in the dependent variable. Immigrants with higher total family income ($80,000 and above); remitted regularly an average of $400 per month, and made frequent (yearly) visits home tended to have formulated repatriation plans. Less likely to have formulated repatriation plans are immigrants who earn reported total family income of less than $80,000, those who did not remit regularly, or averaged less than $400 per month in their remittance behavior. The fewer visits immigrants made home, the less likely there are to formulate plans about possible repatriation. Immigrants who own or are building a home in Africa, including those who have set up a business, (or plan to set up one at home) tended to have formulated definitive plans for repatriation compared with those immigrants who do not own a home (and are not planning to build one) as well as those who do not own a business (and do not plan establishing one).

Taken together, the importance of economic variables in predicting African immigrant repatriation was expected in light of the centrality of economic variables in the motivation of Africans to come to the United States. The desire for self-improvement, to enhance human and social capital potential, and to make enough money to assist in providing for extended family relatives have been behind the drive and ambition of African émigrés all over the world. The chance to live and work in the United States provides demonstrated or measurable ample economic opportunities which cannot be had in Africa if these migrants had stayed at home in Africa. Those who hold baccalaureate and post-baccalaureate degrees may be fortunate to find work in the civil service or find employment with financial institutions and corporations that pay higher salaries with fringe benefits including housing, medical, and transportation subsidies. With the proliferation of institutions of higher learning in Africa coupled with the rise in the number of graduates who are unemployed or underemployed, the privilege to enter the United States is life-altering and significant in achieving social mobility.

As indicated above, owing a home or operating a business in Africa prior to repatriation is a major consideration and undertaking if the decision to return is going to be acted upon. Home ownership confers achieved status. For the immigrant living abroad who is able to undertake this feat, ownership of a home is an affirmation that the migrant does not intend to sever ties with their homeland. Among Ghanaians for example, it is fashionable to build a home while abroad and rent it out until such time that the migrant decides to return home. Rents are usually paid two to three years in advance. With the money from the rented property, a second or even a third home may be built or acquired. Typically, when African immigrants refer to "home," they do not mean the homes that they pay a mortgage or own free and clear. The reference is always to the ancestral home. This is where the soul resides no matter the transnational, class, educational, and income or immigration status of the immigrant. Traveling abroad to work solely to save enough money to repatriate home to build a house is a major driving force spurring both regular and irregular forms of African migration to the West in general.

Access to business opportunities or the desire to establish a business following repatriation is a significant consideration in forming the decision to repatriate. Again, this finding is not surprising. As a group, Africans are very entrepreneurial. A rapidly emerging economy, Africa offers tremendous business opportunities for the immigrants who have the opportunity to replicate small businesses that they see in the migrant destination in the home country. For those immigrants who are able to establish a small business at home prior to repatriating, transitioning from the West to home is facilitated or enhanced by gainful employment which can provide source of income and economic security following the return. Remitted funds sent from the United States may be used in starting such a business which may be operated by family members. Because it may be staffed solely by family members, overhead costs are low. The opportunity to own a business (no matter the size), is a catalyst for migration in Africa's emerging economies. Money made while abroad can be used in purchasing consumer items to stock and open a new shop. Alternatively, the funds may be used as security to leverage loans from financial institutions to start a business venture. The opportunities presented for operating a small business venture is also the motivation behind intra-African or regional migration. For many Africans, migration (whether within Africa's borders or outside) is a strategy whose goal is to gain access to the capital resources necessary for starting a business.

Equally significant influences weighing on the decision to return home were the frequency of home visits, subjective social class of immigrant (SES), and the cost of living in Africa. Immigrants who visited home more often (compared to those who did not) tended to develop and implement various strategies to ensure a successful transition and return migration or repatriation. Similarly, class status affected the decision to return home. Generally, the African immigrants who identified their class status as middle to upper class were more likely (than those immigrants who identified their class status as lower class) to have formed a decision about returning home. Immigrants who had rationalized and given due considerations to the estimated costs of repatriating to and living in Africa versus tended to be more decisive in their plans to return home. Repatriating to live in Africa entails significantly lower cost of living unless the returnee prefers to shop at the exclusive shopping centers catering to the expensive imported commodities and items that immigrants are accustomed to in the West. Items are bought and sold only in foreign currencies. A reasonably cheaper alternative is go purchase items at the local markets using the local currency. On the other hand, favorable foreign exchange rates may favor the returnee by boosting their purchasing power.

Immigrant assessment of the political uncertainties prevailing at home was one of the best predictors of the decision to repatriate. A major factor spurring African migration outside the region, this variable was statistically significant in predicting repatriation outcome. Immigrants with a more positive assessment and perspective of past, current, and future climate of political in(stability) in Africa tended to be more favorable about their short and long-term repatriation plans compared with respondents who were negative in their assessment of political conditions of Africa. We included a general variable intended to capture respondent's overall favorability of Africa (conceived as Africa rising and measured by respondent's understanding of the future economic role of Africa in global affairs) in the regression analysis. The intent was to allow respondent's to cast a future imagination of how rising democratic and civil institutions including robust economic outcomes (a trend already taking hold in a number of countries such as Ghana, Mozambique, Botswana, Angola, Uganda, South Africa, Lesotho, and Swaziland) will affect the repatriation plans of the immigrants. Overall, the results indicate that immigrants who scored "Africa rising" higher tended to hold a more positive outlook about their prospects of repatriating home compared with those immigrants who scored Africa's future prospects very low or negative.

Immigrant preferences to live in close proximity to relatives and also have access to healthcare were both positively related to how the immigrants formed their intent to repatriate. Respondents who indicated the presence of a strong network of family and kinship networks seemed to be more prepared about what the repatriation process entails compared with those whose kinship and familial networks are weak. Through the auspices of the family, returnees are often able to locate and (redefine) their new role within the complex network of extended relatives. The presence of close family members may facilitate the transition to repatriation. Family members can also assist in the re-entry process by providing valuable information or assisting the returnee learn about cultural expectations as these are always in a state of flux.

The ability to have access to affordable and quality healthcare (while a significant predictor in the decision to return home) was not as strong as anticipated. This finding may be linked to the fact that following repatriation, returnees still have access to the medical and health systems of the West. The medical and health benefits that they have earned in the West means that in cases of urgently needed care that cannot be obtained in Africa, returnees can come back to the United States at regular intervals for medical checkups, fill their prescriptions, and come back to Africa. Returnees may opt to perform simple medical procedures in Africa. Access to healthcare and medical services are confined to the larger urban administrative and commercial centers of Africa. For returnees who settle in rural areas, constraining factors may include traveling long distances to access quality health services and the lack of medical specialists. Poor conditions of service for medical and allied health personnel have decimated the ranks of African-trained medical and health staff. Africa's nurses, pharmacists, and doctors have all joined the caravan of professionals headed to the West for better wages and working conditions. The majority do not to return. The few who do return set up their own private clinics or find employment with government-run hospitals and clinics. Others organize medical missions to Africa under the auspices of nongovernmental organizations that they have set up in collaboration with international agencies and bodies working to provide healthcare and medical assistance to remote regions of Africa.

Based on the results from the statistical analyses, we offer the following tentative conclusions about the factors predicting African immigrant repatriation. First, we conclude that demographic variables (age, marital status, years of schooling, gender, and year of immigration) were not strong predictors of the decision to repatriate. Second, economic variables (total family income, immigrant subjective class membership, frequency and amount of remittance, cost of living, savings and retirement investments) including home and business ownership offered more explanatory power in accounting for the variance in the decision to return. Cultural variables (including immigrant preference to live closer to family members, access to medical and health services, and frequency of home visits) were significant in influencing the decision whether to repatriate or not.

The use of aggregated data to model the factors influencing the repatriation decision-making behavior of African immigrants may be masked by country-specific cultural, social, economic or political factors thus making it difficult to specify exact proximate factors. The sheer diversity within the African immigrant population is another methodological issue confronting students of migration who are interested in specifying models to account for repatriation. Differences within and among nations and geopolitical entities in the region (tribal, clan, cultural and normative differences, including religion) renders the task of studying migrant repatriation arduous. A preferred approach is to use a case study approach whereby African immigrants from specific nationalities, clans, or educational or occupational groupings, and ethnic categorizations to better understand the factors that converge to explain the decision-making processes of African immigrant repatriation. An alternate approach is to collect data on returnees who have already settled to develop a comprehensive and systematic documentation of the demographic characteristics of returnees and the factors behind their decision to repatriate. Compiling a census on returnees will provide African central governments with baseline data to assess the potential role that returnees can play in national reconstruction and development.

Data on who is returning, reasons for returning, skills and occupational background of returnee, and returnee assets and resources are pertinent considerations for maximum utilization of the human and social capital of all returnees. While we speculate that there might not be significant differences in repatriation among African immigrants who migrate to the West compared with those who migrate to non-Western destinations (for both groups, economic, cultural factors may dominate the decision to return), we nonetheless suggest systematic research to identify if there are any possible sources of variations in repatriation plans that are caused by destination or place-specific attributes (for example, public sentiments toward immigrants, linguistic barriers, opportunities to pursue educational goals). Data that are collected on returnees must be incorporated in the formulation of policies at the national level to stem the tide of Africa's brain drain and address Africa's perennial human resource needs. As a growing number of African countries (including some in Latin America, the Caribbean, and Asia) continue to become a region of emigration to the more advanced developed economies, their governments must deliberate the full impact of the loss of human resources and skills to other destinations of the world (Pellegrino, 2001; Schmidt, 2008).

Alternative Explanations of African Immigrant Voluntary Repatriation

Predicting the factors that account for African immigrant repatriation is complex and multifaceted. This is not surprising considering the segmented or multidimensional aspects of repatriation in general, and more specifically, the internal economic, social, and economic conditions in many African countries. The findings from this study suggests that immigrant conceptualization of current and future economic well-being and the consternations they associate with the processes of re-entry or resettlement are critical components in identifying the correlates of returning home to Africa. International migration to core economies of the world will continue to dominate African migrations for the foreseeable future. For the short-term, the continued exodus of both skilled and unskilled Africans to core countries will have a detrimental effect and even slow the pace of development in the region. In the long-term, however, the contributions and added value that these immigrants will bring to their respective countries is immense. In this light, it is expected that several of the countries may even continue to promote the migration of their citizens in anticipation of the long-term gains and contributions these migrants bring to national development and sustainable development. Knowing full well that the bulk of their citizens never sever ties with their homelands upon migration is, in of itself, sufficient explanation on the part of the central governments of Africa to not be overly concerned about addressing the factors spurring outmigration in the first place. For most African immigrants abroad, matters of home have an existentialist import. It is the tie that binds them to their homeland that will continue to motivate these immigrants to play pivotal roles in nation-building whether they repatriate or not, and irrespective of how many trans-national migratory cultures they straddle. Predicting return migration is not a linear postulation. There are complex and intervening variables that intersect to predict the possibility of return migration among African émigrés currently domiciled in the United States. Beyond the statistical representations of the determinants of African immigrant reverse migration lie alternate theoretical explanations that can be postulated to account for the return flow of African immigrant populations back to the continent.

One of the preferred approaches to unraveling the determinants of return migration is to examine reverse migration within the specific context of the nation-state and the structural economic relationships specific countries have with global nodes of capitalist production and manufacturing systems (Cohen 2006). This approach emphasizes the structure and organization of the nation-states to which the immigrants will be returning to. Understanding of the economic, social, cultural, and political culture of the returning society is pertinent to the understanding of the formulation of migrant intent or motivation to return home. Structures at home that may facilitate or ease the transition of repatriation and resettlement are important considerations as prospective returnees formulate the decision to return. Ability of the nation-states and their central governments to develop a seamless program that will aid the transition and settlement of returnees and asset transfer are equally salient as the decision to return is being formed. Areas of economic and social organization within the nation-states where returning migrants can make potential investments in the development of the nation-states are important.

For Africa's central governments, this will entail the development of infra-structural services to facilitate not only the removal of bureaucratic obstacles but also the streamlining of business feasibility studies, including production and marketing information to assist returning migrants with assets to invest at home. We suggest that political patronage must be eschewed in the process of determining the locations, sites, and places where diaspora-driven returning migrant investments can be directed. African governments must work in tandem with their citizens abroad to identify areas of economic and social development where diaspora and returnee investments can be directed to maximize output and efficiency.

The governments must remain an important actor and stakeholder in the migrant configurations to repatriate. By its nature, the state is positioned to determine (through stated objectives, policies, and goals regarding national development) the direction, scope, and depth of micro and macro development projects. It (through a combination of public and private resources) can play a major role in terms of the types and forms of economic and business activities and where these can be located to achieve optimum advantage for investors (migrant returnees). It is in these areas where African governments need bilateral or multilateral assistance from the core countries. This will suggest the need for a systematic effort on the part of African central governments to integrate migrant returnee relocation and asset transfer schemes into robust centrally planned economic and industrial development initiatives to funnel resources to sectors of the domestic economy where the potential for economic revitalization projects can be launched, implemented, and supported. Considering the problems facing African central government and public sectors (corruption, thievery, patronage, pacification of tribal, ethnic, clan interests and cronies), the inclusion of private partners in determining returnee investments and divestiture is critical in ensuring accountability and transparency of asset utilization. At a minimum, the role of the state will be to provide the infrastructures and economies of scale if returnee investments in entrepreneurial ventures are to become viable and sustainable. The central government may also partner with private institutions to provide adequate job training for low technology-based economic ventures utilizing local resources for production of goods for local consumption and for regional export. Africa's central governments can utilize immigrant returnee asset transfer and allocation to decentralize their economies to achieve an equal distribution of business activities between rural and urban places. As indicated, there is an urban bias in the allocation and distribution of business ventures (small or large-scale) to the economic detriment of the rural areas of Africa. The penetration of business ventures to the rural locations utilizing in part returnee investments can help stem the tide of rural youth population drift to urban centers in search of non-existing jobs. This will also arrest, in part, the growing problem of urban squatter sprawls and formation of shanty-towns caused in part by a massive drift of rural to urban population. Rural economic depression, lack of jobs, poor living conditions, and political neglect are few of the problems facing Africa's rural sector (Amin, 1974; Mabogunje, 1970; Todaro, 1969; 1976; 1994; Arthur, 1991).

Comprehensive analyses are needed to map out the settlement and relocation habits and preferences of returnees. Understanding the motivations (economic, social, political, or psychological) behind returnees' repatriation is critical for the development of public and private-based programs and policies to channel their assets to existing growth or new areas of Africa's economic systems. Students of migration will have to formulate new paradigms and theoretical models to address or incorporate the complex nature of African immigrant returnee motivations. While it is expected that a majority of returnees may opt to resettle in urban areas due to infrastructural services and relatively better amenities when compared with the rural areas, evidence from the data collected suggests that some of the returnees favor resettlement in small to medium cities, especially those that will provide adequate land, transportation networks to facilitate mobility, health care infrastructure, and access to financial institutions and ample recreational opportunities. The cities meanwhile will continue to remain the choice of initial resettlement due to its comparative advantage and economies of scale. The preference for small to medium size towns for resettlement is appealing because the bulk of Africa's population is still rural. Due to rapid urbanization, conditions in the megacities of Africa are less conducive for returnees who want sufficient land and perhaps also the opportunity to live in close proximity to their hometown. The hometown culture is innate. It is a place where Africans generally (migrants and nonmigrants alike) return to because of the ancestral significance. Among the Akans of Ghana (for example), the ancestral home is the place where the *ntoro* (soul) and *moyga* (blood) resides. Frequently, several immigrant returnees choose to build a home or set up a business in the ancestral, tribal home because such an effort signifies status, prestige, and honor. Among those who migrate from the ancestral birthplace to an urban area for work, many maintain the cultural ties to the ancestral home with regular visits during cultural and religious observances. Others make it a point to build their dream home in this location even though they may already have built a house in the urban place they migrated to.

For migrant returnees with advanced degrees and highly-skilled credentials but not necessarily with significant financial assets to transfer home, developing a scheme to evaluate the human resource and manpower needs of the countries is pertinent. Such an approach, it is contended, must include the development of skill typologies for different categories of employment to assist the national governments in formulating targeted policies of returnee employment and placement in critically short-supply sectors such as technology, healthcare, agriculture, finance, and education. Developing theoretical models to elucidate how these migrant professionals have circulated in the various migratory domains in the core countries of residence is equally significant in modeling the future relocation and resettlement objectives.

Understanding the form(s) of their migratory behavior (regular or irregular migration, refugee status, naturalized or nonnaturalized status) may help determine appropriate relocation and repatriation strategies and policies which the central governments of Africa may initiate to facilitate smoother repatriation and transition. Developing of theoretical models to anchor such policies may also determine the long-term viability of migrant returnee incorporation into society. The return process may pose challenges for some returnees as it involves some degree of resocialization. Some returnees may have to learn how to re-enter and find their place among cultures and societies they had left for decades. Brief visits home do not acculturate the migrant visitor to the full range of rapid changes socioeconomic, cultural, and political occurring throughout Africa due largely in part to the dispersion and penetration of global technologies and new media of communication that has proliferated all across the region. Immigrant returnee cultural shock is not out of the question. Cultural conflicts over normative expectations (if not handled properly) may serve as a barrier not only to future integration but could potentially forestall long-term plans for permanent repatriation.

If children are involved in the repatriation process, their educational needs, assimilation or acculturation may have to be considered. Children's ability to balance the expectations of the West against the expectations of child culture in Africa may prove daunting and be fraught with issues pertaining how to navigate intercultural boundary markers. Depending on the age of the children, the negotiation and social construction of identity may entail a hybrid of multiple identities, some African, some American, including other identities constructed through associative interactions with peers or media technology and secondary institutions. For children who frequently travel to Africa with parents during holidays, the transition following repatriation may not be too traumatic and life-altering. A growing number of Africans in the West regular send their children home to live with extended relatives over a long period of time. Some may be sent to Africa to attend prestigious and elite preparatory schools. While in Africa, their sole preoccupation is prepping for college admission and entrance tests. The strategy is to take advantage of the education offered by quality private schools in Africa. High scores on standardized college admission exams translate into scholarship at prestigious schools in the United States. At the same time, the culture of school failure endemic in the public school system has given cause to some of the immigrants to consider other viable options such as sending children home to be educated.

An emerging pattern of African immigrant repatriation is symbolized by the return plans of dual professional couples usually with postgraduate credentials acquired in the West. These couples adopt a returnee plan based on the need to preserve their economic and class status in the West. The goal is to ensure that irrespective of their relocation or repatriation plans, it is important to safeguard their social security benefits, including being able to tap into the health care system in the West should the need arise. Repatriation plans may also be influenced by whether or not they have acquired the requisite travel documents to enable them travel to Europe, Canada, or Australia and New Zealand. It is significant to note that these professional couples maintain an elaborate network of friends, associates, and family members who are living in other parts of the world. For some of them, opportunities to attend annual professional conferences, present papers, attend short seminars to hone their skills, and travel throughout the West for recreational reasons is desirable. For this group of African émigrés, decisions about future repatriation involve multistage planning and implementation of strategies to repatriate. Typically, one couple (mostly the husband) will resettle home first for a protracted period of time. A portion of the couple's assets are transferred during this first phase. While home, the husband may oversee the building of the family's house, start a new business for the family, and manage the family's remittances and resources to other family members. The other partner stays behind in the West, mostly providing care-giving to underage children, working, paying all the bills, and managing the family's home. The wife who is abroad may come home for visits with or without the children but will eventually return. This pattern of repatriation serves an instrumental purpose: it enables the family to organize its resources at home and abroad. At the same time, it positions these families for a smoother transition once the decision is made to repatriate. These groups of Africans typically will maintain a transnational sojourner identity, neither committing to limit their repatriation plans to one specific country nor the other. They will continue to circulate for brief periods at a time in different advanced economies at times staying with extended relatives or friends in the diaspora. Having a split household may also create financial burdens on some of these families but many are able to garner the resources they need to straddle multiple societies sometimes working for a brief period at a time and at times, holding full-time employment. Straddling between the place of origin and the destination enables some of the migrants to participate in the affairs of the home society and at the same time maintain their economic, social, and cultural foothold in the country of destination.

A key question in rationalizing and modeling the determinants of return migration of African immigrants abroad is the class implications return migration may pose for countries with already fragile national identity caused by incessant intra and inter-ethnic, clan, and tribal schisms. Returning migrants may return with considerable assets which could destabilize existing social class structures and heighten tension by highlighting the already wide gap between Africa's growing new rich, elite, and the majority underclass poor. The identities and lifestyles they express (returning migrants) and manifest (particularly those that are Western) may contradict African normative and cultural expectations which may result in social tensions. Returning migrants from abroad are well-positioned to become middle or upper class upon return. Most adopt and import the lifestyles they are accustomed to while living in the West. Some of them shop in stores where they can purchase foreign goods using foreign currencies. A growing number of them live in gated communities and drive imported SUVs. Their children, if any, attend private schools where the tuition is paid in foreign currency as well. For the average African nonmigrant who did not have the opportunity to travel abroad, these opportunities are hard to come by let alone to have the financial means to afford such lifestyles. Disparate or unequal wealth and income distribution constitutes a growing problem in Africa with the potential to destabilize some of the countries of the region. For returnees who show off their western consumer items, this may cause resentments which may result in the targeting of returnees by criminals and fringe groups. Their presence may also spur irregular or unplanned migrations solely for economic reasons among some of the poor to destinations in and out of Africa where they hope to earn enough money performing menial jobs with the goal of returning home once they have acquired enough savings to start their own business or build their dream home. The intentional or unintentional creation of class-tiered societies emanating from return migration of African abroad could redefine the future of African immigrant-sending and labor-exporting countries in ways that governments may not fully grasp and hence be able to control. With their assets, skills, ideas, new ways of thinking, and beliefs acquired in changing global domains, some of the returnees might agitate and advocate for political, economic, cultural, and social reforms beyond the capacity of the African governments to handle. In the short-term, this might destabilize fragile democracies and threaten the rule of entrenched autocracies. In the long-term though, returnees may position themselves at the vanguard of positive change, mobilization, and coalition building with other interest groups and social movements to effect social changes in Africa. This is already happening.

Beyond the statistical data shedding light on the proximate determinants of return migration among African émigrés is another major alternative theoretical explanation. This is what we describe as the epidemiological factor. Epidemiology broadly speaking deals with the health status of a population. The institution of basic health care across Africa, particularly in sub-Saharan Africa where the bulk of African immigrants arriving in North America originate from, is in most cases undeveloped or in other cases nonexistent. Infant mortality rates are among the highest in the world. Crude birth rates also remain higher than any other region of the globe. So are mortality rates and schedules. Due to improving health care conditions, nutritional standards, rising educational levels, and sanitation standards, significant strides have been made to lower fertility and mortality rates but a majority of Africans, particularly rural dwellers and the uneducated have yet to become beneficiaries of Africa's slowing improving health care and medical system. More specifically, not much is known about the post-migration health status of Africa's immigrant population in the United States and the West in general. There is also a dearth of information about the pre-migration health status of these immigrants. The age structure and composition of the African migratory population to the West show that as a group, African immigrants tend to be relatively young with the majority of newcomers aged between twenty-five and forty-five years old. As such, many of them are in the prime of their lives. In Africa, many of them had to confront perennial health problems like malaria, fever, cholera, HIV, AIDS, tuberculosis, and other diseases which may be attributed to the poor socioeconomic conditions. Certainly nutritional and living standards improve significantly when the immigrants arrive in the United States. Following their migration, the opportunity to access the healthcare system in the United States improves the odds that if there are any underlying health and epidemiological issues, these can be diagnosed and effective treatment sought.

As they form their repatriation plans, access to affordable health care weighs heavily on the decision to resettle or return to Africa. While several of the immigrants recognize that they cannot rely on the healthcare sector of Africa to meet their health and medical needs, they seem not to allow this handicap to stymie or thwart their motivation to repatriate. Due to the assets they transfer home, several are able to gain access to private health care cash-and-carry system. This service is far out of reach for ordinary Africans who depend on the oft crowded public-funded hospitals and polyclinics usually located in the large urban centers to access their healthcare and medical needs. For returning migrants who are naturalized citizens or have acquired legal resident status, the opportunity to come back to the West to access medical care and treatment for ailments is an added advantage. For returnees, therefore, while the question of access to healthcare may feature significantly in their motivation to repatriate, it alone is not the *sine qua non* of the decision to return. It remains a significant consideration but not the overarching determinant of the decision to repatriate. The presence of extended relatives in Africa who are available to offer assistance for elderly care-giving is considered far more necessary than immigrant consternations about whether or not they will have access to healthcare should they form the decision to repatriate. Africans rely on their extensive family networks to care for their elderly in their own homes. The cost of elderly care in the United States is very expensive and can wipe out post-retirement savings. For racial and ethnic minority elderly citizens, a potential challenge living in a nursing home is alienation and marginalization. Hence, the preference among African immigrants to repatriate so that they can take advantage of the family-based elderly care resources available to them at home notwithstanding the poor medical and health care system. One finds therefore that immigrant class status at the point of repatriation and knowledge about existing resources in Africa and elsewhere in the world to meet their total medical care are far more influential in determining their decision to repatriate than the status or quality of health care and medical services in Africa.

The modeling of African immigrant repatriation from the West will have to accentuate the roles played by kinship networks and extended family relationships. Families do form and constitute migratory streams. The institution of family is an agency of economic and social production whose assets are its numerous members who are related by blood or marriage. Among African immigrants, the decision to migrate in the first place are often played out within the nexus of the extended family system and the complex system of migratory networks that Africans often create to facilitate rural-urban, regional, and now increasing, international migration. Families and households cooperate by pulling their resources together to support members who are best positioned to become successful in the West either by pursuing cultural (attending school) or economic goals (working). Family-sponsored migration has become the dominant form of economic and cultural incorporation of Africans into the global economy. Families that have a sizeable number of its members abroad typically fare better economically than those that do not have any relatives living abroad. Often, migrants will remit the entire family no matter how meager the remittances.

These kinship networks also play a pivotal role in the formation of the decision to repatriate. Prospective candidates contemplating repatriation may often discuss their plans with extended family members. These relatives can assist returning immigrants with valuable information about home including the timing of repatriation, political and economic conditions at home, where to settle, type of business activities to engage in, and household assistance before and after repatriation and resettlement. If the returnee sets up a business, extended family members can often be relied upon to work-for-pay thereby minimizing potential staffing problems. Following repatriation, extended family members may assist in the integration of the returnee into community social life. Depending on how long the returnee has been away from home, the presence of extended family members willing to assist the returnee navigate official bureaucracies is important if the outcome of the return is to be successful. Additionally, they may assist returnees in becoming reacquainted with other family members, sharing information about births and deaths, and providing up-to-date information about family oral history during the period the returnee was domiciled abroad. Harnessing the collective human and social capital resources of extended family members is significant in not only spurring migration but also a major influencing factor in the pre- and post-return process. For returnees without this support, the return process can prove daunting and traumatic.

Germane to the understanding of African immigrant repatriation is a holistic assessment of the role(s) played by mutual aid and benevolent associations that African immigrants typically form to express their cultural and normative institutions. Formed along ethnic, alumni, clan, hometown, or village associations, these migrant networks are also at the forefront of marshalling the resources of their members to aid not only the successful return of their members to the place of origin but also champions the socioeconomic and cultural development of their respective regions. While they may channel funds to aid in the construction of roads, schools, bridges, and clinics, these associations and networks have become important cogs in terms of how migrants formulate the reasons for repatriation. The networks may provide business opportunities for their members; provide access to land for development projects, and lobby political leaders and stakeholders for representation in decision-making affecting their respective communities and members (Owusu, 2000). The African presence and experience in international migration suggests that understanding the totality of the processes of primary, secondary, or tertiary migrations or repatriation among Africans will suggest a comprehensive and organic approach that incorporates the multiple dimensions of the institutional structures and fabric that Africans construct to give content to their movement in both familiar and unfamiliar domains.

CONCLUSION

Meticulous attention ought to be given to the processes underlying the repatriation behavior of African immigrants. A question of interest is whether African immigrants' notions about local and transnational identities are reformed at home upon repatriation. If these transnational identities are replicated at home in Africa, it is worthy for research to investigate whether there are resistances emanating from how those immigrant who have resettled and repatriated reinterpret and adjust their transnational identities to fit the local scene in Africa. The need for research studies in this area is critical because not much is known about the reverse migration and repatriation behavior of African émigrés. Specific questions needing attention are whether there is a relationship between the frequency of remittances and the probability of repatriation. Researches on the economic, cultural, and political integration of immigrant returnees in the affairs of their respect countries are equally warranted. Issues pertaining to how returnees relate to their social structures and the roles that they play following repatriation are also needed. Having acquired transnational identities, returnees often move and live in multiple spheres of activities. If they had become naturalized citizens of the United

States, how do they negotiate and articulate the meaning of citizenship at home in Africa? What are the responses and consequences of naturalization and citizenship for the returnees as they forge inclusion or exclusion in the affairs of the home society? Are there specific impediments that are often encountered by returnees and how do they resolve these problems? For developing regions in Africa, what should be the proper role of the central governments in the migrant repatriation process? Are there resources that can be provided by the central governments to tap and harness the capital and human resources that the returnees have acquired living abroad? To what extent do the returnees become change agents and advocates of new ideas, new ways of thinking, and become sources of social, political, and cultural transformation? How do returning immigrants contest traditional norms and at the same time map out new vistas of opportunities for themselves and their home societies at large?

There is also the possibility that repatriation may not always involve resettlement or repatriation to Africa but rather to a third country or region outside the continent. Several African immigrants also have relational ties with family and friends in Europe, Canada, and in other parts of Asia. For those immigrants who have acquired American citizenship, possibilities exist that the repatriation process may be embarked upon in stages. Upon leaving the United States, some may settle on a temporary basis in Europe, Canada or Asia where they have relatives. This temporary sojourn may last for a while before final preparatory steps are made to settle permanently in Africa. This process of piecemeal repatriation is facilitated by the transnational identities and massive network of relatives and friends that some of the immigrants have been able to establish over the years. Transitional or temporary repatriation to a location other than Africa achieves the purpose of allowing the returnees to gradually ease some of the uncertainties that are associated with outright repatriation. Returnees may engage in transitional repatriation while making arrangements for a new house to be completed or an old house to be sold.

To a large degree, the incorporation and inclusion of African societies into the core economies and cultures is going to come about through the returning migration and continued ties that several of Africa's immigrants abroad are able to establish with their home countries. The driving force behind this new change is phenomenal. Its speed, pace, and outcomes are far more visible everywhere in Africa today than hitherto acknowledged. Reverse migration and its outcomes are doing in many parts of Africa what decades of bilateral and multilateral foreign-aid have failed to do in remarkable fashion: that is, alter the lives of a significant number of African populace. What is unique about this people-driven social force is that it transcends the ethnic, tribal, and clan divisions that have dominated the African landscape since the post-independence era. Improved transportation efficiencies and new media technologies will dominate and impact how the outcomes of these migratory returns are played out in Africa and in the rest of the world. As the golden age of African global migrations continue to unfold, its parameters are going to broaden to include the contributions that its returning migrants abroad will make to the overall development of the continent. Nonetheless, the role of immigrant returnees in socioeconomic and cultural development in Africa will ultimately hinge on the quality of the social and human capital resources that these migrants are able to build in the West, the receptiveness of the core and advanced countries in structuring their immigration policies in accordance with their own economic, labor and security needs, the stability of African political regimes and institutions, including the democratization of civil institutions, and above all, the (in)ability of the African governments to develop seamless policies and programs to identify and mobilize the collective resources of African migrant returnees for sustainable growth and development. Projected shortfalls in both skilled and unskilled labor in the African immigrant destination sources in the West will continue to influence the volume, source, and direction of foreign-born including African labor and migration to the West (McDonald and Kippen, 2001). African migrants in the worldwide diasporas are going to continue defining their identities often by linking them with the interplay of economic, social, political, and cultural issues and developments that are going on in their respect homelands. This is significant in light of the fact that the majority African immigrants have interests in the overall ascendancy of Africa in global and international affairs Hence, the imperative for to link migrants to the economic development processes at home (Orozco, 2008).

As they contemplate whether or not to repatriate, African immigrants living abroad are going to rely on government-initiated policies at home to preserve their assets and class status. Part of the ruling elite class, some of these returning migrants are going to look for programs at the macro-state level that will support their lifestyles, normative structures, and political culture. Balancing the needs of its returning migrants who are relatively well-off against the dire and pressing needs of its massive poor will pose a serious challenge to many of the African governments with a sizeable returning immigrant population such as Ghana and Nigeria. Economic, social, and political security conditions prevailing in Africa will determine the scope and magnitude of African immigrant diaspora repatriation. These in turn will influence the robustness of the asset transfers that will be initiated by returning migrants. Africa's returning immigrants from the West will forever have dual or multiple presences in world economic and cultural centers. As Portes (1997) maintained, this simultaneous presence will involve continued negotiations about the role(s) these immigrants will play in nation-building and development. Both returning migrants and their African leaders have a fresh opportunity to re-make Africa by forging a strong partnership that will permit the mobilization of collective resources to promote economic and social development in the region. By all accounts, only few of the African governments are currently positioned to tap into and utilize this collective mobilization of diaspora re-patriation resources for maximum gains. The formalization of diaspora-led development projects into national reconstruction efforts will be critical if African governments including those from other developing economies are to mobilize the resource and human capital transfers of their transnational citi-zens from abroad and promote migrant returns and diaspora developments.

REFERENCES

Adepoju, A. (2002). "Fostering Free Movement of Persons in West Africa: Achieve-ments, Constraints, and Prospects for Intraregional Migration." *International Mi-gration* 40 (2): 3–25.

———. (1991). "South-North Migration: The African Experience." *International Migration* 29: 205–21.

Agyemang-Konadu, K; Takyi, B.; and J. Arthur (2006). *The New African Diaspora in North America. Trends, Community Building, and Adaptation,* (eds.). Lanham, MD: Lexington Books.

Ammassari, Savina and Black, R. (2001). *Harnessing the Potential of Migration and Return to Promote Development: Applying Concepts to West Africa.*: Sussex Migration Working papers No. 3. Sussex Centre for Migration Research, United Kingdom.

Amin, S. (1974). *Modern Migrations in West Africa.* Oxford: Oxford University Press.

Arthur, J. (2000). *Invisible Sojourners. African Immigrant Diaspora in the United States.* Westport, CT: Praeger.

———. (1991). "International labor Migration in West Africa." *African Studies Re-view* 34 (3): 65–87.

———. (2008). *The African Diaspora in the United States and Europe.* England: Ashgate.

———. (2011). *African Diaspora Identities. Negotiating Culture in Transnational Migration.* Lanham, MD: Lexington (Division of Rowman and Littlefield.)

Baerga, M. and Thompson, L. (1999). "Migration in a Small Semiperiphery: The Movement of Puerto Ricans and Dominicans." *International Migration Review* 24 (4): 656–83.

Cohen, R. (2006). *Migration and its Enemies. Global Capital, Migrant Labour and the Nation-State.* England: Ashgate.

Dodoo, F. Nii-Amoo (1991). "Earnings Differentials Among Blacks in America." *Social Science Research* 20: 93–108.

——. and Takyi, B. (2002). "Race and Earnings: Magnitude of Difference Among African Americans." *Ethnic and Racial Studies* 25: 193–941.

Gordon, A. (1998). "The New African Diaspora. African Immigration to the United States." *Journal of Third World Studies* XV: (1): 79–103.

Holtzman, J. (2000). *Nuer Journey. Nuer Lives. Sudanese Refugees in Minnesota.* Boston, MA: Allyn and Bacon.

Kandil, M. and Metwally, M. F. (1999). "The Impact of Migrants' Remittances on the Egyptian Economy." *International Migration Review* 37 (1): 159–169.

Logan, B. I. 1992. "The Brain Drain of Professional, Technical and Kindred Workers from Developing Countries: Some Lessons from the Africa-US Flow of Professionals (1980–1989)." *International Migration.* Volume 30: 289.

——. 1999. "The Reverse Transfer of technology from Sub-Saharan Africa: The case of Zimbabwe." *International Migration.* Volume 37 (2): 437–63.

Mabogunje, A. L. (1970). "Systems Approach to a Theory of Rural to Urban Migration." *Geographical Analysis* 2(1): 1–19.

McDonald, P. and R. Kippen (2001). "Labor Supply Prospects in Sixteen Developed Countries: 2000-2050." *Population and Development Review* 27 (1): 1–32.

Muschkin, C. (1999). "Conseqiences of Return Migrant Status for Employment in Puerto Rico." *International Migration Review.* Volume 28 (1): 79–102.

Orozco, M. (2008). "Diasporas and Development: Issues and Impediments." In Brinkerfoff, J. *Diasporas and Development* (ed.). Boulder, Colorado: Lynne Rienner, 205–30.

Owusu, T. (2000). "The Role of Ghanaian Immigrant Associations in Toronto, Canada." *International Migration Review.* Volume 34: 1155–81.

Peil, M. (1995). "Ghanaians Abroad." *African Affairs* 94 (376): 23–34.

Pellegrino, A. (2001). "Trends in Latin American Skilled Migration: "Brain Drain or Brain Exchange"? *International Migration.* Vol. 39 (5): 111–25.

Portes, A. (1997). "Globalization from Below: The Rise of Transnational Communities." *ESRC Transnational Communities Project.* Working Paper WPTC-98-01.

Robinson, J. (2002). *Development and Displacement* (ed.). Oxford, England: Open University.

Schmidt, B. (2008). *Caribbean Diaspora in the United States.* England: Ashgate.

Sheffer, G. (2007). "The Diaspora Phenomenon in the Twenty-First Century: Ideational, Organizational, and Behavioral Changes." In Totoricaguena, G. (2007). *Opportunity Structures in Diaspora Relations* (ed.). Reno, Nevada: Center for Basque Studies, 187–214.

Takyi, B. and Konadu-Agyemang, K. (2006). "Theoretical Perspectives on African Migration." In Konadu-Agyemang, K.; Takyi, B., and J. Arthur. *The New African Diaspora in North America* (eds.). Lanham, MD: Lexington Books, Rowman and Littlefield, 13–28.

Thomas-Hope, E. (1975). "The Adaptation of Migrants from English-Speaking Caribbean to Select Centres of Britain and North America." Paper presented at the annual meeting of the Society of Applied Anthropology, 1991.

Todaro, M. (1969). "A Model of Labor Migration and Urban Unemployment in Less Developed Countries." *The American Economic Review* 59 (1): 138–48.

———. (1976). *Internal Migration in Developing Countries.* Geneva, Switzerland: ILO.

———. (1994). *Economic Development (*5th Edition). New York: Longman.

Totoricaguena, G. (2007). *Opportunity Structures in Diaspora Relations* (ed.). Reno: Center for Basque Studies, University of Nevada.

Chapter Fourteen

Africans in Global Migration: Still Searching for Promised Lands

As the social reality of international migration becomes a poignant aspect of socioeconomic and cultural development throughout the world, it is not surprising that Africa too has become part of this dynamic process. In an increasingly globalized world the movement of people is now more transnational and involves an increasing number of people than before particularly those from the developing world. New and more effective and efficient transportation and communication technologies coupled with transnational protocols regarding the free movement of people, goods, and services are major aspects of his new social reality. Perhaps, a major influence on the new global migrations has also been the desire among the world's impoverished to search for opportunities beyond the geographic boundaries of their homelands. Economic exigencies are therefore critical components of the transnational drive through migration and population mobility. The stark economic differences between the developed economies of the North and the emerging economies of the South and the systems of global social stratification embedded in this division also lie at the heart of this new migration. Irrespective of the driving forces underpinning the increased rise in international migration across the world, one thing remains certain. An important aspect of international migration is the recognition that the diasporas that are formed as these migratory behaviors are accentuated have been recognized *as* a potent force in development particularly in the migrant origination countries. What we have learned from this process is that though the short-term benefits of international migration for migrant-sending countries are hard to predict, in the long-term, there is a growing understanding that migration, diaspora structures, and development are intertwined and have a central role to play in promoting sustainable economic and social development in migrant-sending countries. This is not to mention the social, cultural, and economic value that migration also brings to the host societies. For the immigrants in the diaspora, while all these facets may not represent the totality of their negotiated identities and realities, it is significant to mention that the entire process(es) involved in the formation of African diaspora identities following transnational migration are oftentimes created or established in a piecemeal manner. This is because diaspora and migrant negotiation of identities in transnational locations is not the exclusive domain of the migrants. Host society institutional and normative structures are centrally involved in determining the outcome of diaspora behavior. After all, the host can use its laws to restrict access to opportunities for immigrant groups. The host society may also create barriers to control immigrant incorporation. It is known that the persistence of ethnic affiliations in particular and the migration, settlement and adaptation process in general need to be understood as immigrants' response to specific social and economic circumstances, opportunities, and limitations that they face in the receiving society, including rejection, racism, and discrimination. This means that as racial and ethnic minorities in a pluralistic American society, the future of African immigrants are inexorably linked with the internal affairs of the body polity of their host societies. The Africans do recognize this and throughout this book, there is recognition among the immigrants that the opportunities that are garnered through migration are not to be taken for granted. Instead, the opportunities offered by migration are constructed and cast within a framework that recognizes that as a process, migration offers Africans from all walks of life new opportunities to redefine their place and role in the social system. In this regard, these immigrants are not the sole actors or proprietors of their destinies. They act upon their host societies. In turn, they are acted upon by their host as well.

In this chapter, we present our thoughts and observations about the current and future manifestations of African global migrations. The scope of our coverage of Africans in global migrations spanned a number of broad and encompassing trajectories of which the major areas are as follows: the formation of migratory racial, ethnic, and gendered identities among African immigrants; business and entrepreneurial formations; institutional structures to support immigrant cultural forms through the formation of mutual benefit associations; the nature of the relationships that these immigrants structure with their home countries; the relationships these immigrants establish with other minorities in the diaspora; professional and labor force participation; and their repatriation plans for the future.

These themes are not isolated or discrete, and independent. Instead, we recognize their interconnectedness and convergences in the emergence of the global migratory identities of Africans as they search beyond their continent for better economic and social opportunities and advancements. The understanding of the intersections of these themes, we believe, is central in link-ing African global migrations to African continental development. In other words, in our view, these themes form a significant aspect of who Africans are, as a people, their hopes, aspirations, and outlook on social life. The interplay of these themes is significant because it lends credence to the idea that often times, diasporas of the kind which Africans are currently engaged in, typically sustains itself and maintains its viability through the creation and establishment of robust structures which enables the members of the diaspora to maintain relationships not only with their homelands but also with the host societies where they are sojourned.

It is evident from the preceding chapters that the migration of Africans to distant lands in search of better economic and cultural opportunities is varied in its form, complex in its manifestations, and yet fluid enough to incorporate the manifold changes in global economic and social systems. From the por-trait of Africans in migration that we have depicted, we can sketch a continent and a people who are yearning for better standards of living and a desire to be-come part of the global and international community. It also reveals a people who are also nervous about the economic, social, and political misfortunes that have persistently plagued the continent. A few countries in Africa have experienced improved economic and social conditions in recent years, includ-ing Ghana, Botswana, South Africa, Uganda, Kenya, and Angola. There is, therefore, renewed vigor and hope that despite the daunting challenges that lie ahead, Africa and Africans are capable of self-empowerment and to use their tremendous human capital and natural resources toward the betterment of all its peoples. At the same time, this renewed hope and vigor is tampered with trepidation that the long-term economic and social development of the continent is being stalled by geopolitical and economic forces operating inter-nally and externally of Africa. Many African scholars have argued that there are still remnants of the colonial order and hegemony that holds a potential to strangle and thus stall the continent's march to selfdom or self-determination. For example, unfair commodity prices of major agricultural commodities like rubber, sugar, and cocoa, including the prices that the advanced countries are willing to pay for minerals like copper, gold, iron, aluminum, and bauxite are too low to enable the African countries to acquire robust foreign reserves receipts to fund basic and much-needed infrastructural improvements such as quality roads, transportation systems, healthcare, and education. This problem is exacerbated by Africa's low levels of industrial and manufacturing produc-tion capacity caused by the mass shipment of the regions raw materials and resources to the developed countries for processing into finished and semi-finished goods which Africans in turn have to purchase from the West. The lack of a strong and sustainable manufacturing base to provide employment for secondary school and university graduates is one of the factors that continue to drive the global migration of Africans in search of better sources of employment and living conditions, a phenomenon aptly characterized as the brain-drain. An associated phenomenon is that when foreign aid is given to assist Africans, it is usually done in such a way by the donor countries to more added-value to the donors than to the aid-recipient country. Structural adjustment programs as preconditions for foreign aid has affected the poor by its emphases on the removal of government-based subsidies for water, electricity, and staple foods like rice and corn, sorghum, millet, and wheat.

To some, the collective destinies of the continent is shaped by the postcolonial political instability and corruption that have fuelled schisms, inter and intra-tribal warfare, genocides, population displacements and cross-border skirmishes. These perennial conditions are inimical to social stability and the creation of a civil society and instructions for nurturing democratic governance structures and institutions. They are also a driving force behind the global migration of Africans in search of safer havens where they can live out to their fullest potential. An assessment of the importance of migration in the development of Africa ought to address the fundamental internal conditions that continue to drive out the continent's skilled and unskilled workers. For Africans, the process of seeking global incorporation through migration is premised on the perception and widely held belief that to date, African governments have failed to demonstrate any capacity to be able to come up with rigorous and sustained programs to ameliorate the plight of the masses. This certainly has caused consternation on the part of most Africans leading to mistrust of government and its role in shaping the economic future of Africans. Even as the forces of globalization continue to alter the economic destiny of the region and be felt throughout the continent and its benefits begin to trickle down, Africans still continue to the leery of the ability of their central governments to fully harness these benefits for the viable future of the continent. In essence, the stalling of economic development internally in Africa and the trickling down of the benefits of globalization while necessary for the future growth of the continent, are not sufficient to ensure a robust revitalization and harnessing of the full potential of the continent toward the achievement of economic independence.

As they reconstitute their cultures in foreign domains after migration, the African immigrants whose experiences are chronicled in this book can be said to represent the multiple and enduring forms of African identities and the unique cultural formations that are often associated with the diversity of cultures found in the region. A common theme that emerged from these chapters is that irrespective of which region of the continent they hail from, African immigrants are engaging and energetic. Their multiple identities render any attempts to categorize them as monolithic nearly impossible. Uniformities in their sociocultural and economic formations as immigrants in their host societies including the United States can be delineated. These uniformities include a strong work and entrepreneurial identity, a strong socialization into core cultural and social institutions such as family, religion, interest in education, and a strong commitment to transnationalism and to use their migratory experiences to bring about the transformation of their home societies. In this regard, we find that African global migrations cannot be reduced to a linear process whereby the migrant destination point becomes the endpoint of the migratory process. On the contrary, the migratory behavior of Africans are such that it is upon reaching their destinations that social, cultural, economic, and political interconnectedness to the continent are strengthened by their meticulous attention to the issues and problems that they have left behind at home. That is to say that, upon entering global migration domain, Africans develop new and sharper lenses that enables them to gain a better understanding of the myriad of issues confronting their continent and the measures needed to address some of these problems. In this regard, migration enables them to reconstruct new images and impressions about their motherland. And once they have formed these new impressions, they use their skills, resources, talents, voices, and ideas to manifest, represent and to promote the affairs of the continent in the day-to-day interactions with the members of their host societies. They seek and agitate for the visible and untainted representation of Africa and its place in the international and global community. It is this representation which serves as the driving force behind African immigrants' strong affiliation and involvement with Africa. That is why they never sever ties with their respective homelands. That is why they seek to forge relationships with stakeholders who are interested in the affairs and well-being of Africans to organize campaigns to bring into sharp focus the needs of the nearly one billion people who live on the continent. African immigrants have also established a variety of national, regional, ethnic, township, and even professional associations to meet needs related to their settlement in a new society, and their homelands. Whether working with non-governmental organizations, churches, charitable organizations, a cross-section of white and black Americans to organize medical mission trips to the continent, operating African grocery, or making presentations about the cultural traditions of Africa, it seems that the African immigrant experience is one whose contexts are varied and dominated by a fervent desire and hope that sooner rather than later, Africa too shall rise and take their place at the table of global affairs. In the meantime, there is the arduous task of nation-building and development which has to occur to lift the millions in abject poverty and deprivation by raising their standards of living. This task, while daunting, is attainable. It is attainable because of the increase in the human capital skills that Africans all over the world continue to build against the backdrop of the vast natural resources that the continent is endowed with. Matching the human capital skills and massive natural resource endowment of the continent will, in the not too distant future, unleash a monumental leap forward toward economic, industrial and cultural growth.

The future manifestations of African immigrant identities will be structured around more globally-defined discourses and narratives such as how to incorporate Africa into the global society and how to harness the continent's vast resources to improve upon the living standards of the people. As the essays in this book demonstrate, structuring the narratives about how Africans will fare in the global community will involve multiple perspectives, conceptual frameworks, and genres. These multiple perspectives will reflect the diverse approaches as well as the complexities of the issues to be resolved. The narratives will involve and reflect the multi-layered forms of social, economic, and cultural developmental approaches. Certainly, Africans will have to play a greater role in defining the scope and direction of these approaches. More importantly, the point has to be stressed by Africans that they will have to play a greater role in finding solutions to the problems that continue to 'push' them out of their homelands to seek greener pastures in the United States, Europe, and other parts of the world.

While it is necessary to understand the causes of the mass migration of skilled and unskilled Africans to globally-structured labor centers, it is not sufficient to unravel the complex and monumental task of positioning Africa in global affairs. Concerted efforts are required on the part of Africa's central governments to understand the transformative impact of globalization and its constituent parts, including its impacts on migration. Policies designed to incorporate the contributions of Africans in the diaspora in fulfilling development initiatives are warranted. To date, African governments have done very little to capitalize on economic and social contributions that their respective diaspora populations can make to national planning and development. The role of diaspora groups and how they operate and in particular their role in fuelling economic and cultural development must be understood and given attention by policy-makers in the migrant-exporting countries in the region. At the same time, it is significant to recognize that merely relying on the economic input and contributions of diaspora populations to spur economic and cultural development will not completely ensure and bring about economic transformation and social change. A comprehensive process of social development involving all stakeholders must be harnessed, including in particular domestic and foreign capital investments as well as bilateral and multilateral economic assistance from donor countries. The goal of such comprehensive approach to tackling economic development issues and finding lasting solutions to the continent's economic and social problem is to retain both skilled and unskilled population. The continued loss of Africa's human resources through outmigration is a major constraint to socioeconomic development. While policies cannot be implemented to completely restrict the international migration of Africans by their central governments, at a minimum, efforts must be made to understand the constraining influences of population and labor mobility at the internal and international levels on economic and social development.

Looking to the future, we expect the migration of skilled and unskilled Africans in search of better economic opportunities outside the continent to continue in a world that continues to globalize. The persistence of this migration stems largely from the sheer magnitude of the economic and social problems currently facing many of the countries of Africa. This migration will intensify as economic, social, and political conditions become worse and intractable. The pace and intensity of this migration will depend on the ability of both the public and private sectors of the African economics to provide employment for graduates. Unmet or unfulfilled economic and social aspirations will continue to be the major driving force behind the continued migration of Africans in search of better opportunities outside the continent. In particular, the ability of Africa's central government to intensify cultural programs aimed at providing vocational-technical training or re-training for displaced school graduates and underemployed rural and urban youths will go a long way in defining the future direction and composition of African global migrations. The continued deterioration of economic and political conditions in the region will compel and promote the migration of unskilled youths who will use migration as a mechanism to raise their living standards and better their lives. For the unskilled rural and urban Africans who have poor educational skills, the search for the promised lands will take some of them to Asia, the Middle East, and Latin America as visa standards are tightened in the advanced countries in the Western hemisphere. This chapter of the African diaspora is currently evolving and its dynamic forms and contents are yet to be unraveled. Despite the uncertainties surrounding this form of migration, it is clear that the picture of Africa in the twenty-first century will be characterized by a vigorous search for ways to find robust and institutional solutions to the persistent problems that have caused economic desperation and intensified the urgency to look beyond the continent for the fulfillment of unmet aspirations and hopes.

Index

About the Editors and Contributors

EDITORS

Dr. John A. Arthur is Professor of Sociology and Criminology at the University of Minnesota, Duluth campus. He received his Ph.D. from Penn State University. His research interests include international migration, the African diaspora, race and ethnic relations, and minorities and the criminal justice system. He is author of several books including *Invisible Sojourners: African Immigrant Diaspora in the United States; The African Diaspora in the United States and Europe; African Immigrant Women in the United States: Crossing Transnational Borders; and African Diaspora Identities: Negotiating Culture in Transnational Migration.*

Dr. Joseph Takougang is Professor of African History in the Department of Africana Studies at the University of Cincinnati in Cincinnati, Ohio. His interests include colonial and post-colonial Africa, with a focus on Cameroon nationalism and post-colonial political developments in Cameroon. A secondary research area focuses on the African Diaspora in the United States. In addition to over a dozen articles in refereed journals and edited volumes, Takougang is also co-author (with Milton Krieger) of *African State and Society in the 1990s: Cameroon's Political Crossroads* (Westview Press, 1998) and co-editor (with John Mukum Mbaku) of *The Leadership Challenge in Africa: Cameroon Under Paul Biya* (Africa World Press, Inc, 2004).

Dr. Thomas Owusu is Professor and Chair of the Department of Geography and Urban Studies, William Paterson University of New Jersey. He earned his B.A from the University of Ghana, M.A. from Wilfred Laurier University in Canada, and Ph.D. from the University of Toronto. His research interests include the changing social geography of North American cities, immigrants and North America cities, dynamics of urban economic and demographic change, and comparative urban development and policy. He has published papers on the social and economic experiences and conditions of immigrants in Canada and the United States in several international journals including *International Migration Review, Journal of Migration and Integration, Housing Studies, The Canadian Geographer, and National Social Science Journal.*

CHAPTER CONTRIBUTORS

John A. Arthur is Professor of Sociology and Criminology at the University of Minnesota, Duluth campus. He received his Ph.D. from Penn State University. His research interests include international migration, the African diaspora, race and ethnic relations, and minorities and the criminal justice system. He is author of several books including *Invisible Sojourners: African Immigrant Diaspora in the United States; The African Diaspora in the United States and Europe; African Immigrant Women in the United States: Crossing Transnational Borders; and African Diaspora Identities: Negotiating Culture in Transnational Migration.*

Janet T. Awokoya earned both her Ph.D. in curriculum and instruction and MA in international education from the University of Maryland at College Park. Currently, she is a Senior Research Associate at the Frederick D. Patterson Research Institute at UNCF, which focuses on educational barriers and facilitators for African Americans and other underrepresented minorities across the P-16 pipeline. Awokoya's research includes the study of African American and Latino education, professional development for pre-service and in-service teachers and identity culture among African and Caribbean immigrants and refugees.

Nemata Blyden (M. Phil, Ph.D., Yale University) is Associate Professor of History and International Affairs at The George Washington University. She is a scholar of Africa and the African Diaspora, with particular interest in the relationship between Africa and its Diaspora as expressed through migration and the "back to Africa" movements in the nineteenth century. Her published work includes *West Indians in West Africa, 1808-1880: A Diaspora in Reverse*, University of Rochester Press, 2000; *"We have the Cause of Africa at heart": West Indians and African Americans in nineteenth century Freetown* in *New perspectives on the Sierra Leone Krio,* Mac Dixon-Fyle and Gibril Cole (eds.): Peter Lang: New York, 2006; *"The Search for Anna Erskine: African-American Women in nineteenth century Liberia* in, *Stepping Forward: Black Women in Africa and the Americas,* Catherine Higgs, Barbara Moss, Earline Rae Ferguson, Ohio University Press, 2002; *"Edward Jones: An African American in Sierra Leone"* in *Moving On: Black Loyalists in the Afro-Atlantic World,* John W. Pulis (ed.) (Garland Publishing, Inc. 1999) and *A Perspective of the African Diaspora in the United States,* published with Fenda Akiwumi, in John W. Frazier, Joe T. Darden, Norah F. Henry (eds), *The African Diaspora in the United States and Canada at the Dawn of the 21ˢᵗ Century* (Global Academic Publishing, 2009)

Msia Kibona Clark is an Assistant Professor at California State University, Los Angeles. Her areas of research are African migrations, African/African American relations, and hip hop expressions. Dr. Clark's work has been published in both scholarly journals and with select websites such as *African Identities, The Other Journal: An Intersection of Theology and Culture, Pambazuka.org, allAfrica.com and PoliticsAfrica.com.*

Hilary Chala Kowino is Assistant Professor in the Department of English at the University of Minnesota, Duluth. His teaching and research interests include African literature, African diaspora literature, postcolonial literature, world literature, cultural studies, gender studies, and critical theories of race, place, space, border, citizenship, and cosmopolitanism. Kowino earned his Ph.D. from Michigan State University. The core of his work challenges the assumptions of conventional belonging by not only exposing a plurality of allegiances and identities that complicate the idea of home, but also oppressed socio-economic and alien feelings that keep subjects out of place. He is currently working on a book project entitled *The Interface between Home and Belonging in African Literature* which examines the conceptions of home in African literature and culture following colonial and global regimes.

Tatenda T. Mambo is a Ph.D. candidate at the University of Calgary, Canada. He holds an MA in Geography from Miami University. His research interests are the brain drain, migration, food security, HIV/AIDS, and urbanization in sub-Saharan Africa.

Mojúbàolú Olúfúnké Okome is a Professor of Political Science at Brooklyn College, City University of New York. She has a doctorate in Political Science from Columbia University, a Master's in Political Science from Long Island University and a Bachelor's in Political Science from University of Ibadan in Nigeria. Her publications include: *West African Migrations: Transnational and Global Pathways in a New Century* (edited with Olufemi Vaughan). NY: Palgrave-Macmillan Publishers (forthcoming, January 2012); *Transnational Africa and Globalization* (edited with Olufemi Vaughan) NY: Palgrave-Macmillan (forthcoming January 2012); *A Sapped Democracy: The Political Economy of the Structural Adjustment Program and the Democratic Transition in Nigeria, 1983-1993* (Baltimore, MD: University Press of America, 1997). Dr. Okome has contributed to numerous book chapters including: "Nigerian Immigrants" In Ronald Bayor, Ed. *Multicultural America: An Encyclopedia of the Newest Americans*, Volume 3, pp. 1595-1655 (Santa Barbara, CA: Greenwood/ABC-CLIO, 2011); (with Elisha Renne) *Àìní obìnrin kò seé dáké lásán, bí a dáké lásán, enu níí yo ni*: Women's Leadership Roles in Aládǔrà Churches in Nigeria and the US" Chapter 8 in Afe Adogame, Ezra Chitando, Bolaji Bateye (eds) *African Traditions in the Study of Religion, Diaspora, and Gendered Societies--a Festschrift in Honour of Prof. Jacob K. Olupona, Book 2*. (Aldershot, UK: Ashgate (forthcoming 2011); "Immigrant Voices in Cyberspace: Spinning Continental and Diaspora Africans into the World Wide Web," In *Gendering the African Diaspora: Women, Culture, and Historical Change in the Caribbean and Nigerian Hinterland.* Judith A. Byfield, LaRay Denzer and Anthea Morrison (eds.) 2010. Indiana University Press; "African Diasporas," In *Diasporas and Development.* Barbara Merz, Lincoln Chen and Peter Geithner. (eds). 2010. Cambridge, Mass.: Harvard University Press, Global Equity Initiative; and "African Immigrant Churches and the New Christian Right," In *African Immigrant Religions in America.* J.K. Olupona and Regina Gemignani (eds.) 2010. New York: New York University Press.

Mary Johnson Osirim is Dean of Graduate Studies and Professor of Sociology at Bryn Mawr College. She is the immediate past coordinator of Africana Studies and Faculty Diversity Liaison at the College. During the past twenty years, she has conducted research on women, entrepreneurship, and the roles of the state and nongovernmental organizations in the microenterprise sectors of Nigeria and Zimbabwe; the development of women's and gender studies scholarship in Anglophone sub-Saharan Africa as well as transnationalism and community development among African immigrants in the United States. She is the author of *Enterprising Women in Urban Zimbabwe: Gender, Microbusiness and Globalization* (2009), co-editor (with Ayumi Takenaka) of *Global Philadelphia: Immigrant Communities, Old and New* (2010) and coeditor (with Akosua Adomako Ampofo and Josephine Beoku-Betts) of a special edition of *African and Asian Studies* on "Researching African Women and Gender Studies" (2008). She has authored over thirty articles and book chapters on these subjects.

Dr. Thomas Owusu is Associate Professor and Chair of the Department of Geography and Urban Studies, William Paterson University of New Jersey. He earned his B.A from the University of Ghana, M.A. from Wilfred Laurier University in Canada, and Ph.D. from the University of Toronto. His research interests include the changing social geography of North American cities, immigrants and North America cities, dynamics of urban economic and demographic change, and comparative urban development and policy. He has published papers on the social and economic experiences and conditions of immigrants in Canada and the United States in several international journals including *International Migration Review, Journal of Migration and Integration, Housing Studies, The Canadian Geographer, and National Social Science Journal.*

Joseph Takougang is Professor of African history in the department of Africana Studies at the University of Cincinnati in Cincinnati, Ohio. His interests include colonial and post-colonial Africa, with a focus on Cameroon nationalism and post-colonial political developments in Cameroon. A secondary research area focuses on the African Diaspora in the United States. In addition to over a dozen articles in refereed journals and edited volumes, Takougang is also co-author (with Milton Krieger) of *African State and Society in the 1990s: Cameroon's Political Crossroads* (Westview Press, 1998) and co-editor (with John Mukum Mbaku) of *The Leadership Challenge in Africa: Cameroon Under Paul Biya* (Africa World Press, Inc, 2004).

Bassirou Tidjani is Professor at University Cheikh Anta Diop, Dakar, Senegal. He received his Ph.D. from University of Madison, Wisconsin. His areas of specialization are business and industrial relations. Dr. Tidjani's has published in journals such as *Industrial Relations/Relations Industrielles; Revue Gestion des Ressources Humaines; Africa Development/Afrique et Développement; International Journal of Cross Cultural Management; and Journal of Third World Studies.*

Ian Yeboah is Professor of Geography at Miami University. He earned a Ph.D. (1994) and a M.Sc. (1988) from the University of Calgary, Canada and a B.A. (Hons.) in the Social Sciences from University of Science and Technology, Kumasi, Ghana (1982). His research and teaching are on globalization and Africa, focusing on urbanization, migration, and poverty.

He has published in journals such as *Area*, *African Geographical Review*, *Canadian Geographer*, *GeoJournal*, *Geographical Research*, *Tijdschrift voor Economische en Sociale Geografie*, *The Geographical Journal*, *Africa Today*, *Social Science and Medicine* as well as numerous book chapters. His recent book titled *Black African Neo-Diaspora: Ghanaian Immigrant Experiences in the Greater Cincinnati, Ohio, Area* (2008) is published by Lexington Books. He is past editor of *African Geographical Review*. He taught at both the University of Science and Technology in Kumasi, Ghana and the University of Calgary before coming to Miami University in 1994.